LITERACY PORTFOLIOS

Using Assessment to Guide Instruction

Roberta B. Wiener
Adelphi University

Judith H. Cohen
Adelphi University

Merrill,
an imprint of Prentice Hall
Upper Saddle River, New Jersey   *Columbus, Oh.*

Library of Congress Cataloging-in-Publication Data

Literacy portfolios: using assessment to guide instruction /
Roberta B. Wiener, Judith H. Cohen

     p. cm.

     Includes bibliographical references and index.

     ISBN 0-02-427472-0 (pbk.)

     1. Reading—Ability testing—United States. 2. Literacy—United
States—Evaluation. 3. Portfolios in education—United States.
4. Language arts (Elementary)—United States. 5. Language arts—
Remedial teaching—United States. I. Cohen, Judith H. II. Title.

LB1050.46.W547 1997

372.41—dc21   96-44644

                                           CIP

Cover photo: © 1994 Scott Cunningham/Merrill
Editor: Bradley J. Potthoff
Developmental Editor: Linda Ashe Montgomery
Production Editor: Patricia S. Kelly
Design Coordinator: Karrie M. Converse
Text Designer: Linda M. Robertson
Cover Designer: Proof Positive/Farrowlyne Assoc., Inc.
Production Manager: Laura Messerly
Director of Marketing: Kevin Flanagan
Advertising/Marketing Coordinator: Julie Shough
Illustrations: The Clarinda Company

This book was set in Adobe Garamond and Helvetica by The Clarinda Company and was printed
and bound by Quebecor Printing/Book Press. The cover was printed by Phoenix Color Corp.

 ©1997 by Prentice-Hall, Inc.
Simon & Schuster/A Viacom Company
Upper Saddle River, New Jersey 07458

Printed in the United States of America

10 9 8 7 6 5 4 3 2 1

ISBN: 0-02-427472-0

Prentice-Hall International (UK) Limited, *London*
Prentice-Hall of Australia Pty. Limited, *Sydney*
Prentice-Hall of Canada, Inc., *Toronto*
Prentice-Hall Hispanoamericana, S. A., *Mexico*
Prentice-Hall of India Private Limited, *New Delhi*
Prentice-Hall of Japan, Inc., *Tokyo*
Simon & Schuster Asia Pte. Ltd., *Singapore*
Editora Prentice-Hall do Brasil, Ltda., *Rio de Janeiro*

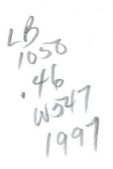
To our husbands, Len and Stuart,
who have shown love, patience, and support throughout this project.

Preface

It has always been our belief that if a student teacher knew one student well then this knowledge could be translated to insights that help with all learners. Thus, as an assignment for a course we teach, The Literacy Practicum, we began to require our college students to do a case study analysis of a student who has difficulty with reading and writing.

The required case study followed traditional practice; thus, our students not only assessed a child's current level of functioning but also investigated background in and out of school and developed a plan for intervention. Additionally, we encouraged our students to assess a child's literacy strategies both through informal means (administration, scoring, and interpretation of an informal reading inventory, an interest inventory, and other batteries, as well as observation in various school settings) and through formal means (review and interpretation of standardized tests administered by the school district). Close appraisal of the child's interactions during actual literacy engagement was always emphasized. That is why, when we first learned about portfolios, we became interested in this concept—because it was congruent with our teaching focus!

Portfolios gave structure to our case study approach. It also added the dimension of collaborative efforts between the teacher and student in assessing literacy strategies through collected works, reading logs, journal writings, other language activities and informal testing. Consequently, our student teachers are now required to produce a portfolio that contains a condensed version of the kind of portfolio that teachers should be involved in throughout the school year. We call this portfolio a **Literacy Assessment Portfolio (LAP)**, to distinguish it from other portfolios that have been described in recent literature. This LAP is meant to provide teachers with an in-depth appraisal of a student's literacy development.

Because we value this process with our undergraduate and graduate student teachers, we propose that teachers use these concepts and implement a LAP with their students. To assist you in doing so, we have written this textbook to explain each aspect of developing literacy assessment portfolios.

TEXT ORGANIZATION

This text is organized so that you will have a firm understanding of the theory of literacy portfolios as part of authentic assessment strategies and to provide you with guidelines for creating and using literacy portfolios successfully in your classroom.

Part I, *Integrating Authentic Literacy and Portfolio Assessment,* contains the theoretical background needed to truly understand the context of contemporary instructional strategies in literacy, the status and development of portfolio practice, current concerns with assessment, and our recommended portfolio model: the LAP. Portfolio practices are thus established as a significant outcome of assessment techniques that align with recent educational reforms in reading and writing instruction. An important feature of Part I is the introduction of the LAP process, which presents important questions to consider if a LAP is to be successfully integrated into a literacy program.

Part II, *Working with the Literacy Assessment Portfolio,* is the how-to of the LAP process. It is in this section that you will find suggestions for assessing the reading and writing entries in a student's LAP with the goal of guiding literacy instruction. Sample entries from actual student portfolios demonstrate how teachers can use the LAP process to diagnose literacy development and individualize instruction to meet the needs of diverse learners. This section also contains suggestions for conferencing with the portfolio so that students, their families, teachers, and administrators all become part of the collaborative process.

In Part III, *Implementing Literacy Portfolios,* Chapter 10 discusses how to begin a portfolio process in any school district. The following chapters describe how educators can adapt the portfolio process to the particular needs of special education students and with students who do not speak English as their primary language. Whether these students are educated in mainstream classes, infusion programs, resource rooms, or other special settings, their literacy needs must be addressed and the portfolio process has much to offer.

Part IV, *Classroom Perspectives,* contains more voices from the schools: reflections about the portfolio process from teachers and an administrator from school districts in New York and other parts of the country who feel that portfolios have made a significant difference in their literacy programs. Sample portfolio entries are used to provide examples of various portfolios. Highlighted are perspectives from two teachers who describe how portfolios can be used with emergent literacy learners and gifted fifth-grade students. Also included is the perspective of an administrator who explains how to begin and implement the process. These educators share with us the frustrations and rewards in initiating portfolio practice and see its evolution in their schools. The essays provide practical ideas supported by the actual portfolio entries of their østudents.

Additional teacher reflections and portfolio samples from elementary and middle school teachers and reading intervention specialists are available as ftp files on the Literacy Homepage for Merrill Education and can be accessed through the URL listed on the back cover of this textbook. Titles for these files are identified in the table of contents.

ACKNOWLEDGMENTS

We gratefully acknowledge the hard work and support of our undergraduate and graduate college students at Adelphi University, as well as classroom teachers and administrators in the following school districts: Hewlett/Woodmere, Lawrence, North Shore, Plainedge, Lynbrook, Three Village, Bedford Hills, all in New York; South Brunswick, New Jersey; and Adams Country Five Star Schools, Colorado. We thank you for sharing your time, insights, and student work to assist in this project's development. Your experiences supplement theory with the reality of the classroom.

Additionally, we would like to thank Linda Montgomery, our developmental editor, for her support of this project through its many phases; Patty Kelly, our production editor; and Luanne Dreyer-Elliott, our copyeditor.

We would also like to thank the following reviewers for their helpful comments and suggestions: Dennise M. Bartelo, Plymouth State College; Donna Camp, University of Central Florida; Martha Combs, University of Nevada; Laurie Elish-Piper, Northern Illinois University; Mary-Margaret Harrington, Southern Illinois University at Carbondale; Patricia P. Kelly, Virginia Tech; Jill P. May, Purdue University; Beverly Otto, Northeastern Illinois University; Timothy Rasinski, Kent State University; Kathy Roskos, John Carroll University; Terry Salinger, International Reading Association; Sam L. Sebesta, University of Washington.

We share with you the delight of learning something new—the literacy assessment portfolio process—and ask that you share with us your ideas about how portfolios can and have worked in your classrooms.

Roberta B. Wiener and Judith H. Cohen

Contents

Part Two
WORKING WITH THE LITERACY ASSESSMENT PORTFOLIO 147

Part Three
IMPLEMENTING LITERACY PORTFOLIOS   239

CHAPTER 12   USING PORTFOLIOS WITH LANGUAGE MINORITY STUDENTS   288

Linda Schlam, ESL Instructor, and Susan Cafetz, ESL Instructor, Columbia University, New York

Part Four
CLASSROOM PERSPECTIVES   305

EXAMPLE A.   USING A LITERACY PORTFOLIO IN FIRST GRADE   306

Lindy Vizyak, First-Grade Teacher, Cotton Creek Elementary School, Adams County Five Star Schools, Westminster, Colorado

EXAMPLE B.   USING A LITERACY PORTFOLIO PROCESS WITH GIFTED STUDENTS   322

EXAMPLE C.   AN ADMINISTRATOR'S PERSPECTIVE: CREATING CONDITIONS FOR CHANGE   334

ADDITIONAL EXAMPLES

The following additional examples of teacher reflections and portfolios are located on the Literacy Homepage for Prentice Hall/Merrill Education and can be accessed through the URL listed on the back cover of this text.

Integrating Authentic Literacy and Portfolio Assessment

1. *Introducing Portfolio Practices*
2. *Changing Views of Literacy*
3. *Observing Authentic Literacy Practices*
4. *Surveying Portfolio Use in Authentic Literacy Classrooms*
5. *Exploring Authentic Assessment Opportunities*
6. *Introducing the Literacy Assessment Portfolio*

CHAPTER

1

Introducing Portfolio Practices

KEY WORDS AND CONCEPTS

Portfolio

Literacy portfolio

Literacy Assessment Portfolio (LAP)

Reading portfolio

Cumulative record portfolio

Showcase portfolio

Writing folder

Portfolio process

Writing portfolio

Integrated language arts portfolio

Benchmark portfolio

Collaborative portfolio

Evaluating children's literacy behavior has always been a concern of classroom teachers; how to fully capture children's growth and accomplishment has been a dilemma. Test scores, report card grades, narrative teacher comments, cumulative record folders, completed assignments, and filled workbooks have traditionally been used to document children's academic accomplishments, but they never gave as full a picture of what children actually do during a school year as does a highly descriptive **portfolio.** A growing number of teachers are using portfolios not only to document children's literacy learning by collecting and reflecting with their students on their actual work but also to foster the development of literacy. Observing students during learning, collecting their work, and collaborating and developing goals with them are essential components of authentic assessment through the use of a portfolio process.

EVOLUTION OF THE PORTFOLIO

The use of portfolios in the workplace is familiar. Artists, models, photographers, and others collect their work in a binder or large portfolio to demonstrate their skills and accomplishments by showing samples of their work. In today's competitive marketplace, many job seekers, including prospective teaching candidates, are using portfolios to seek employment. Encouraged to collect and save their projects, papers, and work samples, college students approach an interview with a large portfolio that clearly and concretely represents their capabilities.

The term *portfolio* has also been widely used in finance. As early as the 1950s, an investment portfolio described a collection of investments specifically chosen according to certain criteria to maximize return (Seger, 1992). Investors were encouraged to periodically review and reflect on the collection to see if goals were being met. However, the use of portfolios in education is fairly recent and can be traced to the mid-1980s, when several trends fostered their use in classrooms. Portfolios can be linked to **writing folders,** which have been an integral part of the writing process movement. Using professional writers as a model, classroom teachers encouraged their students to maintain a collection of their writing in a folder to work on and periodically review. It was important to accumulate students' ongoing work and provide a safe place to store and collect their writing. Ultimately, when these works were edited, polished, and ready to publish (i.e., share with other students), they were often displayed in another folder that showed the students' finished pieces. These writing folders, often called *portfolios,* showcased students' writing accomplishments. As teachers began to incorporate the use of reading logs, self-reflective journals, and other written responses to literature as part of daily classroom practice, they saw the need to save these collections as well, and hence the contents of **literacy portfolios** began to emerge. This practice was a natural outgrowth of changing methodologies for teaching reading and writing.

Early childhood teachers have traditionally saved students' work in large folders that contain artwork, dictated stories and pictures, or stories using invented spelling. These work folders have been an important aspect of tracing a child's development from a nonreader and nonwriter into an individual whose emergent literacy was evolving. An accumulation of a student's work can easily be reviewed and reflected on to document accomplishment, identify instructional needs, and show growth over time.

Because of the dissemination of many reports in the 1980s criticizing the quality of the schools and a general concern that schools were failing, the need to document learning outcomes increased. Many called for the use of new forms of educational assessment, because traditional forms of assessment were being rethought as literacy instruction was transformed. Critics called for assessment methods that were both congruent with newer classroom practices and fairer to all students, allowing for greater sensitivity to differences in gender, ethnicity, and race. With the call to restructure schools, create site-based management, and provide for teacher empowerment, dramatic changes were required not only in curriculum and instruction but also in assessment practices (Gomez & Schenk, 1992).

As part of this accountability movement, reading and writing were targeted as essential curriculum areas and scrutinized to determine if teaching and learning were effective. A major shift in the theory of language arts teaching called for integrative literacy methodology, as well as more direct application of language skills across curriculum areas. The portfolio collection was adopted by many as a new form of what came to be called *authentic assessment,* a form of assessment that could readily demonstrate what students were actually doing in the classroom.

DEFINING THE PORTFOLIO

Although portfolios are becoming widely used and discussed, their definition is confounded by different notions of purpose, type, and format. Seger (1992, pp. 115–116) used an excellent metaphor to describe the evolution of the portfolio phenomenon and the confusion over its definition, "Defining *portfolio* from such multiple notions would be like an early biologist trying to define *mammal* when presented with a whale, a human being, and a bat." Ambiguities about portfolios exist, but an often cited and widely accepted definition was developed by the Northwest Evaluation Association that has been refined by Arter and Spandel (1992), who define a student portfolio as

> a purposeful collection of student work that tells the story of the student's efforts, progress, or achievement in [a] given area[s]. This collection must include student participation in selection of portfolio content; the guidelines for selection; the criteria for judging merit; and evidence of student reflection. (p. 36)

A review of the literature about portfolios reveals several essential features:

- Entries for the portfolio are collected in a semipermanent holder, where they should be kept safe but must be readily available for the student's and teacher's use. Reading and writing folders are often used to provide materials from which students and teachers select entries for the portfolio.

- Products chosen for a portfolio are the result of collaboration between student and teacher, but the contents must reflect the student's ownership and reflection. Criteria for a portfolio collection should be jointly established by the students and teacher to shape the contents of the collection.

- Works chosen for the collection reflect established criteria. A portfolio collection is *not* a random accumulation of items but results from a purposeful review of potential entries chosen to demonstrate various criteria. Works chosen can reflect the range of the student's abilities, growth in the student's accomplishments, or demonstration of student's special pride in a particular outcome. A table of contents or letter of introduction demonstrates how the collection reflects a meaningful system of organization.

■ Significant to the portfolio collection are the student's thoughts, often shared with the teacher, that reflect on such concerns as the student's interests, the student's perceptions of the literacy process, evaluation of the literacy products in the collection, literacy goals, and how the student's literacy behaviors have changed. Ultimately, self-reflection leads to a sense of ownership and pride in one's own unique accomplishments.

■ Works chosen for the collection present a chronological development over time to document the student's progress with literacy. It is therefore essential that all portfolio entries be dated.

■ Works chosen document the student's ability to use reading and writing for learning in a variety of meaningful ways. Crucial to this concept, the materials chosen reflect authentic, or real, classroom activities and have not been constructed just for the portfolio.

■ Entries demonstrate a variety of tasks showing the ability to purposefully use reading and writing in various contexts.

■ Portfolios also contain communications between students, between students and teachers, as well as between students and their families.

■ Portfolios often contain teacher-completed checklists, anecdotal observation, or informal assessments (miscue analysis, running records, etc.) as well as audiotapes or videotapes of the student's literacy performances.

THE PORTFOLIO PROCESS

In this text we refer to a **portfolio process** and specifically recommend the use of a particular form of portfolio that we call a **Literacy Assessment Portfolio (LAP).** We feel that the portfolio process is distinguished from the simple collection of work into a portfolio, because it is an ongoing process of conferences, collaborations, and dialogues and includes the following:

■ Self-reflection by the student, who thinks about and chooses the portfolio selections

■ Dialogue among students as they collaborate, edit, conference, or select projects for their portfolios

■ Self-reflection of the teacher, who observes, describes, and analyzes the student's literacy strategies

■ Dialogue between the student and the teacher during portfolio conferences as they reflect on the student's literacy development

■ Dialogue between students and family that demonstrates how literacy skills are evolving

■ Dialogue among the student, the student's family, and teacher, who all use the portfolio as the centerpiece for describing, evaluating, and celebrating the student's literacy development

Portfolios are also a vehicle for dialogue between members of an instructional team so that they can clearly understand a student's daily performance. This dialogue process can be continued by using the portfolio as means of providing accountability among the school, families, and other concerned individuals, often called *stakeholders,* who want clear evidence of student achievement and progress. Obviously, under this scheme a portfolio process involves changes in instructional strategies and is more intricate than the simple collection of student work in a new kind of folder.

In summary, by viewing a student's portfolio, the observer should have an excellent picture of the unique features of an individual student's literacy growth and accomplishment. According to Paulson, Paulson, and Meyer (1991), a portfolio becomes a true portfolio

> when it provides a complex and comprehensive view of student performance in context. It is a portfolio when the student is a participant in, rather than the object of, assessment. Above all, a portfolio is a portfolio when it provides a forum that encourages students to develop the abilities needed to become independent, self-directed learners. (p. 63)

The portfolio concept is growing in acceptance, and the trend appears likely to continue. Graves (1992) cautions that portfolios have quickly become popular, sometimes without appropriate reflection, "In a few short years, states and school systems have moved from reading about portfolios to mandating them as evaluation instruments for large school populations [and their] possibilities . . . may be lost . . . in the rush to mandate their use" (p. 1). Graves acknowledges that the portfolio process has multiple applications with particular usefulness in evaluation and instructional decision making. Learning to use portfolios well takes effort and training and may require shifting priorities, changing instructional practices, and certainly managing time more carefully.

The Advantages of a Literacy Portfolio Process

Why should teachers and schools support the use of portfolios? The following list of advantages that flow from the use of portfolios in a literacy program is quite compelling:

Portfolios increase our knowledge about each child as well as increase each child's self-knowledge. The portfolio process gives the teacher a portrait of or window into the interests, abilities, goals, learning strategies, and outcomes of individual students. Each portfolio is truly a unique reflection of its creator. From the variety of cover illustrations to the stimulating array of entry types, each portfolio clearly can be used to learn more about even the most introverted students. Because the process requires self-reflection as well as collaboration, thoughtful dialogue between the student and the teacher creates instructional opportunities. The portfolio process is augmented by teacher observation of the student in various instructional settings, so the teacher gains a wide range of insights into how an individual child learns and functions in various educational contexts including:

- Background knowledge about the student's life outside of school: interests, hobbies, preferences, experiences, reactions, and attitudes
- Insights about the student's ability in reading in many different types of materials in multiple contexts, across subject areas
- Information about the student's ability in writing with various genres in many contexts
- Knowledge about the student's use of language skills throughout the curriculum
- Observations of the student's ability to engage in self-reflection and use of metacognitive strategies

- Documentation of developmental growth throughout the school year in literacy
- Awareness of the student's goals and priorities
- Demonstration of the student's ability to engage in collaboration with peers and to use constructive criticism and feedback
- Opportunities for the student to demonstrate self-initiative, as well as self-monitoring strategies
- Knowledge of how the student's sense of self can be enhanced

Teachers who use the process with primary students in Juneau, Alaska (Juneau School District, 1993), commented positively on how portfolios have helped them know children better:

It certainly lends itself to analyzing each student's strengths and weaknesses in depth. It's ongoing and process oriented. You learn by doing it.

The process of observing children and their learning has been incredible—most valuable. Language arts, ongoing learning, myself frazzled, but it's been worth it!

Portfolios improve the quality of teaching. A major benefit of the portfolio process is its ability to merge instruction with assessment and thereby improve teaching. The teacher's ongoing involvement in evaluation is central to the relationship between assessment and instruction. As teachers observe children and meet with them to discuss and reflect on their work, they receive valuable information about how each child is progressing. These data are then used to make informed instructional decisions: what needs reinforcement, what has been acquired, what the child is now ready to attempt, what materials work particularly well, what motivates the child, and how best to proceed and succeed with each individual child.

A key to the success of the portfolio process is the authenticity of the entries that can be collected, because they are the direct outcome of instructional practices and classroom assignments. Because the very product of instruction is the medium by which the teacher assesses the child, there is compatibility between assessment and instruction. As each child interprets the assignments and produces work that indicates unique capacities and experiences, the evaluation process becomes part of who that child is. Consequently, the diversity between children, given the variability in life experiences, capacities, and language skills, is reflected in the portfolio process; there is complete harmony between how to assess and how to instruct, regardless of the wide range of differences between students.

Recent research has been conducted to determine if authentic assessment strategies change the nature of instructional practices. Gooding (1994) found that the use of alternative assessment does influence the relationship between teacher and student as well as modify the learning environment and organizational pattern of the classroom. Teachers who use alternative assessment reported they gave students more opportunity to make decisions regarding both assessment and instruction and generally moved away from teacher direction to a more student-centered focus using a variety of classroom organizational patterns. This study was conducted with a limited sample; however, it documents the changes that teachers informally report when they reflect on how authentic assessment and portfolio use have helped them rethink and modify many of their practices.

The role of the teacher in authentic assessment is pivotal. Teachers are asked to suggest the tasks that are to be used for assessment; teachers decide collaboratively with students on the criteria for successful performance through the creation of rubrics and other rating systems; and teachers and their students score the work themselves. When teachers are given such responsibility for creating assessment systems that are both meaningful and reflective of their teaching priorities, the insights obtained from assessment provide ideas and information for future instruction.

Portfolios enhance students' ownership of their own literacy behavior. Too often, students view education as something that happens to them. Their passive involvement in school activities often results in students completing assignments required for promotion or graduation without any meaningful participation. Many students never develop the attitude that they are responsible for their own learning during the elementary and secondary school years, even though they are responsible for doing the work. This model dramatically changes, however, when a portfolio process is used, because the process is built on the premise that the students own and are accountable for their work; responsibility for the contents of a portfolio resides with the individual student. Rather than externalizing the need for literacy improvement, the portfolio process requires that students become decision makers and acknowledge that their education is part of their identity. Students' successes and triumphs with learning, as well as their disappointments, become internalized as their own, based on self-evaluation and no longer limited to assessment built on decontextualized grades, comments, or red marks from an external evaluator. The medium of the portfolio becomes the source for self-reflection and self-evaluation. When students are guided toward introspection, they become more committed to what they have done and what they have learned.

Educators have long recognized that children need to be sufficiently motivated for meaningful and long-lasting improvement in literacy growth; however, implementation has been elusive. Frequently, motivation has been associated with rewards for short-term successful performance, instructional materials chosen with high interest themes, or through a positive, personal relationship between the teacher and the student. Rarely are unsuccessful readers and writers motivated to improve; rarely, if ever, do poor-achieving students think of literacy development as being a high personal priority of any benefit in their lives. In rare cases, improvement has been noted in postsecondary young adults who find that literacy is a necessary survival skill in the adult world. Educators have reported seeing even the most disabled reader motivated to learn to read a driver's manual to obtain a license. The importance and status attributed to driving are obviously powerful motivators. But reading and writing improvement throughout the grades have rarely been priorities in the lives of students who have been identified with reading and writing failure. Intrinsic motivation has been absent.

The portfolio movement recognizes that, for meaningful improvement to take place in literacy, the student must be central to this process. The concept of children owning their literacy development is an outgrowth of the child-centered philosophy. According to Harp (1993), "for children to have ownership of their learning they must have choice and direction in that learning" (p. 10). When students have meaningful decision-making power in the portfolio process, they can become intrinsically motivated to improve their literacy skills. When literacy learning becomes a priority for students, the likelihood of significant improvement is realized. Nothing is more satisfying for a teacher than to hear students reflect on themselves as readers and writers and note pride of accomplishment. The portfolio process uniquely provides this opportunity.

Portfolios promote accountability by fulfilling district/state mandates for literacy evaluation. The renewal of public confidence in education is a key to developing a collaborative relationship built on mutual respect, and therefore documenting the result of literacy instruction is of prime importance. While many speak globally of the necessity for restructuring schools, most community residents want to take pride in the quality of their local schools and want reassurance that the educational establishment is adhering to community values and graduating literate students. No child who graduates from school without the ability to read and write independently will ever be viewed as a school success, and the public wants the schools to demonstrate accountability for outcomes of literacy instruction.

Consequently, evaluating students' reading and writing ability is a priority in state-mandated testing programs. Virtually all states evaluate language ability. In 1992 to 1993, forty-five states formally tested reading, and thirty-five states formally tested writing as part of mandated statewide evaluation programs (Barton & Coley, 1994). The portfolio movement is gaining national recognition as an additional, viable means of documenting literacy improvement and providing helpful information about the processes and products that are outcomes of literacy instruction. Portfolio use is becoming a reliable and valid form of assessment and is emerging as a part of district evaluation programs throughout the country.

There is a growing acknowledgment that authentic and performance-based assessment can overcome many of the perceived disadvantages of standardized testing. Many states are currently using a variety of assessment formats to balance their current programs including the use of writing samples, performance events, and portfolios along with norm-referenced and criterion-referenced tests. To overcome limitations when standardized literacy tests are used, it is important that teachers be involved in the development of statewide evaluation programs that use portfolios and other authentic assessment techniques. Teacher empowerment initiatives have acknowledged the primacy of the classroom teacher in making decisions about the kinds of tasks that are truly authentic and how outcomes should be evaluated so that the information garnered will have validity for instructional purposes and can better generate trustworthy data needed to make important decisions. The concern then becomes balancing authentic assessment and other indicators of student ability with the need for reliable measurement used in important decision making. Valencia, Hiebert, and Afflerbach (1994) feel that this will take time, but it is worth the effort:

> It has taken decades and millions of dollars to create the assessment system we now have. It would be naive to believe that we could create an effective new system in just a few years. We need to move slowly and cautiously into these new arenas, but we must move. The alternative is to remain in an assessment environment that has not worked very well for any of us—least of all for students. (p. 299)

Portfolios enhance many partnerships including collaboration between families and school, between teachers, as well as between teachers and administrators. Education is a partnership among students, teachers, administrators, and families, and the more effective these partnerships are in communicating with each other, the more likely that educational procedures will result in joint approval. Parents have sometimes felt left out of the partnership. The portfolio concept provides a meaningful opportunity for parents to become more involved in their children's literacy growth through a dialogue with both their children and the teacher using the portfolio as a centerpiece. One parent who was asked to write a letter to her son after viewing his portfolio commented, "I can really see how much your spelling has improved this year, and I truly enjoyed reading your poetry! I never knew you were such a talented poet!"

October 31

Dear Parents,

This has been a wonderful two months of school. I want to thank you for your cooperation and support for our program. As you know, I will be taping your child reading as part of our portfolio and discussing his/her reading periodically. We have completed our first taping, and we would like you to listen to it and enjoy it. Please put on your listening ears, so you can pick out what your child is doing well, and discuss the tape with him/her.

In the folder, you will also find my analysis of the reading and any notes I may have taken. Your child also included an evaluation of his/her reading and evaluation of a written response to a piece of literature.

I recently sent you a short note explaining what your child would like to work on before our next taping (end of November). I discussed some techniques you and your child might use to help accomplish his/her goals. If you would like additional help, please let me know.

Please return the folder and everything in it tomorrow. I would appreciate it if you would answer the questions below.

Thank you,
Mrs. Eisenhauer

FIGURE 1–1 Letter to parents of students in a third-grade class (Courtesy of Wendy Eisenhauer, Marion Street School, Lynbrook, Long Island, New York.)

Before teachers and school districts mandate that portfolios be kept and used to evaluate students' literacy skills, their reasons for doing so should be clearly explained to parents. Parents have always relied on letter grades and percentage scores as validation of their children's progress, and this traditional practice is not easily replaced. Individual teachers must inform parents about their use of portfolios and ask for their assistance with the practice. For example, Wendy Eisenhauer, a third-grade teacher in Lynbrook, New York, periodically writes to parents and explains the latest portfolio entries. She also asks that parents review their child's literacy portfolio and provide her with information from their perspective (see Figures 1–1 and 1–2.) Significantly, Eisenhauer asks parents for their assistance and feedback, and she reports the most positive reaction to this approach, with no parent unwilling to assist.

When parents understand the portfolio process, they willingly assist teachers in understanding their children. One parent from Juneau, Alaska (Juneau School District, 1993), commented how the portfolio process enhanced her confidence in the teacher's ability to work effectively with her child, "I was glad to see the classroom teacher become just as aware of my child's attitude as I was. I know the teacher is better able to teach my child knowing this information."

Sharing portfolio information with parents is central to effective conferencing. Teachers report that parent conferences centered around discussing student portfolios provide concrete information that explains the student's level of achievement, the instructional goals and techniques, and the student's growth. Portfolios provide an occasion for parents to see their child grow and reflect on their learning. One parent noted that her child took more pride in her

What progress has your child made in reading?
She has been reading more fluently and sounding words out more.

What do you feel your child does well when reading?
Tries to figure out the word before asking for help.

Where do you think your child needs to improve?
Sounding out more and understanding what she has read.

What do you plan to do to help your child?
Getting books with tapes.

In what ways (if any) did the reading portfolio help you? All comments are important to me and your child, and we value your input.
Helped me understand what she needs help with. I felt listening to the tape was a great idea.

FIGURE 1–2 Completed questionnaire from a third-grade teacher to parents after review of their child's portfolio. (An audiotape of the child reading aloud at various times during the school year was included in the portfolio.) (Courtesy of Wendy Eisenhauer, Marion Street School, Lynbrook, Long Island, New York.)

work and was willing to rewrite and edit her stories because they would be kept in her portfolio.

Another part of the educational partnership that has become increasingly evident is the number of children educated by instructional teams. These consist of a reading teacher, speech and language teacher, bilingual or English as a second language teacher, and the resource room teacher or other special educators working in conjunction with the mainstream teacher. Frequently, psychosocial personnel form other partnerships with classroom teachers. When these multidisciplinary teams collaborate to discuss a child—whether for diagnosis, program placement, monitoring the child's progress, or creating an individual educational plan (IEP)—examining actual work products provides tremendous insight into the child's capacity and performance. When children are reviewed to determine if interventional services are appropriate, the portfolio process is an important tool in educational decision making.

The partnership between the school administrator and classroom teacher is also enhanced by the portfolio process. Because supervision is necessary for accountability as well as promoting teacher growth, building and district administrators search for ways to be of constructive assistance. Teachers are required to demonstrate what goes on in their classrooms and the outcomes of instruction. Student-produced portfolios are an excellent way for teachers to concretely show their curriculum goals translated into assignments, to provide samples of the level of student work produced, to demonstrate how this process contributes to their knowledge about children, and to describe how the process assists with instructional decisions. One elementary school principal, who supports the use of language arts portfolios, asked to be assigned to work with a group of children on their portfolios. She felt that she needed to understand more about the day-to-day realities of portfolio use in a classroom before she could meaningfully understand the process and interact appropriately with the teachers in her school.

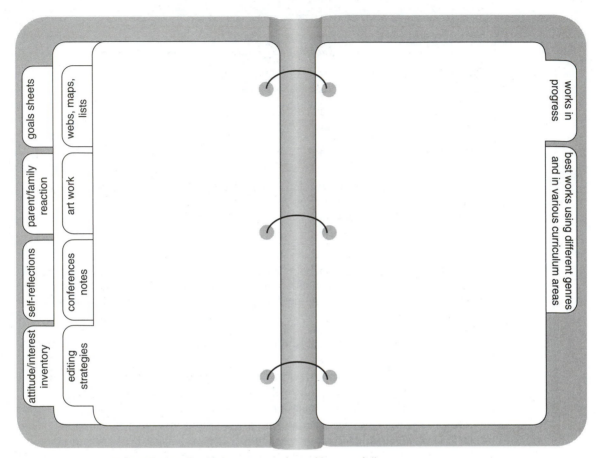

FIGURE 1–3 Typical contents of a writing portfolio

TYPES OF LITERACY PORTFOLIOS IN CURRENT USE

A review of the literature and discussions with educators across the country reveals that different forms of portfolios with various formats are used, but many teachers use **writing portfolios, reading portfolios, integrated language arts portfolios** (often including emphasis on content areas), and **cumulative record portfolios** for assessment. (See Figures 1–3 to 1–6).

Jenkins (1996) proposes another model for describing portfolios that focuses on whether the teacher or the student has primary responsibility for the assessment and creation of the portfolio. She describes writing portfolios that fall along a continuum that reflects basic differences about the nature and purpose of portfolio assessment. This model is helpful for describing all portfolios and distinguishes between **benchmark portfolios,** which are teacher-directed to document accountability for literacy progress, and **showcase portfolios,** which are student-directed to portray accomplishment, and **collaborative portfolios,** which combine

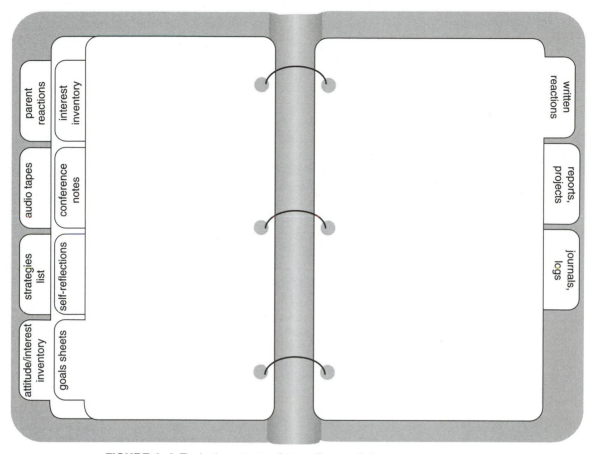

FIGURE 1–4 Typical contents of a reading portfolio

aspects of both of the other kinds of portfolios through a process of student–teacher shared responsibility for assessment, self-evaluation, and portfolio contents.

Some portfolios are limited to use in individual classrooms where teachers adopt the portfolio concept and modify it for their own particular purposes. In some schools, teams of teachers work together and agree on the kind of portfolios that they will assemble to promote consistency and continuity in practices. Other school districts prescribe the contents of portfolios and require that all teachers become involved in the same process to ensure standardization and consistency. In several states, pilot projects are creating guidelines for state-wide portfolio use.

Some teachers have independently embraced the portfolio process through self-education (reading professional literature, sharing ideas with colleagues, attending conferences, and/or taking college or in-service courses) and consequently find the use of portfolios to be an important part of their individual instructional programs. They create portfolios customized for individual classroom use. However, conversations with other teachers reveal a

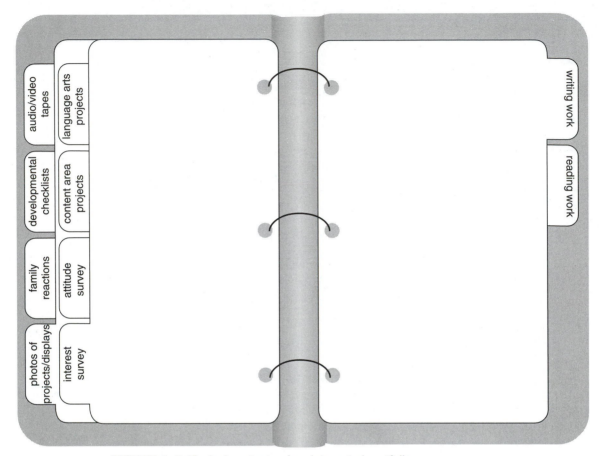

FIGURE 1–5 Typical contents of an integrated portfolio

markedly different attitude. When portfolio practice has been mandated without dialogue and professional development, teachers can perceive it to be merely another unneeded educational fad. Many teachers fear that portfolios create an enormous time burden without having any real benefit. If teachers do not understand and endorse a prescribed portfolio process and do not appreciate its worth, both as an instructional and assessment tool, the process will fail.

Calfee and Perfumo (1993) conducted a survey of portfolio practice in 150 different sites across the country. Three themes emerged:

- Teachers enlisted in the portfolio movement showed an intense commitment and sense of personal renewal.

- The technical foundations for portfolio assessment appeared infirm and inconsistent at all levels.

- Portfolio practice shied away from standards and grades and emphasized narrative and descriptive reporting.

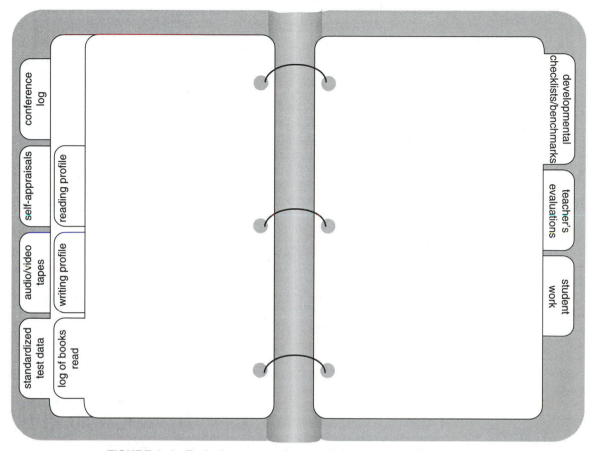

FIGURE 1–6 Typical contents of a cumulative record portfolio

The researchers concluded that reactions to the portfolio concept are varied and complex and that portfolio practices sometimes resulted in "virtual anarchy" as a "pendulum swing" reaction to teachers' bias against traditional testing practices. Conversely, if portfolios are used as part of broad educational changes, then "this 'package' offers the opportunity for fundamental reform in U.S. schooling" (Calfee & Perfumo, 1993, p. 536). Thus, it seems clear that portfolio assessment needs to be part of a coherent theory of educational practice. The movement is likely to falter, however, if teachers, who are already burdened by the number of external mandates, see portfolios as an additional demand without direct benefit.

The use of a portfolio requires redirection in teaching processes and in adoption of a different model and philosophy of literacy teaching and learning. Graves (1992) reminds us that the portfolio movement is still in its infancy and that "the health of the portfolio movement will be measured in the diversity of its practice and the breadth of its use, whether for evaluation or instruction" (p. 12). While there is great benefit to the adoption of portfolio practice, careful thought and planning clearly are needed for effective implementation.

The use of portfolios arises from a context of new thinking about how reading and writing should be taught, learned, and evaluated. In the next chapter, we will trace how the portfolio process evolved from traditional models of reading and writing to a new view of language and literacy that provides the framework and foundation of literature-based, integrated instruction and assessment. In Chapters 3 and 4, we will describe the dynamic changes in literacy instruction and then survey how literacy portfolios provide a complementary aspect of new teaching and assessment strategies. In Chapter 5, the movement from traditional assessment to authentic assessment will be portrayed as well as discussions of changing views of literacy assessment. Chapter 6 contains a proposal for the use of a specific form of a literacy portfolio, the LAP, and describes a process for its implementation.

REFERENCES

Arter, J., & Spandel, V. (1992, Spring). Using portfolios of student work in instruction and assessment. *Educational Measurement: Issues and Practice,* pp. 36–44.

Barton, P., & Coley, R. (1994). *Testing in America's schools.* Princeton, NJ: Educational Testing Service.

Calfee, R., & Perfumo, P. (1993). Student portfolios: Opportunities for a revolution in assessment. *Journal of Reading, 36,* 532–537.

Gomez, M. L., & Schenk, J. (1992). *What are portfolios? Stories teachers tell.* Paper presented at the meeting of the AERA, San Francisco.

Gooding, K. (1994, April). Teaching to the test: The influence of alternative modes of assessment on teachers' instructional strategies. Paper presented at the meeting of the AERA, New Orleans, LA.

Graves, D. (1992). Portfolios: Keep a good idea growing. In D. Graves & B. Sunstein (Eds.), *Portfolios portraits* (pp. 1–12). Portsmouth, NH: Heinemann.

Harp, B. (1993). The whole language movement. In B. Harp (Ed.), *Assessment and evaluation in whole language*

programs (pp. 1–18). Norwood, MA: Christopher Gordon.

Jenkins, C. B. (1996). *Inside the writing portfolio.* Portsmouth, MA: Heinemann.

Juneau School District (1993). *Language arts portfolio handbook.* Juneau, AK: Author.

Paulson, F. L., Paulson, P., & Meyer, C. (1991, February). What makes a portfolio a portfolio? *Educational Leadership,* pp. 60–63.

Rhodes, L., & Shanklin, N. (1993). *Windows into literacy.* Portsmouth, NH: Heinemann.

Seger, F. D. (1992). Portfolio definitions: Toward a shared notion. In D. Graves & B. Sunstein (Eds.), *Portfolio portraits* (pp. 114–126). Portsmouth, NH: Heinemann.

Valencia, S., Hiebert, E., & Afflerbach, P. (1994). Realizing the possibilities of authentic assessment: Current trends and future issues. In S. Valencia, E. Hiebert, & P. Afflerbach (Eds.), *Authentic reading assessment* (pp. 286–300). Newark, DE: International Reading Association.

Changing Views of Literacy

KEY WORDS AND CONCEPTS

Historical perspective	Metacognitive strategies
McGuffey Readers	Integrative model
Reading models	Whole language
Cognitive model	Literature-based teaching
Information processing model	Thematic units
Interactive model	Basal reading
Behaviorists	Emergent literacy
Schema	Authentic learning

A student who is preparing for job interviews asked for some advice. She said, "I've learned a lot about whole language, using children's literature, and other new ways of assessing reading and writing that I'd like to use when I have my own class. But during student teaching, I've seen some very traditional teaching with basals and worksheets. Which is the real world? Do some teachers use the older methods, while new teachers like me implement the new ones? Will I be expected to do what everyone else is doing? Or is everyone in the process of changing? I'm really confused."

In the past few years, a revolution in education has resulted in modifications in philosophy and pedagogy across the curriculum. Change is reflected in new terminology, innovative strategies, refocused goals, and new assessment practices to determine learning outcomes. Until recently, reading, writing, and communications skills, traditionally called *the language arts,* were viewed as separate though related fields. Newer perspectives on literacy and its development have transformed classroom practices.

HISTORY AND BACKGROUND OF READING AND WRITING INSTRUCTION

Reading is a complex and enigmatic phenomenon, easy and natural for most children and adults, difficult and painful for others. With Johann Gutenberg's invention of movable type in 1455, the primacy of the written word was established and a new form of communication, for the first time available to the poor as well as the rich, was introduced to the world. This giant step allowed for dissemination of written ideas, preceded by another profound historical marker centuries earlier: the Greek invention of vowels. The Phoenicians had earlier provided an alphabet with only consonants, which was quite cumbersome. The combined Greek and Phoenician alphabets eliminated the need for thousands of images, as in hieroglyphics and ideographs. Instead, twenty-four symbols provided a manageable code to transmit and record information and ideas with greater ease, resulting in the alphabet systems we use today. Simply having printed materials available did not indicate, however, how best to teach children or adults to process it. There has been much experimentation with a variety of pedagogical strategies and techniques in an attempt to effectively instruct children in how to read and write.

The first readers, used for instructional purposes in classrooms in America, were called *hornbooks.* Adapted from England, hornbooks were used from the 1670s throughout the colonial period. They consisted of wooden paddles containing the alphabet and religious prayers covered with a thin sheet of animal horn. These were replaced by books with nationalistic or moralistic themes, emphasizing diligence and virtue, with titles such as "Charity to Orphans," "Danger of Bad Habits," and "The Love of Country and Home" (N. Banton Smith, 1934-1965). These were followed in the mid-1830s by the ***McGuffey Readers,*** which became so popular they were used for approximately forty years. This series had illustrations, introduced new vocabulary for each story, and had a different book for each grade. Most had biblical, patriotic, or moral themes, but there were also stories about children and animals. To the contemporary ear, the sentences seem choppy and artificial, and the selections are of questionable literary quality. *McGuffey Readers* ultimately were replaced by other readers that were used daily in most schools. Spot probably became the most famous dog in America along with, of course, those renowned siblings Dick and Jane. Basal readers became "the most widely used materials for teaching reading in the elementary schools of the U.S." (Burns, Roe, & Ross, 1992, p. 310).

READING RESEARCH

The study of reading was never stagnant, as N. Banton Smith (1934/1965) pointed out in her definitive history of *American Reading Instruction*. Research began in the 1880s and has been fairly continuous. Theoretical concepts often drove instruction, and many different **reading models** were developed. For example, in the early 1900s, Huey (1908) thought of the reader as receiving useful mental disciplines and learning good judgments and values from the author. The student was perceived as an empty vessel that was filled with the author's ideas. Half a century later, the perspective of reading and instruction drastically changed. Stauffer (1969) conceived of reading as a **cognitive process:** setting a purpose, reflecting, and then accepting or rejecting the ideas presented—a problem-solving view. Figure 2–1 provides an overview of the evolution of reading process models.

Frank Smith (1971, 1983a, 1983b) altered the prevailing view of the reading process by emphasizing comprehension, using perceptions based on communication systems. In Smith's **information processing model,** the reader recognizes visual features and regularities in language that provide a basis for generalizations that are necessary to generate meaning and are affected by unique psychological and sociological factors. In his seminal book, *Understanding Reading* (1971, p. 28), Smith connects speech, writing, and reading by noting that "reading is an aspect of language, only superficially different from the comprehension of speech. . . . [M]any of the skills employed by a child in learning the regularities of spoken language may also be employed in learning to read."

Other models emerged. LaBerge and Samuels (1974) discussed a subskill model having a hierarchy where reader comprehension proceeds from "distinctive features, to letters, to letter clusters, then to words," referred to as the *bottom-up approach.* McCracken (1962), Smith, and whole language supporters view reading as *top-down:* It is holistic and reader focused (rather than text oriented), and readers make predictions using clues from the passage. Reading in this model is a natural and fluid process. An **interactive model** integrates top-down and bottom-up theories, postulating that they occur simultaneously (Rumelhart, 1976). Here, readers use both word identification and meaning cues, depending on the difficulty of the material. In 1973, Goodman put a new spin on reading by calling it a "psycholinguistic guessing game" where readers use their prior knowledge and experiences as well as clues in the text to make predictions about meaning. Meaning and comprehension emerged as essential, although models varied. Reading was considered both an affective and cognitive process involving interpretation, not merely the decoding of graphic symbols, but translating print into meaning. Some demurred; the best known was perhaps Rudolph Flesch, who in 1955 wrote the (in)famous *Why Johnny Can't Read.* Flesch insisted that

	Theoretical Literacy Models	Teaching Models	Models of Reading Comprehension

Early 1900s	Behaviorist
	
	Mental discipline
	   Author provided moral values
	   Student perceived as empty vessel to be filled with author's concepts (Huey, 1908; Gray, 1948; and others)
		Bottom-up
		   Phonics
		   Sight words
		   Splintered skills
			Transmission view
			   Discover the author's intent
			   Meaning as memory
			   Recall
			   Author's message

1960s	Cognitive processes
	   Problem solving
	   Varying levels of comprehension (Stauffer, 1969; Harris, 1961; and others)
		Basal
		   Eclectic
		   Skills focus
			Translation
			   Derive meaning of text
			   Study skills
			   Vocabulary development
			   Word recognition skills

1970–1980	Information processing (F. Smith, 1971)
	Psycholinguistic language interaction (Goodman, 1973)
	Sociolinguistics
	Interactive model (Rumelhart, 1976)
		Top-down
		   Individualized reading
		   Language experience approach
		   Critical thinking
		   Thematic Units
		   Student centered teaching
			Interactive
			   Text and reader together unlock meaning
			   Word and meaning cues
			   Mapping
			   Self-monitoring

1980s	Schema theory
	Metacognition
			Transactional
			   Poststructural
			   Reader response theory
			   Whole language
			   Challenge ideas and assumptions
			   Can always reinterpret text

1990s	Whole language
	Reading as literature
		Integrative
		   Whole language
		   Literature based
		   Integrated Language arts	

FIGURE 2–1 Evolution of reading process models.

reading was phonics based, a decoding not a comprehension process, whereby graphemes (letters) are translated into sounds and sounds into words. He claimed that other concepts, especially the whole word method, caused reading failures as well as many of our political and social problems!

CHANGING LITERACY MODELS IMPACT INSTRUCTION

As models changed, instruction changed. When reading instruction was influenced by **behaviorist** principles, there was a sequential presentation of sound–symbol relationships followed by skill instruction emphasizing decoding and literal comprehension. Although current literacy texts include traditional techniques for word recognition and vocabulary instruction, they also include newer theories and additional strategies that contribute to more authentic instructional approaches.

Cognitive-Interactive Perspectives

Just as behaviorism overshadowed other theories for awhile, interactive perspectives now predominate; these are based on psychological principles that highlight higher order thinking skills. Two exciting conceptual models, schema theory and metacognitive strategies, demonstrate how comprehension, knowledge, and understanding are influenced by how individuals process and store information.

Schema Theory. Schemata are the clusters of knowledge an individual acquires through life experiences and are defined and explained as

- "Mental file folders in which all the information related to an event, object, or person is kept" (Tompkins & McGee, 1993, p. 142)
- Knowledge packed into units or structures that represent concepts stored in our memory (Rumelhart, 1981)
- "[Representing] what a person knows about a particular concept and the interrelationships among known pieces of information" (Burns, Roe, & Ross, 1992, p. 210)
- Capable of being enlarged with additional data gleaned from new experiences and activities because they are a network of dynamic, changing mental representations (Pappas, Kiefer, & Levstik, 1990)

Schema theory explains how past knowledge contributes to reading comprehension. Comprehension is achieved when knowledge from the text is assimilated into an already existing set of data organized as schemata, which helps the reader interpret, reconstruct, and elaborate on information read. The new data fill in any missing gaps of concepts already stored, or help to develop new information. Schema theory—activating prior experiences and developing a cognitive structure of knowledge—is a holistic perspective of comprehension. Every teacher knows the frustration of trying to get students to grasp information for which they have no background or prior knowledge. Schema theory helps by explaining that people understand what they read only if it relates to what they already know (Cooper, 1993).

Semantic mapping and webbing are symbolic ways to diagram the relationship between schemata or concepts. They indicate how ideas are related. These strategies are taught to students so they can visually organize and connect prior knowledge with new information (see Figures 2–2A and B).

Metacognitive Strategies. *Metacognition* is a contemplative intellectual process. It is the ability to reflect on one's own cognitive processes and be aware of one's own activities while reading and problem solving, according to Baker and Brown (1984). They describe the features of metacognition as knowing oneself as a learner (and activating prior knowledge in preparation for reading); regulating oneself (knowing how and what to read, setting a purpose); checking oneself (evaluating one's performance); and repairing (being aware of a comprehension problem and doing something about it). Metacognitive skills can be taught as involving four steps (see Figure 2–3):

1. Plan: Ask prereading questions.
2. Strategize: How will I do it?
3. Monitor: How am I doing?
4. Evaluate: How well have I done?

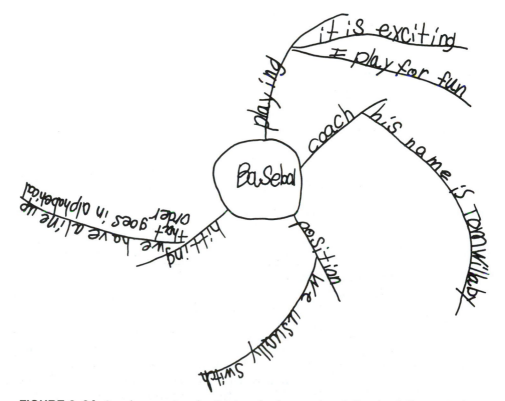

FIGURE 2–2A Sample semantic webs. (A) A student's semantic web for a baseball story. Each strand relates to the core topic.

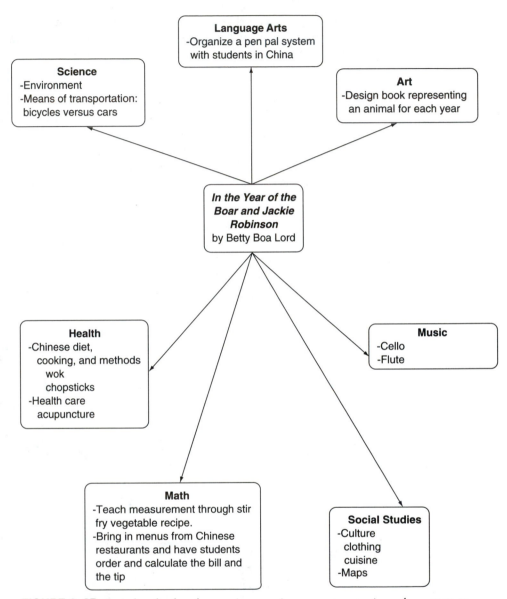

FIGURE 2–2B A teacher-developed semantic map using a story to organize and construct an integrated unit.

Readers draw on their schemata that have been activated from earlier experiences to reconstruct meaning and make sense of the material. Metacognition helps readers focus on *how* they read. It is not enough to be able to summarize, predict, or infer; readers must learn to maximize their reading potential, to monitor themselves, to reflect. To "know that one knows" (to perceive that one understands) it is necessary to

1. Know why a reading strategy works.

2. Know when understanding doesn't take place.

3. Know when understanding occurs.

4. Know what you need to know.

The more fluent the reader, the better the reader's use of metacognitive strategies. Gunning (1992) suggests that such self-awareness is developmental; therefore, older readers do better than younger ones. Although it develops automatically for some, it can be a learned strategy. Teaching metacognition as part of the instructional process empowers students to construct meaning by monitoring and reflecting on their own thinking.

Students are not passive recipients of information but are active learners engaged in meaningful interactions with text, which stimulate prior knowledge and contribute to self-monitored reading strategies.

Integrative Methodologies

The **integrative, holistic model** of reading began to take hold in the early 1980s. It emerged from researchers and practitioners who regarded the reading process in a fundamentally different way. Reading was reconceptualized to emphasize relevant and meaningful reading and writing activities that integrate all language processes. To determine factors that contribute to students becoming fluent readers and successful learners, researchers examined classroom environments and found that authenticity was an essential component. *Process* as well as *products* were emphasized, and the implementation of portfolios for literacy assessment emerged so that actual (authentic) learning strategies and products could be collected and reflected on. Thus, a new movement appeared on the educational horizon called *whole language,* often referred to as an integrative model. The methodological approaches associated with whole language encompass integrated learning, literature-based reading, and thematic reading. The term *whole language* contains the unifying principles and philosophies they all share.

Whole Language. Definitions of **whole language** vary, yet the conceptual commonalities are the focus on language, learning, and the learner. Baumann defines whole language as "the simultaneous, integrated teaching of reading, writing, speaking, and listening within a context that is meaningful to the language-learner" (1984, p. 3). Froese calls it "a child-centered, literature based approach to language teaching that immerses students in real communication situations whenever possible" (1991, p. 2). Yatvin (1992) provides a pedagogical definition: Whole language is the belief that language learning depends on the learner's motivation and self-confidence, and the integration of real language use into learning activities. Brountas (1987) explains that whole language

- Views reading and writing as developmental—as natural as learning to talk.
- Surrounds children with literature. Brountas poetically states that "literature is to children as a rainbow is to sky" (1987, p. 58).
- Keeps language whole and natural.
- Integrates all the language arts by presenting reading, writing, listening, and speaking as related elements of a single unit.

Know myself as a learner: activate prior knowledge.	Plan: Ask questions before reading
Regulate myself: Do I understand what is taking place?	Strategize: Set a purpose, know how and what to read
Check myself: Do I know what I'm reading?	Monitor: How is my performance? Am I doing OK?
Repair: Do I know how to correct the problems I am having?	Evaluate: How well have I done? Do I understand what I have read?

FIGURE 2–3 Eight components of metacognitive strategies.

■ Regards reading and writing as thinking processes.

■ Uses a thematic approach that integrates language arts with other curriculum areas.

■ Views parents as partners.

■ Is a shared teacher–learner responsibility.

The Bureau of English and Reading Education (*English and Reading Education News,* 1989), N.Y. State Education Department, indicated that whole language is a philosophy whose beliefs include the following:

■ Children learn by constructing meaning from the world around them.

■ Reading and writing skills develop simultaneously, not sequentially.

■ Language learning flourishes where risk taking is encouraged.

■ Errors should be viewed as attempts to make sense of one's world.

■ Reading/writing/listening/speaking complement and support each other.

■ Successful readers must have encounters with natural and complete texts.

■ Time must be provided to practice in functional and realistic settings.

Goodman (1986) emphasizes language as the focal point: Language is empowering; language development is a holistic personal-social achievement; and language learning is easy when it is whole, real, and relevant. He believes that, philosophically, whole language "is supported by four humanistic-scientific pillars. It has a strong theory of learning, a theory of language, a basic view of teaching and the role of teachers, and a language centered view of curriculum" (p. 26).

Literature-Based Teaching. Those who endorse the integrative language model and reexamined instruction now focus on quality literature as the basis for teaching literacy. Literature offers new ways of exploring the world and new worlds to explore—the stuff a child's brain thrives on (F. Smith, 1983a). In Norton's book *Through the Eyes of a Child* (1995, p. 4), she explains how children's literature entices, motivates, relays new knowledge about virtually every topic imaginable at all levels of difficulty, and affects personal development and understanding of our cultural heritage. Literature in the classroom is no longer considered recreational reading or a time filler when other work is finished. Instead, quality children's books are the foundation of literacy learning. Real literature touches children in special ways; children don't just learn *how* to read, they *choose* to read (Hornsby, Sukarna, & Parry, 1986). Literature programs promote a desire to read and positive reading habits. Tompkins and McGee (1993) identified several benefits derived from a literature-based reading program:

- Literature provides entertainment and aesthetic experiences that illuminate the human condition. It is enjoyable as well as educational.

- Positive experiences with literature ensure that children will become not only fine readers but also lifelong readers.

- Involvement with literature helps children appreciate literary styles including the flow and rhythm of language. Tompkins and McGee (1993) cite the high correlation between experiences with literature and the sophistication of linguistic development.

- Literature has a strong influence on reading development. Students read more when they read literature, and extensive reading is essential for fluency.

- Students in literature-based programs read 50 to 100 books a year as opposed to reading an average of seven minutes daily and only one or two reading textbooks in traditional classes.

- Exposure to good literature enhances writing, and according to F. Smith (1983a, p. 84), "The only source of knowledge sufficiently rich and reliable for learning about written language is the writing already done by others . . . one learns to write through reading."

- Literature enhances social and cognitive development. Students learn to view problems from different perspectives; they learn to make connections between characters in literature and their own lives; they learn to respect cultural diversity.

In this approach, students apply literacy skills in a variety of contexts throughout the curriculum. Reading to learn and to enjoy replaces learning to read as a goal, and applying reading and writing across the curriculum is a primary focus. When holistic models of literacy instruction are adopted, learning flourishes, and teachers appear to be revitalized when these curricula changes are enthusiastically implemented.

Thematic Learning. Traditionally, all classroom subjects were treated separately and distinctly. A look at teachers' daily plan books probably indicates sections set aside for each curriculum area: spelling, arithmetic, reading, social studies, and so on. Fragmentation of learning, however, is yielding to current ideas of integrating concepts and applying literacy skills across the curriculum. This is often accomplished through the use of themes that combine and relate subject areas to a unit, topic, or issue. A piece of literature can often be the springboard for integrative learning when studied in terms of genre, theme, or plot, or when related to knowledge in content areas such as history, science, and geography.

As Figure 2–4 illustrates, the literature approach lends itself to thematic, interdisciplinary, holistic learning. Norton (1992, p. 7) emphasizes the National Commission on Social Studies in the Schools' recommendation for using literature to develop the understanding of history: "We need black and white, male and female, Native American, Asians and Hispanics, not necessarily balanced to reflect the exact composition of the class, but balanced to reflect the reali-

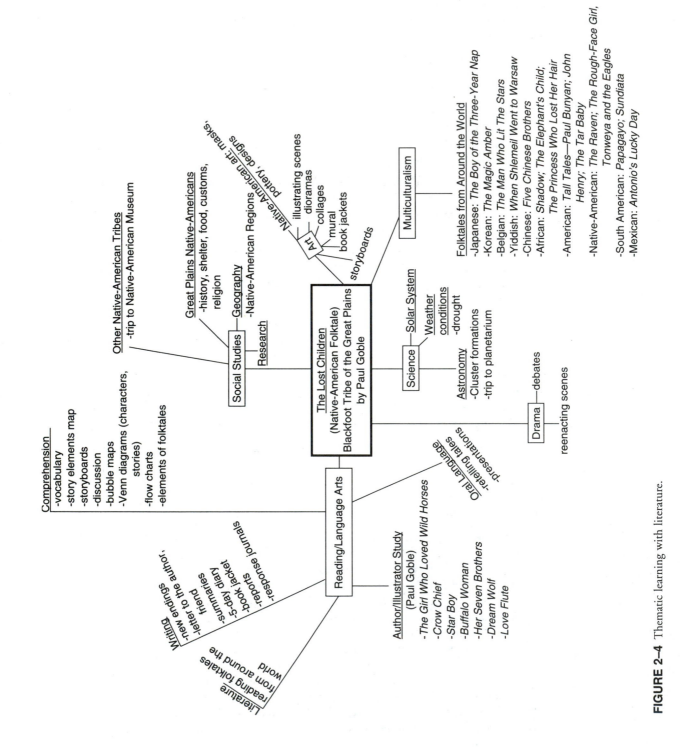

FIGURE 2-4 Thematic learning with literature.

28

ties of the world and of the cultural landscape of our country." Heroes and heroines from literature not only provide prominent role models but make the past come alive.

Teachers are often advised to befriend school librarians because of the immeasurable help they provide. This is an especially good suggestion when using a literature or thematic approach. Whatever topic is studied, school and community librarians can suggest appropriate videos and tapes, fiction and nonfiction trade books, poetry, and folklore that relate to the theme, engage the students, and supplement any text.

SO, HAVE THEY THROWN AWAY BASAL READERS?

In spite of new information about literacy, **basal reading** remains "as American as apple pie." Basal readers are used by 85% to 95% of elementary school teachers, and "virtually every American identifies basals as the focus of reading instruction" (Duffy & Roehler, 1993, p. 11). Many school boards, teachers, and parents view basals as an institutional part of our schools.

Basals are structured texts with stories for each grade level and accompanying workbooks that focus on word recognition, comprehension, and skill reinforcement. Children are assigned to ability groups determined by a standardized reading test or a test designed by the basal publishers. Instruction is uniform: Read the story (most often orally), have a discussion, work on specific skill exercises in the workbook. The lessons are teacher directed with a detailed manual, which suggests the format for introducing the story, new vocabulary, and comprehension questions. There is a classroom management system with planned activities and answer-oriented exercises. Diversity in learning or teaching is not encouraged. Duffy and Roehler (1993) indicate that basal teachers are more like technicians who follow someone else's plans rather than professionals who make their own instructional decisions. Although new teachers find the manuals reassuring, experienced teachers who are required by district policy to use basals often find them constricting.

Teachers lose the forest for the trees when they focus on workbook and skill responses, which are often integral to a basal series. Many children view reading only as what occurs during basal reading time. Even when engaged in a related activity (listening to a story, working on a newspaper lesson, or reading social studies material), children and teachers may complain "we didn't have reading today" because they weren't working in a basal group.

Gambrell (1984) studied the amount of time children spent reading during teacher-directed sessions, and her results indicate very little sustained, contextualized reading. In third grade, for example, each child read orally for about *one-fourth minute* and silently for about *five minutes* during a twenty-three-minute reading lesson; first and second graders spent even less time during longer reading sessions.

Story involvement, uninterrupted reading, and reading for its own sake are not part of basal instruction. Children are exposed to sustained reading of complete works of literature only as an add-on during recreational reading or library time. The joylessness of the process too often turns students into aliterates, meaning they have the ability to read but choose not to do so. Bright youngsters are bored and unchallenged, and less-able children become frustrated by their inability to make sense out of print.

Linguistic scholars are also critical of the basals, because the structured and controlled vocabulary creates stilted language that does not reflect natural speech. Children bring a much more intricate language structure to reading. Story lines in basals are often banal with little literary merit, and guided instruction and frequent literal questions interfere with pleasurable reading.

Poor Reading Success

Basalized instruction apparently has not led to overwhelming reading success. Too frequently students read poorly and ineffectively. Kozol (1985) claims that one-third of Americans can't read well enough to function adequately in society, while one million children between twelve and seventeen cannot read above a third-grade level.

These dismal literacy trends are supported by research:

- One in five Americans cannot read well enough to perform simple tasks (Werner, 1986).
- The majority of nonreaders are under fifty, and many attended high school (Bowen, 1986).
- The illiterate population is expanding at an estimated rate of 2.3 million a year (Rohter, 1986).

Economic, social, political, and educational factors have contributed to problems of illiteracy in this country, and basal reading programs are certainly not the primary cause. However, it is acknowledged that appropriate strategies in literacy teaching can result in more favorable outcomes. As we will see, more child-centered curricula with immersion in a language-rich environment empower students, develop self-confidence, and produce motivation and enjoyment for reading.

Combining Basals and Other Approaches

Is it possible to incorporate a more language-oriented pedagogy into a basal format? Publishers have been trying to make inroads in this direction. Newer editions include journal writing, some metacognitive strategies, and even portfolio use. They often include poetry, folktales, and selections from popular children's literature. Unfortunately, only parts of children's stories are excerpted, which has led to the coining of a new term, the *basalization* of literature (Goodman, 1988).

Jewell and Zintz (1990) state that "basal series have potential for productive use as one component in a balanced literacy development program" (p. 240). Other researchers (Buckley, 1986; Eldredge & Butterfield, 1986) report on programs that combine various approaches. Some classes use basals three times a week and literature twice a week; some use the basals as a springboard for reading other books.

NEW DIRECTIONS

Overemphasis on oral reading, skill and drill reinforcement, underemphasis on higher level thinking skills, and the omission of writing as a partner in literacy have led to a search for more *language-oriented* programs. Goodman (1986) said that teaching doesn't make language learning happen; it supports its development. More recently, Gillet and Temple (1994) explained that reading is primarily a language ability and that learning to talk and learning to read have many parallels. Scholars generally agree that children learn to read and write as naturally as they learn to speak if provided the appropriate environment.

> All proficient readers have acquired an implicit knowledge of how to read, but this knowledge has been developed through the practice of reading, not through anything that is taught in school. The learning process is identical with that by which infants develop a set of internal rules for producing and comprehending spoken language without the benefit of any formal instruction. (F. Smith, 1983a, p. 12)

Literacy experts maintain that children's life experiences help them interpret text. This social-cultural perspective strives to create a "literacy club" environment, which includes parents, teachers, and children. How did we arrive at such concepts? When did we move from talking about reading to talking about literacy? What models led to integrating reading and writing?

Impact of New Literacy Models on Classroom Practice

From Reading to Literacy: Rethinking the Terminology. The focus has shifted to a finer understanding of language development, to establishing new reading and writing models, to teaching thinking skills, and to developing new methods for assessing behavior through portfolios. Terminology also has changed, reflecting the extent of this pervasive, ideological movement. Most significant and noticeable is the fact that researchers, authors, and educators now prefer the term *literacy* to *reading*. This is both a semantic and a conceptual change that reflects current thinking and contemporary perspectives in the field. *Reading,* although enigmatic and complex, is a narrower concept and refers to communication of ideas, thoughts, and emotions from the writer to the reader—an intricate process that transforms printed symbols into ideas and meaning. *Literacy* is a broader concept, which encompasses reading, writing, speaking, and listening, and still more. It implies fluidity, wholeness, and integration rather than separate, isolated disciplines, skills, and subskills. *Literacy* is the holistic term that reflects current views of reading as an authentic thinking task, involving students' ongoing awareness of the process and their progress in the continuum of learning experiences.

Wells's (1990) definition of a literate person goes beyond the "reading as meaning" model to a view that the reader's involvement with the text empowers action, feeling, and thinking in the context of purposeful social activities.

New Models' Impact on Early Literacy Development. Another recent concept, **emergent literacy,** reflects a dramatic change in how early literacy behavior is perceived. It is a relatively recent term, usually credited to Marie Clay (1966, 1967), a New Zealand educator and early whole language advocate. Emergent literacy replaces the concept that a child has a distinct prereading or readiness phase. It postulates that literacy does not begin at a specific age but is natural, developmental, and continuous from birth. It emerges because of the innate capacity to use language as well as environmental experiences with oral language, and symbols— early encounters with reading and print.

Early childhood, bilingual, and linguistic specialists have all acknowledged the oral language expertise of children. Literature on language acquisition is replete with references to the remarkable ability of young children to acquire the complexities of language. Pinker (1994) researched visual cognition and child language acquisition and says "all languages are acquired with equal ease, before the child turns four . . . the 3 year old then is a grammatical genius" (pp. 273, 276). Children, it appears, are really young language prodigies who understand and use semantic and syntactic cues to develop language proficiency so well that by age six they have an oral vocabulary of about 20,000 words and are, according to Brown and Bellugi (1964), able to construct sentences they've never heard but are very well formed.

Thus, emergent literacy models recognize that reading and writing abilities are stimulated by active involvement with language and immersion in a print-rich environment: being read to daily, observing parents read a book or newspaper, and noting street signs and fast-food restaurants. Children come to school with a wealth of prior knowledge and varying amounts of print awareness from home and social environments.

Implications and Applications of Integrated Literacy

The acceptance of language as whole, integrated, and interrelated has led educators to restructure the classroom in terms of methodology and pedagogy. A literacy-centered environment has emerged where literacy is celebrated as the primary focus of the curriculum and where children are the center of the class. In these classes, children self-select reading material and confer and collaborate with one another. They work together as well as independently, so that teachers have no need to form ability groups and therefore avoid labeling children. The following features highlight the literacy-centered, literature-based, integrated classroom: (a) Thematic units are developed and integrated into various content areas; (b) process writing is implemented and products assessed; (c) cooperative learning is encouraged for unit work, peer editing, and assessment; (d) folders store logs and journals as well as other written material; (e) discussions stimulate critical thinking, and metacognitive strategies are encouraged; (f) goal setting is established; (g) activities are relevant and authentic. (See Figure 2–5.)

Authentic Reading and Writing

Newer approaches to literacy learning have a dual emphasis on language and authenticity. For children to be able to make sense of their world, reading, writing, and speaking interactions must be authentic and purposeful. The Center on Organization and Restructuring of Schools at the University of Wisconsin says authentic instruction results in higher order thinking, depth of knowledge, connectedness with the world beyond the classroom, substantive conversation, and social support for student achievement (Wakefield, 1994, p. 4).

Some teachers have difficulty choosing authentic activities. For example, can reading the Big Book *Brown Bear, Brown Bear, What do You See?* (Martin, 1983) with a kindergarten or first-grade class be considered an authentic activity? Definitely! Experiencing the book, turning pages, recognizing the repetition of words and rhyming patterns, reading with a partner, noting the relationship of illustrations to text, choral reading with other children, and later selecting the smaller version of the same book to read—all this involves children with real reading activities. Compare this with another exercise where children are told to copy the letter *p* or "Circle the letter that is different in this row: *t t p t.*" The Big Book lesson engages the child in print with colorful visual illustrations that are age appropriate, pleasurable, and language focused. The other is an isolated drill in a decontextualized setting, which the child cannot relate to any other life activity and ultimately has little to do with enhancing literacy.

When authentic situations are difficult to create in the classroom, literacy activities can still be genuine and require meaningful use of reading and writing. For example, the fifth-

•Students are
in a print-rich
environment

•Collaboration,
cooperation, and peer
interaction are encouraged

•Folders are maintained
that store reactions to
literature in the form of
reading logs and journals

•Teachers encourage thinking
Critical analysis
Discussion

•Thematic units are
developed integrating
literature with other
curriculum areas

Best works

•**Writing** ⟶ WORK in Progress

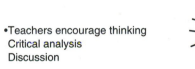

Is taught as authentic
and meaningful

•Self and peer editing: from rehearsal ⟶ to
drafting ⟶ through various stages of
editing ⟶ to the final product or
"publication" or "authorship"

FIGURE 2–5 Features of a
Literacy-centered class.

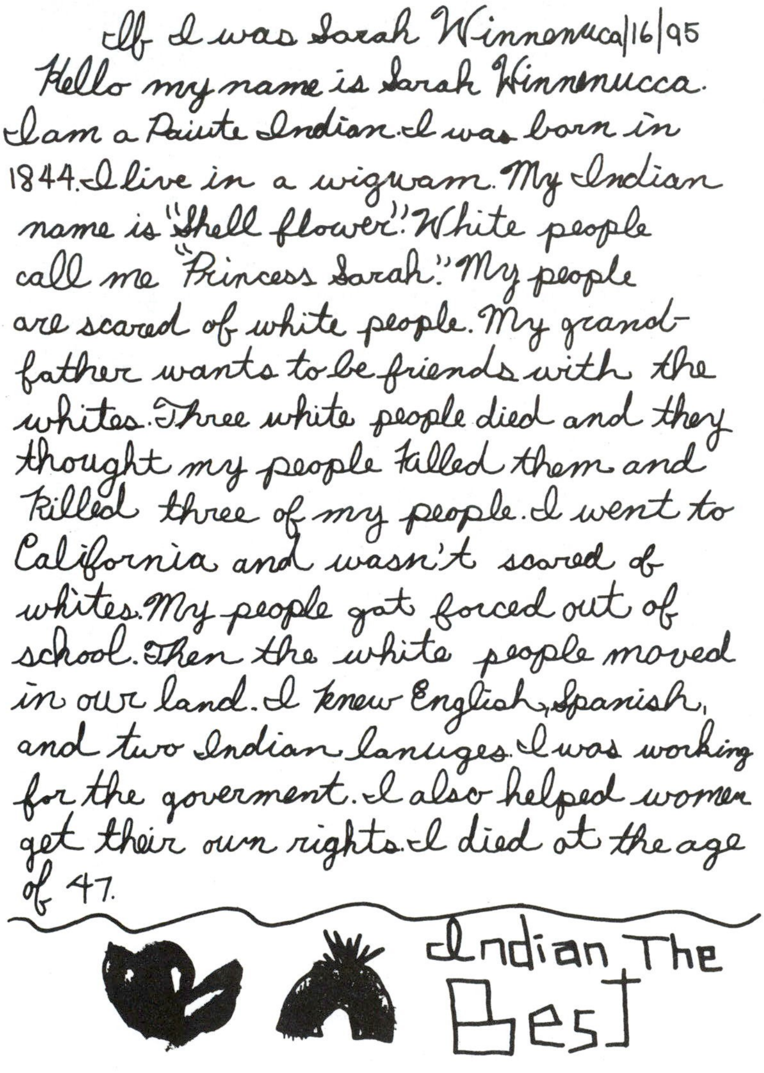

If I was Sarah Winnenuca|16|95

Hello my name is Sarah Winnenucca. I am a Paiute Indian. I was born in 1844. I live in a wigwam. My Indian name is "Shell flower". White people call me "Princess Sarah". My people are scared of white people. My grandfather wants to be friends with the whites. Three white people died and they thought my people killed them and killed three of my people. I went to California and wasn't scared of whites. My people got forced out of school. Then the white people moved in our land. I knew English, Spanish, and two Indian lanuges. I was working for the goverment. I also helped women get their own rights. I died at the age of 47.

Indian The Best

FIGURE 2–6 A fifth-grade student's character journal entry.

grade student writing in a character journal, pretending to be the Paiute Indian Sarah Winnenucca in a historical novel, may not be engaged in a truly authentic activity, but this activity is meaningful and purposeful in terms of understanding other cultures and identification with a character in literature. (See Figure 2–6.) The child has real control over the activity through self-selecting the character, deciding how much time to spend on the reaction, determining the moral dilemmas, reflecting on how she would react to the problems, and deciding what to write about. It is not a decontextualized assignment in a workbook that is unrelated to a personalized reading experience. Similarly, Figure 2–7 shows a third grader's literature-based report, which reflects an integrated reading–writing assignment. The student wrote a letter to an imaginary cousin in China, revealing the student's understanding of the book *In the Year of the Boar and Jackie Robinson.* Rhodes and Shanklin (1993) explain that

Dear Fourth Cousin,

Hi, how are you? I came to like baseball because Mabel my friend taught me how to play. I like to play and listen to baseball. My favorite team is the dodgers and my favorite player is Jackie Robinson. He is my favorite player because the first time I played baseball I scored points and my team called me Jackie Robinson. I got to meet him when I got to give him the key to the school,

Love,
Shirly TempleWog

To:

Fourth Cousin
House of Wong
ChungKing, China

FIGURE 2–7 A third grader's literature-based letter.

"in authentic reading and writing students are constructing meaning to communicate and have substantial control over the event" (p. 72). When engaging in authentic activities, one need not worry about transfer of learning from a theoretical to a real situation, which behavioral psychologists say is difficult at best. To learn to write a business letter, instead of being assigned the topic, students might be asked to write a letter of complaint or praise to a company of their choice, regarding a real product, for example, "The sneakers I bought lasted only three weeks before they started to fall apart" or "The flowers we ordered from your shop for Mom's birthday were so beautiful."

When developing authentic literacy activities, teachers should ask

- Is the reading or writing that the child is engaged in useful for communication purposes?

- Are the processes and goals realistic?

- Are the activities meaningful?

CONCLUSIONS

Changing concepts and models of reading instruction have moved literacy teaching in dynamic ways. The dual emphasis on language and authenticity has resulted in classrooms in which children are perceived as part of a literacy community. The environment is one where reading and writing activities, processes, and products are taught, observed, collected, and assessed in a manner that is congruent with these new directions and perspectives.

REFERENCES

Baker, L., & Brown, A. L. (1984). Metacognitive skills and reading. In P. D. Pearson (Ed.), *Handbook of reading research* (pp. 353–394). New York: Longman.

Bowen, E. (1986, May 6). Losing the war of letters. *Time,* p. 68.

Brountas, M. (1987, November/December). Whole language really works. *Teaching K–8,* pp. 57–60.

Brown, R., & Bellugi, U. (1964). Three processes in the child's acquisition of syntax. *Harvard Educational Review, 34.*

Buckley, M. (1986, April). When teachers decide to integrate the language arts. *Language Arts,* pp. 369–377.

Burns, P., Roe, B. & Ross, E. (1992). *Teaching reading in today's elementary schools* (5th ed.). Boston: Houghton Mifflin.

Clay, M. (1966). *Emergent reading behavior.* Doctoral dissertation, University of Aukland, New Zealand.

Clay, M. (1967). The reading behavior of 5 year old children: A research report. *New Zealand Journal of Educational Studies, 2,* 11–31.

Cooper, J. D. (1993). *Literacy: helping children construct meaning.* Princeton, NJ: Houghton Mifflin.

Duffy, G., & Roehler, L. (1993). *Improving classroom reading instruction.* New York: McGraw-Hill.

Eldredge, L., & Butterfield, D. (1986). Alternatives to traditional reading instruction. *Reading Teacher, 40,* 32–37.

English and Reading Education News. (1989, Spring). Albany, NY: The Bureau of English and Reading Education. The New York State Education Department.

Flesch, R. (1955). *Why Johnny can't read and what you can do about it.* New York: Harper Brothers.

Froese, V. (Ed.). (1991). *Whole-language: Practice and theory.* Needham Heights, MA: Allyn & Bacon.

Gambrell, L. (1984). How much time do children spend reading during teacher-directed reading instruction?" In J. Niles & L. Harris (Eds.), *Changing perspectives on research in reading/language processing and instruction.* Rochester, NY: National Reading Conference.

Gillet, J., & Temple, C. (1994). *Understanding reading problems: Assessment and instruction.* New York: Harper-Collins.

Goodman, K. (1973). Reading: A psycholinguistic guessing game. In R. Karlin (Ed.), *Perspectives on elementary reading.* New York: Harcourt Brace Jovanovich.

Goodman, K. (1986). Basal readers: A call for action. *Language Arts, 63,* 358–363.

Goodman, K. (1988). Look at what they've done to Judy Blume!!: The basalization of children's literature. *The New Advocate, 1* (1), 29–41.

Gunning, T. G. (1992). *Creating reading instruction for all children.* Boston: Allyn & Bacon.

Harris, A. (1961). *How to increase reading ability.* New York: McKay.

Hornsby, D., Sukarna, D., & Parry, J. (1986). *Read on: A conference approach to reading.* Portsmouth, NH: Heinemann.

Huey, E. Burke. (1908). *The psychology and pedagogy of reading.* New York: Macmillan.

Jewell, M. G., & Zintz, M. (1990). *Learning to read and write naturally* (2nd ed.). Dubuque, IA: Kendall/Hunt.

Kozol, J. (1985). *Illiterate America.* New York: New American Library.

LaBerge, D., & Samuels, S. J. (1985). "Toward a theory of automatic information processing in reading." In H. Singer & R. Ruddell (Eds.), *Theoretical models and processes of reading* (pp. 689–718). Newark, DE: International Reading Association.

McCracken, R. A. (1962). Standardized reading tests and informal reading inventories. *Education, 82,* 366–369.

Norton, D. (1992). *The impact of literature based reading.* Upper Saddle River, NJ: Merrill/Prentice Hall.

Norton, D. (1995). *Through the eyes of a child.* Upper Saddle River, NJ: Merrill/Prentice Hall.

Pappas, C., Kiefer, B., & Levstik, L. (1990). *An integrated language perspective in the elementary school.* New York: Longman.

Pinker, S. (1994). *The language instinct.* New York: William Morrow.

Rhodes, L., & Shanklin, N. (1993). *Windows into literacy: Assessing learners K–8.* Portsmouth NH: Heinemann.

Rohter, L. (1986, April 13). The scourge of adult literacy. *The New York Times,* p. 33.

Rosenblatt, L. (1985). Viewpoint: Transaction versus interaction. *Research in the Teaching of English, 19,* 96–107.

Ruddell, R., Ruddell, M., & Singer, H. (1994). *Theoretical models and processes of reading* (4th ed.). Newark, DE: International Reading Association.

Rumelhart, D. E. (1976). Toward an interactive model of reading. In S. Dornic (Ed.), *Attention and performance* (Vol. 6). Hillsdale, NJ: Erlbaum.

Rumelhart, D. E. (1981). Schemata: The building blocks of cognition. In J. Guthrie (Ed.), *Comprehension and teaching: Research reviews.* Newark, DE: The International Reading Association.

Smith, F. (1971). *Understanding reading—A psycholinguistic analysis of reading and learning to read.* New York: Holt, Rinehart & Winston.

Smith, F. (1983a). *Essays into literacy.* Exeter, NH: Heinemann.

Smith, F. (1983b) Reading like a writer. *Language Arts, 60,* 558–567.

Smith, N. B. (1965). *American reading instruction.* Newark, DE: International Reading Association. (Original work published 1934)

Stauffer, R. G. (1969). *Directing reading maturity as a cognitive process.* New York: Harper & Row.

Tompkins, G., & McGee, L. (1993). *Teaching reading with literature.* Upper Saddle River, NJ: Merrill/Prentice Hall.

Wakefield, J. (1994). Restructuring educational psychology courses: Creating labs for authentic instruction and assessment. *Educators Forum, 10,* p. 4.

Wells G. (1990). Creating conditions to encourage literate thinking. *Educational Leadership, 47*(6), 13–17.

Werner, L. (1986, April 21). 13% of U.S. adults are illiterate. *The New York Times,* p. 1.

Yatvin, J. (1992). *Developing a whole language program for a whole school.* Midlothian, VA: Virginia State Reading Association.

Children's Literature References

Cleary, B. (1983). *Dear Mr. Henshaw.* New York: Morrow.

Lord, B. (1984). *In the year of the boar and Jackie Robinson.* New York: Harper & Row.

Martin, B., Jr. (1983). *Brown bear, brown bear, what do you see?* New York: Holt Rinehart & Winston.

Morrison, D. (1980). *Chief Sarah: Sarah Winnemucca's fight for Indian rights.* New York: Atheneum.

Observing Authentic Literacy Practices

KEY WORDS AND CONCEPTS

Emergent literacy	Writer's workshop
Parental roles	Dialogue journals
Reading to children	Literature response journals
Print-rich environment	Personal journals
Invented spelling	Buddy journals
Integrated literacy	Learning logs
Reader's workshop	Character journals
Literature circles USSR/DEAR	Conferencing
Story frames/story grammars	Middle schools
Thematic units	Modeling

Mr. Romero's classroom: Children work in small clusters at tables. Children's books are the focus of the reading program. There is process writing and peer editing. Reader's and writer's workshops meet regularly. Student, teacher, and parent conferencing are ongoing. Journal writing occurs several times a week. Children reflect in their learning logs. Critical thinking and self-monitoring are goals. Students and teacher maintain portfolios of children's works; these are the heart of assessment and instruction. Students work at various learning centers. An author's study changes monthly. Books are everywhere. Children's written and creative arts are displayed.

Does this describe the kind of classes you attended in elementary school? Or did you have three reading groups, weekly compositions, monthly book reports, and dittos after each lesson? Mr. Romero's classroom illustrates what we refer to as a community of learners and views literacy as integrative and transactive (McNeil, 1992). This chapter reveals why authentic classroom environments like Mr. Romero's are gaining favor across the country and abroad.

EMERGENT LITERACY AND YOUNG LEARNERS (GRADES N TO 1)

Early language learning is now referred to as **emergent literacy.** This means that even in the first few months of life, children come in contact with environmental print—written language in the forms of signs and labels, TV commercials, or toy-like books—and these early contacts with print begin the lifelong process of learning to read and write (Neuman & Roskos, 1993). Young children engage in language learning, both in spoken and written form, long before they enter school. Our complex, high-tech, visual society has an abundance of print and symbols, so very young children are immersed in a language-laden world.

Before this view of beginning literacy, *reading readiness* was considered a prerequisite to learning how to read. This meant children had to have certain prereading skills, such as knowledge of the alphabet, number awareness, recognition of symbols (square, circle), as well as other perceptual and motor skills before they could begin a reading program. Readiness was determined by giving a standardized reading readiness test. Children who scored poorly were given special instruction in developing a hierarchy of skills. Durrell (1958) suggested early training in letter names and sounds, followed by applied phonics and then practice with a meaningful sight vocabulary. The lack of emphasis on language development, recreational reading, storytelling, sharing activities, and vocabulary enhancement are noted by their absence.

The Dimensions of Early Literacy

Current research has provided us with new insights into young children's *written* language abilities and how reading and writing develop simultaneously (Tierney & Shanahan, 1991). Scribbles and single-letter representations are as significant to written language as babbling and holophrases (one-word sentences) are to speech. Early writing goes through developmental phases from picture writing, to scribble writing, to a random letter phase to invented spelling shown in Figure 3–1 and ultimately to conventional writing. Studies from Teale and Sulzby (1989) indicate that there are many dimensions to early literacy, which include the following:

- Readiness for print comes considerably earlier than six years of age. The range has been extended to include youngsters fourteen months and younger.

- Literacy is not only a cognitive skill but a multidimensional activity that includes social, linguistic, and psychological factors.

- Literacy is enmeshed in a child's surroundings; it is a natural part of daily life.

FIGURE 3–1 Jen's story and picture of Grandma's house, showing early use of invented spelling

"I love to dance. I love to go to the zoo. I love to go to Grandma's house."

If children practiced writing as often and with as much freedom as they practice speaking, they would be equally proficient in both forms of communication. The young toddler who says, "Granny goed home already," is allowed and encouraged to experiment. It's only since the 1980s that a new understanding of the relationship among oral language, reading, and writing has resulted in educators' incorporating new writing methods in the classroom. These recognize and encourage invented or creative spelling (spelling a word as it sounds) as necessary experimentation for written language. Invented spelling (Figure 3–2), also referred to as developmental spelling, implies a progression from one stage to another as a child's writing ability develops.

In emergent literacy classrooms, teachers must capitalize on the multidimensional abilities of youngsters. Although children are natural and curious learners, Durkin (1989) cautions that the factors necessary for school success and the development of early reading and writing abilities, whether called emergent literacy or reading readiness, do not develop in a vacuum, and that those youngsters who sprout very quickly and easily often come from highly literate home and school environments. The others, she warns, emerge much more slowly unless teachers know what to do to help their development.

Parental Roles with the Emergent Learners

Although parents play a vital role throughout a child's school life, the significance of the home in the development of language and literacy success cannot be overstressed. Parents are children's first teachers, and their influence has a direct bearing on literacy development

> June 17
>
> We went to Steping Sone pack. We wont in the Play scaP it was e fun. We Went in the SPrinc als

"We went to Steppingstone Park. We went in the playscape. It was fun. We went in the sprinkles."

FIGURE 3–2 Emergent literacy: Jen's story showing invented spelling.

(Doiron & Shapiro, 1988; Freeman & Sanders, 1989; Keshian, 1963). Verbal interaction with infants, reading to young children, and engaging in print-rich and manipulative play all correlate highly with early success in reading and writing. Vygotsky's (1962) studies of very young children and their language development emphasized the environmental significance of an adult role model (parental, teacher, older sibling) to stimulate and facilitate language and cognitive growth. Piaget's (1952, 1955) seminal research provided insights into how language and thought develop. He indicated the necessity for very young children to interact and experiment with oral language, which develops from inner speech, to speech for oneself, to socialized speech. The presence of others, children or adults, is necessary to nurture language, which is intimately related to cognition and thinking.

The profound relationship among language, home environment, learning, and schooling was investigated and reported on by the Plowdon Commission (1969) in a thorough longitudinal study, undertaken in England, and disseminated throughout the world. It underscored the importance of parental involvement, or partnership, for the successful education of children. The Bullock Report (1975) confirmed and reemphasized the weighty role of the early environment and parents in the language development of children and the positive impact and relationship to reading performance.

Even in homes where there is little overt reading and writing, children are still exposed to environmental print through mail, newspapers, signs on stores, labels on food items, street and road signs, TV ads, and so on. Yet many parents are unaware of the critically important role they play in the language and literacy development of their children. Teachers must *help* parents become educational partners in enhancing children's literacy experiences. Although parents know they must provide comfort, love, and support, they may not understand how influential they can be in educational matters. This can be communicated through formal and informal conferences, parents' nights, and class newsletters that encourage and invite active participation in their children's class. Ideas should be provided indicating how to help young children achieve school success in reading and writing and might include:

- Encourage the scribbling and invented spelling of young children.

  Read to children.

- Point out labels in the supermarket and on food items in the kitchen.

  Read aloud to children.

- Engage children in frequent conversation.

  Read daily to children.

- Use "good talk sessions"; answer children's questions without annoyance and with full sentences.

  Read picture books and fairy tales to very young children.

- Enlarge on children's responses by helping them advance from one conceptual level to another. When a child points to ice cream in a picture book, the parent expands on this with "yes, that's pink and looks like strawberry ice cream, and that's your favorite, isn't it?" This technique is called *scaffolding.*

  Read funny stories and rhyming books.

- Ask children questions to encourage thinking and speaking interactions.

  Read chapter books.

- Share personal experiences about growing up, humorous experiences, and so on.
  Read tall tales.
- Tell stories to the children about family and friends.
  Read contemporary children's literature.
- Take children on nearby trips to parks, shops, the library.
  Read favorite stories over and over.
- Go to special places such as farms, zoos, museums, camping, and famous sites. Use new and unfamiliar words to expand vocabulary, for example, baggage, departures, arrivals, depot, lantern, chalet, display case, and dairy.

Parents should be made aware that talking with children is essential for language development. Varied experiences combined with discussions expand vocabulary and conceptual knowledge of the world, which adds to the child's schema. At a later time, when reading about something similar in school, the child's prior knowledge is activated ("Oh, yes, I remember when I went to a dairy farm and saw milking machines"), and since the child can relate to and identify with the material, comprehension is greatly enhanced.

Reading to Children. The importance of reading to children, both at home and in class, cannot be overemphasized. Research is replete with evidence on the relationship of reading to children and school success (Anderson, Hiebert, Scott, & Wilkinson, 1985; Taylor & Strickland, 1986). Strickland and Morrow (1990) suggest specific interactions when reading with children, such as praising, questioning, directing discussions, modeling dialogue, and relating to life experiences.

The daily ritual of reading to the child, the closeness of child to parent, and the routine and pleasure of sharing a favorite book or exploring a new story, without pressure or threat, is what is most important. The parent is developing a warm and nonthreatening reading relationship; the child is developing a positive connection—books/pleasure/parents. In addition to this affective dimension, the young child is also becoming familiar with books: learning how to turn pages, realizing one reads from top to bottom and left to right, becoming comfortable with print, recognizing certain letters and especially becoming accustomed to formal book language. The more children hear familiar stories, the more they internalize the structural and linguistic features of narrative texts (Sulzby, 1985, 1994). Burns and Roe (1992, p. 55) suggest a number of useful activities for parents:

- Listen patiently and supportively when the child struggles to express ideas.
- Share mail so the child can see that writing can communicate messages.
- Point out familiar signs, and encourage the child to read them.
- Provide writing materials, and encourage writing messages, shopping lists, and letters.
- Model good reading practices by reading books for your own pleasure.
- Carry on conversations with your child; answer questions and explain.
- Share newspapers and magazines and look for familiar words.
- Sing songs, recite nursery rhymes, play guessing games.
- On trips use words like flight attendant, baggage area.
- Visit the children's section of the library; allow the child to get a library card and check out lots of books.

Creating a Print-Rich Classroom Community

Teachers in preschool, kindergarten, and 1st grade foster literacy learning while aware of the developmental nature of children: Children grow and learn, socially, physically, and educationally, at different rates. Their interests and attention spans vary. Some write using sentences, others scribble and barely print their name. Some will read with ease, others have had little formal contact with books. Yet all are part of the community of literacy learners; all contribute verbally by sharing stories and experiences; all listen to peers and the teacher reading aloud and imparting information; and all share their new reading and writing products with classmates.

Teachers note differences yet promote growth for all. This means that one doesn't just teach reading and writing but creates a sense of community where learners are interested in

I love when we learn about Mars.

FIGURE 3–3 Jen's science journal entry: November (grade 1).

each other's ideas. Progress in reading and writing as well as speaking and listening is maintained in the literacy portfolio. The writing of a first-grade youngster differs from month to month. Figures 3–3 and 3–4 illustrate significant changes in Jen's spelling and sentence structure in her science learning journal in just three months. Similarly, how a child reads in October will be substantially different in fluency and context than reading that is done in May.

A **print-rich environment** is a classroom filled with books of all types, easy and more difficult, wordless and predictable books, myths and fables, magazines, typewriters, computers, a writing and reading center and other labeled learning centers. Samples of children's work are displayed prominently; children-authored books (from the class or other grades) are available; reading and writing folders are within reach and labeled. There are language experience and other group stories and charts in the room; there may be a Riddle of the Week or

We had science. Today we learned about mammals. They have backbones. They have hair.

3/1/97

We hao science. Tobay we

learned about mammals.

Tay hav Back Bones.

Tay hav har

FIGURE 3–4 Jen's journal entry: March science (grade 1).

Focus of the Week (colors, pets, favorite book characters) as well as books for paired reading (i.e., Cowley, 1987, *Mrs. Wishy Washy*) and for personal reading (picture books, familiar stories). The room abounds with pictures, labels, charts, drawings with captions, individual and group stories, and **books and books and more books.** The objective is for children to be comfortable when interacting with books and print. Exposure to various genres and activities might include:

Predictable books repeat the same pattern of phrases throughout the text, which encourages children to join in and participate when that refrain is reached. The students love the familiarity and repetition and don't seem to tire of hearing them read again and again. *The Very Hungry Caterpillar* (Carle, 1975), *Chicken Soup with Rice* (Sendak, 1962), and *Love You Forever* (Munch, 1987) are examples.

Wordless picture books have pictures but no words. Children verbally create their own stories based on the illustrations, and stories change with each telling as children learn to elaborate and include their own experiences and background. Oral language skills are enhanced as well. Some favorites include *A Boy A Dog and A Frog* (Mayer, 1971), *Pancakes for Breakfast* (dePaola, 1978), and *The Gift* (Prater, 1987).

Language experience stories (LES) have been used for years and have become part of integrated reading and writing formats. The philosophy was articulated by Van Allen and Allen (1968):

What I think about I can say.
What I can say, I can write.
What I can write, I can read.
What I can read others can read, too.

The teacher writes down what the child says without correction on paper or the chalkboard. Large newsprint on an easel is preferable because it can be kept and added to each day; it is easy to flip back to previously written stories, and read about "Our New Gerbil" or "Fun on Our Spring Trip." This is an authentic method of integrating oral and written language and reading, since children see their words written down and then read them back just as they said them. LES are usually group stories, based on shared experiences.

Caption pictures occur when children draw a picture about an experience, a part of a book, or something that pleases them (pet dog, cat, or new bicycle). Early in the year, the teacher asks what caption to write under a picture, just one or two sentences to describe it. After a few weeks, the children are asked to write, as best they can (invented spelling), about the picture or to label objects in the picture. The captioned pictures of several youngsters can be put together and made into a co-authored book.

Book making is another important technique for creating a community of readers and writers, and it's a good transition from group story writing to individual writing. Children see the fruits of their labor, their completed book, in the classroom where it is shared with others. The books that are made can be simple, with children illustrating the cover and several pages stapled together, or they can be more complicated, made with binding, glue, and stitching. Parents or grandparents may volunteer to work on a bookmaking project that creatively combines art, following directions, reading, writing, and socialization skills. Simple or elaborate, all the books are displayed, read by others, or given as gifts to the family. The concept of authorship starts here.

FIGURE 3–5 A sample of a first-grade journal entry with the teacher's encouraging comments.

Journal writing can start in emergent literacy classes with children recording their reactions in a daily journal. Figure 3–5 shows a page from a first grader's daily journal entry and the teacher's encouraging comment on an attached note. This is discussed extensively with intermediate grades.

Many forms of reading and writing contribute to emergent learning. In one first-grade class, the children wrote daily stories with the teacher, made caption pictures, and kept a Joke and Riddle Book. Additionally, the class maintained three journals: a science, a literature response, and a self-esteem journal. A youngster reported on fifteen books in her literature response journal, which included *Miss Nelson Is Missing* (Allard, 1977) and *Hekedy Peg* (Wood, 1987) (Figure 3–6). When story writing, even young children may be provided with a format to assist them with their editing. Figure 3–7 shows a simplified editing sheet that is used with emergent learners. Although in first grade, the children are learning skills such as incorporating reading into the writing process, sharing and socialization (peer editing), and following organizing guidelines.

Writing in this environment is risk free. Children are not afraid to express themselves in print when asked to react to a trip, an experience, or book they read, because they are taught not to be concerned about accuracy in spelling at this stage. In emergent literacy classes, children communicate their ideas without concern for correctness of spelling. Writing workshops encourage all forms of written expression, and folders and portfolios track the progress and growth being made.

Even very young children can be engaged in written expression as long as handwriting and spelling are held to appropriate standards. The concept of **invented spelling** is to encourage the young child to become part of a literacy awareness community. Strickland describes it as spelling attempts that children create independently, from their own personal

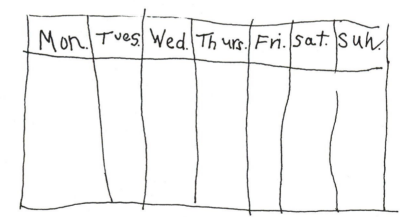

3/10/97 HECKEDY PEG
Audrey Wood
The children were overjoyed
and KNOW exactly what They
Monday asked for a Tub of butter
Tuesday asked for a pocket
knife Wednecaay asked
for a china pitcher
Thursday asked for a pot
of honey Fridat asked
for a salt saturday
asked for crackers
and Sunday asked
for a Bowl
of egg pudding

Mon.	Tues.	Wed.	Thurs.	Fri.	sat.	sun.

FIGURE 3–6 A page from a literature response journal (first grader).

encounters with print. In kindergarten, she says, children discover "print as a tool of authority" (Strickland & Morrow, 1988, p. 70). Scribbles, pictures, and all forms of spelling are seen as acceptable communication from the young child. For example, "Mye Dg Fze" under a picture of a dog that a kindergarten youngster has printed, is not hard to interpret and provides an opportunity to engage in a dialogue with the child about the fuzzy pooch. The child learns that she has communicated, that reading and writing are interconnected, and that she is engaged in the process.

FIGURE 3–7 Editing sheet for original story "The Scary Ghost."

Recording expression of personal thoughts is the important first step in writing, not the accuracy of words. In this new concept of spelling—also referred to as *inventive, creative, temporary, or developmental spelling*—young children express themselves in print by experimenting with letter–sound relationships in their own unique and often unconventional way. Figure 3–8 clearly documents the beginning of graphophonemic awareness. Print is a tool whose developmental nature should be understood as children move from the concrete world of drawings, to the representational sphere of letter formation, and on to a transitional stage that allows them to invent their own spelling so they can express their ideas in print. Frank Smith (1983) has said that children need to see themselves as members of the writing club before they can begin to read like writers. (Older children often use invented spelling in their journals or in first drafts of a writing project. If the writing is for themselves, not for others to see, it is acceptable. The objective is to encourage thinking, and recording of ideas. However, older students are expected to revise and correct spelling and grammar for all work that is to be published, or shared with others.)

I am going to bring my dog to school

October 6, 1996
I am going to
brg my dog
to solo.
I Love my dog.

FIGURE 3–8 Invented spelling sample. Note that several words are correctly spelled and others have a good graphophonemic relationship.

INTEGRATED LITERACY APPLIED TO PRIMARY AND INTERMEDIATE LEARNERS (GRADES 2 TO 4)

Teachers working in grades 2 to 4 have an opportunity to see how a literacy based program flowers from its budding growth in K to 1. The nurturing environment first established with the very young child must be maintained for continued development. Some of the ingredients of the integrated class change as the children's needs and experiences expand. Children are now more able to reflect on how they use language functionally: for oral discussions, for informational and recreational reading, and for various writing projects. Pedagogically, the teacher must create authentic, relevant learning opportunities that motivate, stimulate, and expand learning. Parents continue to be encouraged to participate in the school life of their children, volunteering when possible for various in-class projects, conferencing, and continuing to read with their children. In some locales where parents' literacy skills are poor, parents can attend community-based parenting and literacy classes, sometimes along with their children. The research is clear that intergenerational illiteracy promotes failure for each new generation.

The goal of the upper primary and intermediate literature-based programs is to develop engaged readers, who can respond to pleasure stories and share research information. Additionally, they should be able to escape into the literary world, perform tasks, and take some sort of social or political action in response to what they read (Alvermann & Guthrie, 1993). Accomplishing this literacy instruction must involve more than the cognitive or mechanical aspects of reading, and yet these cannot be ignored. All teachers using integrated literature programs should provide skill instruction and reinforcement as the need emerges from authentic contexts. For example, if a child writes a story that requires use of the possessive form, the teacher should teach a minilesson on this skill in the context where it arises naturally. Figure 3–9 outlines the features of an integrated literacy classroom.

Organizing for Instruction

In a language/literature approach, there is often whole class involvement and infrequent grouping based on ability; children are not separated into bright and slow readers and learn-

Features

• Literature is celebrated.

• Children are surrounded with books. They make choices and self-select the books they read.

• Teachers avoid labeling children with ability levels.

FIGURE 3–9 Literacy-centered class.

ers. Many researchers are dissatisfied with ability groups and the traditional three reading groups. Slavin (1988), Sorenson and Hallinan (1986), and Dawson (1987) are just a few of many critics who found (1) grouping fosters negative self-concepts and poor self-images, especially for children who are in the low group, and (2) evidence is lacking that grouping by ability is associated with any advantages. Other types of grouping patterns, however, for supplementing whole class instruction can be useful: interest groups, skill reinforcement groups, project groups, and so on. Teaching literacy only through achievement groups appears to stifle many children's opportunities to learn.

In integrated reading programs, all children are recognized as capable learners; some are fluent readers, and others less so; some are advanced writers, and others are at a more rudimentary stage; some are great storytellers, and others are wonderful listeners, but they all have the ability to think, reflect, and interact as an important part of the community of language users. A variety of practices create this reading community. Reutzel and Cooter (1991) suggest that they all include these four elements:

1. Students should feel a sense of ownership of their time; they should be able to choose how they spend their reading time.

2. The activities must encourage the integration of reading, writing, speaking and listening.

3. The teacher must set an example of the importance of reading (especially through modeling).

4. Opportunities must be provided for sharing reading strategies and ideas and assessing individual progress.

Dynamics of an integrated reading–writing classroom are illustrated in Figure 3–10.

Literacy Strategies for Teaching and Learning

Unique features of integrated learning and teaching must be implemented to create an environment that nurtures a special community of literacy learners. Some distinctive attributes that are appropriate for grades 2 to 4 are described next:

Reader's Workshop. The reader's workshop is related to the writing workshop, having as its aim helping children make sense out of print. The focus is self-selected reading—setting aside enough time for meaningful reading, reactions, and projects. It is a flexible way to organize the literature-based classroom where children read, discuss, and share their ideas as part of a community of readers. Cooper (1993) highlights important components of the reader's workshop:

1. Teacher share time: The warm-up or motivating time of five to ten minutes when the teacher gets the children excited about literature. This might be done by reading a story or sharing an experience. (This is often used in grades 2 to 3.)

FIGURE 3–10 Dynamics of an integrated reading–writing classroom.

■Honors the process

■Honors the progress   } of learning

■Honors the product

2. Minilesson: A short five- to ten-minute lesson that introduces vocabulary or background information that is related to the unit or narrative. It may also teach a strategy or a skill that is needed by the whole class or a small group.

3. State-of-the class conference: Usually a five-minute period when the teacher assesses what the students are doing. Often, teachers use a clipboard or self-adhesive note tags for quick notes. They might indicate "Erik—working on journal" or "Debra—still shy in discussions." As students are observed, the teacher decides if a conference is needed, or if a child can be encouraged to participate in a discussion group, or if a certain skill needs to be taught.

4. Self-selected reading and responding: This is the heart of the reader's workshop, and there are several parts to this: The children choose material with which they are comfortable and read at their own rate. While they read, the teacher circulates, does incidental teaching, and conducts miniconferences. The children read and make entries in their journals (perhaps new or interesting words, notes, comments about a character, and of course, the title and author of the book they are reading). Literature response time involves journal writing, participating in a literature circle, or conferencing with a classmate about the book being read. During student-share time, students contribute to the community of readers by sharing their questions, attitudes, and ideas. Sometimes, instead of having one large group, the teacher divides the class into small sharing groups of three to five students.

The reader's workshop incorporates these reading strategies for about an hour or more each day. This allows enough time for students to select a book, read without interruption, take notes, and share some reactions with others.

Literature Circles. The social aspects of writing and reading are considered integral to the literature circle concept. A literature circle is a form of discussion group and is similar to a literature study group but less formal. Children who have read or are reading the same book (multiple copies should be made available) meet in a circle of four to five students. Several circles can assemble at the same time, each discussing different books. The circle meets for about fifteen minutes, and children reflect on their feelings about the book, discuss issues they think are pertinent, and share how the book relates to their lives. One should aim for "grand conversations" (Eeds & Wells, 1989), not banal chatter. Teachers should model this technique for several weeks when it is first introduced by joining a circle, listening, and participating in dynamic discussions, and then moving on to another circle. Students can be grouped by the teacher based on their social interactions or can be self-selected. Care should be given to balancing the groups, as they can easily become social clusters or ability groups.

USSR/DEAR. Uninterrupted sustained silent reading (USSR or SSR) and drop everything and read (DEAR) are practices that include modeling along with sustained reading. Everyone in the class reads at the same time, including the teacher. In some schools, blocks of time are set aside for silent reading, and all faculty as well as staff participate. The advantages of this practice are apparent: The youngsters see that reading is important for everyone, not just children; they observe their teacher engrossed in a book; there is silence in the class, so no one is disturbed; children choose their own reading material, usually books or children's magazines and therefore are interested in what they are reading. Since books are self-selected, not imposed by the teacher or a basal reader, they are on a comfortable, recreational reading level. It is a self-motivating procedure with no competition, since all read at their own rate. A caveat is in order: It is important for the teacher to read as well. This modeling is essential to demonstrate the personal value of reading in an authentic reading environment.

Story Frames/Story Grammars. **Story frames** help children with comprehension by providing a structured outline for literature that highlights the elements of plot, characters, setting, problem, and resolution. There are a variety of story frame formats. A class chart can direct children to think about relevant story elements while reading or when writing in their response journals. Children should be encouraged to choose different items to write about each time, so that they do not get bored with a single format or routine and so they also experience independence and some control in self-selection. A chart may list the following elements from which the children are asked to select five:

1. Choose one character from the story. Why is that character important to you?
2. Who are the main characters? Was there someone you did or didn't like? Explain why.
3. Compare two characters. What traits are similar, which are different?
4. What are two main things that happened in the story?
5. Could you think of a different ending?
6. What words give you clues to where the story takes place?
7. How did you feel while reading the story? Use sentences and avoid "happy" and "sad."
8. What was the funniest, saddest, or strangest part?
9. What are some interesting or unusual words this author used?
10. When did the story take place: in the past, the future, or the present? How do you know?
11. Why should or shouldn't someone else read this book?
12. What kind of book was this (mystery, science fiction, biography, folktale, historical fiction, humor, narrative fiction)?

Many variations can be devised for story frames. For example, Figure 3–11 demonstrates a story frame using a modified cloze format. Norton (1992) suggests using the following generic story grammar for all forms of literature to aid and enrich comprehension:

- *Setting and normal circumstances:* Where and when does the story take place? What are the circumstances surrounding the characters?
- *Problem or adverse incident:* What is the problem? What causes the main character to take action?
- *Characters' reactions:* How does the main character act after encountering the problem? Is there someone to help or advise? How does the character change?
- *Corrective action:* What does the main character do to solve the problem? Does the character get help?
- *Resolution of the problem and new circumstances:* How does life change for the characters at the end of the story? What do the characters learn as a consequence of their experiences?

Thematic Units. **Thematic units** combine the holistic view of literature based reading and integrated literacy. Not only are reading and writing integrated, but content areas across the

STORY FRAME

Student Name _____ *Date* _____

The book I just read is titled _____ and is

written by _____. The setting takes place

in _____. I know this because _____

is the character I liked best in this story. The person I didn't like too much was _____

because _____. One part of the story I liked

best was _____.

Two words I didn't know were _____ and _____.

I do _____ I don't _____ want to read

another book by this author. This was: fiction _____ poetry _____

mystery _____ biography _____

science _____ science fiction _____

folktale _____ history _____

historical fiction _____ sports _____

animal _____ other _____

Shared with _____ *(teacher or partner)*

FIGURE 3–11 Sample story frame.

curriculum are linked together. A thematic unit is a sequence of related lessons that are developed around a common theme or issue and may continue for approximately two to six weeks. The literacy activities incorporated into the unit are essential for acquiring new information or creating background. Themes can be built around an author, a literary genre, a broad concern, or an important book. A thematic unit often evolves from a content area subject where literature is interwoven with science, math, art, social studies, writing, and music. Figure 3–12 shows part of a fourth-grade thematic unit on the study of mammals that illustrates a combination of research, art and writing activities, and student collaboration. Fig-

---

MIXED-UP MAMMAL

Select one or two friends to work cooperatively with in groups of two or three. Look at several mammals, study their features—how they move, etc. Now create a new mammal creature that is a mix of three or four other mammals.

Your group will consider the following:

1. The new mammal's habitat.
2. What the mammal eats (its diet).
3. How the mammal moves through the environment.
4. Any special features it has that would help it to survive.

Next your group will draw a picture of this new mammal. (Clay animals, paper puppets, and paper maché animals will be used for a group project.) Each group member will write a description of the new mammal, telling about the features you have included and why your creature has these special adaptations.

After the project is completed, the class will display the illustrations of the new mammals in the class. The class will view each group's mammal and guess the identity of the mixed-up mammal.

FIGURE 3–12 Sample assignment from a fourth-grade thematic unit (student teacher Michael Bonacore).

ure 3–13 indicates one youngster's contribution to the unit. For meaningful unit activities and discussions, multiple copies of the same core books along with books on similar topics should be available. After whole class discussion during which conceptual background knowledge is established, unit goals are formulated, and children select an aspect of the topic they wish to work on and who they want to collaborate with or decide that they prefer to work alone. The learning culminates in a final project the learning and is shared with the class, so that discussion, reflection, and expansion of knowledge take place in a social milieu, or what we have been calling "a community of learners."

Thematic topics can cover such diverse domains as friendship, spiders, consumerism, ecology, and multiculturalism, or there can be a focus on issues such as war, family relationships, and courage. Whatever the topic, it expands outward from the study of core books to other subject areas to include the following:

■ *Literature:* Study vocabulary, organization, self-questioning strategies, literary elements (theme, characterization, plot).

■ *Music:* Research the kind of music and instruments that were played during a historical period. Recordings, instruments, dances, and composers may be listened to, investigated, and discussed.

■ *Art:* Learn what kind of art was produced during a period. Who were some famous artists at the time? The teacher should determine if local museums display art of the era.

■ *Social studies:* Research the politics and issues of the day, how the economy and the people were affected, the clothing worn, the jobs that were available. Map studies can

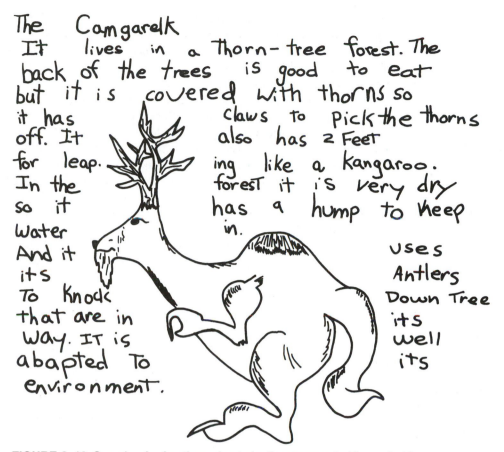

The Camgarelk
It lives in a thorn-tree forest. The back of the trees is good to eat but it is covered with thorns so it has   claws to pick the thorns off. It   also has 2 Feet for leap.   ing like a kangaroo. In the   forest it is very dry so it   has a hump to keep water   in. And it its To knock that are in way. IT is abapted To environment.

uses
Antlers
Down Tree
its
well
its

FIGURE 3–13 Sample of a fourth-grade student's response to Figure 3–12.

determine where important events occurred or the movement of key characters from place to place.

- *Writing:* Students can write a character journal by imagining what it's like to be a character they read about in their core book. They can keep a learning log or project journal while reading their book or while doing research and record foreign words, new expressions, unusual sites, as well as questions that can be addressed during conference time or whole-class interaction and share time.

- *Other subjects:* Math and science can also be included as well as activities such as debates, report writing, role playing, and dramatizations.

Unit study extends the knowledge of the children by expanding the resources used for learning. Dry textbook chapters are replaced by historical fiction and informational books that bring to life a particular era and expand knowledge. Teachers who are required to use a standard textbook can supplement it with trade books, reference books, and primary source materials (newspapers, diaries). Include a good balance of fiction and nonfiction, and reinforce reflective brainstorming and extensive planning with the entire class. Learning opportunities should combine individualized study, group work, and whole-class instruction so that youngsters can use their particular learning strengths, talents, and interests. Students with reading disabilities can fully participate in thematic study, provided they are given materials of appropriate difficulty. Obviously, access to a variety of multilevel materials on relevant topics is critical for individual learning to take place.

Thematic units are developed through careful preplanning and proceed through several stages: topic selection to brainstorm the subcategories and related subject areas, choice of appropriate research materials, ascertaining who (often a self-selection process) is to investigate a particular area, and determination of the methods of sharing the final projects with the class, parents, or others. When the unit is complete, the children have a powerful sense of ownership, because they have been active and involved from its inception to its completion.

Webbing. Webbing is a strategy that is used successfully with thematic units. It connects a topic to various other ideas and subtopics and graphically shows relationships between concepts. See the sample multicultural web in Figure 3–14. Pappas, Kiefer, and Levsti (1990) describe webbing as a schematic technique or a semantic map that is a mental representation

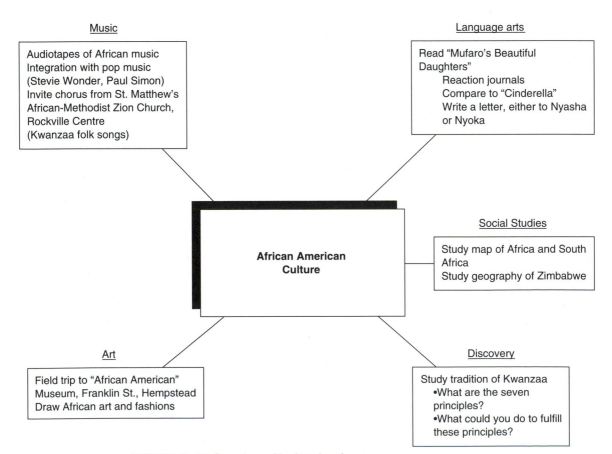

FIGURE 3–14 Sample multicultural web.

of relationships that takes one theme into many directions by fleshing out the topic and moving into various categories and subcategories.

When brainstorming, students use prior knowledge and share experiences with the class. As they verbalize ideas, the teacher records information and creates various categories and subheadings within which to organize the concepts generated. Students add to their knowledge through brainstorming and sharing. Their schema is enhanced even before they begin to research their topic, and they are provided with an organizational structure that helps them see relationships and organize thinking.

The web can look like a spider's web or an octopus with many tentacles, but the center always contains the theme, focus, or core book being studied. Its branches may reach out into other related content areas; may focus more narrowly by looking at the literary elements of a particular book; or may highlight a particular subject or historical period that branches out into subheadings to include literature (Figure 3–15 shows a web developed as part of a unit).

K-W-L. The K-W-L technique may be implemented with webs or other prereading activities. The children brainstorm to determine what they already **know** and what they **want** to

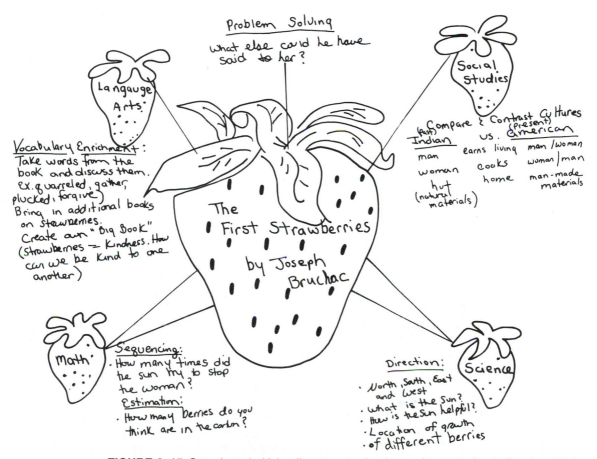

FIGURE 3–15 Sample web: Using literature to develop an integrated unit (fourth grade).

know before research begins. When the research is completed and the projects are shared, the students look at the original web and determine what they *learned* from their thematic study. This process incorporates metacognitive strategies as youngsters become reflective about what they know and set goals for reading. It is useful as both a whole-class strategy and for students doing individual research.

Writer's Workshop. The focus and style of teaching reading has changed because of our understanding of the developmental nature and interconnectedness of early language development, speech, reading, and writing. This has led to profound changes in the way we teach writing. In classrooms that incorporate a whole language philosophy and an integrated literature approach, it would be rare to see writing or reading taught as independent subjects; instead, they are combined into the entire (whole) language curriculum.

Writer's workshops parallel the reading workshop concept, although writing workshops appeared many years earlier. Emphasis is not as much on the product as on the process; thus, the technique is referred to as *the process approach* to writing, or *process writing.* It does not negate the importance of the finished product but emphasizes the steps that a student uses to write and underscores the reciprocal relationship between thinking, reading, and writing. Since students should become proficient and comfortable with all forms of communication, their written language skills should flourish just as naturally as their oral expression.

Graves (1983, 1994) developed instructional strategies and defined stages for students and teachers to use so that a positive writing climate is created that differs greatly from what many recall as the traditional weekly composition assignments. Teachers who implement Graves' concepts involve students in the various stages of writing: prewriting, composing, revising, editing, and publishing. Group sharing and teacher conferences round out the process. These are modeled after the process that adult and professional authors use. The writer's workshop creates a special environment that allows for appropriate blocks of time so that students are not rushed; encouragement of students so they feel a sense of pride and ownership in their work; understanding of the mechanics of writing so that editing and rewriting are meaningful; and frequent and positive feedback so students do not get discouraged. Teachers' demonstrations and minilessons provide the necessary modeling.

Writing is a holistic process that grows along with other forms of expressive language. Reading is not perceived as preceding writing; writing is not taught after beginning reading instruction. In the integrative model, reading and writing support each other, and the current emphasis on early writing is one positive outcome. New terminology includes *ownership* and *authorship,* which relate to appreciation of both process and product. Students move through the following stages from prewriting to the finished product: selecting the topic (brainstorming); drafting (first product, often using invented spelling); composing (additional drafts, based on teacher and peer conferencing); proofreading/revising (adding, deleting, rearranging,); editing (correcting spelling, using conventions of grammar, rewriting); publishing (the final product, ready for the public); authorship (sharing finished work with others and inculcating respect for the student's voice in the writing); and ownership (a feeling of pride in the final product). Ideas are expressed without critical interference, and thus the role of assessment changes. To acknowledge the child's ownership, the teacher has gone from decision maker and evaluator to the trusted adult whom Daniels says, "responds to meaning, to the story or message the child has to share" (1990, p. 110). He compares this to respectful conversation between people interested in each other, where there is no advice giving or correction. Instead, the teacher responds, connects to personal experience, reacts to content, discusses, and asks empathic questions. Graves (1994, p. 18) explains that the teacher creates a community of writers and sets the tone by demonstrating the power and the meaning of writing. Regard for children's writing and awareness that some writing is private and other writing is meant to be shared has led to the extensive and elaborative use of journals, logs, and diaries.

Journals and Logs. Journals have become staples in many classrooms, even those not fully committed to a whole language orientation or to process writing. Teachers realize that just as one becomes a better reader through daily reading, one becomes a better writer through daily writing. "Journals provide students with records of their own thoughts, ideas, and observations, and so invite them to reread, revisit and perhaps revise past thoughts," says Bromley (1989, p. 9).

While journals have always been used as a private repository of an individual's thoughts and feelings, journals can also contain an ongoing response to a book being read, reactions to literature, or questions the student has and wants to discuss during conference time or in a small group. Student journals can also include predictions about outcomes, responses to story frame questions, copies and interpretations of figurative language, as well as records of individual teacher conferences. The integration of reading with writing is apparent; it puts private thoughts and reflections into written form.

There are at least a dozen different types of journals or logs used for various purposes, and creative teachers may find additional categories for their own instructional goals. Journals always connect reading, writing, and thinking and thereby contribute to making the classroom a community of writers.

Dialogue Journals. Using **dialogue journals,** children communicate by having a conversation in print with the teacher or another significant adult in which they discuss topics from daily life: their weekend, a visit to a relative, a movie they saw, a birthday celebration they attended, a school experience, or anything else they wish to share. Teachers respond to the children's entries with some of their personal feelings, "I also love the circus, especially the clowns." The teachers' interactions are useful for modeling correct spelling and grammar, but teachers *should not* mark, correct, or grade the entries. The focus of the dialogue should be responding to content and not to the form of writing. Figures 3–16 and 3–17 show a dialogue between a student teacher and a third-grade youngster whose mother is expecting a new baby. All children appear to enjoy this personal interchange with their teacher. Youngsters learning English as a second language, students with learning disabilities, or children with immature language development can use dialogue journals as long as their creative spelling is accepted. Older students also respond very well to interacting in this fashion with the teacher.

Teachers find engaging a youngster in a dialogue journal a most effective way of knowing a student better. A child who is shy or having a learning problem may not readily converse with a teacher in a public setting, but in dialogue through the journal, the child can be responsive and blossom because of the personal attention and interaction—all done through writing! One teacher commented that she was amazed by the sensitive and thoughtful entries of a child she generally found uncommunicative.

Literature Response Journals. Children respond in writing to the books they are reading by reacting to and keeping track of various ideas and concepts in reading logs or **literature response journals.** The goal is for students to learn to be reflective and introspective about something they are in the process of, or have just finished, reading. These journals are often used instead of book

Dear Angela,

I know this must be a very exciting month at your house. My brother is having a baby in March, and everyone is getting so excited. There are so many things to get ready for a new baby. Please tell me some of the ways your family is getting ready to welcome your new baby.

Yours truly,
Mrs. Murphy

FIGURE 3–16 Student teacher's dialogue journal with a third-grade student.

Feb 8th, 1996

Dear Mrs. Murphy,
Well we're running out of room to put all the baby's stuff so my dad is going to knock the wall down and make another room out of it. We all are so excited. I'm getting my own room soon and we're all going to take my momy on next Monday to Toys "я" us to buy more baby stuf and get a nice wooden crib to put in the baby's room.

Figure 3–17 Student's response to the dialogue journal entry in Figure 3–16.

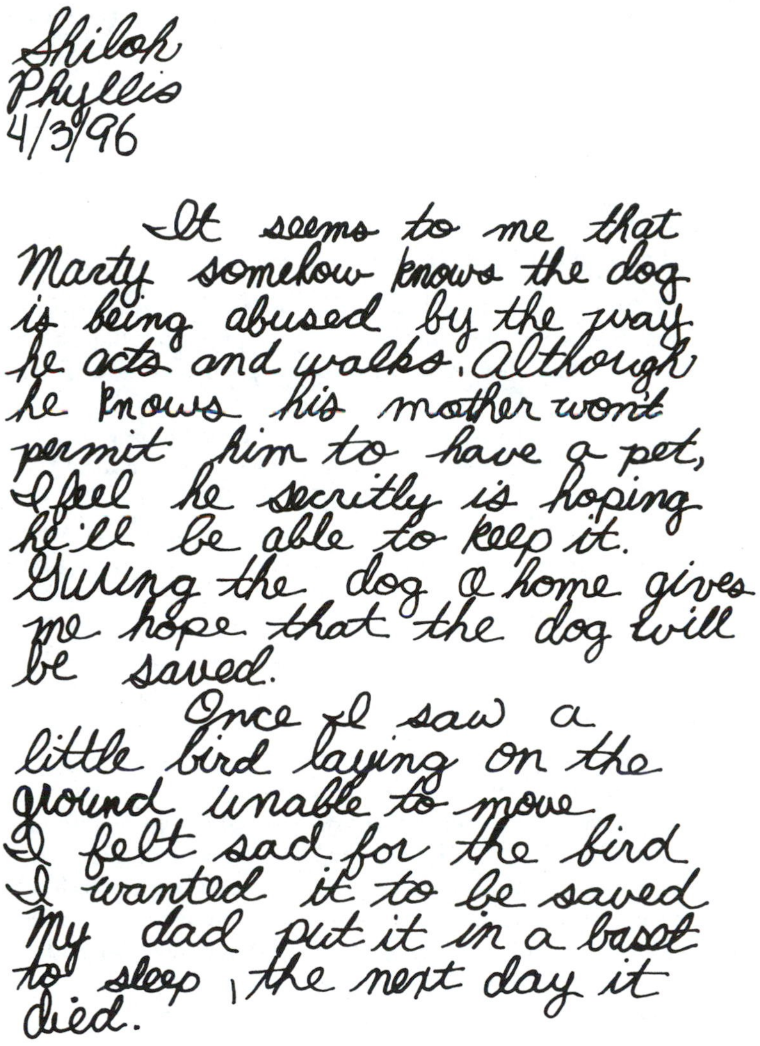

Shiloh
Phyllis
4/3/96

It seems to me that Marty somehow knows the dog is being abused by the way he acts and walks. Although he knows his mother won't permit him to have a pet, I feel he secritly is hoping he'll be able to keep it. Giving the dog a home gives me hope that the dog will be saved.

Once I saw a little bird laying on the ground unable to move I felt sad for the bird I wanted it to be saved My dad put it in a baset to sleep, the next day it died.

FIGURE 3–18 A fourth-grade student's personalized literature entry.

reports. The teacher can see how well students comprehend, the level of intellectual involvement, strengths and weaknesses in literacy skills, areas that need assistance, and how the children relate the book to their lives. Figure 3–18 indicates how a student made a personal connection with an incident in her life with the book she was reading. To avoid copying or parroting text and to provide some focus for students, Kelly (1990) suggests three simple prompts for students to answer:

1. What did you notice in this book?
2. What are your feelings about the book?
3. What does this story remind you of in your own life?

Since some students need assistance to respond spontaneously or critically to a book, teachers can provide a personal checklist or create a classroom chart that lists various ideas that all can refer to for guidelines. Students can select three items from the list when reacting to a book in their literature response journal:

- Describe a situation you think is realistic or silly.
- Write about a character you disliked or really liked.
- Write a short summary.
- Identify (talk about) some feelings you had while reading.
- What one new word did you learn that you never knew before?

Free Writing or Personal Journals. In **personal journals,** the topics that children write about are self-selected and may be intended for their eyes only. Students express thoughts and feelings on subjects they choose because they are of personal concern or interest and reflect ideas, dreams, experiences, creative stories, and so on. These may be assigned weekly, or a particular time is set aside for daily contemplation and commentary (the first fifteen minutes in the morning, the last twenty minutes of each afternoon or after returning from lunch). Students soon become accustomed to putting their personal thoughts in print. If the teacher wants some sharing of these journals, it's suggested that the child select the entry, since some writings may be of a sensitive nature and therefore should be kept private. This journal is very much like a diary, and the teacher may want to read and display some literary diaries to help launch this format, for example, *Anne Frank: The Diary of a Young Girl* (Mooyart, 1967), *Diary of a Rabbit* (Hess, 1982), *Dear Mr. Henshaw* (Cleary, 1983), *The Diary of Nina Kosterina* (1968), *Amazing and Death Defying Diary of Eugene Dingman* (Zindel, 1987), and the recent *Zlata's Diary* by twelve-year-old Zlata Filipovic (1994), who shares her own reflections on war-torn Bosnia.

Buddy Journals. Students pair up and write to one another through their **buddy journals.** Buddy journals are similar to dialogue journals, except that instead of student and teacher communicating through writing, two students correspond and engage in a dialogue. Again, corrections are not made, but the content is responded to; it is a conversation through print. This activity is a variation of pen pals where two people who have not met each other correspond; here, the correspondence is between two classmates or buddies. A number of adaptations can be tried: buddies in two different classes, schools, or from different grade levels; a second language learner paired with a native speaker; or a young student with an older remedial student. The personal and authentic nature of writing and reading merge into a meaningful and purposeful exchange of feelings, attitudes, and experiences. Deep friendships and attachments can develop from these writing relationships.

Project Journals. The project journal format grew out of the writing across the curriculum movement. In this approach, students keep track of their learning experiences in various content areas and write about trips taken, visitors to the classroom, and observations in science labs. They keep detailed notes on the growth of the bean seedling, the class gerbil, or a consumer awareness project. These journals not only record what is going on but are an accounting of various themes and units. Students might include special social studies reports, detail the responsibilities of various members of a debate team, integrate a mythology and social science project, relate a literary reading to a scientific or historical occurrence, or write about a musicale they had or an artist they learned about.

Learning Logs. **Learning logs** are sometimes called content journals, but they differ from project journals in that they have a more directed focus. Learning logs sometimes use the K-W-L model referred to previously. Students reflect on their accomplishments and record their attitudes, goals, or achievements. Metacognitive strategies are overtly reinforced in this journal or log, where students consciously think about their thinking and learning. For example, students can be directed to answering, What is it that I know and don't know? How did I learn something new? How do I know I know something new? Where did I locate the information? This process contributes to the students' schema by making them consciously aware of their thinking strategies. They maintain a written record of this reflective process (Figure 3–19). Learning log entries are especially useful as part of the literacy portfolio for self-assessment and evaluation of accomplishments.

Poetry Journals. Students are encouraged to write their own poetry or to keep records of their favorite poems and note the variety of poetic types: humorous poems, puns, haiku, rhyming and nonrhyming poetry, and so on. Additionally, ideas for future poetry projects are included as well as personal poetry collections. The poetry journal can be a repository of other poets' works or for trying one's hand at poetry. Creativity thrives in environments where risk taking is encouraged, and journals provide a perfect private place to experiment with different poetic forms. Teachers can initiate this journal by sharing their favorite poems, reading aloud limericks or alliterative poems, reading favorite children's poets such as Shel Silverstein's *Where the Sidewalk Ends* (1974) and *A Light in the Attic* (1981) or Rudner's modern fairy tales such

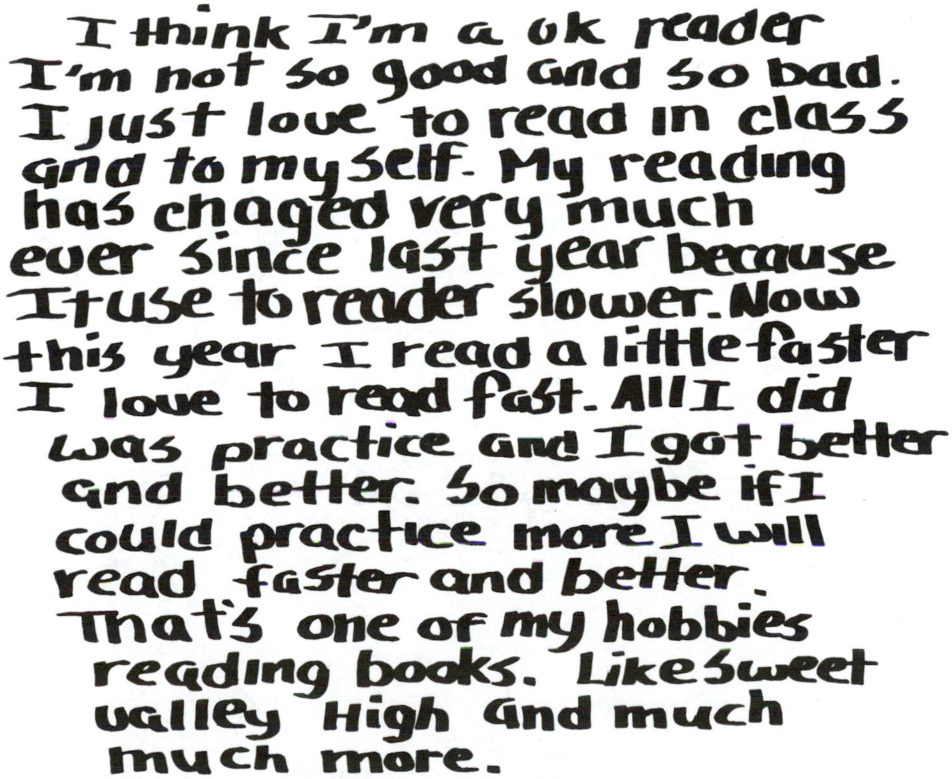

I think I'm a ok reader I'm not so good and so bad. I just love to read in class and to myself. My reading has chaged very much ever since last year because I t use to reader slower. Now this year I read a little faster I love to read fast. All I did was practice and I got better and better. So maybe if I could practice more I will read faster and better. That's one of my hobbies reading books. Like Sweet valley High and much much more.

FIGURE 3–19 A fifth-grade student's self-reflection in a learning log (bilingual, born in the United States).

as *The Littlest Tall Fellow* (1989b) and *The Bumblebee and the Ram* (1989a) or Prelutsky's *My Parents Think I'm Sleeping* (1985) and *The New Kid on the Block* (1984).

Another motivating resource is Janeczko's (1990) *The Place My Words Are Looking For: What Poets Say about and through Their Work,* a book in which poets share their personal experiences. Poetry is an idiosyncratic genre, however, and children should be encouraged to play with sounds and words and sensitive ideas. Since poetry is meant to be read aloud (that's why there are poetry readings in libraries and bookstores), students can be taught to read published poems aloud and encouraged to try sharing their poems in this fashion with others as well.

Process Writing Journals. Process writing journals evolved as part of the writing process movement. Gillet and Temple (1994) suggest using composition notebooks for this journal, since all drafts and edited versions are to be included for students, teachers, and parents to see the progress made in writing from the beginning through the various stages to the completed or published works. Figure 3–20A and B documents the progression in one third grader's writing from a web to the first draft after a teacher conference. Figure 3–20C shows the edited and rewritten story ready for publication.

Revisions (editing) can result from writing conferences with the teacher, peer collaboration, or personal reflection. This journal may also reveal the mechanics of writing skills, such

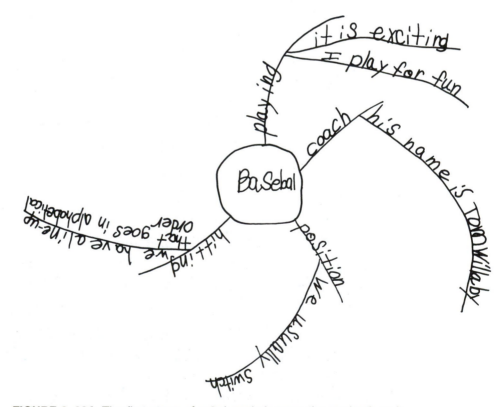

FIGURE 3–20A The first stage of a 3rd grader's story, the student's web.

Baseball is Me

#I play baseball for the fun of it. I don't get really nervous. I've been through almost all of the ^{league} league

They are
∧Tee-Ball, Farms and I'm going into the minors

I've been playing for 4 years. It's really fun.

¶My favorite positions are first base and pitcher.

But I love hitting the best. My coaches

name is Tom   I don't know what
position I will play this year. All my
coaches gave me balls. I have 5
trophies.

FIGURE 3–20B The second stage: the story draft.

Baseball is Me

I play baseball for the fun of it. I don't get really nervous. I've been through almost all of the leagues They are Tee-ball, Farms and I'm going into the Minors. I've been playing for 4 years. It's really fun.

My favorite positions are first base and pitching. I love hitting the best. My coaches name is Tom. I don't know what position I'll play this year. All my coaches gave me balls. I have 5 trophies,

FIGURE 3–20C The third stage: the finished story.

as summary paragraphs, using supporting details or practice with expository writing. Students use the journal as a place to practice skills that the teacher has demonstrated.

Dialectical Journal. Edwards (1992) describes these journals as "a methodical training format for improving thinking skills." It structures students' responses to written material by providing focus questions or formats and a place to record the readers' thinking in response to what was read. Although some children can do this naturally or with minimal practice, others have difficulty honing their thinking skills, and this is one strategy that is suggested. In this journal, the page is divided into three columns: (1) What It Says (the text), (2) What It Means (interpreting text), and (3) What It Means to Me (personalizing text). This procedure requires students to interpret text material in stages, from a literal level to a more interpretive, problem-solving level. The students thereby can see how their thinking has evolved. Obviously, students need direction in using critical thinking strategies and goals that realistically reflect their age and ability.

Character Journals. **Character journals** are a variation on the theme of literature journals but are more specific and focused. Hancock (1993) describes this journal as appropriate for adolescents, but it is successfully used in lower grades as well. "The students," said Hancock (p. 42), "make diary-like entries in the voice of the literary character." By assuming the role or writing to a certain character, students become personally involved, placing themselves in the same or similar circumstances. Figure 3–21 is an example of a 5th grade student writing in the voice of a contemporary queen who is jealous of Snow White's youth and beauty. (Note the time line.) Self-awareness and critical comprehension are heightened as students try to imagine themselves in a particular situation or living in a different time or place and then pretend to be that personality. These journal entries are often powerful, intense, and emotional. Some children use dialect when they become the character, or they use the quaint language of a period.

Take-Home Journal. Sometimes called a go-home journal, the take-home journal differs from the others in that it is designed for student–parent or student–parent–teacher communication. The children write about and share some school event, activity, or special project with their parents. (Primary grade youngsters often draw pictures as well.) The parents respond in writing, so children see that writing and reading are not merely a school function but that adults interact this way as well. With three-way communication, some teachers find it effective to color code the paper, for example, blue for the teacher's letter, white for the student's entry, and yellow for the parent's response. Bromley (1989) suggests that a different child could be chosen each week to share, if the child wants to, a parent's entry with the class. Although this type of journal keeps lines of communication open, monitors literacy development, and informs parents of school activities, the downside is the possibility of lack of parental response or inappropriate parental concern. An occasional note or newsletter may help avoid disappointment resulting from a nonparticipating parent or a parent who doesn't understand the focus of the journal.

Special Journals. Other journals record special events, topics, people, or ideas. Some suggestions are special words, great quotes, famous people, funny (or weird) newspaper items, animal stories, favorite sports stories, admired book characters, and silly riddles. Children choose their own special area of interest to record, often based on their hobbies or unusual experiences. Cartoons and jokes are especially attractive to many students, especially the more reluctant learners.

Several other journal formats are occasionally mentioned, such as problem-solving, note-taking, or daily-group journals. Some are subsets of, or related to, the journals discussed pre-

I was jealous. I'll admit that. My beauty was very important to me. Plus it was fading. What Would I have left? And I knew Snow White was far more beautiful than me. I'd never had these worries before. I wasn't prepared to grow old!

Snow White Grows Up

2 years
8 years
13 years
17 years

FIGURE 3–21 Sample character journal entry of a 5th grade student: A contemporary Snow White.

viously. A variety of pedagogical strategies may have to be implemented and frequently changed so that children do not get bored with a particular journal format. One type of journal can be assigned for several months and then changed to another to stimulate fresh ideas. Some older children have unfortunately learned that writing means correction marks all over a page and will therefore have to relearn and trust that this new form of daily writing is functional, enjoyable, and often private. They will need reassurance that their journal will not be graded and that, just as good readers become better readers by reading, writers get better by writing.

The following practices will help create successful journal involvement:

- Set aside enough time for journal writing, at least fifteen minutes each day.

- Encourage but don't insist on the sharing of some journal entries; that is, personal or free-entry journals may be kept private.

- Peer sharing is important, especially with process writing, learning logs, and project journals.

■ Brainstorming on potential themes and topics should be initiated every few weeks so that students don't feel "all written out" and new ideas are generated.

The classroom can be organized so that Monday is free writing day or personal journal day and Wednesday is literature response journal day. Journals can be continued for several months and then filed for a while but available for the student who may want to continue writing in them. Another format might then be introduced, for example, buddy journals on Monday and Thursday (providing enough time for the students to write and exchange their journals with one another).

It is essential that writing become a comfortable, nonstressful activity and that journals be authentic experiences that allow students to think things through, record personal insights, reflect on their social and educational world, and essentially write for themselves.

Conferencing. **Conferences** are a vital part of literature-based, integrated thematic programs and are discussed in depth in Chapter 9. They are essential to writing and reading workshops and the portfolio process because they provide an opportunity for children and teachers to discuss various topics, especially the books being read and current and past writing. Graves (1991) calls conferences the heart of good teaching. During informal conferences teachers stop by students' desks as they read independently or in small groups and inquire about journal entries or any issues they would like explained. Formal conferences may include discussions about literature response journals, reading logs, book lists, future selections, and goals. The teacher notes interests, strengths, and weaknesses.

In summary, innovative literacy methods allow primary and intermediate students to develop ownership of their literacy and fully interact with the instructional program. They learn to maintain their own records, share book experiences, take part in paired or partner reading, deliberate in journals, and engage in peer collaboration. Teaching strategies incorporate minilessons for targeting specific topics or skill deficiencies noted from conferences and observations. All strategies are designed to fully engage students in authentic reading and writing opportunities.

INTEGRATED LITERACY INSTRUCTION APPLIED TO MIDDLE SCHOOLS

A number of strategies can be adapted from younger students and implemented with older youngsters and vice versa. But the teen years have special psychosocial-educational concerns and issues that certain techniques are particularly apt for that population.

Understanding the Special Needs of Adolescents

Preteens and adolescents are unique. They are funny, sad, irritable, happy, moody, angry, irreverent, and conventional—often at the same time. This is a transitional stage of development that bridges childhood and adulthood, a critical time that can be challenging and exasperating. Teen years are difficult, with profound changes taking place physically, emotionally, and socially. Parents now take a back seat to friends, cars, the telephone, and part-time jobs.

Intense peer relationships are teens' highest priority, and everything, including reading and schooling, seems to pale beside this obsession. Goodlad's (1984) research confirmed that friends appear to be the most important aspect of school at this stage. Instead of bemoaning this phenomenon, teachers must understand and use it to educational advantage.

Middle schools often include various grade combinations. Consequently, while some middle schoolers are clearly adolescent, others are childish and prepubescent. Vacillating emotions, intensity of feelings, worries about attractiveness, and bouts of low self-esteem all compete with learning and schooling. The egocentric behaviors and self-importance of the young child reappear at this time, and the curriculum must reflect teens' needs and concerns so they don't become disenchanted and add to the already high dropout rates. Extending and incorporating authentic reading and writing experiences and assessments becomes essential.

Adolescents complain that learning is "booooring" and they never read "good" books. Why are they unmotivated to read when there is a wonderful world of adolescent literature available? It appears that few classrooms allow teens to select materials that relate to their lives—that are applicable or authentic experiences. Literacy instruction at this level often means lack of variety in the type of books made available to teens and insufficient time taken to implement integrated thematic instruction. It's important for younger students to have time set aside for extended and extensive reading (SSR, DEAR), and it is equally critical for middle schoolers. Goodlad (1984), when investigating schools across the country, found that only 6% of the elementary school day was spent on reading. It is even more startling to learn that less than 3% of a middle school student's day is spent reading! What messages are children getting? If reading is important, then why is so little time provided? If writing is significant, why is so much writing assigned for homework and not practiced in school?

Time Constraints

Primary grades usually are self-contained with flexible blocks of instructional time, while middle schools are departmentalized with content often taught in fifty-minute periods. To implement integrated curricula, the amount of time devoted to thematic learning must be increased. This can be accomplished when teachers work in teams so curricula can be combined and instructional time can be adjusted. Through collaborative planning and flexible scheduling, a student-centered, interdisciplinary curriculum, rather than a subject-centered approach, can be established where content is related to, and made meaningful to, the students.

To create an effective writer's workshop, students need time; Graves (1994) suggests about three hours a week. Classes should be scheduled back-to-back or combined for writing instruction to truly be effective. If writing across the curriculum and thematic learning are to become realities, then social studies or science can become part of the writer's workshop. Allington (1994) suggests reconfiguring the school day and week: "Teachers need long blocks of time to teach and children need such time to learn. . . . Perhaps it is time to schedule literacy lessons on only Monday and Tuesday—but all day Monday and Tuesday." He explains how flexible modules allow students to read whole books, research a topic thoroughly for an oral presentation, compose a really well-formed story or report, and implement process writing from drafting to final copy. Additionally, middle schoolers need time for uninterrupted reading and time to assimilate and reflect on concepts and collaborate with classmates.

Teacher Modeling

The role of middle school teacher is multidimensional: advisor, counselor, educator, facilitator, and role model. Students watch carefully to see if promises and commitments are carried through. In integrated classes where literacy is intertwined with other subject areas and students are given choices for self-selected literature, writing topics, and journal entries, the teacher's reading and writing behaviors will be carefully noted. During reader's workshop, does the teacher read? During writer's workshop, does the teacher write? Do teachers do the corrections or encourage student collaboration and editing?

Nancie Atwell (1987) was a teacher in a middle school in rural Maine. In her books, she shares practical ideas and her experiences and transformation from a traditional English teacher to a teacher who truly collaborates with and models learning. She says "I write with my students, I show them my drafts. I ask for their responses in writing conferences. . . . I read with my students, I show them what I'm reading and I talk about and lend my books." What Atwell is describing is an authentic learning environment. Her classroom overflows with books that adolescents love. Each year she surveys her students, then adds and deletes books based on the students' ratings. She demonstrates how trust, honesty, and authenticity help get students hooked into literacy learning: reading and writing become real, enjoyable, and meaningful tasks.

Instructional Strategies

Six points are itemized by Heller (1995, p. 186) to foster middle school literacy development:

1. Provide guidance through a balance of direct instruction and student-centered activities that are supported by the reading/writing process.
2. Integrate listening to, talking about, reading, and writing a variety of prose and poetry.
3. Allow middle schoolers the freedom to talk about their learning. Foster conversation, reaction, and free expression of ideas and feelings.
4. Teach grammar, mechanics, and spelling in the context of meaningful connected text.
5. Choose the best adolescent literature you can find for read-aloud sessions.
6. Help students develop a strong sense of self-esteem and discover who they are through daily reading, writing, and responding.

To achieve an integrated thematic literacy curriculum in the middle schools, the following activities should be implemented:

Journal writing

Teacher modeling

Teaching teams

Conferences

Life preparation

Writer's workshop

Flexible time

Reader's workshop

Student collaboration

Portfolio assessment

Adolescent literature

Teacher collaboration

Minilessons

Emphasis on metacognition

Preparation for high school

Many of the new strategies examined in previous sections for intermediate grades can be extended into the middle school program. Instead of anthologies and excerpted novels, middle schoolers must be provided whole reading selections they can relate to; fortunately, well-written adolescent fiction is now available in abundance. Newspapers and magazines provide excellent up-to-date readings in all curriculum areas and are motivating because of their adult focus and enormous range of topics. At this stage of development, the curriculum can become more student driven with appropriate teacher direction. Students collaborate with peers in unit studies and engage in meaningful literature discussions. Self-reflection is emphasized as students assess their knowledge and progress. Reading and writing workshops have shared teacher–student planning and decision making. Teachers focus minilessons on specific skills and metacognitive comprehension strategies. Classroom management shifts to accommodate this type of interactive learning.

Studying, Learning, and Remembering. Middle school literacy curricula emphasize critical thinking and independence in working and studying. According to Irvin (1990, p. 138), "Most students read not only for their own pleasure, but also to acquire information relevant to a test, report, project, or some other assignment."

Note Taking. Middle schoolers, no matter how attentive or intelligent, cannot mentally store everything and must therefore (re)learn to take effective notes. Notes are especially important when reading informational or content material and to respond to concepts from journals or reports. Data gathering from research texts, encyclopedias, CD-ROM, and trade books requires note-taking skills, not merely jotting down data, but reflecting on what is read or heard and critically determining the significance to the topic under investigation. Tompkins and Hoskisson (1995) suggest a format where the page is divided into two columns; one is headed *Take Notes,* the other *Make Notes*. Under "Take Notes," students jot down factual or notable information; later they add to the "Make Notes" side reflections or questions they wonder about. This format makes use of both efferent and aesthetic learning.

Library and Reference Skills. In our highly technological age, no teacher or curriculum can provide students with all the information that might be needed in the next century. But students can be equipped with the abilities to locate any information they may need. While library skills have always been important, computer databases and other technology now require a complex sophistication. To become an independent learner, students must know how to retrieve and use reference materials via computer terminals, on-line systems, CD-ROM, and microfilm. Students engaged in independent and group thematic research projects have excellent opportunities to use library resources and multimedia communication centers.

Writing across the Curriculum. Middle schoolers need to become familiar with writing research reports as well as other forms of oral and written discourse: journals, narratives, letters, requests, applications, memos, poems, plays, newspaper articles, reviews, and so on (Vacca & Vacca, 1989, pp. 275–276). Writing a laboratory report requires strategies quite different from a critical analysis of a persuasive editorial. Though students may be competent writers in one area, they may need assistance in writing in other curricula areas or in responding to essay questions that are frequently used in secondary settings.

The writing process approach can be used in writing across the curriculum; however, some stages need to be redefined for communicating expository information. As students become involved in brainstorming, drafting, sharing, revising, and editing, they focus on the specific purpose for writing, and how they organize, evaluate, and present information to successfully share it. Good organizational skills (preoutlining, webs, or maps) aid in presenting information so that it is cogent and logical. Vacca and Vacca (1989, pp. 275–291) detail how the writing process can be effectively implemented with content area learning.

Literature across the Curriculum. An essential focus of this text is the use of quality literature, trade books, and nonfiction materials that integrate learning and creative assessment as the core of an excellent literacy program. At the middle school, quality literature can be used to expand students' subject matter knowledge, increase exposure to literary forms, and gain satisfaction from recreational reading.

Sustained silent reading of literature becomes difficult, as noted earlier, when there are time management constraints. These are resolved when content teachers team up to combine classes, which creates larger and more flexible time periods. This also allows time for sharing of projects and specific genres (especially plays and poetry), which are not merely enjoyable but provide a common literacy experience when there is a wide range of reading ability in the class.

To enhance integrated thematic literature units in subject areas Irvin (1990, pp. 158–166) suggests these steps:

Step 1. Brainstorm ideas, topics, or themes related to a unit in the content area. This defines topics related to the subject and books that can be used.

Step 2. Identify titles and locate books. Librarians should be consulted about the resources on specific topics. *(A to Zoo, The Hornbook Magazine).*

Step 3. Provide shared literary experiences and dwell on the book experiences. This sharing can be through read-alouds or collaborative reading.

Step 4. Consider alternative ways to share books and extend book experience.

"Literature can enliven and enrich the teaching of content area classes by telling the stories of the people who made the events of social studies and science happen" (Irvin, 1990, p. 167).

Critical Thinking Skills. Adolescents are in what Piaget (1955) termed the *formal operational period* in terms of cognitive development, thinking, and language skills. It is not until this highest phase of development is reached that logical reasoning emerges and students can truly understand concepts that are not related to previous or direct experiences. Adolescents have the developmental ability to be reflective and critical thinkers and can effectively implement metacognitive strategies. They can now genuinely think about what they are thinking and understand the process when reconstructing meaning. To think critically, to reflect on what is known, to understand prior knowledge brought to the text, and to consciously process new information and ideas is essential to learning, thinking, and problem solving and requires certain developmental maturity.

When meaning is constructed and ideas are actively processed, the process takes two forms, according to Rosenblatt (1978). She coined the terms *efferent* and *aesthetic learning* to describe distinct thinking processes that affect reading and listening behaviors. Efferent learning requires thinking that uses knowledge, information, and generalizations received from the text. It is essentially objective, making sense of the material, adding to one's schema, relating to other information already known. Aesthetic learning requires different processing and is subjective and personal. It relates to the emotions and experiences one has before and during reading or listening, not the information one derives from the experience. Rosenblatt describes the emotional aspect as the stuff of memory, thought, and feeling that become part of life experiences to be reflected on. The ability to use both efferent and aesthetic meaning appears to be circular: We relate our personal reactions to objective information, and we relate objective knowledge to our personal feelings when we engage in active learning. Both processes are nurtured by authentic experiences.

Middle School Conferences. Conferences between the student and teacher are always important, especially so for adolescents, who are notoriously egocentric and enjoy talking about themselves, their friends, their progress, and achievements. This is a time to have the individual attention of the teacher and discuss items that range from personal to instructional to evaluative. Several types of literacy conferences are appropriate to the middle school: parent conferences, workshop conferences, peer conferences, editing conferences, planning conferences, whole class conferences, and evaluation conferences. Most are one-on-one and relatively short. The purpose varies with the requirements of the student, the goal of the conference, and the teacher's need to be in touch with what is going on in the class and with each student.

During the writing conference, for example, it has been suggested that teachers not criticize or even correct a student's work. Atwell (1987) points out that all writers feel vulnerable; they often expose their innermost feelings to others. Therefore, during the conference, teens should be treated with dignity and courtesy and not feel threatened as a writer. Atwell (1987) provides some excellent guidelines:

- Keep conferences short.
- Don't tell writers what should be in their work.
- Respect the students' ownership of their writing.
- Resist making judgments.
- Avoid contrived praise.
- Ask global questions such as "tell me more about that" or "I don't quite understand that."

Peer conferences need careful preplanning, especially to avoid the tyranny of one's peers. Teachers must model good conferencing techniques and hold discussions on do's and don'ts so that peer conferences will result in sensitive, thoughtful, and useful interactions. Conferences with parents are just as vital. As noted throughout this book, parental involvement is critical to school success. When conferencing with parents, include students and use the Literacy Assessment Portfolio (LAP) as a focus for discussion. Parents need to *see* how the adolescent is progressing, and providing authentic portfolio materials is the best indicator of growth, improvement, and work in progress. The student can take pride in ownership and explain the contents. It's a time for teachers to articulate instructional goals and discuss students' actual performance.

Preparing for Adult Literacy. The middle school is not too early to establish the literacy strategies students will need in employment, recreation, and as active citizens. Esteem and independence develop through the use of functional reading and writing strategies in many contexts, for different purposes, by applying critical thinking and problem-solving skills.

The contemporary workplace, the complex literacy demands of daily life, and the competitive nature of postsecondary schools require increasingly proficient literacy skills. Mikulecky (1989) suggests introducing real-life literacy activities in all curriculum areas: a science teacher should use pamphlets, labels, medicine instructions, catalogs, and weather information; math teachers may consider ads, newspapers, magazines, banking forms, and cookbooks to enrich their programs. Additionally, authentic materials help the at-risk student with self-esteem, maturity, and independence.

Implementation of authentic strategies can be uncomplicated, since materials are easily obtainable and quite inexpensive (newspapers and magazines) or free (bank forms, job applications, and train schedules). When students see that what they learn in school is essential for daily living, literacy activities take on validity and motivation for learning is heightened.

CONCLUSIONS

All the new directions in literacy learning discussed in this chapter are pieces of an integrated literacy mosaic that can be implemented in all grades. The key to success may be twofold: (1) careful planning and sharing of new ideas and strategies with students and (2) appropriate teacher training in authentic instruction and portfolio assessment techniques. Even if children have had prior experience with integrated literacy, it is still necessary for teachers to establish their own style and classroom model. Persistence and patience are needed for the smooth operation of protocols, management schemes, innovative teaching techniques, new record-keeping devices, and portfolios.

It takes time to plan and establish new learning environments. For example, a successful writer's workshop requires paper, pencils, scissors, tape, staples, computers and printers, thesaurus, dictionary, wall charts suggesting do's and don'ts of writing rules, spelling guides, record-keeping devices, and arrangements for portfolios and conferencing areas. For Reader's Workshops one must plan and organize for minilessons, shared time, uninterrupted reading time, student collaborations, and conferences.

A classroom climate must be developed that promotes a literature-rich community of readers and writers. A philosophical belief in this model and careful teacher and class preparation are the foundation for success. LAPs are the natural outgrowth of this approach. They provide the opportunity for student progress to be assessed and encouraged and allow instructional strategies to be adapted to students' literacy needs.

REFERENCES

Allington, R. (1994). The schools we have. The schools we need. *The Reading Teacher, 48,* 14–29.

Alvermann, D. E., and Guthrie, J. T. (1993). *Themes and directions of the National Reading Research Center. Perspectives in reading research,* No. 1. Athens, GA: University of Georgia and University of Maryland at College Park.

Anderson, R., Hiebert, E., Scott, J., & Wilkinson, I. (1985). *Becoming a nation of readers: The report of the Commission on Reading.* Washington, DC: National Institute of Education.

Atwell, N. (1987). *In the middle: Writing, reading, and learning with adolescents.* Portsmouth, NH: Heinemann.

Blachowicz, C., & Lee, J. (1995). Vocabulary development in the whole literacy classroom. *The Reading Teacher, 45,* 188–195.

Bromley, K. (1989). *Journaling: Engagements in reading, writing and thinking.* New York: Scholastic.

Bullock, A. (1975). *A language for life.* London, England: Her Majesty's Stationery Office.

Burns, P., Roe, B., & Ross, E. (1992). *Teaching reading in today's elementary schools.* Boston: Houghton Mifflin.

Cooper, J. (1993). *Literacy: Helping children construct meaning.* Princeton, NJ: Houghton Mifflin.

Daniels, H. (1990). Young writers and readers reach out: Developing a sense of audience. In S T, (Ed.), *Reading and writing together: New perspectives for the classroom.* Norwood, MA: Christopher-Gordon.

Dawson, M. M. (1987). Beyond ability grouping: A review of ability grouping and its alternatives. *School Reading Review, 16,* 348–369.

Doiron, R., & Shapiro, J. (1988). Home literacy environment and children's sense of story. *Reading Psychology, 9,* 187–202.

Durkin, D. (1989). Emerging readers. *The Reading Teacher, 42,* p. 633.

Durrel, D. (Ed.). (1958, February). Success in first grade reading. *Boston University Journal of Education, 150.*

Edwards, P. R. (1992). Using dialectical journals to teach thinking skills. *Journal of Reading, 35,* 312–317.

Eeds, M., & Wells, D. (1989). Grand conversations: An exploration of meaning construction in literature study groups. *Research in the Teaching of English, 23,* 4–29.

Freeman, E. B., & Sanders, T. R. (1989). Kindergarten children's emerging concepts of writing functions in the community. *Early Childhood Research Quarterly, 4,* 331–338.

Gillet, J. W., & Temple, C. (1994). *Understanding reading problems: Assessment and instruction* (4th ed.). New York: Harper Collins.

Goodlad, J. (1984). *A place called school.* New York: McGraw-Hill.

Graves, D. (1983). *Writing: Teachers and children at work.* Exeter, NH: Heinemann.

Graves, D. (1991). *Build a literate classroom.* Portsmouth, NH: Heinemann.

Graves, D. (1994). *A fresh look at writing.* Portsmouth, NH: Heinemann.

Hancock, M. R. (1993). Character journals: Initiating involvement and identification through literature. *Journal of Reading, 37*(1), 42–50.

Heller, M. F. (1995). *Reading–writing connections.* White Plains, NY: Longman.

Hewlett, S. A. (1991). *When the bough breaks: The cost of neglecting our children.* New York: Basic Books.

Irvin, J. (1990). *Reading and the middle school student.* Boston: Allyn & Bacon.

Janecczko, P. B. (1990). *The place my words are looking for: What poets say about and through their work.* New York: Bradbury.

Kelly, P. (1990). Guiding your students' response to literature. *The Reading Teacher, 43,* 464–470.

Keshian, J. G. (1963). The characteristics and experiences of children who learn to read successfully. *Elementary English, 40,* 615–616.

McNeil, J. D. (1992). *Reading comprehension: New direction for classroom practice.* New York: HarperCollins.

Mikulecky, L. (1989). Real-world literacy demands: How they've changed and what teachers can do. In D. Lapp, J. Flood, & N. Farnan, (Eds.), *Content area reading and learning.* Englewood Cliffs, NJ: Prentice Hall.

Neuman, S., & Roskos, K. (1993). *Language and learning in the early years.* Fort Worth, TX: Harcourt Brace Jovanovich.

Norton, D. (1992). *The impact of literature-based reading.* Saddle River, NJ: Merrill/Prentice Hall.

Pappas, C., Kiefer, B., & Levsti, K. L. (1990). *An integrated language perspective in the elementary school.* New York: Longman.

Piaget, J. (1952). *The origins of intelligence in children.* New York: International University Press.

Piaget, J. (1955). *The language and thought of the child.* New York: Meridian.

Plowden, B. (1969). Children and their primary schools: A report of the Central Advisory Council for Education. London: Her Majesty's Stationery Office.

Reutzel, D., & Cooter, R. B., Jr. (1991). Organizing for effective instruction: the reading workshop. *The Reading Teacher, 44*(8), 548–555.

Rosenblatt, L. M. (1978). *The reader, the text, the poem: The transactional theory of the literary work.* Carbondale: Southern Illinois University Press.

Slavin, R. E. (1988). Ability grouping and student achievement in elementary and secondary school. *Educational Leadership, 46*(1), 67–77.

Smith, F. (1983). *Essays into literacy.* Exeter, NH: Heinemann.

Sorensen, A., & Hallinan, M. (1986). Effects of ability grouping on growth in academic achievement. *American Educational Research Journal, 23,* 519–542.

Strickland, D., & Morrow, L. (1988). New perspectives on young children learning to read and write. *The Reading Teacher, 42*(1), 70–71.

Strickland, D., & Morrow., L. (1990). Integrating the emergent literacy curriculum with themes. *The Reading Teacher, 43,* 604–605.

Sulzby, E. (1985). Children's emergent reading of favorite story books: A developmental study. *Reading Research Quarterly, 20,* 458–481.

Sulzby, E. (1994). I can write! Encouraging emergent writers. In K. Paciorek (Ed.), *Early childhood education 94/95* (15th ed., pp. 204–207). Guilford, CT: Dushkin.

Taylor, D., & Strickland, D. (1986). *Family storybook reading.* Portsmouth, NH: Heinemann.

Teale, W., & Sulzby, E. (Eds.). (1989). *Emergent literacy: Young children learn to read and write.* Norwood, NJ: Ablex.

Tierney, R. J., & Shanahan, T. (1991). Research on the reading–writing relationship: Interactions, transactions, and outcomes. In R. Barr et al. (Eds.), *Handbook of reading research* (Vol. 2, pp. 245–280). New York: Longman.

Tompkins, G., & Hoskisson, K. (1995). *Language arts: content and teaching strategies.* Saddle River, NJ: Prentice Hall.

Vacca, R., & Vacca, J. (1989). *Content area reading.* Glenview, IL: Scott, Foresman and Co.

Van Allen, R., & Allen, C. (1968). *Language experience in reading.* Chicago: Encyclopedia Britannica.

Vygotsky, L. S. (1962). *Thought and language.* (E. Haufman & G. Vakas, Eds. and Trans.). Cambridge, MA: MIT Press.

Wells, G. (1990). Creating the conditions to encourage literate thinking. *Educational Leadership, 47*(6), 13–17.

Children's Literature References

Allard, H. (1977). *Miss Nelson is missing.* Boston: Houghton Mifflin.

Carle, E. (1975). *The very hungry caterpillar.* New York: Philomel.

Cleary, B. (1983). *Dear Mr. Henshaw.* New York: Morrow.

Cowley, J. (1987). *Mrs. Wishy Washy.* San Diego, CA: The Wright Group.

dePaola, T. (1978). *Pancakes for breakfast.* New York: Harcourt Brace Jovanovich.

The Diary of Nina Kosterina. (1968). New York: Crown Publishers.

Filipovic, Z. (1994). *Zlata's diary.* New York: Viking.

Hess, L. (1982). *Diary of a rabbit.* New York: Scribner.

Mayer, M. (1971). *A boy, a dog, a frog and a friend.* New York: Dial.

Mooyart, B. M. (Ed.). (1967). *Anne Frank: the diary of a young girl* (rev. ed.). Garden City, NY: Doubleday.

Munch, R. (1987). *Love you forever.* Ontario, Canada: Firefly Books.

Prater, J. (1987). *The gift.* New York: Viking.

Prelutsky, J. (1984). *The new kid on the block.* New York: Greenwillow.

Prelutsky, J. (1985). *My parents think I'm sleeping.* New York: Greenwillow.

Rudner, B. (1989a). *The bumblebee and the ram.* Louisville, KY: Art-Print and Publishing Co.

Rudner, B. (1989b). *The littlest tall fellow.* Louisville, KY: Art-Print and Publishing Co.

Sendak, M. (1962). *Chicken soup with rice.* New York: HarperCollins.

Silverstein, S. (1974). *Where the sidewalk ends.* New York: Harper & Row.

Silverstein, S. (1981). *A light in the attic.* New York: HarperCollins.

Wood, A. (1987). *Heckedy peg.* Orlando, FL: Harcourt Brace Jovanovich.

Zindel, P. (1987). *Amazing and death defying diary of Eugene Dingman.* New York: Harper & Row.

Surveying Portfolio Use in Authentic Literacy Classrooms

KEY WORDS AND CONCEPTS

Literacy products
Literacy processes
Writing portfolio
Reading portfolio

Integrated language arts
or reading/writing portfolio
Cumulative record portfolio

I recently asked Craig, a fifth-grade student, how his year in fifth grade had gone. He replied, "Let me show you my portfolio and then we can really talk." He returned with a large loose-leaf note-book entitled **"My Fifth-Grade Portfolio."** *It was decorated with animals and contained many different entries, including:*

About the author	*Cartoons and comics*
Class pictures and events	*Class autographs*
Writing pieces	*Artwork*
Letters from parents	*Reactions to reading*

Craig was quick to point out that in addition to this end-of-year portfolio he had a sep-arate writing folder and another loose-leaf notebook that contained his reading log and all of his responses to reading done during the year. The portfolio made it quite easy to understand how fifth grade went for Craig. It was a year full of projects, with special emphasis on read-ing and writing poetry, and certainly it was a year of considerable growth and reflection about literacy.

It is evident both from Craig's perspective as well as from teachers' perspectives that a portfolio has become an important aspect of literacy instruction. As Chapter 3 described, teachers have incorporated many newer methods of authentic literacy into their instructional programs. Likewise, they now use portfolios as a means to more authentically assess the lit-eracy development in their students, to promote student self-reflection, and to provide essen-tial information for more effective instruction. When teachers thoughtfully implement portfolios into their classrooms, they are faced with many questions, including the following:

- What kind of portfolio should I use?
- What should be collected in the portfolio, and how should the contents be organized?

This chapter provides a survey of current portfolio practices and attempts to provide teach-ers with guidelines to assist them. A literacy portfolio is an essential ingredient in an authen-tic literacy classroom.

CHOOSING PORTFOLIO CONTENTS

A literacy portfolio should include evidence of both literacy products and processes. Given the new theories of literacy—that reading and writing involve the active participation of the student in reconstructing meaning—then portfolio contents must show evidence of both stu-dents' **literacy products** (the outcome of reading and writing activities, which might be in the form of essays, narratives, logs, and journals), and **literacy processes,** or strategies used during reading and writing. For example, teachers often want to know what students do when they encounter an important but unfamiliar word during reading. However, traditional forms of reading assessment have long focused on literacy outcomes and do not provide this kind of process information. Because much of reading and writing involve internal, cognitive processes, evaluating students' literacy strategies is much more complicated and elusive than collecting literacy products but can be addressed by the literacy portfolio process. Techniques such as self-reflective questionnaires, student-composed literacy biographies, informal reading assessments, and teacher–student conferences provide important information about students' literacy processes.

Rhodes and Shanklin (1993) suggest that teachers can also be guided by two questions when they think about what to include in a portfolio:

1. What does this information reveal or demonstrate about a student's development?
2. How will this information help make instructional decisions for this student? (p. 421)

For example, if a teacher is trying to determine if student-selected poetry belongs in the portfolio, the teacher might decide that including poetry demonstrates that the student is learning a new genre.

Paulson, Paulson, and Meyer (1991) provide eight guidelines to consider when teachers involve students in a portfolio process. Answering the question, "What makes a portfolio a portfolio?" they say that all portfolios

1. Should contain information that demonstrates the student has become involved in self-reflection
2. Reflect a process where the student is directly part of choosing the entries
3. Should not be similar to students' cumulative folders and should contain scores and other cumulative folder data only if they become meaningful as part of a portfolio collection
4. Should document the student's activities including the portfolio's purpose, goals, contents, standards, and judgments
5. Can serve an instructional purpose during the school year, but the end of the year portfolio should contain data that the student wishes to display
6. May have a variety of purposes, with an almost universal purpose of demonstrating progress in the instructional program, but multiple purposes should not conflict with each other
7. Should document the student's growth in terms of skills, school performance, interests, and attitudes
8. Should be based on a support structure where students are shown portfolio models that demonstrate how collections are created and how other students reflect on the contents (pp. 62–63).

An essential component of any portfolio is an explanation of how the entries are chosen and the system by which they are organized. Students should include a table of contents or write a letter to the reader in which the contents and the reasons for specific entries are described. Figure 4–1 is a letter written by a third-grade student to her parents in which she describes her portfolio. The reading test that is mentioned is a running record.

Careful organization of portfolio contents not only helps the reader understand how the portfolio was assembled but more importantly requires that both the student and teacher

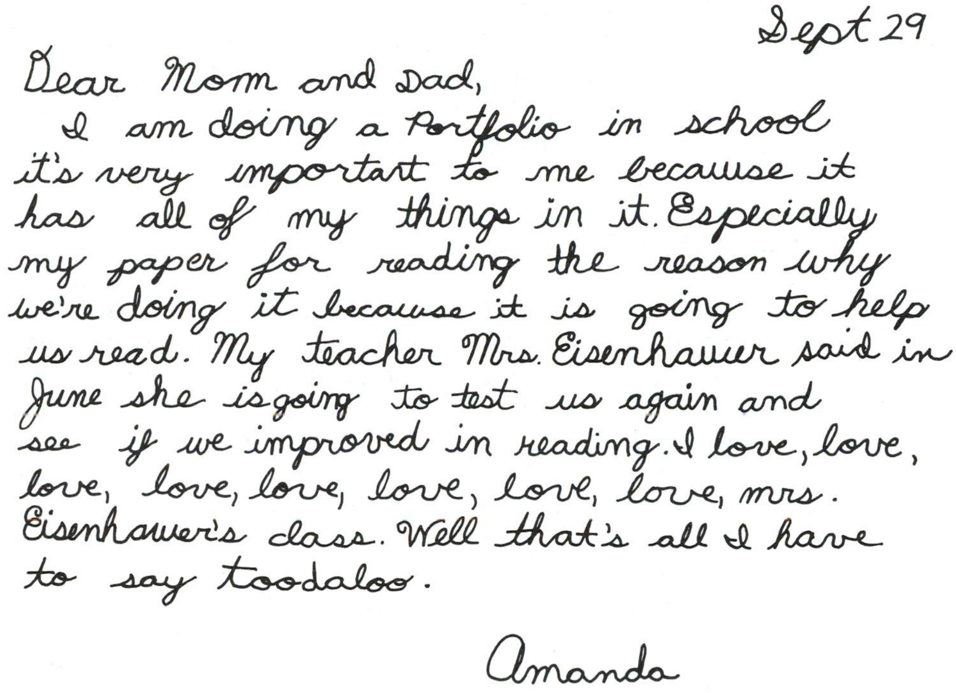

Sept 29

Dear Mom and Dad,
    I am doing a Portfolio in school it's very important to me because it has all of my things in it. Especially my paper for reading the reason why we're doing it because it is going to help us read. My teacher Mrs. Eisenhauer said in June she is going to test us again and see if we improved in reading. I love, love, love, love, love, love, love, love, mrs. Eisenhauer's class. Well that's all I have to say toodaloo.

                                        Amanda

FIGURE 4–1 Sample letter from a third-grade student introducing her portfolio to her parents.

reflect on the criteria for the collection. No two students' portfolios will be identical, and that is to be desired. In fact, depending on the amount of independence a student is given in choosing portfolio contents, the collection will vary widely. Portfolio contents should reflect variation between students in terms of interests, attitudes, goals, strategies, and abilities. "Above all, a portfolio is a portfolio when it provides a forum that encourages students to develop the abilities needed to become independent, self-directed learners" (Paulson et al., 1991, p. 63).

Another dynamic that needs to be explored during the initial phase of deciding on contents is determining who will be responsible for choosing portfolio entries. Jenkins (1996, p. 11) provides a useful survey for teachers to complete that will help them resolve this dilemma. She suggests choosing among student control, teacher control, and joint control as alternatives for taking responsibility about entry selection, portfolio access, product assessment, goal setting, conferencing, and sharing contents. Deciding on the purpose of the portfolio will help make such determinations logical. If a portfolio is to be used primarily for accountability, then teachers may feel totally responsible for choosing entries that reflect accomplishment of developmental benchmarks. However, if a portfolio is to be used to celebrate and showcase student accomplishment and promote student self-assessment, then the student's choice should prevail. Jenkins (1996) feels that a collaborative portfolio process combines the best of both benchmark and showcase portfolios; "we create the collaborative portfolio by merging copies of the child's selections and reflections with our choices and analyses (and those of parents)" (p. 18). This collaborative model accomplishes three goals: It engages children in self-assessment and goal setting, assesses progress, and collects data for instructional interactions. The Literacy Assessment Portfolio (LAP) process recommended in this text, which is fully described in Chapter 6, endorses this collaborative model.

Several fairly consistent patterns emerge from a survey of current portfolio practices. These are summarized and categorized in the balance of this chapter.

WRITING PORTFOLIOS

The most widespread use of portfolios has been the writing portfolio, evolving from the writing folder. Writing instruction has changed dramatically in recent years. Teachers are now aware that a piece of writing is the product of different stages of writing that involve activities such as making lists, taking notes, attempting drafts, sharing with peers, conferencing, editing, revising work, and finally publishing pieces. Students need a repository for the work as it evolves through these stages. Collecting writing pieces as works in progress gives teachers the opportunity to see the evolution of a piece of writing through its development and provides information about the process of writing used by an individual student. When students value the outcome of their writing efforts and take pride in their accomplishment, they want a place to store finished pieces in a semipermanent fashion for both display and review. Writing folders with collected students' work are a means of publishing student work for display, for teacher conferences, and for communicating and sharing with families, and they are sometimes used for acquainting next year's teacher with the student's work. In some districts, the final products of the writing process can be found in folders often called Best Works Folders. These folders are closely aligned with recommended portfolio practice because students are responsible for choosing the contents and are self-reflective in deciding why a piece is meritorious. Figure 4–2 contains a third-grade student's reasons for choosing entries for his writing portfolio.

Trends Creating the Need for Writing Portfolios

As the writing process approach became nationally recognized as a model of good writing instruction, writing folders proliferated. Rarely can one find a classroom where students are not engaged in composing a piece of writing over several days and then storing their work. While the contents of these folders vary to include such other writing-related items as writing skills checklists, self-editing guidelines, conference notes, feedback from other students, and teacher evaluations, they share a common feature in that they are an outgrowth of the writing process philosophy of instruction.

Many state-wide testing programs require the collection of students' writing. Since many states have incorporated actual student work into their writing assessment systems, teachers have become aware of the need to collect student writing that can be analyzed for diagnostic and assessment purposes. For example, New Mexico uses a portfolio system for statewide assessment (Rael & Travelstead, 1993). Each school year, teachers are given a list of writing prompts and criteria for good writing to use with their students. They develop lessons around these prompts using a writing process approach, and thus the students write on assigned topics. Students' best efforts are collected in writing portfolios, and in the spring the State Education Department selects one of the prompts for scoring. The students' writing samples for the particular topic are then scored against criteria that have been widely distributed.

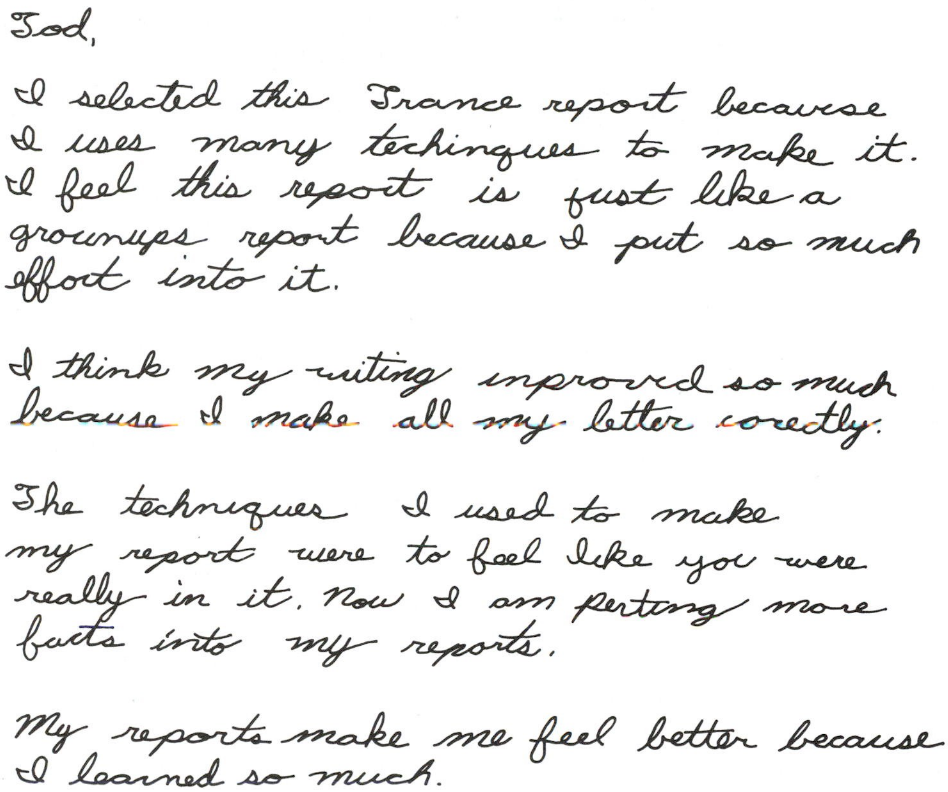

Tod,

I selected this France report because I uses many techinques to make it. I feel this report is just like a grounups report because I put so much effort into it.

I think my writing improved so much because I make all my letter corectly.

The techniques I used to make my report were to feel like you were really in it. Now I am perting more facts into my reports.

My reports make me feel better because I learned so much.

FIGURE 4–2 A third-grade student shares his reasons for choosing an entry for his portfolio.

The introduction of computer-assisted instruction (CAI) and word processing have also contributed to preserving students' writing. When all writing was the product of handwritten efforts, students who experienced graphomotor problems were physically limited in their ability to produce a large amount of writing or were certainly reluctant to recopy or revise. Older students often resisted the suggestion that they edit their writing because of the time and effort needed. Editing and revising are intensive and laborious without the use of a computer. As students were introduced to keyboarding and schools put computers in the classroom or in computer labs, a marked increase in writing productivity resulted. Students were motivated to write more with the aid of word processing, and their ability to produce legible copy with ease of revision became evident.

Writing Portfolio Contents

A writing portfolio should contain evidence of both process and product. (Hill & Ruptic, 1994, p. 17; Rhodes & Shanklin, 1993, p. 420; Tierney, Carter, & Desai, 1991, pp. 73–74). *Writing process* entries reveal how a child goes about writing and in particular what strategies are employed. The evidence of writing process measures can include prompts students use during their writing (i.e., word webs, semantic maps, lists, etc.), their thoughts about their writing, as well as copies of their work in progress. Rhodes and Shanklin (1993, p. 420) also suggest including process measures in a writing portfolio, which can include, among other items:

Topics lists

Self-reflections

Webs and artwork

Writing strategy checklists

Conference guides

Author's circle tapes and notes

Because many students have difficulty beginning a writing task, they are often helped by group brainstorming, compiling lists of suggested topics, or referring to guided questions. During the drafting phase, notes from conferences (both with peers and the teacher) may prove helpful. The use of prewriting techniques such as concept maps, semantic webs, and word maps are also widely used to assist students with organization of their thoughts before and during composing. These aids can be included to document strategies used to lend coherence to writing. When students self-edit, they can be assisted by checklists and wall charts labeled with titles such as "Skills I Know" or "What to Look for When I Edit." Often, students edit their works collaboratively in peer editing groups or by having another student sign off that the work has been reviewed by a peer.

When deciding what product measures to include in a writing portfolio, it is usual to incorporate those that reflect day-to-day assignments and activities. Particular attention should be given to having students attempt a variety of age-appropriate writing (personal narratives, reports, persuasive essays, letters, poetry, etc.) as well as projects that integrate writing in different curriculum areas. Many teachers now require students to respond to books they've read in various ways, including response logs and literature journals as a replacement for the traditional book report. These are often more reflective reactions that show evidence of different levels of understanding as well as a reader's affective response to a piece of literature. Tierney et al. (1991) suggest a list of writing products that can be assembled to show evidence of work on underlying instructional goals:

- Written responses to literary components such as plot, setting, point of view, character development, and theme
- Items that are evidence of development of style, organization, voice, sense of audience, choice of words, and clarity
- Writing that shows growth in use of skills such as self-correction, punctuation, spelling, grammar, appropriate form, and legibility
- Writing that illustrates evidence of topic generation (pp. 73–74)

In the development of writing skills in the young student, or in the student just beginning to acquire English language skills, the relationship between writing and illustrations is most important, and the inclusion of students' artwork as a supplementary form of expression is encouraged. Artwork not only personalizes a student's writing but also helps to communicate ideas or a sequence of events and often is a motivating factor. For the older student, illustrations as well as diagrams, charts, and tables should be encouraged.

Figure 4–3 provides a summary of what often constitutes a writing folder.

student's writing ⟶ collected in works in progress folder ⟶ entries chosen for writing portfolio

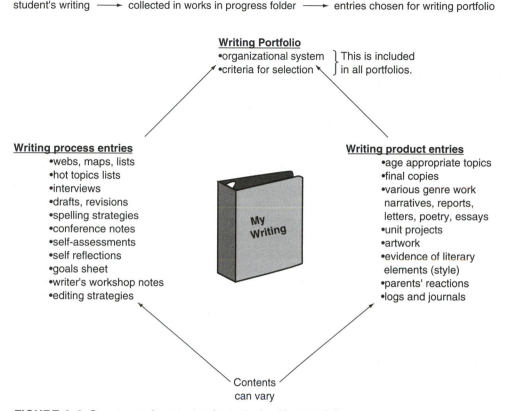

Writing Portfolio
•organizational system ⎱ This is included
•criteria for selection ⎰ in all portfolios.

Writing process entries
•webs, maps, lists
•hot topics lists
•interviews
•drafts, revisions
•spelling strategies
•conference notes
•self-assessments
•self reflections
•goals sheet
•writer's workshop notes
•editing strategies

My Writing

Writing product entries
•age appropriate topics
•final copies
•various genre work
 narratives, reports,
 letters, poetry, essays
•unit projects
•artwork
•evidence of literary
 elements (style)
•parents' reactions
•logs and journals

Contents
can vary

FIGURE 4–3 Summary of contents of a typical writing portfolio.

Management of Writing Portfolios

Writing portfolios must be accessible to students and have ample storage with a secure pocket so that small items are not lost. Many suggest that a writing portfolio be divided into two phases: works in progress and published writing. Teachers have often stored these writing folders on open shelves in a convenient location, in cardboard or plastic filing boxes, or in file cabinets, or students can keep folders in their desks. Many teachers prefer to use an informal folder approach for work in progress and reserve the writing portfolio for those special pieces that are selected according to predetermined criteria and are carefully stored.

Ongoing monitoring by the teacher ensures that the goals of the portfolio process are met. It must be emphasized that without establishing and using criteria for selection of entries, writing portfolios can quickly become large, cumbersome assortments of student work without instructional or personal significance. Writing conferences are an excellent time for the teacher to guide a student in shaping portfolio contents. Regardless of whether teachers adopt portfolio practice for other uses, the writing portfolio clearly is essential for those who use a writing process approach.

READING PORTFOLIOS

There has been a major shift in our understanding of what constitutes literacy, with consequent changes in the manner in which instruction is conducted. Today, many literacy experts feel that "children learn to read, write, speak, listen and think by having real opportunities to read, write, speak, listen and think as opposed to completing contrived exercises that involve marking, circling, and underlining" (Cooper, 1993, pp. 6–7). Restructuring literacy teaching has resulted in more integration of the language arts, reliance on thematic units, extensive use of quality literature as the medium of instruction, cooperative learning, and the application of literacy strategies across curriculum areas with assignments designed to mirror actual, "authentic" literacy demands.

The reading portfolio process is viewed by some as an opportunity to better understand the student's literacy processes by examining strategies that students use in a wide variety of activities each day. The portfolio process also incorporates and promotes the reader's self-reflections, also called metacognition. This is defined as an individual's ability to self-monitor by engaging in such activities as rereading, self-questioning, purpose setting, and predicting and thereby being aware of and in control of the functioning of the mind (Burns, Roe, & Ross, 1996, p. 703). During reading, metacognitive awareness helps the student select strategies that are useful for succeeding with certain literacy tasks. The portfolio process is particularly well suited to directing students to engage in thoughtful reflection about what and how they read and therefore has important instructional implications for teachers.

Reading Portfolio Contents

The contents of a good reading portfolio, one that will truly give the teacher and the student a full appraisal of reading ability, must incorporate both product and process measures. A survey of the literature regarding reading portfolios also indicates that the contents can be divided into the following categories:

- Measures that reflect and analyze students' decoding and vocabulary skills
- Measures that reflect and analyze students' comprehension skills
- Measures that require students to write as a reaction to reading across content areas with different forms of text and for different purposes
- Measures of students' reading interests and attitudes
- Lists and logs of students' actual reading experiences
- Projects or products that are the outcomes of reading assignments
- Teacher's progress notes, conference notes, or observational notes about the student when the student is engaged in reading activities
- Appraisal of the students' reading skills outside the school environment

Figure 4–4 summarizes the contents of a typical reading portfolio.
Rhodes and Shanklin (1993) describe the contents of an ideal reading portfolio:

Process Measures

Metacognitive interviews

Tapes of oral reading

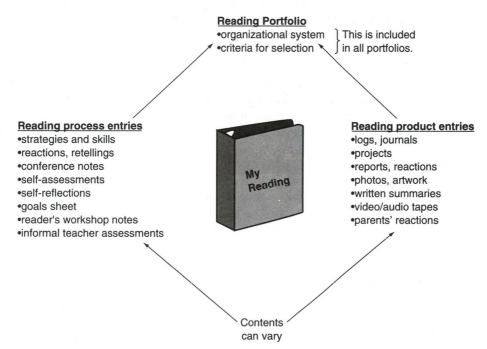

student's reading activities ⟶ recorded by logs, reports, tapes, projects, etc. ⟶ entries chosen for reading portfolio

Reading Portfolio
•organizational system } This is included
•criteria for selection } in all portfolios.

Reading process entries
•strategies and skills
•reactions, retellings
•conference notes
•self-assessments
•self-reflections
•goals sheet
•reader's workshop notes
•informal teacher assessments

My Reading

Reading product entries
•logs, journals
•projects
•reports, reactions
•photos, artwork
•written summaries
•video/audio tapes
•parents' reactions

Contents
can vary

FIGURE 4–4 Summary of contents of a typical reading portfolio.

Self-assessment of processes

Goal setting

Strategies used by the student, called "Strategies I Use"

Photographs/videos of student's reading

Reading discussions

Product Measures

List of books read—teacher or student selected, at home and school

Written retellings of reading

Reading/learning log entries

After-reading projects—sketches, story maps, sociograms

Photographs of products—literacy-related art, social studies and science projects

Videos of student plays

Self-assessment of products

Goal setting

Parent responses to portfolios (p. 420)

Reading portfolios can include numerous other types of entries.

Literature Log. Classrooms that use literature-based approaches to reading frequently use a technique called a *literature circle,* where a group of students engage in meaningful discussions after reading. Depending on the age and experience of the students, or with some training, these groups can be student led. Portfolios will frequently contain tape recordings or notes from these literature discussion group meetings.

Reading Log. Students record what they read during school and at home in log entries that are included in almost all reading portfolios. Reading journals and logs are extensively discussed in Chapter 3. Their inclusion in a portfolio is a most important indicator of how much reading a student is engaged in; the type, difficulty, and variety of books read; and the reaction to what is read.

Reading Projects. Many teachers give formal assignments for students to complete after they have finished a chapter or an entire book. These assignments have taken the place of the traditional book report and are often in the form of projects (i.e., write an advertisement for the book, create a bookmark or book jacket, etc.). These projects provide insights into depth of comprehension and personal reactions.

Self-Assessments. Many teachers who use portfolios for reading also include self-assessment forms that help appraise the students' general perceptions of themselves as a reader, their reading interests, their goals, and their specific reactions to something that has been read. These self-reflections can take many forms. Some teachers ask that students write a literacy biography for their reading portfolio that tells their individual history as a reader and also focuses on their self-identified literacy goals for the year. Students often keep a daily journal. A popular topic for an entry is a personal reaction to something they have read. Teachers can also provide a reading response sheet to guide students in responding to their reading selections, as shown in Figure 4–5.

Documenting the Use of Decoding Strategies. Teachers still place a heavy emphasis on teaching decoding strategies, especially during the primary grades or when they work with disabled readers. Therefore, appraising a student's decoding strategies is frequently perceived to be an important part of reading assessment, and analysis of these strategies is incorporated into reading portfolios in the form of administration of informal reading inventories, running records, and miscue analysis. Taped, oral readings by the student, obtained at several points during the school year, may be included to show changes in reading fluency and document growth over time. Tape recordings must be preceded by a clear identification of the child's name, date of the taping, and the source of the material read. In one third-grade class, the teacher, the students, and the parents found oral tapings valuable, because they present a clear demonstration of how a student's ability changes during the year. Figure 4–6 is a letter to parents prepared by the teacher, Mrs. Eisenhauer, explaining how they can use the taped reading to assist their children's reading. Of particular interest is Mrs. Eisenhauer's emphasis on reading strategies, the use of content material (often thought to be more difficult for young children), orientation toward the child's growing success, and enlisting the parents' help.

Observational Data. Another source of valuable information for the reading portfolio is composed of observational data collected by the teacher. Goodman's concept of kid watching

Date: *Oct 25 1994*

Reading Response Evaluation

Why do you feel this is the best response you've written so far this year?

I thought this respons was good because it tolld alot of informaion.

What would you add or change? *I would add more detal because I newor right alot*

Would you read another book by this author? Why? *I would because he is my favort athor and I like his books*

What do you think you can do to improve the way you respond to literature?

I would rigt more infmaion and detal abrot the book because my storys don't have alot of infmion in them

FIGURE 4–5 A completed reading response sheet from a third-grade student.

has given renewed attention to observing children and recording insights gained through informal assessment (1978). Information such as how long a child can sustain attention, the student's individual work habits and preferences, and how the student relates to other learners can be gained only from observing the child at work. Some teachers find that making notes on small self-adhesive tags is an easy method of keeping track of individual student behavior. These notes can be affixed to the student's portfolio or contained in a teacher notebook. Other teachers use a clipboard with lined paper to record their daily observations about students. Some teachers create an observational loose-leaf book with separate sections devoted to each child so that a chronology of behaviors can be documented throughout the school year. Whatever system a teacher employs, it is essential to allocate time to observe and document individual student behavior on a regular basis. Notes that the teacher takes after a conference with a student about the portfolio or an ongoing literacy project provide additional valuable information.

Content Area Projects. In classrooms where there is particular emphasis on reading applied to content learning (especially evident in intermediate grade and middle school portfolios),

February 10

Dear Parents,

Your child has completed a third taped reading and evaluation of a reading response. We'd like to share it with you, so you can note the progress your child is making and continue to take part in our plans for improvement.

This time we taped a selection from our social studies text for the purpose of monitoring our strategies for reading factual material. We discuss reading techniques in school that will improve our recall and understanding of this type of material. At the beginning of the taping, I asked your child what techniques if any s/he uses before reading factual material. Listen carefully to see if your child mentioned any of the following prereading strategies:

1. Read the title or subject heading.
2. Think about everything I know about the subject before reading.
3. Look at any pictures, graphs, maps, etc.
4. Look at any words in bold type.
5. Predict what the passage will be about.
6. Think about what I'd like to learn about the subject.

Your child will probably mention some of these techniques, and you may want to encourage him/her to use them while reading content area books for reports or for pleasure. Using them will help improve your child's recall and comprehension.

Enjoy this tape with your child, and please let me know where you see your child making the most progress and what areas you and your child feel you'd like to focus on next.

Your child and I thank you for your continued support and interest.

Mrs. Eisenhauer

FIGURE 4–6 Letter to parents of students in Mrs. Eisenhauer's third-grade class in Lynbrook, New York, informing them about using a taped reading.

reading portfolio entries often include products that are the outgrowth of subject area assignments. Research projects resulting from reading in the content areas are important entries in the reading portfolio. Including research reports and other forms of content area studies (these projects can include pictures or multimedia displays and written projects) demonstrates to students that reading has practical significance in learning across the curriculum, exposes students to different contexts for using their reading skills, and meaningfully incorporates research strategies into the reading curriculum. Obviously, reading and writing efforts on thematic and integrated language arts units should be included in the portfolio collection.

Family Information. Input from parents and families about portfolio contents is an additional welcome entry. To promote cooperation between the family and the school, parents should be actively included in the process. Some teachers do this by sending the portfolios home regularly. Students are encouraged to share their portfolios with their parents, and parents are asked to add an entry into the portfolio, noting that they have viewed the contents, discussed the portfolio with the student, and responded to the portfolio and their child's work.

Other Reading Portfolio Contents. An organizational framework for a reading portfolio is necessary, whether in the form of a table of contents or a letter to the portfolio reader. This helps reinforce the criteria for entry selection, helps students take responsibility for choosing portfolio entries, and makes the ongoing monitoring and conferencing about the portfolio contents much more efficient.

Use of Standardized Test Data. A critical issue with regard to the reading portfolio has been whether standardized test scores obtained both from district-wide testing programs and state assessment systems should be included in a reading portfolio. Many educators find that these traditional data add to a fuller picture of how the child functions as a reader. Others feel that such information is often unreliable, is not helpful in terms of instructional decision making, and contaminates an authentic assessment model. Before test data are included in a reading portfolio, we strongly recommend that consideration be given to whether the data should be shared with a student, given the student's age, maturity, and reading level. Students who do not succeed on standardized tests can easily be defeated by having such data reproduced in their portfolio, which has been geared to documenting growth and success. Also, these data must be interpreted in the context of other information learned about the student through authentic assessment. For example, is the performance reported on standardized tests compatible with the work that the child has produced in the classroom setting? If there appears to be a significant discrepancy between standardized test scores and classroom performance (often in the direction of a depressed test score and better class performance), what explanation can be given for the divergence in performance data? Such factors as the child's language and experiential background, test-taking behavior, motivation, and attention span as well as the content of the standardized test as compared with school curriculum are all variables that must be considered because they dramatically impact on a child's test performance.

A reading portfolio will reflect the goals of the reading curriculum as well as the reading activities used in the classroom and is highly individual, based on each child's interests, goals, and abilities. Such diversity is not only expected but is encouraged. A good portfolio collection, according to Tierney et al. (1991), will demonstrate variety, "Collections will undoubtedly differ from classroom to classroom and from student to student depending upon teacher and student interests, cultural background, grade level, and many other variables" (p. 74).

INTEGRATED LANGUAGE ARTS, OR READING/WRITING, PORTFOLIOS

Many educators now recognize that the language arts are most effectively taught in an integrated fashion. This is particularly evident in classrooms that use a whole language methodology for teaching reading and writing and that may use literature-based teaching, thematic teaching units, or reading and writing process activities. When reading and writing instruction are integrated and a portfolio process is used, it logically follows that the portfolio reflects classroom practice and thus contains evidence of reading and writing as well as other language arts activities.

A number of researchers have commented on various types of integrated portfolios. Valencia's (1990) early and widely cited article on portfolios was seminal in proposing a portfolio process that suggested a range of almost limitless entries; "the key [was] to ensure a *vari-*

ety of types of indicators of learning so that teachers, parents, students, and administrators [could] build a complete picture of the student's development," and the contents of a portfolio [grew] from curricular goals and instructional priorities (p. 339). Portfolio contents could therefore include a variety of language activities: reading logs, daily work, writing at various stages, class tests, checklists, unit projects, and audio/videotapes.

In another widely cited article about portfolio collection, Au, Scheu, Kawakami, and Herman (1990, p. 574) support the concept of an integrated portfolio. They describe six aspects of literacy that should be reflected in a portfolio: student ownership, reading comprehension, writing process, word identification, language and vocabulary knowledge, and voluntary reading. Further, they propose that the portfolio collection portray these literacy characteristics by containing an attitude questionnaire on reading and writing, a response to a literature task (including a checklist), a writing sample, a running record, and a voluntary reading log.

Tierney et al. (1991) recommend that portfolios represent "students as readers and writers . . . and this allows the student's continuous literacy development to be accurately documented" (p. 74). Their proposed list for portfolio entries includes a wide assortment of language arts activities, such as:

Favorite poems, songs, and thoughts

Writing samples from across the curriculum

Logs, journals, and reports

Audio reading tapes

Conferences notes

Literature extensions including artwork

Rhodes and Shanklin (1993, pp. 416–418) recommend a collection process that reflects both reading and writing activities. They suggest that teachers keep reading and writing folders that contain student-collected chronological entries of their ongoing work and that these folders should be reviewed with particular pieces selected and put into a Current Year Portfolio. Hill and Ruptic (1994, pp. 20–28) also recommend a portfolio process that requires teachers to keep separate reading and writing collections of students' work. While teachers are encouraged to maintain separate folders for reading and writing, it is evident that the two collections are parallel by assessing both language process and product. Together, they reflect total literacy development. Suggested contents include attitude and interest surveys, logs, responses to reading and writing, and content area projects. These authors also advise teachers to keep an ongoing diagnostic notebook that records the student's literacy development in both reading and writing.

Farr and Tone (1994) also provide a very comprehensive and easy-to-use guide to creating portfolio collections and recommend various entries with emphasis on the students' role in selection to reflect their interests and language applications. For these authors, the reading–writing log is a centerpiece of the portfolio, but they also describe many other entries that "depict and promote the student's development as a language user" (Farr & Tone, 1994, p. 49). From the preceding examples, it seems evident that portfolio collections reflect integrated literacy methods with heavy emphasis on reading and writing development.

The portfolio process used at the Rider College lab school is described by Glazer and Brown (1993, pp. 34–37) and reflects the literature-based, language arts program employed in this clinical setting. They feel that the portfolio process should be viewed as "windows for learning about students," best achieved by including entries reflecting a variety of language skills. Collected work samples are chosen by the students to reflect their accomplishments, and entries that contain data most helpful for planning instruction are also included.

Developmental Language Arts Portfolios

Many school districts are using portfolios that include reading and writing activities as well as activities that document students' growth in all language arts and therefore include developmental checklists for speaking and listening ability as well. These checklists are completed by the teacher at various points during the academic year to document progress. Teachers from Juneau, Alaska, use an integrated literacy approach, and their Language Arts Portfolio echoes this philosophy by including assessment of reading, writing, listening, and speaking (see Juneau School District, *Language Arts Portfolio Handbook,* 1993). Consequently, their portfolio is an integrated language arts portfolio, which presents a comprehensive assessment of a child's educational accomplishment in language ability. The contents reflect this multi-dimensional curriculum and require teachers to document all phases of the language arts.

The portfolio used in Juneau contains the following entries collected during the four quarters of the school year: Student Reflection Letter, A Reading Continuum (a behaviorally oriented scale that assesses the student's development in essential skill areas), Reading Samples (using a running record form of analysis), Reading Attitude Survey, Writing Continuum (parallels the reading continuum concept as it pertains to essential writing skills), Writing Samples (scored according to district guidelines), Written Teacher Narrative (statement describes the student's performance and progress in reading, writing, listening, speaking, literacy interests, and suggestions for parents), and Speaking/Listening Narrative (a description of observed behavior in speaking and listening). Optional entries include favorite pieces chosen by the students, teacher anecdotal observations, oral language cassette tapes, developmental spelling lists, reading logs, and drawings and illustrations by the child. The Juneau portfolio collection is noteworthy both as an early example of district-wide portfolio adoption and for its attempt to document growth in all language areas.

Portfolio Performances or Demonstrations

Some teachers have students present portfolio projects in the form of a performance or oral report often assessed through the use of a collaboratively designed evaluation system called a *rubric.* Consequently, speaking and other communication skills become an important aspect of a student's ability to share information. Such a practice is part of a sixth-grade exit project used in the South Brunswick, New Jersey, schools to demonstrate that students are eligible for graduation and prepared for middle school work (see King-Shaver & Spicer, 1993). These projects integrate research skills, reading and writing ability, as well as speaking and presentation skills. Students are also reminded about the importance of listening, both when they are an audience for others' presentations and when they are involved in research that may include interviews. In this school district, community residents, local professionals, and students enrolled in teacher education programs at nearby colleges are all invited to participate as assessors, so that each sixth-grade student is individually evaluated by an "expert" trained in the use of a uniform scoring rubric.

In North Shore, Long Island—a school district that endorses the use of integrated port-folios—a team of special education teachers in a middle school has their students participate in a school-wide presentation of independent research in social studies. These teachers find that the oral/aural presentation format is especially important for their students who may be struggling with reading and writing skills. A successful oral presentation enhances the students' feelings of self-worth. It is evident that many school districts use a portfolio process that attempts to reinforce the interrelationships among all of the language arts.

CUMULATIVE RECORD PORTFOLIOS

Some school districts see the portfolio process as a collection designed not only to support the instructional program, but also to promote accountability by adding to information contained in cumulative record folders and other forms of standard assessment information traditionally kept by school districts. Maintaining record folders (often called permanent record cards) has been important to demonstrate compliance with state-mandated testing and record keeping, and it has also been useful in documenting longitudinal change and achievement over time. These records also follow children if they leave one school district and register in other districts within or out of state. Cumulative record folders have tradi-tionally contained the following assessment data: standardized test scores (required both by state education departments and local school districts), individual diagnostic evaluations (frequently the product of a referral to the Committee on Special Education and often stored in separate files), report cards, health and attendance records, and less frequently anecdotal teacher comments. The traditional cumulative record folder has been criticized by some as being the repository of information of little use to teachers, often ignored by teach-ers, filled with unreliable or irrelevant data, and too often a reflection of outdated assess-ment practices.

Districts that embrace portfolios as part of a district-wide, uniform assessment system do so with the belief that the authentic nature of the portfolio process is a true reflection of both instructional priorities and the actual achievement of students. However, restructuring district-wide assessment procedures is a formidable task replete with problems. The Lawrence/Inwood school district in New York is representative of school districts that are proponents of the portfolio process and have found them useful as part of longitudinal, cumulative records. This school district created a district-wide portfolio process through a series of steps using committees of both administrators and teachers and was designed to reflect the concerns and reciprocal respect between teachers and administrators in the change process (Peppe & Petraglia, 1992).

Change in this district's program was an outgrowth of the widespread use of the writing process in the elementary schools. As teachers became convinced that reading quality litera-ture encouraged good writing, students were exposed to a variety of reading materials that soon replaced basal readers. Whole language instruction became the district philosophy, with emphasis on obtaining meaning from the reading of whole stories before skills were rein-forced in a meaningful context. The result of this change in philosophy not only was seen in instructional practices but also created a necessity to change assessment; a process of assess-ment was needed that would parallel and reflect the district's whole language practices. The district eventually adopted a reading–writing portfolio that was an outgrowth of several years' work and reflects the belief that teachers' observations, students' self-reflections, and analysis of classroom tasks are the most valid tools for language arts assessment. The K–6 Reading/Writing Process Assessment Portfolio is contained in a sturdy, three-part folder with required core elements and encourages teachers to include other entries under an optional elements category:

Core Elements

- Language Literacy Profile (for use in kindergarten)
- Reading Development Checklist (grades 1 to 8)
- List of Books Read Independently
- Form: Am I Developing as a Reader?
- Student Teacher Conference Log
- District Writing Folder—a standardized rubric by which to evaluate students' writing samples

Optional Elements

- Reading journals
- One-minute assessment
- Student interest inventory
- Audio/videotapes
- Photographic records
- Other projects
- Other formal and informal records such as running records and anecdotal records

The elementary folder was designed to be an end-of-year compilation of entries chosen from classroom portfolios kept for each child. This folder accompanies the child from kindergarten through sixth grade. Even after seven years of development and piloting, it is still seen as a work in progress, subject to annual revisions suggested by committees that meet in the summer. English and reading teachers in the district's middle school created a different portfolio for their students. While it is too soon to formally document effects of the new portfolio, it is quite evident that Lawrence has moved a long way from the traditional cumulative record system to a change in assessment strategies using a portfolio process based on mutual cooperation between teachers and administrators.

Other professionals in the assessment field have discussed the worth of using portfolios to document longitudinal change in literacy growth. Hill and Ruptic (1994) propose that a learning profile accompany students from kindergarten through grade 5 and be composed of representative samples from each year's collection. A reading and writing continuum follows students' development in essential literacy areas. Rhodes and Shanklin (1993, pp. 418–419) propose that a permanent portfolio be assembled for students so that each new teacher can benefit from prior assessment. Concern is expressed that the number of items in such a permanent folder should be limited, or its usefulness will be outweighed by the unwieldy size of a long-term collection.

Many states have begun initiatives that are likely to result in mandated portfolio practices to create new forms of permanent records. Issues that have been raised about large assessment programs that use performance-based techniques have addressed such areas as the reliability of limited sampling of student performance, concern about equity issues that result from assessment decisions, the opportunity of students in varying geographical areas to receive quality education, and the tension of creating systems that are sensitive to individual priorities and allow for wide variations but are still reliable and consistent (Pearson, 1994, pp. 218–227).

CONCERNS

The growing use of portfolios has raised several significant concerns. For example, it is important to separate the effects of using a classroom portfolio process from using portfolios in larger assessment programs, which results in portfolios being used for making high-stakes decisions such as program placement, promotion, and graduation. Some feel the need to be especially cautious because of the serious ramifications of misinformed decision making. Researchers also caution that too much emphasis has been placed on how to create portfolios without understanding and analyzing how portfolios are actually used. Gomez and Graue (1994) caution that while portfolios have opened a new conversation about teaching and learning, too much emphasis has been placed on the form of portfolios without analyzing the effects of their use. Their research describes current portfolio practice by a small group of teachers who were identified as being quality educators by peers, administrators, parents, and children. Unfortunately, the researchers found that assessment with portfolios often replicated much of traditional, standardized measures because portfolios tended to be cumulative and linear, were permeated by the context of accountability, were quantitative rather than integrative, and focused on reporting data that all too often focused on students' deficiencies rather than strengths. In summary, these researchers feel that any act of assessment is essentially interpretive and relies on the lenses of the observer, who creates meaning from portfolio contents. While portfolio assessment has promise, Gomez and Graue warn that "the outcomes of portfolio assessment are bounded by historical and social contexts, by institutional constraints, and by personal perspectives on teaching, learning and learners."

Arter and Spandel (1992) share similar concerns about the ability to draw accurate conclusions from portfolios. They caution that portfolios, as a form of performance assessment, can have a number of problems:

> The work in the portfolio may not really be representative of what the student knows and can do, the criteria used to critique the product may not reflect the most relevant or useful dimensions of the task, the work that a student puts in the portfolio may make the viewer wonder what is authentic about it, there may be aspects of the portfolio process that make a student unable to really demonstrate what he or she knows or can do, and the conclusions drawn from the portfolio can be heavily influenced by the person doing the evaluation. (Arter & Spandel, 1992, p. 38)

CONCLUSIONS

In summary, Graves (1992) cautions that educators should "slow down and learn" about portfolios before "rac[ing] to use portfolios with large populations" (p. 2). He suggests seven principles that should be heeded when a portfolio process is used:

- Involve the students.
- Help the staff keep portfolios of their own.

- Broaden the purpose of portfolios.
- Keep instructional opportunities open.
- Reexamine issues in comparability.
- Study the effect of school policy on portfolio practice.
- Enlist the ingenuity of teachers (p. 3).

There is great benefit to be obtained from using portfolios as well as a great deal to learn and understand about the process. It is evident that portfolios are not simply folders that contain students' work. According to Harp (1996), teachers need to know that portfolios involve "a collection that is carefully, thoughtfully and critically evaluated," require an effective management system, and can be time-consuming (p. 140).

Chapter 5 explores the replacement of traditional assessment practices with more authentic assessment opportunities. The use of a literacy portfolio is now another means by which teachers can assess the literacy skills of their students, and portfolios have become a major focus in changing assessment strategies.

REFERENCES

Arter, J., & Spandel, V. (1992, Spring). Using portfolios of student work in instruction and assessment. *Educational Measurement: Issues and Practice*, pp. 36–44.

Au, K., Scheu, J., Kawakami, A., & Herman, P. (1990, April). Assessment and accountability in a Whole Literacy Curriculum. *The Reading Teacher, 43*(8), 574–578.

Burns, P., Roe, B., & Ross, E. (1996). *Teaching reading in today's elementary schools.* Boston: Houghton Mifflin.

Cooper, J. (1993). *Literacy.* Boston: Houghton Mifflin.

Farr, R., & Tone, B. (1994). *Portfolio and performance assessment.* New York: Harcourt Brace.

Glazer, S., & Brown, C. (1993). *Portfolios and beyond: Collaborative assessment in reading and writing.* Norwood, MA: Christopher Gordon.

Gomez, M. L., & Graue, M. E. (1994). Possibilities, not panacea: A case for rethinking the processes of portfolio assessment. Unpublished paper. University of Wisconsin-Madison. Madison, WI.

Goodman, Y. (1978). Kid watching: An alternative to testing. *National Elementary Principal, 57,* 41–45.

Graves, D. (1992). Portfolios: Keep a good idea growing. In D. Graves & B. Sunstein (Eds.), *Portfolios portraits* (pp. 1–12). Portsmouth, NH: Heinemann.

Harp, B. (1996). *The handbook of literacy assessment and evaluation.* Norwood, MA: Christopher-Gordon.

Hill, B., & Ruptic, C. (1994). *Practical aspects of authentic assessment: Putting the pieces together.* Norwood, MA: Christopher Gordon.

Jenkins, C. B. (1996). *Inside the writing portfolio.* Portsmouth, NH: Heinemann.

Juneau School District. (1993). *Language arts portfolio handbook.* Juneau, AK: Author.

King-Shaver, B., & Spicer, W. (1993). What is worth assessing? Authentic assessment in South Brunswick. *Focus on Education, NJASCD,* pp. 38–44.

Paulson, F. L., Paulson, P., Meyer, C. (1991, February). What makes a portfolio a portfolio? *Educational Leadership,* pp. 60–63.

Pearson, P. D. (1994). Commentary on California's New English-language arts assessment. In S. Valencia, E. Hiebert, & P. Afflerbach (Eds.), *Authentic reading assessment: Practices and possibilities* (pp. 218–227). Newark, DE: IRA.

Peppe, R., Petraglia, M. (1992, Winter). Toward a reading/writing assessment portfolio. *Holistic Education Review, 5* (4), 24–30.

Rael, P., Travelstead, J. (1993). *Statewide student assessment requirements.* Santa Fe, NM: New Mexico State Department of Education.

Rhodes, L., & Shanklin, N. (1993). *Windows into literacy.* Portsmouth, NH: Heinemann.

Tierney, R., Carter, M., & Desai, L. (1991). *Portfolio assessment in the reading-writing classroom.* Norwood, MA: Christopher-Gordon.

Valencia, S. (1990, January). A portfolio approach to classroom reading assessment: The whys, whats, and hows. *The Reading Teacher, 43*(4), 338–340.

CHAPTER

5

Exploring Authentic Assessment Opportunities

KEY WORDS AND CONCEPTS

Assessment   Criterion-referenced tests
Evaluation   Informal assessment
Diagnosis   Alternative assessment
Standardized or formal tests   Authentic assessment
Norm-referenced tests   Performance-based assessment

"So, how'm I doing?" This is the familiar phrase associated with former New York City Mayor Ed Koch, who is famous for asking people on the street to evaluate his work as mayor. Mayor Koch, similar to most of us, wanted feedback about his performance. There's a general impression that it's possible to answer questions about performance and other complicated inquiries by accumulating data and that by analyzing the data, judgments can be made with greater precision. Americans have a preoccupation with measurement, and they believe that the most reliable means for decision making is looking at numbers, because numbers do seem powerful and scientific.

THE CURRENT CONTEXT OF LITERACY ASSESSMENT

Numbers and data have an extraordinary impact on the field of education, especially when we seek feedback about just how well we, our schools, teachers, programs, policies, and students are doing. Recently, this has become more evident, given the close scrutiny imposed on the education community by all who are concerned about schooling. Huge amounts of money are spent on the industry of education, and therefore reassurance is needed that those in this business know what they are doing and are accountable for producing good results. There also appears to be a consensus that the best way to answer questions about performance is to look at test data—scores and numbers. Trust in numbers appears to be fueled by the belief that if educators can produce sufficient and precise data then education can be objectively demonstrated and verified.

Concern Over Quality of Education Impacts Literacy

The quality of American education has been a national concern for many years. The general conclusion reached by recent national indicators is a decline in school achievement between the years 1967 and 1980 (Hopkins, Stanley, & Hopkins, 1990, p. 411). According to Ravitch (1995, pp. 3–4), evidence seems to indicate that American schools are failing to fulfill their mission because students are at best mediocre in achievement when compared with peers from other industrial nations. Unfortunately, this decline is echoed by recent data about students' literacy ability ("Decline," 1995, p. A18). The political and social climate demand more from American schools, because without a cadre of literate and technologically sophisticated employees, our industries suffer and decline. Many social critics feel that the schools are falling short of their essential mission and categorize them as "anti-intellectual" and "anti-achievement" and call for swift reform (Crebbin, 1993). The public wants reassurance that when students leave high school they have the literacy skills needed to gain employment or productively continue their education. Students who do not possess appropriate literacy skills at the completion of their formal education are not only a personal failure but an indication of an educational system not accomplishing an essential mission.

This heightened concern about the quality of education caused a systemic demand for accountability and often resulted in an increase in the number of state-wide testing programs that rely on norm-referenced, standardized tests. Schools today spend more time and money measuring student performance than ever before. While it is hard to be specific about the amount of testing that is routinely a part of schooling, even conservative estimates describe the number of standardized tests administered as staggering. Although standardized tests are routinely criticized by academics, their sales are booming (Worthen, Borg, & White 1993). One commentator, who estimated that approximately 20 million school days each year are devoted to children taking multiple-choice tests, believes this is not time well spent, because it robs students of vital instruction (Mitchell, 1992). A recent report concluded that during the past twenty years schools have been undergoing an explosion in testing (Barton & Coley, 1994). Testing is not teaching; time allocated for testing diminishes time spent teaching.

Before education reforms could be planned and actualized, an appraisal seemed in order, with a consequent movement to create national assessments to determine if educational standards and goals were being met. Part of this concern with assessment, however, has been the recognition that traditional forms of educational assessment may not evaluate the skills that students need in today's world and that assessment must focus on critical thinking, application of knowledge, and problem solving. Unless new forms of assessment are designed to measure more complex thinking strategies, schools are not likely to reform their curricula to meet the new goals (Ravitch, 1995).

Testing students has become a seemingly efficient, although time-consuming and expensive, way of providing answers to the questions that have been asked about our schools and students. There is skepticism, however, that test data alone do not truly, reliably, or fairly answer the profound questions to which educators want and need answers. Sizer (1995) documents the reliance on test data as a solution to education's ills with great reservation: "One of American educators' greatest conceits is the belief that people can be pigeonholed, in effect sorted by some scientific mechanism, usually the standardized test" (p. 58).

State-Wide Testing Programs Increase Literacy Assessment. All states have instituted state-wide testing programs to (1) demonstrate accountability, (2) show instructional improvement, (3) evaluate programs, (4) diagnose student needs, (5) place students in special programs, and (6) demonstrate that students are eligible for high school graduation. All schools presently evaluate students attending elementary school in mathematics and language ability (most commonly reading and writing) and frequently test children in the areas of science and social studies as well. Children have become accommodated to routinely taking tests for many different purposes throughout their academic careers, but has large-scale testing in any way resulted in improvement? According to Wiggins (1990), it has not, "Can an increase in testing ever yield improved quality in schools? To suggest that it can is akin to saying that more accounting results in higher-quality products or services in business, or that more taking of one's temperature will lead to better health" (p. 36). Wiggins feels that concern with quantities has overtaken the need to examine the qualities of schooling.

Assessment Compared to Evaluation. There is confusion about terminology, and it is important to distinguish between terms that are often used interchangeably. **Assessment** can either refer to the assessment of individual students or the assessment of an entire educational system (Worthen et al., 1993, p. 67). In both instances, *assessment* refers to an ongoing process during which data are collected from a variety of sources to aid decision making. Traditional forms of assessment have relied heavily on test data, but assessment information can be obtained from other activities that result in a performance that can either be quantified or described. *Assessment precedes evaluation.* **Evaluation** refers to a value judgment about the quality, effectiveness, or worth of an educational program or the performance of an individual based on analyzing data collected during the assessment phase (Worthen et al., 1993,

p. 68). This value judgment is often used to decide if educational objectives are being met; by relying on assessment data, the evaluation process is both objective and reliable. Assessment data can and should be collected by having students engage in different activities that make assessment multidimensional, yet too often assessment is reduced to the administration of tests alone. Again, testing is only one means of obtaining assessment information, but it has been the means most heavily relied on.

Criticism of Standardized Tests

A growing disenchantment has been building regarding the testing industry and in particular with the overreliance on the multiple-choice test format. When teachers look at the data generated by the many tests given to their students, they question whether or not the data truly provide answers to the important questions they ask. This is especially true regarding literacy assessment, which often produces data that compare students with each other but fail to inform teachers by providing essential information needed to be more effective. Educators also wonder whether the format of these tests, with their heavy reliance on measuring recall of discrete bits of information, can reliably describe the complex and integrative intellectual processes that students will be expected to use in a technological society. Additionally, tests developed and administered on a national basis have been criticized as being insensitive to gender, race, ethnicity, and culture—all of which impact on children's knowledge and learning. Critics also look at the sometimes traumatic effect of poor test performance on children's lives and question the value of making life-altering decisions based on test scores. In a society that purports not to limit educational opportunities, poor test performance of many minority students has resulted in decreased educational opportunity and in new forms of de facto segregation in tracking by achievement. Many admit that even the best tests shed no light on the really important questions of how students think and learn.

Assessment programs that rely heavily on test scores as the sole means of describing student performance are flawed for many reasons. Figure 5–1 provides an overview of the current criticisms of contemporary testing programs.

The challenge for the education community is not to simply abandon the practice of using standardized tests, as they do have positive aspects worth considering, but rather to create programs that assess learning through the use of multiple measures. Therefore, there is a growing impetus to explore alternative assessment approaches outside the realm of the traditional, standardized tests, and this has created a debate about the best means to evaluate students, programs, and schools. Many are rethinking the definition of assessment and trying to decide the best means for determining student progress to make more informed decisions about teaching, policies, and programs.

Essential to the debate over the best forms of assessment is reconsideration of several factors that are intimately involved in education measurement including forms of evaluation, processes to be measured, roles of participants, the examination of learning contexts, the interdisciplinary nature of knowledge, as well as increased respect for gender differences and the role of cultural diversity. This has had an impact on literacy assessment that resulted in two nationally prominent literacy groups redefining the model of assessment: "Quality assessment, then, hinges on the process of setting up conditions so that the classroom, the school and the community become centers of inquiry where students, teachers, and other members of the school community investigate their own learning, both individually and collabora-

1. Test scores are too often the product of a one-time collection of data.

2. Tests are often developed for a national market and do not reflect the characteristics of local education programs.

3. Tests at best require that a student perform on a small number of tasks, which may not reflect the variety of behaviors that the student uses.

4. The finite amount of information measured by tests often doesn't correspond to local curriculum objectives and education programs.

5. Student performance on tests can be dramatically affected by mood, well-being, and attention on any given day.

6. Test formats often require only passive behavior from students, as they ask the student to recognize "right" answers rather than reconstruct meaning or demonstrate understanding.

7. Tests often measure what is easy to evaluate without the thoughtful consideration of essential and significant learning and knowledge.

8. Tests are constructed to produce results that provide data along a hypothetical bell-shaped curve and thereby divide students into comparative groups rather than describe students' various strengths and weaknesses.

9. Tests are biased toward groups in the mainstream based on culture, race, and economic and social conditions. Students who are not from more privileged communities, or whose cultural backgrounds diverge from the hypothetical mainstream culture, often do not perform as well.

10. Tests produce results that may be influenced by the gender of the test taker rather than an actual appraisal of competency.

11. Tests require competence with mainstream English language, regardless of a student's knowledge of the subject. Given the increasingly pluralistic nature of our school population and the large numbers of children for whom English is not the dominant, home language, or for children whose language skills reflect dialectical and lexical differences, performance is often negatively affected.

12. Tests are constructed outside of the teaching/learning process and are therefore far removed from the individuals who are affected by their outcomes.

13. Tests seem to obfuscate data about individual students and mislead by appearing to be more trustworthy than the informed opinions of those who deal with students on a daily basis.

14. Tests are administered in an atmosphere of secrecy that makes them truly external to the teaching/learning process.

15. Tests tend to dominate the formation of curriculum, and the trend toward "teaching for the test" is well documented. Unfortunately, too often, tests drive the curriculum rather than the reverse.

16. Giving tests, scoring tests, and preparing students for tests are all time-consuming and expensive, both because of the funds allocated as well as time expended for testing that could be spent on teaching.

FIGURE 5–1 Summary of current criticisms of contemporary testing programs.

tively" (International Reading Association, 1994, p. 7). Literacy assessment should not fall only on students and teachers, because various members of the school community have different but interacting interests, roles, and responsibilities, "and assessment is the medium that allows all to explore what they have learned and whether they have met their responsibilities to the school community" (International Reading Association, 1994, p. 7).

CURRENT ASSESSMENT PRACTICES IN LITERACY

Literacy assessment, as literacy instruction, is undergoing a marked change; a change seen by some as so dramatic that it is a second revolution in educational assessment, with the advent of objective testing in the historical scientific movement being the first such revolution (Jongsma & Farr, 1993, p. 516). This revolution in literacy assessment is associated with three major concerns in contemporary education: (1) the need for educational reform; (2) the perceived disharmony among curriculum, pedagogy, and assessment; and (3) the search for standards. Although, historically, the fields of reading and writing have been rife with continuing controversies over instructional practices, at no time in the past has the controversy been as pronounced as it is presently over literacy assessment. In the past, the greatest debates were over choice of methodology, but today attention is focused on how literacy skills should be assessed and how assessment can transform literacy instruction.

Purposes of Literacy Assessment

The debate over how to best evaluate learning and literacy has recently begun to have a dramatic impact on day-to-day classroom practice. Teachers have complained about the burden that standardized tests place on curriculum and pedagogy and have expressed disappointment with the lack of practical information that often dominates assessment. Others question whether tests in reading serve any legitimate purpose at all. Frank Smith (1982) has this to say about the "mania for measurement":

> Tests are a major element in the consciousness of every classroom. Teachers spend a large part of their time preparing children for tests, and helping children recover from tests. Yet no test ever helped a child learn anything. Children do not need tests to know whether they understand something, and teachers do not need tests to discover whether children are making progress. (p. 208)

According to the International Reading Association (1991), all literacy assessment should be purposeful, and the primary reasons for assessing are (1) to inform learning and instruction and (2) to address accountability concerns through evaluating program effectiveness. Therefore, literacy assessment can provide the following important information.

Information about the Individual Child
- *Determine a child's individual capacity to profit from instruction.*
- *Determine if a child is making continuous and appropriate progress throughout the grades.* Literacy tests measure the child's achievement at specific grades (often, grades 4 and 8 have been targeted for evaluation). Because early reading failure is seen as an indicator of the likelihood of academic problems in later years, monitoring progress is important to decide whether interventional instruction is needed.

■ *Diagnose a student's individual ability in reading and writing skills and strategies.* To assist in providing appropriate instruction, tests are administered to more specifically analyze the student's abilities.

Information for Program Placement

■ *Determine if a student needs special services. Literacy tests are used to screen for special program placement.* This includes the evaluation of handicapping conditions or the need for interventional assistance (i.e., remediation in reading, writing, enrichment or gifted programs, or instruction in English as a second language, etc.).

■ *Determine the appropriate level of placement in a reading program.* Literacy tests indicate students' general level of reading ability, skill deficiencies, and their capacity to profit from reading materials of varying levels of difficulty.

■ *Determine if a student is ready for formal reading instruction.* Reading tests (traditionally called reading readiness tests) have been administered to young readers to determine if they are likely to succeed with formal reading instruction. While newer concepts of emergent literacy replace the term *reading readiness,* testing young children before entrance into first grade continues. There is growing concern that these formal tests are inappropriate and should be curtailed because of the particular dynamics of young children and the belief that standardized tests do not yield trustworthy data.

Information for Accountability

■ *Determine the effectiveness of programs of instruction.* Group achievement tests of language skills are routinely conducted. Such data can be used by teachers and administrators to help assess the effectiveness of teaching and various instructional materials, methods, and programs.

■ *Determine mastery of basic skills in reading and writing.* State-wide competency tests in basic language skills are commonly administered and not only demonstrate whether individual students have the appropriate ability but also assist in decisions about promotion, graduation, and eligibility for special programs, as well as monitor program effectiveness. As public opinion regarding declining student achievement has become even more evident, the competency testing movement has grown.

■ *Provide a means of communicating to others.* Teachers have traditionally used assessment to provide information about a student's literacy ability to teachers, parents, administrators, or the student.

Information to Guide Intervention

While literacy assessment has been an important part of ongoing student evaluation as well as data provision for decisions about teaching and program effectiveness, its use for diagnostic purposes has been a vital cornerstone of interventional teaching. According to Gillet and Temple (1994, p. 8), **diagnosis** is defined as a "process of identifying a learner's deficits" with the goal of applying the appropriate and most effective form of remediation. Remedial instruction has long been based on a medical deficit model, which requires the specific description of a student's deficits before appropriate instruction can be prescribed to "cure" the problem. This model fostered the extraordinary reliance on standardized tests as essential to diagnostic intervention. According to Bond, Tinker, Wasson, and Wasson (1989), the efficacy and supremacy of standardized testing in the field of literacy has often been unquestioned: "Whenever possible, standardized test procedures should be used [for diagnosis]" (p. 93).

Perhaps because of the proliferation of assessment in literacy instruction and wide reliance on such test data, more emphasis has recently been placed on current standards for literacy assessment. In 1994 a joint task force on assessment of the two most prominent professional organizations in literacy, the International Reading Association (IRA) and the National Council of Teachers of English (NCTE), published a guide devoted to establishing standards for the assessment of reading and writing. The organizations acknowledge that within the past 30 years research has produced "revolutionary changes in our understanding of language, learning and the complex literacy demands of a rapidly changing democratic and technological society" (IRA/NCTE, 1994, p. 5). However, these organizations remind educators that theoretical advancements also impact assessment, and to enhance the application of knowledge to assessment, "we must outgrow the limitations of our own school histories and understand language, literacy, and assessment in more complex ways." Any educator who is involved with literacy assessment is encouraged to review the eleven goals established by these organizations that speak to the fair, equitable and sound use of assessment in any literacy application. The goals are listed in Figure 5–2.

Forms of Literacy Measurement

Assessment in literacy has predominantly relied on both *standardized* or *formal* as well as *informal* techniques for data collection.

---

1. The interests of the student are paramount in assessment.
2. The primary purpose of assessment is to improve teaching and learning.
3. Assessment must reflect and allow for critical inquiry into curriculum and instruction.
4. Assessments must recognize and reflect the intellectually and socially complex nature of reading and writing and the important roles of school, home, and society in literacy development.
5. Assessment must be fair and equitable.
6. The consequences of an assessment procedure are the first, and most important, consideration in establishing the validity of the assessment.
7. The teacher is the most important agent of assessment.
8. The assessment process should involve multiple perspectives and source of data.
9. Assessment must be based in the school community.
10. All members of the educational community—students, parents, teachers, administrators, policy makers, and the public—must have a voice in the development, interpretation, and reporting of assessment.
11. Parents must be involved as active, essential participants in the assessment process.

FIGURE 5–2 Standards for the assessment of reading and writing developed by the IRA/NCTE Joint Task Force on Assessment in 1994.

Formal Assessment in Reading. Educators have believed that measures of formal assessment provide specific, objective, precise, but too often unchallenged data about children's literacy ability. Ironically, no other form of literacy assessment has caused such extensive criticism among reading educators as have standardized tests. According to Pikulski (1990) they "are routinely criticized for their limitations if not for the harm that they do to progress in literacy assessment and instruction" (p. 686). Yet their widespread use persists. A **standardized test** samples reading "in a controlled and systematic fashion" (Heilman, Blair, & Rupley, 1994, p. 383) and is composed of a set of tasks presented under similar conditions to measure an aspect of an individual's behavior (Worthen et al., 1993, p. 77). The essential components are a standard set of directions, a standard amount of time for administering the test, a standard system for scoring the test, and a standard set of test questions.

Standardized tests are either norm-referenced or criterion-referenced, and these frameworks aid in interpreting test data. **Norm-referenced tests** are tests that have been given to a large number of male and female students who represent a variety of racial, ethnic, and economic groups and are from different geographical regions. This is done to determine average test behavior for students at different ages and grades. *Test norms* are created by summarizing the performance of the groups who took the test during its development (Worthen et al., 1993, p. 77). Norm-referenced tests are therefore useful for determining how well an individual's performance compares with the average performance of the peer group, and these tests are not used to evaluate an individual's specific ability in detail. Norm-referenced achievement tests are used to determine how much a student has learned in the past and are frequently used in literacy assessment to evaluate student progress, to determine program effectiveness, and to screen students for program placement.

The other major framework used for interpreting standardized test data is criterion-referenced assessment. **Criterion-referenced tests** indicate specific knowledge and skills that a student possesses on predetermined criteria that function as benchmarks of performance (IRA/NCTE 1994, p. 41). In literacy assessment, they determine how well a student answers questions that the test makers feel reflect essential skills. Consequently, these tests are composed of many questions that focus on determining mastery of discrete subskills. Criterion-referenced tests have been widely used to describe a child's strengths and weaknesses based on the belief that reading can be reduced to a list of component subskills (Burns, Roe, & Ross, 1996, p. 565). Some educators view criterion-referenced tests favorably, because they seem to be less competitive than norm-referenced tests, which compare one student with others, and seem to provide information about specific abilities. Other educators, however, view criterion-referenced tests as a product of an outmoded theory of reading that reduces complex behavior to a list of specific subskills. According to the IRA/NCTE Standards on Assessment, "Neither frame of reference [norm or criterion referenced] is particularly illuminating instructionally" (IRA/NCTE 1994, p. 41).

Frankly, it is often difficult to determine if a literacy test is norm- or criterion-referenced based on an examination of its content or its application. In general, norm-referenced tests are composed of questions that survey larger domains of general reading behavior, whereas criterion-referenced tests measure narrower and specific aspects. In reading assessment, however, overlap in test content is frequent because both types of test usually provide scores in the categories of comprehension, vocabulary, and decoding. Test experts, in fact, often feel that "scores from any test can be interpreted either in a criterion-referenced manner or in a norm-referenced manner" (Worthen et al., 1993, p. 74). Once a student's skill mastery is determined on a criterion-referenced test, it can be compared with grade level expectations, since "no test can be independent of a context" (Maggart & Zintz, 1992, p. 601).

Standardized tests are traditionally used to assess general reading ability and therefore are called reading achievement or reading survey tests. Another category of standardized tests are diagnostic tests used to provide a profile of an individual student's reading ability. Achievement and diagnostic tests are administered either individually or in groups, and their major strength is their apparent efficiency in ease of administering, and scoring, as well as their perceived ability to provide objective, scientific data.

Because standardized tests are widely used in assessing literacy programs, determining students' progress, or placing students in different programs, their importance cannot be overstated. According to Rhodes and Shanklin (1993), these traditional tests need to be understood both by teachers and parents because their use has grave consequences; these tests are primarily responsible for the "sorting" and "labeling" of children with important implications for educational opportunities and for success in later life (p. 366).

Criticism of Standardized Reading Tests. The extensive commentary and criticism of standardized reading tests not only repeats the concerns raised about all standardized tests but also negatively reviews how standardized tests are used in reading assessment. Several of the most common criticisms follow:

- These tests do not reflect advances in theory that view reading as an interactive process between reader and text in a specific environment with the goal of reconstructing meaning.

- Scores often do not indicate actual performance and represent the child working at an inflated frustration level or may show the child working at a depressed level of ability, which is due to factors unrelated to literacy.

- Various groups have extreme difficulty performing on standardized reading tests, which may be more a reflection of background, sex, and culture than actual reading ability. Such important decisions as placement in special education programs, placement in lower track classes, and consequently stereotyping or labeling ability as an attribute of group membership are too often the outcome of poor performance on standardized reading tests and certainly can diminish a child's educational opportunities.

- Regardless of the form of the test score being used, test data demonstrate competitive ranking and provide only summary data, which is not helpful for instructional purposes.

- Reading tests overrely on literal recall of information and do not measure other cognitive skills.

- Test formats are predominantly multiple-choice, which gives students the impression that there is only one right answer to a problem and certainly does not reflect the practical and diverse applications of reading.

- To produce test scores that fit a normal curve, test questions may be chosen based on their ability to discriminate between children rather than on the importance of what is being measured.

- The use of time limits on tests imposes a false requirement, and this does not represent reading behavior in real situations.

- Standardized reading tests are developed external to the teaching/learning process and often are not reflective of curriculum goals and emphases.

- Students are not involved in self-evaluation and often get no information that provides realistic feedback to help them value, monitor, and take responsibility for their own literacy development. Reading tests can demoralize many children, diminish their sense of self by focusing on what is not known, and ultimately rob children of the motivation needed to succeed. Too often, they reinforce a sense of failure by focusing on weaknesses instead of strengths, and they do not provide insights about strategies students use when they read.

- Because of the importance and reliance on standardized tests, there is a strong tendency to have literacy curricula conform to the content measured by tests.

- Test questions and reading passages provide isolated, decontextualized measures of reading behavior. True reading behavior should be evaluated with longer passages of varying formats, read for different purposes. The current form of measurement usually provides only a very limited sample of a student's behavior measured for a very brief period of time.

- The form of reporting reading test data may be esoteric, complex, or incomplete, is easily misinterpreted and misunderstood, and often does not provide practical information needed for instructional decision making.

Valencia and Pearson (1986) find that assessment practices have not kept abreast with newer theories:

> The tests used to monitor the ability and achievement of individual students and to make policy decisions at the school, district, and state level have remained remarkably impervious to advances in reading research. If we are ever to witness the full impact of this new research upon instruction—if we are to foster a healthy link between assessment and classroom instruction—we must develop new measures of reading. (p. 4)

Pikulski (1990, p. 686), however, feels that it is an "inescapable conclusion" that standardized tests will continue to be widely used. He therefore suggests three options: curtail misuse and misinterpretation, improve the tests, and use other assessment procedures that put standardized test scores in context. Test publishers are keenly aware of these major criticisms, and there have been efforts toward revision, with changes in test format that include passages of longer length with a variety of content material and different genres; passages that require reading in practical situations; and more testing of vocabulary in context. Additionally, attempts are being made to analyze incorrect responses and identify process strategies. Several new tests now require that students respond to questions in writing rather than through a multiple-choice format (Burns et al., 1996, p. 570; Farr, 1992, p. 34).

Basal reader tests are often used for literacy evaluations as part of basal reader instruction and appear to have attributes of standardized tests but have not been subjected to the formal standardization process. These tests usually measure the specific vocabulary and reading skills introduced in the basal program and have been criticized as viewing reading behavior through a fragmented skills model that measures complex behavior in isolation by using short bits of text taken out of context. Basal publishers, however, have begun to revise their testing programs to offer alternatives to their traditional forms of assessments, going beyond conventional unit and skills tests to assess oral and silent reading skills. Some publishers now provide observational checklists, open-ended questions, student self-evaluation forms, conferencing guidelines, student journals and log forms, information about collecting student work and incorporating it into portfolios, and use of longer passages with more factual content.

Informal Assessment in Reading. Classroom teachers have always required and relied on specific and readily available assessment information to help them make instructional and curricular decisions and to evaluate growth in their day-to-day work with students. These techniques are often informal and are easily distinguished from formal, standardized tests. Although some educators are comfortable with standardized tests because they seem to be objective and scientific, growing awareness that standardized testing has significant drawbacks has resulted in a renewed interest in informal assessment. Most significantly, informal strategies are more in tune with the newer literacy theories and are especially sensitive to the learning behaviors of individual students.

Informal assessment strategies recognize classroom teachers as reliable experts in knowing their students. According to Wolf (1993), "Many have come to believe that the most valuable and valid information about student learning comes not from an isolated and decontextualized 'snapshot' of student performance, but from those who work closely with students on a daily basis" (p. 519). He suggests that the term *informal assessment* be changed to *informed assessment,* because this is a process that knowledgeable teachers use when they observe and document students' performance in different ways and in different contexts over long blocks of time during daily classroom activities.

According to Burns et al. (1996, p. 543), the key elements of observation, interaction, and analysis are essential to the use of informal techniques for literacy assessment. This process requires that teachers be trained to carefully observe children so that they can describe literacy behaviors in actual practice; interact with children to question, clarify, respond, and coach literacy behaviors; and finally analyze the information about students' literacy behaviors that has been collected. Obviously, record keeping is an important part of any informal system so teachers can note what they observe in a convenient and meaningful manner for subsequent reference and analysis.

Since teachers have traditionally relied on their own literacy assessment through observing and working with their students, a wide variety of informal assessment techniques has emerged. These informal strategies include

- Teacher-made tests, inventories, and checklists
- Observing, questioning, and conferencing with students
- Anecdotal records
- Assessing student work

Even though informal literacy assessment provides meaningful information about individual student's reading and writing ability, concerns and limitations about these techniques should be noted. Informal assessment requires that teachers work with and observe students on an individual or small group basis, and therefore time management is an issue. These techniques incorporate subjective impressions that teachers form based on ongoing observation. This subjectivity can be a drawback, as teachers can be biased for or against individual students, which obviously invalidates the assessment. Classroom teachers must become proficient with the use and interpretation of informal assessment techniques. As the population of learners continues to become more diverse through inclusion of many non–English-speaking children and children with handicapping conditions, teachers need familiarity with the use of informal assessment techniques appropriate for these special populations as well. Unfortunately, this is not part of most preservice teacher education programs.

The use of individually administered informal reading inventories (IRIs) has had a significant impact on informal assessment. An IRI is "an individually administered reading test . . . composed of a series of graded word lists and graded passages" (Johns, 1994, p. 82). With the publication of Gray's first oral reading test in 1915, the measurement of reading behavior changed dramatically. The IRI developed in response to teachers' need for more practical information detailing the processes and strategies students use during reading. The concept underlying this form of test is that teachers can both observe and interrupt the reading process of individual students through an interactive form of assessment conducted with materials that correspond to those used in the classroom. IRIs can be created by the teacher or purchased from a publisher, or they may come from a basal reading program.

With the current need for alternative assessments that go beyond standardized and criterion-referenced tests and the growing recognition of the value of a portfolio process, IRIs have received renewed attention. Bader and Wiesendanger (1994) describe the IRI as an individual, systematic, and detailed means of monitoring student progress that significantly adds to information collected in a literacy portfolio to appraise students' reading strategies. Many reading portfolios call for an individually administered, informal diagnostic survey such as provided by an IRI. The Literacy Assessment Portfolio (LAP) process that is described in the next chapter also recommends that an IRI be administered to every student to complement other information contained in the portfolio.

Published IRIs are frequently accompanied by other informal assessment tools including interest inventories, student goal sheets, decoding inventories, and writing evaluation checklists. Listening to students read orally, recording their errors (now often called *miscues*), analyzing error patterns, and then assessing whether the students understood or remembered what they read have become a very significant means of individual reading diagnosis by use of the IRI.

THE MOVEMENT TO ALTERNATIVE, AUTHENTIC ASSESSMENT

The concerns raised about the overreliance on large-scale assessment systems and the decision-making process that is heavily influenced by data from standardized tests have resulted in a strong movement toward the use of alternative assessment measures. This is quite evident in the field of literacy, where the use of portfolios is one alternative to standardized testing and informed educators are exploring other more informal means to learn about their students, valuing such techniques as informal tests, open-ended questions, interviews, observations, performance evaluations, collections of student work, learning records, logs, projects, exhibitions, and demonstrations. Many feel that these alternatives more fully, accurately, and realistically describe student performance as an integral part of an ongoing teaching–learning–assessment process.

Defining Authentic, Alternative, and Performance Assessment

This new means of describing student performance, commonly called **alternative assessment, authentic assessment,** or **performance-based assessment,** is defined as using a variety of assessment techniques over an extended period of time "to capture the quality of a student's work or of an educational program" (Mitchell, 1992, p. 20). Essential to this concept is the principle that such assessment requires the performance or "demonstration of understanding and skill in applied, procedural, or open-ended settings" (Baker, O'Neil, & Linn, 1993, p. 1210). To simplify, authentic or alternative assessments use a variety of means to measure day-to-day performance in school subjects instead of relying on tests. Authentic assessment techniques often rely on collecting performance from "real" learning activities (Crafton, 1994). Some refer to these practices as "alternative assessment," because they do not rely on standard assessment practices of multiple-choice testing; Hiebert, Valencia, and Afflerbach (1994), however, use the term *authentic assessment,* which focuses on behavior that "reflect[s] the actual learning and instructional activities of the classroom and out-of-school worlds" (p. 11). To simplify, authentic or alternative assessments use a variety of means to measure day-to-day performance in school subjects instead of relying on tests.

The terms *authentic assessment* and *performance assessment* are often used interchangeably but they are not identical. According to Meyer (1992), with "performance assessment the student completes or demonstrates the same behavior that the assessor desires to measure," while in "authentic assessment the student not only completes or demonstrates the desired behavior, but also does it in a real-life context" (p. 40). All definitions of alternative assessment share two essential features (Worthen, 1993):

1. They are viewed as *alternatives* to multiple-choice standardized tests.
2. They require *direct* examination of student *performance* on tasks that are significant and important for daily living.

For most educators the concept of authentic assessment is not radical or innovative, because the term reflects practices that teachers have traditionally found to be important. According to Heibert et al. (1994), authentic assessment includes informal strategies, the use of "informal reading inventories, classroom tests, teacher observations and evaluation of students' written work" (p. 6), that have a longer history than standardized tests. These researchers feel "teachers have always viewed their ongoing interactions with children as occasions for assessing students' learning processes, abilities, and accomplishments" (p. 6). These techniques should not be perceived as revolutionary, and according to Maeroff (1991), the change in assessment focus comprises only a "gentle upheaval" because good teachers have historically used such methods to monitor the progress of their students. However, now that these approaches are being extended beyond individual classrooms, they pose a challenge to traditional ways of mass testing (p. 274).

Authentic assessment focuses on the procedures and formats used for data collection. Hiebert et al. (1994) describe data collection as falling on a continuum from traditional procedures (a standard task given to all students with specific directions, such as requiring a written response to a topic) to less traditional procedures (presentations, projects, and portfolios). Authentic assessment tasks can also vary in terms of response formats (short oral responses or longer written responses) and scope of the task (daily journal entry or cumulative research project) and are heavily influenced by the audience with whom assessment data will be shared, the age and number of students assessed, and goals specified for assessment. Educators now have many assessment options. Figure 5–3 indicates the essential differences between traditional and authentic assessment (Crafton, 1994, p. 30).

Authentic literacy assessment uses techniques that more realistically and fully describe how a student performs complex tasks that reflect daily activities. Hiebert et al. (1994) succinctly describe the goal of authentic literacy assessment to be assessing "many different kinds of literacy abilities in contexts that closely resemble the actual situations in which those abilities are used" (p. 9).

Authentic assessment activities translate curriculum objectives into classroom practices that increasingly require students to apply a wide variety of language and learning skills across subject areas and simultaneously make connections between different disciplines. These require students to use cognitive skills that will ultimately be necessary for them to function as literate adults.

Authentic assessment includes a wide variety of activities. These could include interest surveys, observational checklists, interviews, conference forms, think-aloud protocols, literature logs, observations and analyses of records from projects, cooperative group activities, and writing folders (Hiebert et al., 1994). The activities chosen should mirror the language and thinking behavior that children are expected to develop during their school years and that in adult life will become important literacy strategies.

Authentic assessment often uses descriptive reporting about student performance quite different from the numerical data obtained from multiple-choice tests. Therefore, there is true authen-

Traditional Assessment	Authentic Assessment
Emphasizes simple behaviors	Emphasizes complex thinking and learning strategies
Stops learning	Allows learning to continue
Isolated event outside of teaching/ learning cycle	Ongoing event, part of teaching/ learning cycle
Reductive	Expansive
Relies on numbers	Relies on words
Extensive use of tests	Use of multiple assessments
Learners are passive recipients of knowledge	Learners as active participants who reconstruct knowledge
Decontextualized from classroom	Part of learning context
Teacher external to process	Teacher is part of process
Relies on evaluation by outsiders	Relies on self-evaluation
Standard criteria for success	Varied criteria for success
Relies on convergent thinking and one right answer	Relies on divergent thinking and multiple answers
Focuses on separate skills	Focuses on integrative applications of learning
Measures traditional subject areas	Uses an interdisciplinary approach

Note. Partially based on Crafton (1994).

FIGURE 5–3 A comparison between traditional and authentic assessment.

ticity in this model of naturalistic data collection. Authentic assessment is, thus, the attempt to "test the actual habits and capacities society views as essential, in the context of actual performances where those habits and capacities can be observed, rather than using tests whose items are proxies for such performances" (Worthen et al., 1993, p. 27).

The Advantages of Authentic Assessment

What then are the generally recognized positive attributes of authentic assessment as compared to more traditional forms of standardized assessment? Authentic assessment is praised for the following: (Baker et al., 1993; Maeroff, 1991; Wiggins 1989, 1990).

- Uses tasks that are open-ended and reflective of actual classroom learning activities that develop important strategies
- Emphasizes higher level cognitive skills applied across disciplines
- Embeds assessment in the actual context of classroom learning
- Requires active performance to demonstrate solutions to more complex problem solving
- Encourages a variety of different kinds of assessments to document a wide range of learning in many different contexts
- Can be used with individual students or with larger groups
- Is perceived as more sensitive to diversity between and among learners
- Requires student choice and self-monitoring
- Incorporates the teacher and student as essential players in the assessment scheme
- Often requires an active, public performance to document learning
- Is scored with the use of multiple criteria arrived at by several judges who have prior training
- Does not require that educational outcomes fit along a hypothetical curve
- Does not dictate arbitrary or unrealistic time parameters for performance and encourages assessment over longer time frames
- Focuses on progress made toward mastery rather than documenting perceived student weaknesses
- Encourages collaborative efforts between teachers, students, and their families
- Provides feedback that is meaningful and relevant to both teachers and students
- Is not needlessly intrusive or overly time-consuming
- Emphasizes essential aspects of learning rather than simply counting numbers of errors
- De-emphasizes demoralizing comparisons between students and instead focuses on individual differences, diversity, and complexity
- Supports and reflects school reform movements and curriculum revision
- Has strategies easily taught to both students and teachers
- Is economical in terms of actual dollar expense for training and materials and time not taken from classroom instruction

Authentic assessment also addresses who should design the task, who should collect the data, and who should evaluate the data collected. Under traditional modes of assessment, the test developer, test administrator, and test scorer were individuals from outside the teaching–learning process, thus ensuring objectivity in test construction, uniformity in data collection, and fairness in data analysis. Authentic assessment proponents believe just the opposite. Those who take on the role of designers, collectors, and evaluators should and must be someone intimately connected to the student and the learning process, because that person is in the best position to know the student. This person is, of course, the teacher. Teachers involved in authentic assessment have commented that in their role as evaluators they gain knowledge about their students while gaining knowledge about their own effectiveness as teachers. These insights help shape the curriculum and assist teachers in meeting student learning needs more effectively, which is the ultimate goal of all assessment.

Another essential aspect of authentic assessment is the incorporation of the student in the process. Many believe that the most valuable form of evaluation is *self-evaluation*. Many teachers, especially those who subscribe to whole language or child-centered approaches, feel that too often students have been omitted from the evaluation process. It is the students themselves who most need the kind of feedback that is an outcome of all good assessment processes. Today, it is recognized that students have the capacity to make informed choices, given criteria and expectations that are age appropriate. They can be guided to become truly reflective about their own behavior and performance. Students who are involved in monitoring their learning are more likely to benefit from assessment by reflecting on their learning and, consequently, to take responsibility for promoting their learning. When this approach is applied to literacy improvement, it is referred to as students' owning their literacy development.

Writing Assessment as a Current Example of Authentic Assessment

In addition to the use of portfolios, the change in evaluating writing is another application of authentic assessment now widely adopted by teachers. The need for assessing writing ability has traditionally served many purposes similar to those previously discussed about assessing reading ability. According to Tiedt (1989), the purposes are (1) instruction management—diagnosis, placement, guidance (2) student screening—selection and certification of minimal competency and (3) program evaluation. Today, because of the impact of newer theories that stress integrated language arts teaching and process approaches to writing instruction, writing assessment is an important part of demonstrating learning as well as providing insight into children's thinking and language strategies. Assessment in writing has also been associated with providing accountability through mandated state-wide testing as well as sharing information with parents about their children's progress with an essential literacy skill.

At one time, assessing students' writing meant measuring what students knew about grammar, punctuation, and spelling, which were considered the essential skills needed for good writing; multiple-choice tests were widely used to measure these basic skills. Now, writing assessment has undergone a dramatic transformation, because it is recognized that knowledge of mechanics alone is not sufficient to measure actual writing ability, and a performance measure (an actual writing sample) is a more accurate means by which writing is assessed.

Although many states still use norm-referenced tests of language usage (to evaluate how much children know as compared to their peers) and criterion-referenced tests (to evaluate

which particular mechanics of writing a child can demonstrate), there is definitely a trend toward direct assessment by scoring children's writing. Instead of measuring what students know about mechanics (i.e., choosing the correct spelling of a word from a list), student evaluation is based on actual performance (i.e., spelling correctly when they write). Not only does this present a more descriptive evaluation of writing ability, but the assessment process informs the evaluator about what and how to teach the child.

In the past, mechanics and skills received primary attention in writing assessment; however, today's teachers are more aware of the multidimensional aspects of good writing and are sensitive to the need and methods by which they can examine an individual's writing to both monitor literacy growth and improve instruction. Obviously, the analysis of actual writing samples is much more labor intensive than machine-scored, multiple-choice tests, but the information acquired through writing sample analysis could not be obtained when writing was measured by knowledge of mechanics alone. Assessment now provides information about such important aspects of children's language and thinking as organization, language usage, composing strategies, editing ability, use of various writing genres, sense of audience, and understanding of the rhetorical task.

CONCERNS ABOUT AUTHENTIC ASSESSMENT

The authentic assessment movement is transforming the evaluation of children's literacy in schools all across the country. However, critical concerns still need to be answered, and Worthen (1993) cautions that the true potential of the movement can be realized only to the extent that the following are addressed:

- Clarify concepts and terminology.
- Establish mechanisms and forums for self-criticism and self-monitoring.
- Build broad-based support and cooperation from teachers as well as ensure teachers' ability to use new assessment strategies.
- Promote technical quality and honesty.
- Balance standardization without negating diversity.
- Find means to measure complex thinking skills.
- Accept new forms of assessment by the public.
- Evaluate the suitability for high-stakes assessment, especially with increased awareness of minority members' performance as well as the ability to defend against legal challenges.
- Decide on feasibility for large-scale assessment programs
- Examine the potential role of technology (pp. 447–453).

With these cautions in mind, Worthen still encourages the application of authentic assessment techniques, because they have a great deal to offer.

Hiebert et al. (1994) also point to the challenges faced by those examining authentic assessment options. For example, policy makers require different forms of data than do classroom teachers or children and their families, and obviously, the use of one assessment strategy will not satisfy all audiences. Decisions about how to best assess students' understanding are complex and may require the use of multiple indicators of performance, which can be cumbersome and complex. Authentic assessment is a collaborative process between children, parents, and teachers, which requires careful preparation and consideration. It is especially valuable in classrooms using thematic units, literature-based learning, and texts of different difficulty levels. Therefore, the lack of standardization in materials used for assessment must also be considered. Hiebert et al. (1994) caution that good intentions alone do not necessarily translate into better assessment practices but that authentic assessment possibilities present the opportunity to more comprehensively and accurately reflect the real goals of quality literacy instruction. Reducing assessment to a restricted notion of reliance on reading short, decontextualized passages and having students respond with predetermined choices does not reflect what is now known about literacy behavior or what is taught in classrooms that use integrated language arts techniques.

CONCLUSIONS

The concern with accountability in literacy education has demanded scientific and objective data. Different constituencies, including state education departments and school administrators, require information that is easily summarized, appears accurate, and seems trustworthy. Tests still have a considerable hold on the education community, and those who choose to ignore the mandate to use tests are in peril of violating state and district mandates as well as alienating parents. Commenting on our nation's fixation with measurement and testing in reading and writing, Smith (1982) says,

> Tests are almost inevitably based on very poor theories of what writing and reading involve; they are constructed by people whose expertise is in test construction, not in writing and reading. . . . When people who have thought about writing and reading are asked to construct tests . . . they will often say that such tests are impossible and unnecessary. . . . Yet test constructors and administrators say that measurement has to be done. So the educational world is polarized between those who argue that poor tests are better than no tests (because they see no alternative to tests) and those who argue that no tests are better than poor tests (because they see the damage that tests can do). Between the extremes is a mass of confused and anxious teachers and students. (pp. 208–209)

Teachers today, however, are becoming more familiar with a variety of other assessment techniques they can use daily to better assess their students and thereby improve literacy instruction. Authentic assessment techniques lend themselves to detailed, descriptive analysis of student behavior. While the information gathered can be especially precise and detailed, it may be difficult to summarize succinctly or to use for statistical analysis. It therefore seems apparent that standardized literacy testing, especially in reading, will continue. However, such tests cannot and should not be the sole measure of a student's literacy ability, especially in classrooms using authentic learning strategies and integrated literacy approaches. Alternative assessment strategies must also be included to provide a full picture of students, which is essential for making reading and writing instruction more effective.

REFERENCES

Bader, L., & Wiesendanger, K. (1994). *Bader reading and language inventory* (2nd ed.). Upper Saddle River, NJ: Merrill/Prentice Hall.

Baker, E., O'Neil, H., & Linn, R. (1993, December). Policy and validity prospects for performance-based assessment. *American Psychologist,* pp. 1210–1218.

Barton, P., & Coley, R. (1994). *Testing in America's schools.* Princeton, NJ: Educational Testing Service.

Bond, G., Tinker, M., Wasson, B., & Wasson, J. (1989). *Reading difficulties: Their diagnosis and correction.* Upper Saddle River, NJ: Prentice Hall.

Burns, P., Roe, B., & Ross, E. (1996). *Teaching reading in today's elementary schools.* Boston, MA: Houghton Mifflin.

Crafton, L. (1994). *Challenges of holistic teaching: Answering the tough questions.* Norwood, MA: Christopher-Gordon.

Crebbin, W. (1993). Evaluation: A political issue. In C. Bouffler (Ed.), *Literacy evaluation—Issues and practicalities.* Portsmouth, NH: Heinemann.

Decline found in reading proficiency of high school seniors. (1995, April 28). *New York Times,* p. A18.

Farr, R. (1992). Putting it all together: Solving the reading assessment puzzle. *Reading Teacher, 16*(1), 26–37.

Gillet, J. W., & Temple, C. (1994). *Understanding reading problems: Assessment and instruction.* New York: Harper-Collins.

Heilman, A., Blair, T., & Rupley, W. (1994). *Principles and practices of teaching reading* (8th ed.). Upper Saddle River, NJ: Merrill/Prentice Hall.

Hiebert, E., Valencia, S., & Afflerbach, P. (1994). Definitions and perspectives. In S. Valencia, E. Hiebert, & P. Afflerbach. *Authentic reading assessment: Practices and possibilities* (pp. 6–23) Newark, DE: International Reading Association.

Hopkins, K., Stanley, J., & Hopkins, B. R. (1990). *Educational and psychological and evaluation.* Upper Saddle River, NJ: Prentice Hall.

International Reading Association. (1991). Resolutions on literacy assessment. Newark, DE: Author.

International Reading Association and the National Council of Teachers of English. (1994). *Standards for the assessment of reading and writing.* Newark, DE: Author.

IRA/NCTE Joint Task Force on Assessment. (1994). *Standards for the assessment of reading and writing.* Newark, DE: IRA.

Johns, J. (1994). *Basic reading inventory.* Dubuque, IA: Kendall Hunt.

Jongsma, E., Farr, R. (1993, April). A themed issue on literacy assessment. *Journal of Reading, 36*(7), 516–517.

Maeroff, G. (1991, December). Assessing alternative assessment. *Phi Delta Kappan,* pp. 272–281.

Maggart, Z., Zintz, M. (1992). *The reading process.* Dubuque, IA: Brown and Benchmark.

Meyer, C. (1992, May). What's the difference between *authentic* and *performance assessment? Educational Leadership,* pp. 39–41.

Mitchell, R. (1992). *Testing for learning.* New York: The Free Press.

Pikulski, J. (1990). The role of tests in a literacy assessment program. *The Reading Teacher, 43*(9), 686–688.

Ravitch, D. (1995). *National Standards in American Education.* Washington, DC: Brookings Institution.

Rhodes, L., & Shanklin, N. (1993). *Windows into literacy.* Portsmouth, NH: Heinemann.

Sizer, T. (1995, January). What's wrong with standard tests. *The New York Times,* pp. 4A, 58.

Smith, F. (1982). *Writing and the writer.* New York: Holt, Rinehart & Winston.

Tiedt, I. (1989). *Writing, from topic to evaluation.* Boston: Allyn & Bacon.

Valencia, S., & Pearson, P. D. (1986). *New models for reading assessment.* Center for the Study of Reading, Reading Education, No. 71. Champaign, IL: University of Illinois at Urbana Champaign.

Wiggins, G. (1989, May). A true test: Toward more authentic and equitable assessment. *Phi Delta Kappan,* pp. 703–713.

Wiggins, G. (1990, January 24). Standards should mean qualities, not quantities. *Education Week,* p. 36.

Wolf, K. (1993). From informal to informed assessment: Recognizing the role of the classroom teacher. *Journal of Reading, 36*(7), 518–523.

Worthen, B. (1993, February). Critical issues that will determine the future of alternative assessment. *Phi Delta Kappan,* pp. 444–454.

Worthen, B., Borg, W., & White, K. (1993). *Measurement and evaluation in the schools.* New York: Longman.

CHAPTER

6

Introducing the Literacy Assessment Portfolio

KEY WORDS AND CONCEPTS

Literacy assessment portfolio (LAP)   Interest inventory
Literacy opportunities   Student portfolio
Cumulative portfolio   Baseline portfolio
Reading log   Summative portfolio
Writing log   Permanent record portfolio
Teacher portfolio   Literacy processes
Background data sheet   Literacy products

At a recent national literacy conference, a panel of educators presented information on authentic assessment and highlighted the use of a literacy portfolio as an important classroom tool. A question and answer session followed the presentation, during which a teacher asked the following: "Today, I've heard a great deal about authentic assessment and the use of portfolios. I've also read about portfolios, and my principal is very eager for us to begin using them. There's so much to learn about that I'm a bit overwhelmed. Can you tell me what kind of portfolio I should be using in my class, and how I can get it started?"

Her question was important and required a thoughtful and detailed answer that unfortunately could not be fully provided in the limited time of the conference session. The following chapter describes a model portfolio process, the Literacy Assessment Portfolio (LAP), and is our response to this teacher's question.

GOALS AND PURPOSE OF A LITERACY ASSESSMENT PORTFOLIO

Much has recently been written about portfolio use, and attention has focused on the various forms of portfolios that teachers have begun using as an integral aspect of language arts instruction and literacy assessment. This chapter describes a particular type of portfolio, which we call the **Literacy Assessment Portfolio (LAP).** We describe the ideal contents, discuss a process for using the LAP, and then present some important issues that need to be clarified before a LAP process can be successfully implemented.

The primary purpose of the LAP is to improve literacy instruction, which is affected in several significant ways when the portfolio process is part of an ongoing teaching and learning cycle. The LAP enables the teacher to monitor a child's progress in reading and writing and affords ample opportunities to gain insights into strategies that the student uses. Additionally, the LAP sets the environment for collaborative learning so that the child and teacher can work together toward improvement in reading and writing. Students' involvement in self-assessing, setting priorities, and taking more responsibility for their literacy development all provide for a maximal educational experience. Information obtained through the LAP process becomes an important aspect of sharing assessment with children, their families, and other members of their instructional team.

Specific purposes of the LAP follow:

- Provide opportunities for realistic and authentic assessment of a student's literacy by observing the student during reading and writing.
- Collect actual student work products and descriptions of literacy strategies that give the teacher a direct opportunity to see the application of reading and writing skills in the broad context of daily performance.
- Create a collaborative relationship between the teacher and student so that instructional goals are appropriate and relevant to actual student needs and priorities.

- Create an opportunity through portfolio conferencing for direct one-to-one instruction that maximizes the quality of teaching through individualized and focused group instruction.

- Assist the student in developing metacognitive and self-reflective reading and writing skills and strategies that encourage responsibility for ongoing development.

- Create a climate recognizing the student's strengths in reading and writing ability rather than focusing on weaknesses or deficits.

- Provide insight that will prove invaluable for jointly establishing appropriate literacy goals and choosing the most effective instructional strategies.

- Share information about the student's actual reading and writing strategies with other members of the instructional team and interested parties.

- Incorporate the child, the teacher, and the family in joint assessment, collaboration, and learning.

The concept behind a literacy assessment portfolio process is that literacy instruction will be enhanced by selectively collecting student work that reflects daily reading and writing behavior used in the classroom, by the descriptive and analytic evaluation of this collection by both the teacher and student, and by the judicious use of other informal techniques. By engaging in the LAP process, the teacher and student learn more about the student's literacy behavior and thereby are better able to

- Accurately evaluate the current status of the student's literacy behavior.

- Reflect and take pride in the student's changing literacy behavior.

- Establish appropriate literacy goals for instruction.

- Choose effective methods of literacy instruction.

- Communicate more effectively with others (parents, school district personnel) and provide a full and accurate description of how literacy is progressing.

Ultimate accountability for literacy teaching is achieved when the teacher understands the individual student's reading and writing strategies and correspondingly when students understand the importance of reading and writing in their lives.

New Roles for Teachers and Students

The portfolio is built on the underlying belief that literacy learning is enjoyable and has practical significance. Effective instruction results from the teacher's understanding of the strategies students use in daily encounters with print, what students enjoy doing, and what is meaningful to students. This process requires new responsibilities for both students and teachers. Students need to be actively engaged in their own literacy development; they can no longer be passive recipients of information and indifferent participants to a sometimes unmotivating instructional program. Therefore, an essential aspect of the literacy portfolio process is the collaborative partnership between teachers and students to determine literacy goals. It is through guided self-reflection—best accomplished before and during the portfolio conference—that students take pride in their developing reading and writing ability. Too often in the past, assessment was external to the teaching–learning process and had little practical impact on daily instruction. Too often, students' opinions and attitudes about what was important to learn and how they learned best were rarely incorporated in instructional decisions. When students reflect on their reading and writing behavior, they establish appropriate goals for continued improvement that will have meaning in their lives. Instructional decision making is the end result of a self-evaluative, collaborative process.

The Teacher's Role in the LAP

The teacher has a very important role when a LAP process is used. Teachers must be acutely aware of each student's reading and writing profile (past and current performances) and must be knowledgeable about literacy methodologies so they can translate assessment data into goals and effective methods of instruction. Consequently, each teacher must develop skills for diagnosing reading and writing processes and must be familiar with a wide range of sound methodological approaches to maximize literacy learning. While this diagnostician/teacher role sounds quite formidable, it is the most effective model for meeting students' needs. Figure 6–1 contains a conceptualization of the process in which LAP assessments interface with instruction, reflection, goal setting, and **literacy opportunities.** Each phase of the model obviously affects and informs the other stages.

When teachers begin to think about the development of a LAP process, they should ask themselves several basic questions:

1. What are the reading and writing strategies that I feel students should be developing, given their age, grade placement, and level of ability?

2. What specific outcomes do I expect from the instructional program?

3. What reading and writing opportunities and activities are appropriate, given the students' interests and abilities and our goals for literacy development this school year?

4. What literacy products should the students and I review that come from daily activities and accurately reflect student learning opportunities?

5. What behaviors and activities should I observe on an ongoing basis that will help inform me about the strategies used by the students?

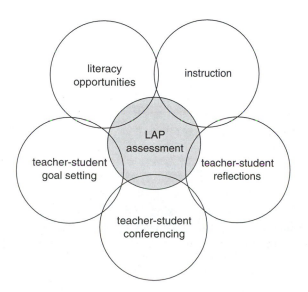

FIGURE 6–1 Model of a literacy assessment portfolio process.

6. How can I translate the assessment knowledge I have gained from working with the students, observing the students, jointly evaluating the portfolio contents, and using other informal assessment techniques into effective whole class, focused group, and individualized instruction?

The aim of the LAP process is not only to maximize growth for the individual student but also to give the teacher an opportunity to reflect on the outcomes and opportunities for dynamic language-based learning for all students in the classroom. Therefore, several aims are vitally important in the development of a quality literacy program for all learners:

- Students should be given opportunities to enjoy quality literature appropriate for their age and development using different genres.

- Students should be given opportunities to expand their conceptual base as well as enhance language development through exposure to literature, both fiction and non-fiction.

- Students should be given the opportunity to grow in written expression through direct instruction, in individual, small, and large group settings; daily writing in various forms in all curriculum areas, especially using journals and logs; writing for various purposes and different audiences; as well as seeing the reciprocal relationship between the reading and writing processes.

- Students should be shown how reading and writing have personal importance in their daily lives, both in school and at home.

CONTENTS OF THE LITERACY ASSESSMENT PORTFOLIO

This conceptualization of a LAP is based on the creation of both a student portfolio and a teacher portfolio, which should be used in a complementary fashion and then integrated into an end-of-year **cumulative portfolio.** This process is based on several assumptions. This LAP process works best in an integrative literacy environment.

Collecting Student Work

Students are encouraged to collect their daily literacy work in "work in progress folders." These become the repository of different projects and products that the students review to select entries for the LAP. Students need to be guided in determining how to choose the entries for the LAP. It's most important that the teacher help the students understand that the purpose of the portfolio process is for *both* the teacher and students to assess ongoing literacy strategies and growth as well as to document how the students change over time. Students will come to realize that literacy learning takes place throughout the day in all activities and especially through unit work in various curriculum areas. Consequently, work produced in all subjects should be considered for the working folders. Some teachers require students to write in journals each day and to keep written work in separate writing folders. Teachers who use a reading process approach may also find that their students need a separate folder for maintaining reading logs and collecting other reading-related work. This obviously can only complement and enhance the work-in-progress concept.

Several techniques have proven useful to assist students. It's important for students to have a tangible concept of what a portfolio is and what it looks like. Teachers are encouraged to gather different types of portfolios from other grades or from previous classes. Students should examine these and discuss the various purposes for collection as well as think about the focus of their own literacy portfolio. Next, students and the teacher reflect on the students' opportunities for using reading and writing throughout the school day and brainstorm the possible products that can be used to demonstrate their literacy ability. Students need to be guided in how to select products from their work in progress or reading and writing folders for the more carefully defined and selective LAP. Some teachers list core requirements for the LAP and provide students with a sheet of suggestions to guide selections. Teachers should conduct minilessons to demonstrate a reflective process that students should use when choosing LAP entries. Some teachers model the process and show their students how they reflect when choosing entries for their own portfolio. Other teachers use individual teacher–student conferences, peer groups, or a buddy system to ensure that students have the opportunity to share with others who are also part of the portfolio creation process.

We recommend that at least four times a year students be required to choose entries for their individual literacy portfolio and participate in a formal conference with the teacher to discuss selections and review the portfolio. The LAP evolves through four different phases and is sequential. Materials are added or deleted based on the portfolio focus of each phase. The focus of these four portfolio phases will vary slightly throughout the school year:

- LAP 1 creates the baseline portfolio in which the student's literacy ability, interests, and background are determined and the initial goal-setting process is begun.

- LAP 2 and LAP 3 are used for monitoring progress toward meeting one's literacy goals, redefining goals as appropriate, and determining the most appropriate methods and materials for literacy opportunities.

- LAP 4 is summative, because it reflects on the entire year's work and growth in literacy development.

Prescribing the specific contents of a LAP should not pose a dilemma. It is essential that the LAP contents reflect each teacher's priorities and be sensitive to individual needs as well as differences among students, school environments, and literacy philosophies. The following section provides suggestions that are culled from a theoretical understanding of factors that promote quality literacy instruction and reflect a review of instructional practices in different types of classrooms in varied locations. The suggestions are not meant to create a standardized portfolio but are provided to guide teachers who are just beginning to implement a portfolio process. We highly recommend that teachers within a school district collaborate with each other as well as with administrators and most importantly with their students to create the outline for a literacy portfolio. It's important to balance the concern that portfolios reflect individuality with the concern that they also incorporate consistent features to promote focus and longevity.

Student Literacy Assessment Portfolio

We recommend that the student's LAP entries contain the items in the following paragraphs (see Figure 6–2).

Introductory Letter. The student should write a statement that describes the purpose of the portfolio, how entries were chosen, and how they are organized in the portfolio. This can also be facilitated by including a table of contents created by the student or provided by the teacher when core contents are mutually agreed on. Students must date each entry so comparisons can be made to determine growth and change. Additionally, students need to be reminded that portfolio contents can come from many sources: authentic reading and writing responses to books, projects in various subject areas, and unit or thematic projects.

A Self-Reflective Piece of Writing. One entry should reflect the students' awareness of themselves as readers and writers. It can be written exclusively for the portfolio (some teach-

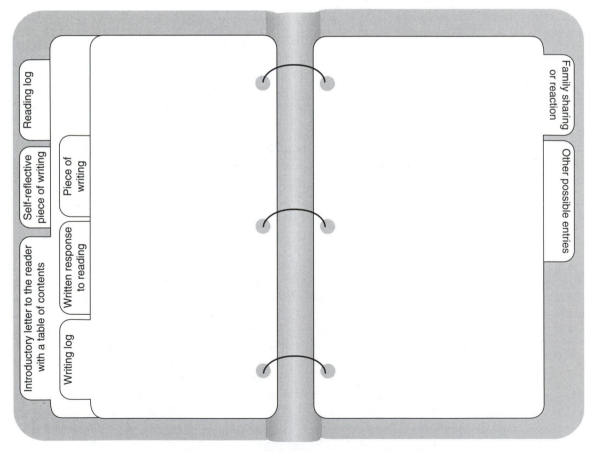

STUDENT'S LITERACY ASSESSMENT PORTFOLIO

FIGURE 6–2 Contents of a student's literacy assessment portfolio.

ers use a survey/questionnaire format), or it can be a piece chosen from the working folders accompanied by a self-reflective essay. Many teachers have found it helpful for the initial self-reflective writing to contain information about the students' interests and attitudes, along with their expectations for the school year. Often, these expectations are transcribed onto a goals sheet. Figure 6–3 is a writing goals sheet that was completed by a fifth-grade student in mid-year.

It is helpful, especially with younger students, to have this self-reflection include a statement about why the piece was chosen. The focus is on students' becoming aware of their own literacy skills so they can comment on their development through the year. Self-reflection can focus on how literacy goals have been worked on and on changes in literacy ability, and it can also be used for analytic thinking about specific literacy projects. For example, a student might answer these questions:

"What piece of writing do you feel most proud of and why?"

"What have you read that has had a strong impact on you? How did it affect you?"

Teachers can also review commercially available materials such as those contained in Bader's (Bader & Wiesendanger, 1994, pp. 16–19) informal reading inventory, which includes student priority surveys; Rhodes's (1993, pp. 2–31) text that contains interviews and attitude surveys that are appropriate for students of different ages and also are translated into Spanish; Vizyak's (1996) text that focuses on primary grade students; forms provided by

Writing Goals for Richard for February through March

1. What I like most about my writing is

   that my spelling is getting better.

2. What I would like to improve the most about my writing is

   sentence structure.

3. I am going to work on ___*organization*___ for the next two months.

4. I'll try to do these things to help reach my goals:

   use spelling checks
   use language skills checklists
   write interesting sentences.

   Signed:_____student

   _____teacher

   Feb. 1

FIGURE 6–3 A writing goals sheet completed by a fifth-grade student.

Sharp (1989, p. 27); and strategies suggested by Miller (1995), Clemmons, Laase, Cooper, Areglado, and Dill (1993), and Fiderer (1995).

Both emergent readers and students with limited literacy skills can include artwork and pictures along with dictated narration to explain the illustrations. Students are encouraged to use art to decorate their portfolios, to personalize them, and to make them distinctive and representative of their interests. A reflective piece might be included to describe the illustrated portfolio jacket.

Reading Log. Students are encouraged to keep track of the amount and kind of reading that they are doing in school and at home. Many teachers invite parent participation in at-home literacy projects through sharing books with their children, listening to their children read aloud, or reading to them. The log of books read can be accompanied by a chart that analyzes the entries according to genre. This encourages diversity in reading choices and can also guide reading selections.

Some teachers require a reaction to each book read, while others simply ask students to log their daily reading. Analyzing or reporting on books read can be individualized based on the age and sophistication of the student. Tedious, old-fashioned book reports should be avoided if a love of literature and reading are to be encouraged and developed.

Writing Log. Parallel to the reading log, students should keep records of their writing that can be analyzed in terms of how often they write, the forms of writing they use, and their audiences. Providing students with diverse writing opportunities promotes frequency and range in writing projects. Some suggest that students integrate reading and writing logs to reinforce the understanding that reading and writing are integral and related aspects of literacy (Farr & Tone, 1994). Whether lists are integrated or separate is not as significant as the necessity for keeping track of how much and what kind of reading and writing students do daily.

Again, for the emergent reader or the student with limited English proficiency, artwork and dictated stories with captions can supplement the writing contributions.

A Written Response to Reading. The form of written response will vary, given the age and ability of the student and the formats the teacher employs. At the primary level, the entry might be in the form of a story grammar, a story frame, a web, or a picture with a dictated reaction or a response using invented spelling. At the intermediate level, the response to literature is more likely to come from a literature response journal, a learning log, or a teacher-directed assignment. Some teachers have successfully used innovative forms of reporting about books such as annotated book marks, book jackets, or book advertisements and commercials. These entries will depend on the instructional program and the kinds of assignments and literacy opportunities that are part of the reading program. For example, teachers might suggest to their students that responses include a statement about a reading selection that had a significant impact on them or a reaction to what they've read explaining why they liked or disliked a book. Students should be encouraged to respond to nonfiction reading material as well as to fiction. Regarding a response to nonfiction material, students might be asked, "What have you recently read that taught you something new?" or "What reading have you done that provided interesting information?" In classrooms where nonfiction trade books are routinely used as well as selections from appropriate newspapers and magazines, students will have a wide range of reading selections from which to choose. Students can also respond to thematic projects or reading they've done for an integrated unit that includes several curriculum areas.

Teachers should be aware that when students respond to reading they construct meaning based on their individual understanding, attitudes, background, and beliefs. Additionally, modes of responding to literature should vary from fact-based, cognitive reactions (summaries) to emotional and aesthetic reactions (impressions of how a theme or character impacts on their lives). When students truly enter into the world of a book, their reactions can be quite personal and compelling.

A Piece of Writing. A selection from the student's ongoing writing should be included in the portfolio along with a statement of why the particular piece was chosen. Figure 6–4 contains a fourth-grade student's explanation for choosing an essay about basketball for her portfolio. In classrooms that have adopted the writing process strategy, the student should include drafts to show how a piece of writing has evolved from brainstorming or list making, to draft stages, to revised copy, up to the final, edited, and published piece of writing. By including work that's part of various stages of writing, students demonstrate how they've applied editing techniques, whether they were done individually or collaboratively. If peer conferencing is part of the process used, then conference notes can be included. For publishing, some teachers require students to share a piece of writing with others to reinforce the concept of

> My brother always brags to me about the New York Knicks. Whenever me and my brother play basketball I try to make a slamdunk but I never can. Basketball is something my family always talks about and fights about.
>
> I picked this topic, basketball, because it is easy to understand and it's my favorite sport. It's easy to tell which person has the ball. It's easy to read the score. I know the positions. I know if it is a 3 pointer or 2 pointer score.
>
> This piece shows how much I know about basketball.

FIGURE 6–4 A fourth-grade student's self-reflections on her basketball story.

the classroom as a community of learners. If this has occurred, then other students' reactions to the piece or a self-reflection about how the writing was shared and received should be incorporated. This provides an opportunity for students to concretely reflect on changes in their writing ability. The use of collaboratively designed rubrics also aids students in self-evaluation and gives them specific guidelines to consider.

Depending on the student's age, interests, and ability, this aspect of the portfolio can be refined to include such assignments as writing in a new genre (attempt at poetry or fable writing), writing that incorporates content area learning (from a project or learning log entry), a student's choice of his or her best work, or work that shows how the student's writing has changed.

Family Sharing or Reaction. Growth in literacy is best accomplished when both the child's family and school personnel collaborate on learning. Information from the home should be incorporated in the portfolio. Feedback from family members is important because it shows interest and concern. It also promotes the opportunity for recognizing growth in the student's literacy ability. Parents may be asked to complete a questionnaire, respond generally to the portfolio collection, or respond to a specific entry. Family involvement results in an additional benefit of making the family well aware of the instructional program and of the teacher's interest in the individual child.

For the emergent reader, a family member might be asked to provide a portfolio entry that describes the student's language skills at home, important family activities or news, or the student's hobbies and other interests. Parents can be asked to participate in reading and writing activities with the child and then write a brief note describing books shared, trips to the library, a TV program or movie that was watched and discussed, or their child's reaction to school activities and related at-home projects. For older students, the family can collaborate by providing reactions, sharing news about relevant events or activities, discussing the application of literacy skills used outside of school, and most especially praising the student's efforts. All of these entries reinforce the family's interest in the child.

Many school projects can be used to enlist parental support of literacy development: book clubs and sales, shared reading activities, read-a-thons, projects that require discussion and interviews with family and community members, and parent volunteers in the classroom. If these activities are part of the school program, they too can be incorporated in the portfolio.

Other Possible Entries. The list of other possible entries for the portfolio is almost endless. Many educators have suggested including audio or videotapes recorded while the student reads aloud or presents a project. Audiotapes can be used to appraise students' reading fluency, and videotapes not only are fun to make and watch but also provide a dynamic record of literacy events in progress. Special educators in particular find that because their students' behavioral changes are often quite gradual, a video or audiotape record shows progress that can be noted only over longer periods.

Other entries can display student projects that are a part of the literacy program. Photographs of a student created model, diorama, or any three-dimensional project are delightful inclusions. Some teachers find it important to lighten the portfolio record and encourage students to keep a joke page, cartoon collection, or other entries that are personal and fun. Pictures from home or meaningful memorabilia can likewise give the portfolio a personal flair.

Integration of literacy activities with content areas should be emphasized, and portfolio entries can document how reading and writing are used across the subject disciplines. In middle schools, instructional teams frequently plan unit and project work to include reading and writing activities in such areas as social studies, science, health, and even mathematics. These interdisciplinary learning activities reinforce how reading and writing are important in subject areas and should be included in the portfolio. It's important for instructional team members to collaborate on goals and contents of middle school portfolios and coordinate their efforts to promote diverse literacy opportunities.

Teacher Portfolio

An essential purpose of a LAP is to help appraise the student's profile of literacy skills. Teachers should create their own portfolio to document each child's literacy behavior. Figure 6–5 contains a summary of the suggested contents for this teacher portfolio. Various means of collecting and storing the information can be used for the **teacher portfolio.** Many teachers use a loose-leaf notebook with individual sections for each child or separate file folders

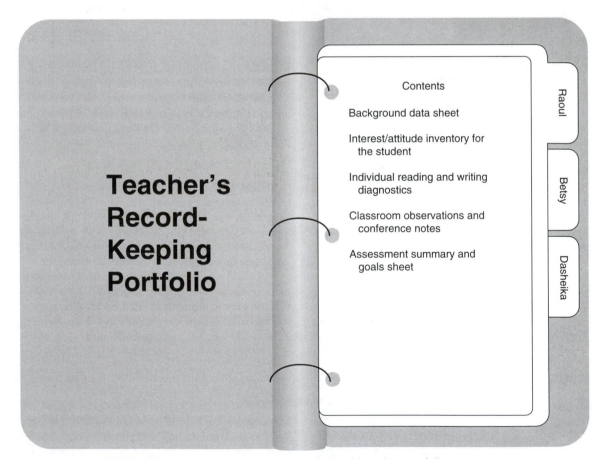

FIGURE 6–5 Contents of a teacher's record-keeping portfolio.

because they are convenient and flexible for storing information. Teachers should choose diagnostic techniques that they are comfortable using and find beneficial for appraising reading and writing skills and strategies. The following is offered as a suggested outline for the contents of a teacher's record-keeping portfolio for individual student evaluations.

Background Data Sheet. It is vital for teachers to be familiar with each child's background. Without knowing the child's family and school history, the teacher cannot fully understand the child. Frequently, this information can be collected by reading a student's permanent record folder; by checking with the school nurse, other faculty, social worker, psychologist or guidance counselor; and through conversations with the child and family members. Rhodes (1993, pp. 147–161) offers excellent suggestions for interviewing parents and children, writing letters to the family, and providing questionnaires that the child and family can complete. The aim is to provide information about literacy involvement at home as well as to learn about special circumstances that might impede or enhance a student's development. Such information can be difficult to ascertain in some school settings and may be especially problematic when children enter a school without previous records. However, the following are important topics to consider as background knowledge about each child:

- Health and developmental history
- Family background

    People with whom the child lives
    Special family circumstances
    Parental employment, interests, or talents
    Places that the child has lived and visited

- Language background

    Language spoken by the family
    Child's language development history

- Child's school history

    Achievement, interventional help
    Results of testing
    Input from other team members involved with the child

Interest/Attitude Inventory. An interest/attitude inventory can be used both to learn more about the individual child and to appraise the child's interests and attitudes about reading and writing. For beginning readers, the inventory can be administered orally, and family members can assist the teacher in recording the child's responses. With older students, the information can be collected through a brief list of questions, an incomplete sentence inventory, and certainly, focused interviews and conferences. The interest inventory is an important focus for the first portfolio conference with the child.

An **interest inventory** should be used to learn more about the child's hobbies (collections), interests (leisure activities, sports activities, and clubs), favorite activities (television programs, favorite books, and movies), and emotional responses to school and learning. Bader and Wiesendanger (1994, pp. 185–186) provide an outline for an interview with a stu-

dent as well as an unfinished sentence test that can be used to reveal underlying student attitudes. Rhodes (1993, pp. 1–31; 56–72) also provides excellent surveys and inventories about reading and writing that achieve the same purpose. Figure 6–6 contains an example of Bader and Wiesendanger's (1994, p. 186) unfinished sentence inventory that was completed by a fourth-grade student. It's interesting to see that the child completing this survey has a positive attitude about herself and school, enjoys reading, likes to swim, and has humanitarian

Unfinished Sentences

1. Sometimes I like to . . . *Draw pictures of animals.*

2. Last summer I . . . *joined a swim team for the first time.*

3. I hope I'll never . . . *get left back.*

4. When I read I . . . *can't stop.*

5. My friend likes to . . . *run 10 blocks in the morning.*

6. I often worry about . . . *dying.*

7. The best thing about school is . . . *the teachers.*

8. Someday I want to . . . *be a judge.*

9. The person I like best is . . . *Mr. B.* (teacher's name).

10. I wish someone would . . . *win the lottery and give it to me.*

11. Learning to read is . . . *fun.*

12. My favorite television show is . . . *The Mommies.*

13. The worst thing about school is . . . *Homework.*

14. I have fun when . . . *I have sleepovers.*

15. The biggest problem with reading is . . . *picking out a book.*

16. After school I like to . . . *swim.*

17. I wish my teacher would . . . *give no homework.*

18. My eyes are . . . *Sparkling Brown.*

19. I would like to be able to read . . . *a 3" book in 1 hour and 30 minutes.*

20. If I had three wishes I would wish for . . . *Peace on earth, Black People and White People be treated equal and children that are handicapped will get better.*

FIGURE 6–6 Unfinished sentence inventory completed by a fourth-grade student. (*Note.* From Bader/Wiesendanger, *Bader Reading and Language Inventory,* 1994, p. 186. Reprinted by permission of Prentice Hall, Upper Saddle River, NJ.

concerns. During a conference, the teacher might choose to discuss the child's interests or concerns and suggest appropriate related reading.

Individual Reading and Writing Diagnostics. Various informal appraisals can be made of a child's reading and writing skills. Some school districts have devised developmental checklists that are completed after lengthy observation of the child. Most schools administer standardized tests that present reading and language arts achievement in terms of norm-referenced scores useful for program placement and evaluation. However, more process-oriented measures should be used to profile each student's reading and writing abilities. Many published informal techniques are available for locating helpful diagnostic techniques (e.g., Miller, 1995; Rhodes, 1993).

The administration of a reading diagnostic in the form of an informal reading inventory (IRI) is vital for obtaining essential information about a child's reading strategies, including reading fluency, decoding strategies, vocabulary skills, comprehension strategies, and the various levels of reading ability for classroom instruction and independent reading. Many commercially available IRIs differ only in terms of story content and grade-level application. Teachers should review several inventories and find one in which story content seems appropriate and motivating for their students. Although administering, scoring, and evaluating an IRI are time-consuming, with experience, most teachers can efficiently complete the essential aspects of such inventories in a short time. The information gathered from the IRI is too valuable to overlook, and time must be allocated for its use. Running records (described in Chapter 7) and miscue analysis are also widely used diagnostic techniques for reading fluency and can be incorporated into this part of the teacher's LAP.

A writing diagnostic is another essential aspect of a literacy profile. Depending on the writing program used in the classroom, a writing evaluation can focus on the strategies used during the writing process (listing, drafting, conferencing, and editing) and can also be used to determine the quality of the written product based on realistic expectations given the child's age, language background, overall ability, and exposure to quality instruction. Any diagnostic should assess the child's ability to express ideas in written form; understand a rhetorical task and use appropriate written forms; organize and develop ideas; use language effectively with appropriate elaboration; use appropriate syntax; form letters to promote legibility; be aware of language conventions and mechanics (capitalization, punctuation, spelling, etc.); and use editing strategies. Many published informal writing evaluation guides often are included with IRIs. Other techniques that teachers can review are assessment systems developed by state education departments as part of holistic scoring of writing samples, rubrics created by teachers working collaboratively, as well as checklists of writing ability at different developmental levels. We encourage teachers to examine these informal techniques and choose a writing process assessment that is compatible with their instructional approach as well as with district and state requirements.

These individual inventories should be administered early during the first phase of the annual instructional program to be included in creation of LAP 1 and then be repeated toward the end of the school year to determine growth and provide information for LAP 4.

Various forms of informal reading assessment are more fully described in Chapter 7 and informal writing assessment is discussed in Chapter 8.

Classroom Observation and Conference Notes. An essential aspect of knowing a child is observing the child in the classroom. Each student should be observed routinely during a variety of reading and writing activities. Such observations help the teacher know more about the child's strategies and study habits, including the ability to focus, attend, sustain interest, work independently, work cooperatively, apply skills to actual reading and writing assignments, be involved in oral discussions, and demonstrate metacognitive reflection. During portfolio conferences, the teacher adds insights to these observational data through one-on-one dialogue. Teachers' reflections after conferencing with students should be accurately and succinctly recorded.

Assessment Summary and Goals Sheet. All of the preceding data should be reviewed so that the teacher can summarize assessment information and then use that data to determine appropriate goals for each student. The goals should be developed collaboratively. Teachers should discuss their students' objectives and then coordinate them with activities that promote acquisition of targeted strategies and outcomes. Consequently, it is essential that teachers know appropriate instructional techniques for reading and writing as well as be familiar with the large quantity of excellent books for children. When goals are discussed, the teacher should keep in mind the student's own priorities. For example, if a student wants to read longer books, then activities to promote sustained reading should be considered. Likewise, a program to enhance vocabulary growth can best be undertaken if the student sees this as important. The teacher should be aware of the student's interests so that instruction incorporates use of high-interest materials. A summary of the teacher's assessment and targeted goals should be carefully noted in the teacher's portfolio.

THE LAP PROCESS

The **teacher's portfolio** and the **student's portfolio** should complement each other. Figure 6–7 shows a chronological scheme of how these two portfolios are created simultaneously and intersect to inform each other. The purpose of LAP 1 is to create a **baseline portfolio.** Both the teacher and student portfolios are used to determine the student's literacy ability, interests, and background. The teacher will administer diagnostics in both reading and writing as well as observe and confer with the student. The information contained in these two portfolios is used to discuss expectations and to establish initial goals. Literacy opportunities (reading and writing activities, projects, and assignments) are suggested and discussed so that the goals are realistic and attainable.

LAPs 2 and 3 are ongoing, **cumulative portfolios** because they provide evidence of progress toward attainment of goals specified in LAP 1, opportunities for refinement of instructional methods chosen, literacy opportunities, and revisions in goal setting. Student self-reflections as well as ongoing observation and insights by the teacher are essential aspects of these LAPs. LAPs 2 and 3 are created at two different times during the school year to focus on developing literacy skills and strategies.

LAP 4 is the **summative portfolio** because it is the culmination of the process. Toward the end of the school year, the teacher and student together select and create the final portfolio that is the outgrowth of the entire year's portfolio process. At this point, the teacher may wish to readminister the IRI and writing diagnostic used for LAP 1 to note changes in reading and writing ability, as indicated by informal measures. Both the student's and the teacher's reflections are used to summarize the student's progress throughout the year. It is also appropriate to discuss expectations for the future that may be passed on to next year's

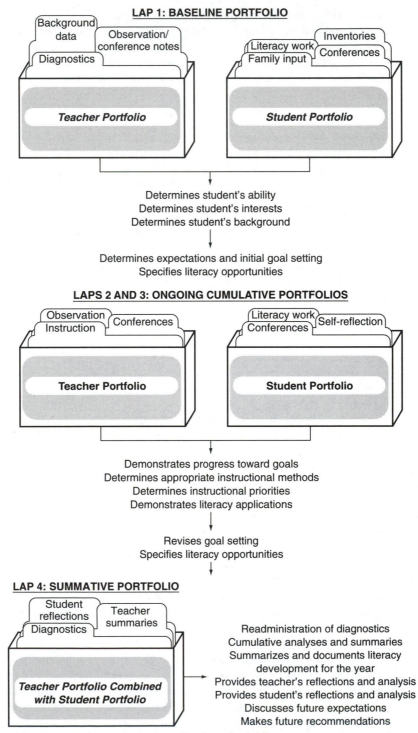

FIGURE 6–7 Chronological application of a LAP process.

teacher as well as possible summer literacy opportunities. Obviously, having family members participate in the process will enhance literacy development at home.

The exact timing of the four LAP stages will be determined by the particular school context. Before formal conferences, teachers should give students ample time to make their final portfolio selections from the material in their working folders. Students should clearly understand the criteria for the portfolio collection and should be aware of their conference date well in advance. To help students be comfortable and familiar with portfolio conferences, a sample conference format should be developed collaboratively. Some have found it reassuring to conduct a demonstration conference so that students can observe the process and become at ease and prepared before their own individual conference. The scheduling of formal portfolio conferences often coincides with marking periods and parent conference days. The portfolios are obviously a rich source of information that can be used for student evaluation in the language arts and interdisciplinary work as well as for sharing with the student's family. Teachers report that the evidence of literacy ability contained in portfolios facilitates assessment in the language arts. More information about conferencing with students and families is provided in Chapter 9.

The ultimate goal of the teacher's portfolio is to complement the student's portfolio. The information contained in both collections should be integrated during conferences and used when choosing instructional priorities, specifying literacy opportunities, planning curricula, and monitoring growth. At the end of the school year, if the portfolio becomes part of a student's permanent record or will be transmitted to the next teacher, then a formal summary report should be created from the teacher's portfolio and combined with the student's portfolio into a **permanent record portfolio.** If the portfolio will be returned to the student at the end of the school year, then a summary letter from the teacher to the student and the family should be inserted into the student's portfolio.

Issues to Be Decided Regarding Implementation of the LAP Process

Many important issues regarding the adoption of a portfolio process need to be addressed before the implementation phase. Arter and Spandel (1992) provide a comprehensive self-test that they encourage teachers to complete before initiating a portfolio process. The survey is intended to resolve issues regarding design, purpose, linkage to instruction, content, assessment, management, and staff development.

The following questions are presented to assist in the development of a portfolio process that successfully integrates literacy instruction with assessment issues. These questions clarify some of the dilemmas teachers encounter when they consider using a literacy portfolio process in their classrooms. Highlighting these issues may assist and promote informed decision making. Figure 6–8 is a summary of this self-survey.

How does the portfolio process complement the philosophy of literacy instruction? Several trends in literacy have had a profound impact on classroom instruction. In an optimum situation, the use of a portfolio process will not be perceived as an add-on but will be incorporated as an ongoing part of the literacy curriculum. The underlying philosophy of literacy instruction and the methodological choices that result should be understood. A portfolio process will work best when

1. How does the portfolio process complement the philosophy of literacy instruction?
2. What should be included in the literacy portfolio?
3. Who decides which entries go into the literacy portfolio?
4. How should portfolios be stored and managed?
5. How can teachers learn to use literacy portfolios?
6. How are portfolios graded and used as part of evaluation, including report cards?
7. What happens to the literacy portfolio at the end of the school year?
8. How can a portfolio be used as part of school district accountability?
9. How can we balance consistency and reliability with the need to create flexible portfolios?
10. What if you try portfolios, and they "flop"?

FIGURE 6–8 Self-survey for teachers to complete before beginning a literacy portfolio process.

■ Literacy instruction reflects the view that the language arts are intrinsically related to each other and that there is a reciprocal, supportive relationship between instruction in reading, writing, speaking, and listening.

■ Literacy instruction uses authentic tasks that demonstrate to students that being literate has value in their lives because it is personally enjoyable and has practical utility.

■ Literacy instruction addresses the individual child's level of ability, readiness for learning, interests, and background. While grade-level expectations for meeting curricula goals should be considered, the teacher focuses on the individual child by knowing what the child is ready to learn, how the child learns best, the child's own goals, and what the child enjoys learning.

■ Integrated language instruction incorporates all aspects of the curriculum, using quality literature (both fiction and nonfiction) with a wide variety of subject area content, often thematically presented, and engages students in active individual and collaborative group participation.

■ The underlying instructional philosophy reflects the view that students, parents, and educators are all partners in helping students become literate and independent learners; therefore, all members of this triad have important roles and responsibilities for enhancing literacy.

■ The philosophy of instruction demonstrates that students' self-reflection and ownership of their literacy behavior are essential aspects of the portfolio process. Students learn and improve when their thoughts and feelings are respected and when they are guided in knowing how to use metacognitive strategies that provide feedback during reading, writing, speaking, and listening activities.

■ Instructional methodology for literacy reflects the most current holistic views that literacy revolves around reconstructing and producing meaning and that strategies are best reinforced in the context of genuine literacy environments. While such a view does not mandate that the classroom be identified as whole language, it does necessitate that skill instruction be undertaken as reinforcement after primary language activities are practiced in a meaningful context.

Many teachers use basals as the primary mode of instruction, and inexperienced teachers often rely on the prescriptive nature of basalized instruction as a starting point in their teaching careers. As noted earlier, basal readers have undergone dramatic transformation. When teachers choose basal instruction, it is hoped that they do so because the newer programs incorporate quality reading material and provide variety in genre and content. In such programs, a literacy portfolio process can be used, especially if core books and chapter books are added to the reading materials. But the primary method of instruction—the quality and content of what children read, how writing instruction is conducted, and the manner in which skills are reinforced—needs to be carefully examined and perhaps revised, or the portfolio process will become only a clerical attachment to a reading/writing program and therefore will be perceived as irrelevant by both teachers and students.

What should be included in the literacy portfolio? For a literacy collection to be meaningful, it should reflect the variety of instructional assignments that are the essential activities in day-to-day literacy instruction. Therefore, entries for the portfolio should be authentic, naturally evolving from ongoing activities, and not contrived to fulfill some notion of a stilted, mandated, literacy collection that does not reflect actual classroom practice. Entries should also reflect the instructional priorities of a program. For example, one teacher who does a great deal of work with poetry in her class of gifted children uses the children's poetry as the central focus of their portfolios. Anyone reading a child's portfolio from this class would be struck by the number of entries that are selected to reflect individual and collaborative attempts at poetry writing and reading.

While some professionals discuss the concern that standardization in a literacy portfolio collection should enhance consistency and reliability, each child's portfolio will be a unique compilation of what is important to that child and a particular teacher, during that time in the child's life, in a given classroom. The notion of standardization needs to be carefully balanced with sensitivity toward instructional priorities and individualization.

All literacy collections need to contain entries that reflect both the **literacy processes** and the **literacy products.** While obtaining products is quite easy (lists of books read, narratives ready for publication), it is vitally important that the collection provide information to gain insights about the underlying processes and strategies that children use. All literacy collections need to be based on selection criteria. While a chronology of entries is important for documenting growth and change, unless the collection is created through a process of critical reflection, it will be too large and unwieldy for meaningful use. Central to the collection should be a system of organization so that both the student and anyone reading the portfolio know why specific entries were chosen and how they are arranged. (Suggestions about portfolio contents are provided both in the beginning of this chapter—as a starting point for those just initiating the process—and in Chapter 4, which describes several different models of current portfolio practices.)

Who decides which entries go into the literacy portfolio? The literacy collection is the product of collaboration between students and teachers. Children need to be shown models of portfolios to understand the concept and to see how others have created a literacy collection. The goals, uses, and criteria for entries for the portfolio collection should be jointly developed and well understood by the students. Folders of ongoing work are the raw materials for the literacy portfolio selections. Teachers should keep a notebook or create a record system to collect information about a child's literacy behavior that will be used for the LAP.

Collaboration between children is also recommended. Research on peer tutoring and peer conferencing demonstrates that when children communicate with each other there are many positive outcomes. Students should be encouraged to share their literacy collections and assist each other in evaluating their work. This process is directly related to other classroom practices that are frequently used as part of the writing process, reading workshops, and literature response circles. Meaningful feedback from others helps students decide which entries to consider for inclusion. In classrooms where peer groups are part of an ongoing instructional program, such collaboration will be a natural outcome. If this is not regularly undertaken and students have little experience working with each other, then ample time needs to be devoted to helping children collaborate in meaningful and supportive ways.

As noted earlier, parents, too, are involved in the portfolio process. Students need a responsive audience for their work, and parents can often supply needed instructional reinforcement. Teachers report that parents have told them that portfolios provide a concrete means of learning about the child's school activities, and discussion about school contributes to the sense that learning is a valued priority for the family.

Ultimately, it is the teacher's job to collaborate with the student on the selections for the portfolio. The teacher guides the young child through the process and helps older students by posing key questions and focusing their thoughts.

How should portfolios be stored and managed? A great deal of the literature about portfolios reflects an inordinate concern over management issues and focuses too extensively on the how-to of portfolio collection. There are simply no right answers to the management questions that will prove appropriate for all teachers in all classrooms. School districts that have implemented a portfolio process have found it necessary to modify the process each year based on teachers' experiences.

Teachers are encouraged to explore various management possibilities on a trial and error basis and share their experiences with colleagues. Part IV contains practical tips from those who have been involved in the portfolio process. The following guidelines provide important considerations regarding storage and management:

- The child's age must be considered. Obviously, young children produce literacy products that are rather large, and therefore, the binder must be of ample size. Students of all ages want to personalize their collections and show their own individuality.

- Privacy is an important issue for many children, regardless of age; parameters need to be established to ensure appropriate confidentiality. The classroom environment needs to support the concept of respect for each other's work. Nothing is more distressing for children than to have their collections lost or mishandled or for a personal, private log to be read by another.

- The folder should be sturdy enough to withstand frequent use but not so costly as to dictate against replacement from wear and tear. Folders, binders, envelopes, storage bins, baskets, cartons, and file cabinets have all been used for portfolio storage.

■ The portfolio should be kept in an area where it is easily accessible to both the student and the teacher. This might be in the child's desk, on a shelf, or in a central file area. Regardless of where the folders are kept, students must be able to locate their own folders independently and feel secure that the contents will be treated with respect.

■ A time management system needs to be created. Students need to know when and for how long they can work on their portfolios. Although no general answers will pertain to all classrooms, for the portfolio to be meaningful students should have regular access to them. Some days they may use their folders only for storing works in progress. Other days they may need to review prior entries. Time needs to be allocated for the student's review of the portfolio before conferences with the teacher. The focus and format of conferences need to be established and known to both the student and the teacher for the time to be most worthwhile. Developing and displaying a calendar for portfolio conferences and sharing the agenda for these conferences make time allocation much more manageable.

How can teachers learn more about literacy portfolios? There are many sources of information about portfolios in general and some excellent information pertaining to literacy collections. The sources in each chapter's reference list will certainly provide excellent professional suggestions. We encourage teachers to join local or regional professional associations and attend conferences that pertain to portfolio use. The International Reading Association and the National Council of Teachers of English provide the most up-to-date and relevant information about literacy instruction. Some neighboring school districts have formed assessment or whole language consortiums for both administrators and teachers.

It is important that teachers involved in portfolios have a support system, ideally, within their own buildings or districts, for sharing information with friends and colleagues. Networks can be established by taking local college courses, summer courses, and in-service classes. Several newsletters assist in putting teachers in touch with each other and provide helpful information. It is vital that teachers using a portfolio process have the support of their school administration. We also recommend that teachers request that portfolios and authentic assessment be topics for in-service education in terms of courses, consultants, and speakers.

Ultimately, the best way to learn about portfolios is to start using the process and learn from experience.

How are portfolios graded and used as part of evaluation, including report cards? The issue of evaluating portfolios is complex and controversial. Some teachers feel strongly that portfolios should be celebrated and examined to provide insights about the quality of students' work in order to make better instructional decisions. These teachers believe that portfolios should not be graded. Others feel that students perform best when they know specifically what is expected of them and that students want evaluative feedback. Therefore, they believe that portfolios should be graded.

The concern over evaluation in our society is apparent, and it is essential that appropriate feedback be provided for students when portfolios are used, whether or not they are graded. Such feedback can be communicated through teacher conferences, conferencing with other students, notes from the teacher, self-evaluations, and checklists. If a portfolio is graded, students should be aware of this, along with the evaluation criteria, during the initial planning stage. Teachers should work with their students to create rubrics so that entries or the entire portfolio can be evaluated cooperatively, using jointly developed criteria. Teachers who do not believe in reducing an entire portfolio to a letter grade or a numerical score should provide students with analysis and thoughtful comments regarding the portfolio work. Students both want and deserve this kind of information from their teachers. We also highly recommend that the report card system be evaluated in light of the portfolio process so that information on the report card can reflect and include portfolios.

What happens to the literacy portfolio at the end of the school year? The decision about what to do with the LAP at the end of the year will be determined by the goals established for the literacy portfolio. Several models based on different purposes for the portfolio collection are described next.

1. *A literacy portfolio established for exclusive use by the classroom teacher.* This portfolio is not used after the instructional year. The teacher may return the portfolio to the student with a special celebration at the end of the year. The teacher should write a summary to the student and family commenting on the portfolio process and describing the literacy program and the student's growth and performance. Teachers may decide to keep several student portfolios each year to use with subsequent classes, and obviously, students need to provide permission for this.

2. *A literacy portfolio established as part of permanent record keeping.* A LAP that is part of the permanent record either will be kept in a central location in the school (along with other permanent records) or will be passed from teacher to teacher throughout the grades for review and additions. This type of portfolio is useful in noting the developmental growth of literacy skills over time. It is also useful in familiarizing each new teacher with the individual student's profile of literacy behaviors, which can help in establishing appropriate curricular goals for the school year.

3. *Variations and combinations of types 1 and 2.* After engaging in an effective portfolio process for a year, teachers probably will want to share the wealth of information contained in a student's portfolio with next year's teacher. Even if a school district does not designate literacy portfolios as an aspect of permanent records, teachers within buildings may still find it useful to pass along students' portfolios. Unfortunately, this process is often not replicated when students are promoted from an elementary building to a middle school or junior high school. If the district does not formally provide permanent storage and transmission of student portfolios between teachers and buildings, then teachers should request this. Obviously, portfolios that are transferred between teachers and buildings need to be carefully culled so that entries provide insights and meaningful information with appropriate examples. In the preceding discussion describing LAP contents, we recommended that teachers create a summary of each student's literacy profile. Such a condensed profile would prove most informative for subsequent teachers.

How can a portfolio be used as part of school district accountability? If a school district contemplates using a portfolio process for monitoring students' literacy development, this should be coordinated with other record-keeping and testing programs mandated by the district or the state education department. Large-scale assessment systems are moving toward performance-based forms of measurement, and portfolios are recognized as making an important contribution to this movement. Data collected from review of individual portfolios containing standardized writing tasks have already been used in many school districts to monitor the effectiveness of instructional programs, track developmental trends in writing, and provide an indication of overall student achievement. According to Simmons (1992), a professional who has done extensive work consulting with districts on portfolio assessment, the time is ripe for using portfolios in large-scale assessment:

> Portfolio assessment has now developed sufficiently at the individual level to be adapted to large-scale settings. To fail to do so, or to settle in the process of change for only the most superficial or highly constrained forms of portfolios, can only perpetuate the inequalities and inaccuracies of the past. (p. 113)

Using a portfolio process helps to eradicate test bias based on factors such as socioeconomic status and therefore has great potential.

How can we balance consistency and reliability with the need to create flexible portfolios? There is concern that if a "portfolio bandwagon" sweeps the country, portfolios will ultimately become products of standardized and rigid mandates. While attempting to demonstrate authentic student accomplishment, portfolios can easily reflect formalistic views of what constitutes a "good" portfolio, which would likely be composed of uniform checklists, typical lists of students' reading, and uniform writing products. Such portfolios would hardly overcome the concerns many have voiced about standardized testing and evaluation systems. Commercial kits are now available that provide teachers with sample checklists and forms to be reproduced to create portfolio collections. Such commercial products may be worth considering as starting points, but they may produce a portfolio process that is essentially insensitive to the diverse concerns of schools and classrooms all across the country. Two researchers who have viewed advertisements that promote the use of "handy folders," "a portfolio storage box," a prescribed list of activities that can be "administered at selected intervals throughout the school year," and "scoring guides and training packages" comment that

> The tacit promise of these professional workshops and products is the development of a generic set of tools that *all* teachers can acquire and apply to the collections of work of *all* children in their classrooms. Such efforts not only echo the problems of standardized tests . . . they make an individual teacher's scrutiny of a student's work appear scientific and plausible . . . and ignore a fundamental dimension of their use—an understanding of the ways teachers construct meanings from these collections of materials. (Gomez & Schenk, 1992, p. 4)

A good portfolio should reflect the goals and curriculum of individual children, teachers, and educational programs; therefore, uniformity and standardization are suspect.

While flexibility in portfolio contents is desirable, there is concern about producing reliable results when a variety of portfolio entries are scored as part of large assessment systems. The issue of interrater reliability is of paramount concern when portfolio entries are evaluated as part of statewide testing programs that can result in high-stakes decisions. More research needs to be done on scorer reliability when portfolio contents reflect diversity. Experience with holistic scoring of writing samples demonstrates that training scorers has a very positive effect on the reliability of scoring outcomes. If portfolios are to be used reliably in statewide assessment systems, then certainly, some level of standardization in terms of suggested contents and means of assessment is needed. In large-scale programs, the use of selected entries, prompted responses, uniform scoring rubrics, and adequate training for scorers are necessary but should be distinguished from the evaluation of portfolio contents for other purposes.

Again, the answer to the question of how to balance consistency with flexibility will depend on the purpose of the portfolio collection. When portfolios are to be reviewed on a mass basis (i.e., throughout an entire state), consistency in form and content are necessitated by time constraints and the need for reliable results. If portfolios are primarily to be used to document individual student growth, to monitor the effectiveness of local instructional approaches, and as an intrinsic part of a methodological approach to literacy instruction, then diversity of contents and scoring systems is not only expected but appropriate and desirable.

What if you try portfolios, and they "flop?" Contributions from teachers using portfolios, which can be found in Part IV, indicate that the process is one of experimentation, revision, and refinement. Even experienced teachers find that their second-year portfolio process was different from the first year, and they expect the process to be modified each successive year. For example, one teacher found that her choice of passages for a running record was boring to the students and therefore not helpful, while another teacher found that she needed to communicate more effectively with parents earlier in the school year.

Every teacher knows that each year contains triumphs and mistakes. Truly, the portfolio process is a learning experience for both teachers and students, and therefore, if the process seems to flop one year, it should be analyzed and discussed to determine why. Some teachers are overly ambitious at the outset and should be cautioned to keep their goals modest and expand the process in small stages. Shared planning and decision making are highly recommended. Teachers should not use portfolios in isolation, and every teacher should have at least one colleague with whom to share and reflect.

CONCLUSIONS

Teachers who have not used a literacy portfolio process quite naturally approach its implementation with a good deal of trepidation. Many issues remain unanswered, ranging from theoretical concerns about authentic assessment practices to practical issues of how to efficiently use a portfolio as part of daily literacy instruction. Gillespie, Ford, Gillespie, and Leavell (1996) have collected questions asked by a large group of secondary teachers introduced to portfolio practice in workshops and have generated answers from the research about defining portfolios, advantages of portfolio assessment, weaknesses of portfolio assessment, portfolio contents, assessing/evaluating portfolios, validity and reliability of portfolios, models of portfolio use, portfolio practice as part of authentic assessment, and the outlook for portfolios. Their review of the research is highly recommended for teachers who want current information generated by specialists in portfolio practice. These researchers encourage teachers to use a variety of assessment techniques to provide more information about students and also to encourage students to think and apply skills in many authentic contexts.

Although the literacy portfolio process is known to have many advantages, teachers undertake the use of portfolios with the realistic concern that their workload may be increased in terms of more time observing students, working with individual students through conferences, note taking, and record keeping. If teachers do not see important advantages in literacy portfolios, such added work will be too burdensome to offset the benefits. Portfolio use not only changes the quantity of a teacher's involvement with students but certainly affects the quality of this involvement. Teachers must recognize the changing roles and responsibilities for both themselves and their students under this strategy, or portfolio use will be reduced to a new fad quickly abandoned.

Teachers should also recognize that there may be no simple answers to their many questions about literacy portfolios. Hopefully, the suggestions contained in this chapter will offer some beginning guidelines for portfolio use. However, the literacy portfolio is still a new strategy and one that needs to be tried and tested in many different contexts in classrooms across the country. According to Graves (1992), the portfolio movement is still in its infancy and "the health of the portfolio movement will be measured in the diversity of its practice and the breadth of its use, whether for evaluation or instruction" (p. 12). The *perfect* portfolio is elusive if not unattainable, and the process is far more important than the product.

REFERENCES

Arter, J., & Spandel, V. (1992, Spring). Using portfolios of student work in instruction and assessment. *Educational Measurement: Issues and Practice*, pp. 36–44.

Bader, L., & Wiesendanger, K. (1994). *Bader reading and language inventory* (2nd ed.). Upper Saddle River, NJ: Merrill/Prentice Hall.

Clemmons, J., Laase, L., Cooper, D., Areglado, N., & Dill, M. (1993). *Portfolios in the classroom—A teacher's sourcebook.* New York: Scholastic.

Farr, R., & Tone, B. (1994). *Portfolio and performance assessment.* New York: Harcourt Brace.

Fiderer, A. (1995). *Practical assessment for literature-based reading classrooms.* New York: Scholastic.

Gillespie, C., Ford, K., Gillespie, R., & Leavell, A. (1996). Portfolio assessment: Some questions, some answers, some recommendations. *Journal of Adolescent and Adult Literacy 39,* 480–491.

Gomez, M. L., & Schenk, J. (1992). What are portfolios?

Stories teachers tell. Paper presented at the meeting of the AERA, San Francisco.

Graves, D. (1992). Portfolios: Keep a good idea growing. In Graves, D., & Sunstein, B. (Eds.), *Portfolio portraits* (pp. 1–12). Portsmouth, NH: Heinemann.

Miller, W. (1995). *Alternative assessment techniques for reading and writing.* West Nyack, NY: The Center for Applied Research in Education.

Rhodes, L. (1993). *Literacy assessment—A handbook of instruments.* Portsmouth, NH: Heinemann.

Sharp, Q. Q. (1989). *Evaluation: Whole language checklists for evaluating your children.* New York: Scholastic.

Simmons, J. (1992). Portfolios for large-scale assessment. In D. Graves & B. Sunstein (Eds.), *Portfolio portraits* (pp. 96–113). Portsmouth, NH: Heinemann.

Vizyak, L. (1996). *Student portfolio—A practical guide to evaluation.* Bothell, WA: The Wright Group.

PART TWO

Working with the Literacy Assessment Portfolio

Using the Literacy Assessment Portfolio to Assess and Guide Reading Instruction

KEY WORDS AND CONCEPTS

Assessment versus evaluation

Anecdotal notes

Reading profiles

Observation checklists

Literature questionnaires

Story retelling

Think-alouds

Running record

Informal Reading Inventory (IRI)

Miscues

Question–Answer Relationship (QAR)

Student Attitude Survey

Low-risk learning environments

Dear Chris Van Allsburg,

Hello! My Name is Cristina R., and I just love your books. You are very talented to be able to write and illustrate like that. I have read many of your books, such as "The Wreck of the <u>Zaphar</u>," "The Widow's Broom," and "The Polar Express." Yet, my favorite is "The Garden of Abdul Gasazi." I love all the <u>betutiful</u> illustrations! They almost seem to make the story come alive! I especially like the end because you do not reveal if the dog <u>realy</u> becomes the duck.*

Now, if you don't mind, I'd like to ask you a few questions:

#1. Why did you use the same dog in "The Widow's Broom," and "The Garden of Abdul Gasazi?"

#2. At what age did you start drawing?

#3. What do you do in your spare time?

#4. Where do you think you got <u>you</u> talents from?

Thanks!

(*see text below)

Sincerely,
Cristina (5th grade)

THE READING ASSESSMENT ENVIRONMENT

In classrooms where basals, workbook activities, and skill sheets are prominent, reading evaluations are often based on formal procedures. However, reading performance is assessed differently in literature-based classrooms and in classrooms where teachers prefer to use less formal, more alternative assessment measures. In the preceding letter to the author Chris Van Allsburg from a fifth grader's assessment portfolio, the teacher can evaluate various aspects of the student's understanding of literature and work on skills that might need attention.* The underlined items refer to spelling errors that need correction. In terms of critical thinking, Christina appears to relate well to the subleties in Van Allsberg's writing and indicates enthusiasm in knowing more about the creative aspects of this author.

The Literacy Assessment Profile (LAP) contains the representative works of each child, like Cristina, that have been selected by both student and teacher along with shared comments about literacy experiences, ongoing projects, completed units, logs, reports, and accomplishments that indicate the progressive nature of learning and reading growth. Teacher and student together inspect, analyze, and reflect on the use of language, the fluency of shared readings, and interest in, and comprehension of, literature so that a thorough understanding of literacy progress and achievements emerges. Meaningful and appropriate literacy goals are jointly determined.

Since reading is complex and multidimensional, when assessing and evaluating students one must look at both cognitive and affective dimensions, which include reading interests, motivation, feelings of self-esteem, and positive or negative attitudes toward reading. The objective is to note students' ability to comprehend critically, read fluently, self-correct, effectively respond to literature discussions, and integrate and evaluate ideas and concepts that are both textually explicit (literal) and textually implicit (interpretive, critical).

Teachers who implement a literature-based, thematic, language approach to teaching literacy have a variety of effective assessment strategies at their disposal. These, along with anecdotal and formal written observations, are also incorporated into the LAP. Surveys, observations, and inventories allow the teacher to monitor and assess reading strengths, difficulties, and problems. Based on these assessments, intervention can be provided through guided instruction—often one-on-one and in small groups—leading to enhanced performance.

READING ASSESSMENT STRATEGIES

Teachers use numerous techniques to assess, analyze, monitor, and appraise reading behavior. As noted previously, both process and product measures are included in the LAP, many of which are informal and holistic and include ongoing observations of students applying their reading skills in authentic classroom situations. The process includes observing and recording actual literacy behaviors. These can identify strengths and weaknesses, reading patterns, cueing systems, oral and silent reading fluency, comprehension, and meaning insights, and can help plan for appropriate instruction based on assessment. For example, Figure 7–1 is a reading comprehension assessment profile included in portfolios in the Lawrence, New York, schools to provide teachers with needed information, such as whether the student can identify story elements and support statements with facts from text.

The following formal and informal reading assessment strategies are suggested for inclusion in a LAP. They will be discussed and clarified in this section:

Anecdotal notes	Miscue Analysis
Observation checklists	Informal Reading Inventory (IRI)
Literature questionnaires	QARs (question–answer relationships)
Audio/videotapes	Reciprocal teaching guides
Story retellings	Reading profiles
Think-alouds	Reading Attitude Survey
Running records	

Anecdotal Notes. During whole class, small group, or minilesson time, while children are actively engaged in a reading activity, the teacher should circulate about the room, observing and taking notes while the students read with partners, confer, discuss books, share their knowledge of story elements, or retell stories. During shared book activities, the teacher can focus on a particular child and record specific reading behaviors, such as vocabulary growth and the ability to synthesize, become engaged in discussions, self-correct, predict, make judgments. Although informal, **anecdotal notes** provide authentic and useful information. They may be recorded in a notebook, on loose-leaf paper, or on self-adhesive notes to be transferred at a later time to the appropriate student's record page. Figure 7–2 is a copy of an anecdotal reading record that a student teacher entered after observing a student learning English as a second language (ESL).

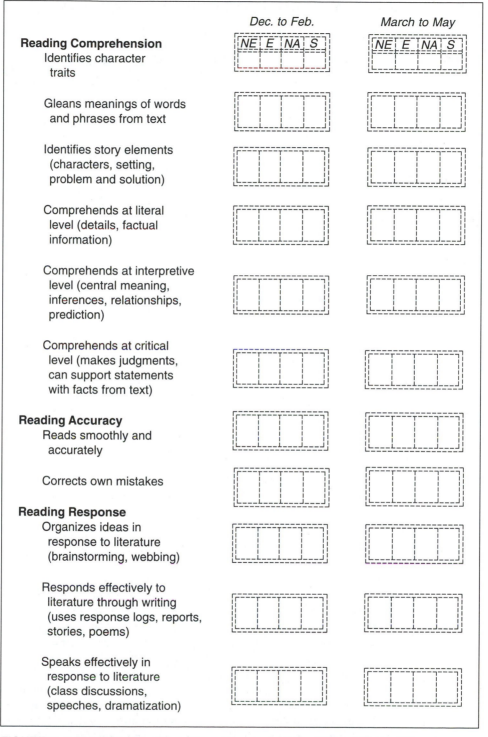

	Dec. to Feb.				March to May			
	NE	E	NA	S	NE	E	NA	S
Reading Comprehension Identifies character traits								
Gleans meanings of words and phrases from text								
Identifies story elements (characters, setting, problem and solution)								
Comprehends at literal level (details, factual information)								
Comprehends at interpretive level (central meaning, inferences, relationships, prediction)								
Comprehends at critical level (makes judgments, can support statements with facts from text)								
Reading Accuracy Reads smoothly and accurately								
Corrects own mistakes								
Reading Response Organizes ideas in response to literature (brainstorming, webbing)								
Responds effectively to literature through writing (uses response logs, reports, stories, poems)								
Speaks effectively in response to literature (class discussions, speeches, dramatization)								

FIGURE 7–1 Reading comprehension assessment profile. Abbreviations: NE, not evident; E, evident; S, sometimes; NA, not applicable. (*Note.* Developed by the Lawrence, New York, school district.)

Anecdotal Reading Record

Date _March 16_   Time _10:45_

Name _Alex_

Subject _Reading_

Setting _Reader's Workshop_

Reading Activity _Read story–discuss_

Observations _Alex was attentive but did not actively participate. He listened_
    but didn't volunteer any answers to questions.

Significance _Alex has an interest in reading but still has trouble interacting_
    with the group. His English has improved greatly, but he rarely volunteers.

FIGURE 7–2 An anecdotal reading record completed by a student teacher for a student learning English as a second language.

Observation Checklists. Checklists allow for structured observations of specific skills, behaviors, and strategies. They can be designed to look at particular oral reading and word identification competencies; to note comprehension strategies, strengths, and weaknesses; or to observe the ability to predict, and set a purpose for reading as in Figure 7–3. Shearer and Homan (1994) suggest that structured checklists be used as a starting point, later followed by interviews and conferences. Assessment information can be used for minilessons and direct instruction. (Once again, this demonstrates how assessment and instruction cannot be separated.) Teachers find checklists useful because items can readily be added or deleted, and they are easy to design. Literature checklists may focus on comprehension of text, metacognitive abilities of the student, and understanding of the story structure, setting, character, and plot.

Sharp (1989) describes checklist models that range from early readers' language usage to identifying students' prior knowledge and thought processes in their interpretations. Checklists using metacognitive insights can be implemented at various times of the year to examine progress and recognize when new strategies are incorporated into the child's literacy repertoire. Rhodes and Shanklin (1993, p. 237) suggest a checklist model with a focused format that includes *before reading* (i.e., uses captions to make predictions), *during reading* (i.e., is aware when text doesn't make sense), and *after reading* (i.e., recalls important information).

The number of items should be limited to features the teacher deems most important. A comments section at the bottom, with remarks, suggestions, and summaries may also be help-

OBSERVATION CHECKLIST
METACOGNITIVE STRATEGIES

Student _____   Grade _____

Examiner _____

	Obs. I		Obs. II	
	Date ____		Date ____	
	DA*	NI*	DA*	NI*
1. Links prior knowledge before reading.	_____	_____	_____	_____
2. Develops purpose for reading.	_____	_____	_____	_____
3. Uses titles and/or illustrations to predict content/events.	_____	_____	_____	_____
4. Verifies predictions.	_____	_____	_____	_____
5. Develops questions to guide reading.	_____	_____	_____	_____
6. Creates visual representations of key concepts (web, outline, etc.).	_____	_____	_____	_____
7. Summarizes.	_____	_____	_____	_____

Summary

_____

_____

_____

_____

Recommendations

_____

_____

_____

_____

*DA = Developing Adequately.
 NI = Needs Improvement.

FIGURE 7–3 A sample observation checklist for structured observation. (*Note.* From *Linking Reading Assessment to Instruction* (p. 155) by A. Shearer and S. Homan, 1994, New York: St. Martin's Press. Copyright 1994 by St. Martin's Press. Reprinted by permission.)

ful. Baskwill and Whitman (1988) caution that although checklists are useful they can be cumbersome and lengthy, and the fact that they "are written in a linear, sequential fashion often misleads people into thinking that is the order in which things must happen" (p. 17).

Literature Questionnaires. **Literature questionnaires** are designed to determine how children react to reading materials. They include items that relate to or question attitudes toward reading or appreciation of poetry, fables, and folktales; understanding of other cultures; knowledge of various literary genres that are enjoyed and read most frequently. A questionnaire with an incomplete sentence format, as in Figure 7–4, allows for self-reflection and can touch on various issues, attitudes, and information, which could be useful for conference discussions.

Other questionnaires might be of the more traditional question and answer type:

- Do you prefer reading fables or poetry?
- Who is your favorite character in a mystery?
- What would you like to learn next? What is your reading goal?
- What kind of books do you like best?
- What do you like to do on weekends and after school?

Audio and Videotapes. Audio and videotaping can be quite valuable in sharing reading behaviors with children and their parents. Teachers record students while they read both familiar and unfamiliar stories. Strategies and fluency can then be analyzed. Does the student self-correct? Use pictoral clues? Is the reading early in the year (October) different from the flow of reading heard on a tape dated later (March)? Taped comparisons can be made when a student self-selects a passage from a favorite book and when the teacher selects the material. Children can record each other during a reader's workshop or shared reading time or when they read to another, perhaps younger child. Figure 7–5A is a youngster's self-assessment

1. I don't like to read about _____.

2. When I read about other cultures _____.

3. I think it's interesting when I read about other people's problems because

    _____.

4. In the book I'm reading now, the part that really got to me is _____.

5. During discussion time, I like it best when _____.

6. The most difficult book _____.

FIGURE 7–4 A sample literacy questionnaire for students' use.

Date:

Listen to your tape as many times as you want. Then answer the questions below.
Use the Good Reader's Lists to help you.

What do you notice about your reading?

I went back and fixed the words I read.

What do you feel you do well?

I try to sound out the words

What did you do when you came to a word you weren't sure of?

I sounded it out and if I didn't know it I asked the teacher

What did you do when you didn't understand what you read?

I go back.

FIGURE 7–5A A student's self-assessment of his taped reading. (Courtesy of Wendy Eisenhauer, Lynbrook, New York, school district.)

of his taped reading. In some schools, the parents are sent the tapes of their child reading several times during the school year. Figure 7–5B is a parent's enthusiastic written reaction after listening to a child's taped reading. In other schools, tapes are considered a significant part of the LAP and are sent along with additional work to the next teacher. When the child goes on to middle school, the tapes, along with other LAP contents, can be sent home. Parents (and the students) often treasure them, because they can listen (or see) the child grow in reading ability over the years.

Videos are an equally powerful assessment tool. Children can be taped in their shared reading group, during whole group interactions, or for specific purposes such as a final unit project. Sometimes teachers videotape individual children during the administration of an Informal Reading Inventory at the beginning and end of the year to demonstrate (to parents, other teachers) reading behaviors and progress.

> *This taping is a great gauge for me. It has terrific timing insofar as it allows me to participate and correct any bad habits Joey may have developed. It has given me an opportunity to understand and know exactly what Joey is doing and how he evaluates himself. This is a very informative tool.*

FIGURE 7–5B A parent's reaction to a child's taped reading. (Courtesy of Wendy Eisen-hauer, Lynbrook, New York, school district.)

Story Retelling. An effective way of monitoring metacognitive processes for comprehending reading material is through **story retelling.** This appears to be replacing more traditional, structured, literal comprehension questions. Emergent readers as well as older students can use this strategy productively. They listen to a story and tell it back, or recall and reconstruct important parts of the story. To make story retellings more effective, Polakowski (1993), a teacher in New Jersey, indicates that directions must be clearly explained to students and include these steps: (1) Tell children they will be asked to retell the story. (2) For portfolio purposes, the story should be read from beginning to end without interruptions. (3) For assessment purposes, the child retells the stories without teacher prompts. (The book is closed during the retelling.)

Through retellings, kindergarteners and first graders internalize linguistic structures, activate their auditory memory, and demonstrate various levels of listening comprehension. In grades 2 and up, story retelling assists the teacher in understanding how students reconstruct meaning from text, what elements of text are significant to them, and if they are aware of story elements such as plot, setting, and characters. Figure 7–6 depicts a story retelling done graphically via a Bubble Map, indicating the story elements from the book *The Witch Has an Itch* (Guthrie, 1990).

Retellings can be tape-recorded, heard orally, or written as summaries. Teachers analyze the tapes and keep records of the child's retelling. Figure 7–7, developed by Polakowski and colleagues (1993), is a story retelling assessment sheet that includes story structure, theme, and plot and text difficulty.

Think-Alouds. Another way of observing metacognitive processes that are otherwise not apparent, although present, is through the use of **think-alouds** (see Figure 7–8). Students are taught to predict, confirm, and elaborate as they verbalize their thinking processes before, during, and after reading. Predictions are based on previewing the text and prior knowledge of the topic. During reading, students confirm predictions and describe whatever difficulties or confusions they encounter with unknown words, comprehension, plot, and so on. After reading, students are encouraged to verify their predictions, summarize what they've learned, and verbally elaborate on and react to the text. "The purpose of think-aloud activities is not to teach students how to talk about strategies . . . but to encourage them to be more aware of the different kinds of strategies they might use when reading" (Tompkins & McGee, 1993).

Think-aloud can be a time-consuming and highly subjective technique. Myers and Lytle (1986) suggest a think-aloud model that includes six categories for teachers to consider as children verbalize their thought processes: monitoring, signaling, analyzing, judging, reason-

FIGURE 7–6 Story elements: a visual retelling using a bubble map.

Child's Name _____   Grade _____   Date _____

Teacher _____   Book Title _____   Author _____

___ Story was read to child
___ Child read alone

Text Difficulty
___ High Predictability
___ Moderate Predictability
___ Advanced Predictability

Response
___ Oral Retelling
___ Pictorial Retelling (Attached)
___ Written Retelling (Attached)

Story Structure	Includes	After Prompt	Comments
Setting/Characters Starts retelling at beginning of story			
Names main character(s)			
Names other character(s)			
Tells when story happened			
Tells where story happened			
Theme Identifies goal or problem			
Plot/events			
Includes all major events			
Tells events in sensible order			
Resolution Tells how problem was solved or goal was met			

Evaluative Comments:

_____

_____

FIGURE 7–7 Sample story retelling assessment sheet. (*Note.* Courtesy of the South Brunswick, NJ, school district.)

1. Teacher models several examples of think-aloud strategies.
2. Students often work in pairs or groups to verbalize their strategies to one another.
3. Enhance students' comprehension.
4. Help children see their thinking, operationally. They verbally express their thought processes.
5. As they think aloud or state what they are thinking, they are constructing meaning from the text.
6. Teacher assesses students' ability to access prior knowledge, see if a selection makes sense, and make inferences and predictions.
7. Collaborative activities (peer interaction) is especially useful as students tell *why strategy was used, how it is used, and when to use it successfully.*

FIGURE 7–8 How to conduct a think-aloud. (*Note.* Based on the theories of J. F. Baumann, 1993.)

ing, and use of prompts. It may also be helpful to focus on the following areas when evaluating think-alouds:

1. The quality of the student's literal understanding of what was read. How many important features did the student comprehend and attend to?

2. The student's ability to differentiate between the relative significance of information presented.

3. The strategies employed during reading. Does the student use context clues and look for compound or root words when encountering an unfamiliar word?

4. Do certain patterns recur?

5. Note the student's emotional involvement with the text and ability to relate material to life experiences.

Running Records. Since it is critical for teachers to profile how students read and to monitor their progress, Clay (1993, p. 20) suggests a procedure called a **running record.** Running records allow the teacher to directly monitor students' decoding skills and are an important addition to the LAP because they are so specific—noting and recording a child's oral reading strategies. Although they may seem arduous, running records become easier with practice. The conventions are rather simple: The teacher notes everything the child says and does while reading; *all* the correct words and *all* the miscues are recorded. Clay notes that "As your ear becomes tuned-in to reading behaviors and you gain control over the recording conventions your records will become more and more reliable" (p. 24).

Some teachers keep a sheet of lined paper next to the text and maintain a record by placing a check for each word read correctly. When there is a miscue—a reversal, substitution, repetition, or omission—it is counted as an error. However, if the child self-corrects, it is not counted as an error. Other teachers duplicate the passage(s) being read and record each miscue on their copy as the child reads. Usually, three different levels of reading are evaluated: (1) *an easy selection,* (2) *a familiar selection* that has previously been read, and (3) *a more difficult selection.*

Teachers vary as to how they implement running records. Some use reading material from trade books, others select materials from basals or children's magazines. It is important to first observe, listen, and record the child reading, then to analyze the oral miscues to determine instructional strategies. In Figure 7–9 the teacher notes the child's effective use of context and some phonics and comprehension problems. Teachers also gain valuable insights into their own administration of running records and instructional activities. Figure 7–10 indicates a teacher's reflections on what she might change or improve in the future: use more specific prompts, choose more engaging reading selections for the running record, and perhaps develop a reading rubric, as well.

Informal Reading Inventories. **Informal Reading Inventories (IRIs)** are similar to running records. Although IRIs can be teacher made, many well-constructed IRIs are available through major publishers. (Some basal programs provide an IRI as part of their package of materials.) IRIs are comparable, in that all have graded word lists to determine sight vocabulary and graded story passages, ranging from preprimer up through eighth, or even twelfth grade. The student is asked to first read the stories orally and then to read others silently. Literal and inferential comprehension questions are asked after each selection is read. IRIs such as the Bader Reading and Language Inventory (Bader & Wiesendanger 1994) distinguish between comprehending and recalling and assess students' ability to retell as well as recall answers.

While the student reads orally, decoding strategies and fluency are assessed. Most IRIs include interest inventories and attitude surveys; some (Miller, 1995) include self- assessments, cloze procedures, semantic inventories, and phonic surveys. When completed, an IRI provides the teacher with a good deal of knowledge about the child's reading behaviors and attitudes as well as the student's independent, instructional, and frustration reading levels.

The **independent level,** also called recreational or pleasure reading level, indicates where the child is most comfortable with written material and therefore makes almost no errors. Library books checked out for enjoyment (as opposed to informational and reporting purposes) should be on this level. It is usually one year below the instructional level.

Word recognition = 99%   Comprehension = 95%

Read more fluently than expected.
Seemed to decode words mostly from context.
Did decode "listen," but initially sounded out "i" sound first.
Reread sometimes—often meaning broke down & she didn't reread. Some reading made no sense at all.
Asked for assistance frequently by looking at teacher.
Main idea—songs—writing
Summary—listen to music teacher & learn to listen to other songs to get ideas.
Comprehension quite good considering error rate.

FIGURE 7–9 Summary of a running record. (Courtesy of Wendy Eisenhauer, Lynbrook, New York, school district.)

Things I Would Do Differently

Next year the child's entire Response Log will be included, and I'll staple the evaluation to the response they select. This will give the stakeholders a chance to see all the responses and will save the time and paper needed to copy them. Also the books read during DEAR are recorded in the back of this notebook and will not have to be copied either.

Keep the baseline piece to 100 to 150 words. The first piece I used was too long, even though the miscue analysis was based on only the first part. The piece was not engaging, and the children lost interest about midway into the piece in many instances.

Borrow at least one other tape recorder, so more than one student at a time can listen to and evaluate the reading at one time. (I thought of this after the first taping, and it works very well.)

Go back to using more specific prompts with children and parents. They seemed to help the parents the most.

Discuss how to select student's best piece more often. I thought the children had a better handle on what to look for after we generated the chart, but I think we need to discuss it more often at conference time, etc.

Use reading selections that are engaging, and perhaps try poetry, textbooks, etc., to evaluate how the child interacts with different genres. (I've already tried these ideas with success.)

Create a rubric for the two writing pieces. I hope to do this for the second selection.

I'm wrestling with the idea of a rubric for the reading portion, but since reading is an ongoing process, perhaps the criteria check-off sheets are enough.

Keeping the parents informed and responding to their responses and comments have made them very receptive and supportive. They feel they are a part of their child's education and have a good handle on their progress and how they can help them. This is something I would not change, I would only improve on it.

FIGURE 7–10 A teacher's plans for revising a running record. (Courtesy of Wendy Eisenhauer, Lynbrook, New York, school district.)

The **instructional level** is often referred to as the teaching level, especially if one is using a graded or basal reader. The student finds the reading material challenging, not too difficult or too easy.

Word recognition = 90%   Comprehension = 75%

The **frustration level** is where reading performance breaks down. Vocabulary and concepts are much too difficult, and the child shows signs of anxiety and frustration.

Word recognition = below 90%   Comprehension = below 50%

Reading/listening capacity level is the level of comprehension a youngster achieves when the material is read *to* the student. Listening capacity is useful to determine if poor readers have the ability to comprehend but are unable for a variety of reasons (insufficient prior knowledge, poor decoding skills, emotional issues) to read and comprehend effectively on their own.

These distinctive reading levels are useful for understanding how a child reads in different situations, how interests can be matched with books, and overall to determine instructional goals for individual students.

When administering an IRI, the teacher records **miscues** from the oral reading passages and analyzes the responses to the comprehension questions. (Deviations or substitutions from the text are not called *errors* to avoid a negative connotation.) Fluency, strategies, and reading attitude are noted as the children read an entire (short) passage. Word lists determine basic sight vocabulary, but comprehension is always the major focus.

When scoring an IRI, teacher judgment plays a large and subjective role: one point is deducted for a major miscue (substitution, mispronunciation), and a half-point is deducted for minor miscues (insertion, omission). Miscues are considered minor when meaning has not been affected by the error.

Additionally, IRI results provide insightful information for literacy conferences with students and parents. Figure 7–11 is part of an IRI summary report that discusses the reading behaviors, motivation, strengths, and weaknesses of Spencer, a 10-year-old fifth grader, as determined by Scott Starkey, a student teacher who administered his first IRI.

The report continues with recommendations to help Spencer become a more effective reader (see Figure 7–12). Starkey offers several suggestions: Question–Answer Relationships (discussed later) for questioning strategies, help with motivation, and the use of cloze and story mapping for improving comprehension and organization.

IRIs may include spelling tests, interest inventories, and self-assessment reports (see Figure 7–13). These contribute to understanding the student's literacy repertoire and assist teacher, child, and parents in selecting appropriate books of interest. In Figure 7–13, the student says he likes scary stories; therefore, books could be suggested that deal with suspense and mysteries, such as *On the Edge* (Cross, 1985), *The Case of the Vanishing Corpse* (Newman), *A Kind of Thief* (Alcock, 1992), or *Encyclopedia Brown Tracks Them Down* (Sobol, 1971).

We suggest that an IRI be given to all students, in the fall and again in the spring, if possible. It is especially useful for noting growth and change in children with reading difficulties and for collaboratively setting instructional goals. The teacher can monitor reading progress and see which strategies have been learned and applied and which still need additional guidance. The summary sheet and fairly detailed recommendations for future instruction should be included in the LAP, along with the student's self-assessment of reading achievements and future goals, preferably in narrative form.

Question–Answer Relationships. Some assessment strategies are also instructional devices; others highlight needs so that appropriate instruction can be implemented. When students appear to have difficulties with various levels of comprehension, a deductive assessment device called **Question–Answer–Relationships** (QARs) may be used. Metacognitive strategies are activated as students are asked to provide text-based or knowledge based responses. The students are given passages of gradually increased length and learn to identify how they know an answer to a question: Does it come from the text, from the youngster's own prior knowledge, or both?

The teacher models the behavior and sets the purpose for each of the readings. The teacher then asks the student to create questions and identify the source used, starting with "in the book" and "think and search" type questions. The student develops questions for each category and explains the relationship between the answer and the question.

Next, the teacher sets a purpose for reading another selection. After the teacher models several examples, the student is asked to label the question that the student created as com-

Strengths and Weaknesses in Reading

I was pleasantly surprised by the IRI. Spencer did very well in all facets of the test. He has an excellent sight vocabulary. He was reading words on the list a few grade levels above his own. He also showed promising decoding skills.

Spencer decoded words from the word list such as *antibiotic* and *contrary*. He succeeded in reading twenty-one words on the seventh-grade level correctly. I stopped there, because he had reached his frustration level. On the sixth-grade level, he did very well, saying twenty-three words correctly. The sixth-grade level proved to be his instructional level. At this point I began to wonder why he was in a low reading group. I discovered no glaring weaknesses while observing the word list portion of the IRI.

We began on the fourth-grade level for the oral reading passages. I wanted to begin with an easy reading passage, for I was still biased by the reading group placement. He answered the questions without a flaw. We discussed the passage, and he admitted to finding it easy. This was good, for he had seemed nervous, as if expecting something highly difficult.

This time I noticed four miscues, mispronunciations, and an omission, and two repeated words. On the questions, his only mistake was forgetting Bill Clinton's hometown. Some answers to higher level questions were adequate, yet uninspiring. This lack of creativity surfaced throughout the testing.

The sixth-grade level showed a dramatic dropoff. He just barely answered the questions. He had trouble with the higher level questions. His comprehension skills do not measure up to his sight vocabulary and decoding skills. He seemed rattled and acted irritated. I decided he'd had enough.

The silent reading part confirmed my view that comprehension is his weakest area. I contributed the dropoff to its being harder and Spencer's being less interested in the material.

I discovered that Spencer is a better reader than I would have previously guessed. I think he has been compared to his very bright classmates. Spencer did very well when motivated; the Alcatraz passage is a great example. Since I administered the IRI, Spencer has come up to me several times to discuss the prison.

FIGURE 7–11 Part of an IRI summary report: The student's reading strengths and weaknesses. (Courtesy of Scott Starkey.)

ing from "the author and you" or "on my own" type questions. After additional modeling and practicing, with the teacher creating some questions and the students creating other questions, questions formulated are analyzed: Did they come from the student, or from the ideas presented by the text, or both?

The next step is for the student to reflect on the source of the questions and the answers and to formulate four types of QARs:

1. "On my own" (ideas come from student's own schema)
2. "Right there" (ideas are directly from the book)
3. "Think and search" (student uses prior information and other resources)
4. "Author and you" (questions combine author's and student's ideas)

This strategy can be implemented once a week, and students ultimately learn to label and analyze their self-created questions for each of the following categories:

Recommendations

Spencer has definite potential to be an outstanding reader. His greatest weakness was comprehension; arguably the most important aspect of reading. He was not deficient in this area, but compared to other areas, this one lagged behind. Fortunately, the weakness is now identified, and remediation can begin. There are a number of different strategies to improve comprehension. The remediation is twofold. Some of the strategies are direct teaching strategies, while another is to teach Spencer to change his own approach to reading.

Some of the different direct procedures include predicting, prereading, cloze procedure, guided questioning, and story mapping. Each strategy could be used during in-class reading.

Prereading activities attempt to activate the student's problem solving and motivation. Motivation is a key help for Spencer. The reading segment on Alcatraz brought this to my attention. When interested, he can do very well. Drawing on background knowledge before reading awakens curiosity and thus makes the reader more focused. This heightened attention is necessary, for without it Spencer misses much of the material.

I would also teach Spencer about the use of analogies. Analogies help students make inferences when they read. Again, an appropriate analogy can help awaken prior knowledge.

If we are reading out loud, guiding questions may help stimulate comprehension. Questioning is a beneficial comprehension strategy, for it encourages reader interaction with the test. These questions again can be derived from the student's prior knowledge. Students using questioning strategies (QARs) do better than their peers. These questions would help keep him focused on the important material.

The cloze procedure could help Spencer enhance his predicting skills. The teacher should be careful to recognize the wide range of possible answers. The problem with the cloze procedure is that it is choppy and interferes with the flow of the story. This could cause a lack of enjoyment. Pleasure is a necessary component of reading.

Story mapping is yet another important skill that could be tried. The student must organize the story into a web. The mental, or visual, representation can stimulate the student in a new way. Spencer may prosper from this type of practice. It is impossible to know, unless it's tried.

FIGURE 7–12 Part of an IRI summary report: recommendations for student. (Courtesy of Scott Starkey.)

1. In the book (text based)
2. Right there (literal)
3. Think and search (literal and interpretive)

1. In my head (critical reading based)
2. Author and me (interpretive and applied)
3. On my own (applied)

Raphael (1982, 1986) emphasizes that the focus of a QAR is more on the source of the answer rather than how correct the answer is. It is a problem-solving, analytical approach to comprehension, which helps youngsters differentiate among literal, inferential, and critical questions and responses. When students understand where information comes from—themselves or the text—it helps them become, according to Raphael, more strategic readers and thinkers. Additionally, this technique is quite self-empowering and adds to a youngster's self-esteem. Templeton (1991, p. 313) says, "This strategy will in part help students learn they are in control, not at the mercy of the text they are reading. It is not always their fault, in other words, if a text is too complicated and/or they cannot find the answer."

Name **Richard**　　　Grade **4**　　Teacher **D. Basilone** Date_____

✱ D. Basilone

SELF-ASSESSMENT DEVICE
(Intermediate-Grade Level)

1. What does a person have to do to be a good reader?

    Read alot.

2. Who is my favorite author? Why do I like to read books or stories written by him or her?

    Ristine he was good horror stories

3. What are the three best things I have read this semester? Why did I like them?

    earth and Lights out Garfield

4. What are the easiest and hardest things about reading for me?

    Made up Words

5. What kinds of books and stories would I like to read in the future?

    Long ones

6. What does a person have to do to be a good writer?

    Spell good

7. What kinds of writing have I done this year?

    Short stories

8. What kinds of writing do I like to do the most?

    Computer writins

9. What piece of writing would I like most to do over to make it better?

    Final Escape the last breakout to happen in jail.

10. What kinds of writing would I like to do in the future?

    none

11. What are the easiest and hardest things for me about writing?

    easy story; editing hard

12. What do I need to work on the hardest to improve my writing?

    Spelling

✱ Student Teacher

FIGURE 7–13 A 10-year-old ESL student's self-assessment sheet. (*Note.* From *Alternative Assessment Techniques for Reading and Writing* (p. 466) by W. Miller, 1995, West Nyack, NY: The Center for Applied Research in Education/Simon & Schuster. © 1995 by the Center for Applied Research in Education. Reprinted by permission.)

Reciprocal Teaching. The reciprocal teaching strategy both assesses and teaches comprehension through metacognitive monitoring (Figure 7–14). The teacher demonstrates four structured comprehension approaches, and then students take turns modeling themselves after the teacher and guiding other students to use the technique. The four strategies for reciprocal teaching are (1) generating questions, (2) summarizing, (3) clarifying, and (4) predicting. The teacher assesses students' ability to use this structured process to become successful, insightful, and independent readers who are aware of their metacognitive processes and understand when and which strategies are being implemented. Most significant, according to Berliner and Casanova (1986), is the students' facility to monitor their own comprehension and to become more cognitively informed about their own thinking processes and how they comprehend text.

ASSESSING CHILDREN'S READING PRODUCTS

The LAP, to be respected as well as effective, must be considered a trustworthy and valuable addition to the classroom. It must contribute to the thorough understanding of each child's literacy strengths and weaknesses and must be a dynamic and viable vehicle for designing instruction based on each child's competencies and performance as indicated by ongoing authentic assessment.

Reading assessment includes the teacher's observations of various strategies, as indicated earlier, and the assessment of the student's collections, which include story maps, story frames, story grammars, reading lists, journals (character journals, reading response journals), reading conference logs, reading goals, and reflective self-assessment reports. These are deliberated on by both teacher and student. Since the reading process is not as tangible as the writing process, writing is often used as a tool to describe reading. The LAPs therefore contain a variety of written materials that exhibit the student's reading responses, understandings, and reflections. Analysis of specific accomplishments, goals to improve areas of weakness, attention to the student's products and reflections and the student's self-evaluations are all essential outcomes.

Reading Lists. Reading lists kept by students provide information as to the types of literature being read, when completed, and so on. Reading lists are an easy way of keeping records that can be used simultaneously with logs and journals.

In Figure 7–15, the teacher can see at a glance that within less than two months, Renee has self-selected books that include poetry, fantasy, and a multicultural dictionary. Additional books by the same authors could be suggested. As the year progresses, the book list indicates Renee's reading interests and the extent of her reading involvement and continues to help the teacher guide her instruction.

Journals and Logs. Chapter 3 discusses the variety of journals and logs that children maintain as an ongoing record and response to their reading. Journal entries should be read and evaluated by the teacher because they provide valuable insights into students' understanding and reaction to what they read. This is especially valuable for determining appropriate instruction to meet individual student needs. Character journals indicate that students understand a book on the creative thinking level and express themselves through the voices

Directions: Follow the steps below in order. **"R"** before the directions means you will read. **"W"** means you will write the answer to a question. To complete this assignment, you will read pages _____ in your text.

    R   Read the title of the section and subtitles. Then skim the first paragraph.

    W   What is this going to be about?

_____

_____

    W   What are two questions you have on this topic that can guide your reading?

_____

_____

    R   Now read the first section.

    W   What words were unfamiliar to you?

_____

_____

    W   What do you think these words mean?

_____

_____

    R   What was unclear to you as you read this passage?

_____

_____

    W   Write a summary of this section.

_____

_____

_____

FIGURE 7–14 Reciprocal teaching guide. (*Note.* From *Linking Reading Assessment to Instruction* (p. 149) by A. Shearer and S. Homan, 1994, New York: St. Martin's Press. Copyright 1994 by St. Martin's Press. Reprinted by permission.

Books I Finished Reading

Name: Renee

Title	Author	Completed
1. *A Light in the Attic* This was a fun poem book. The pictures are silly too.	S. Silverstein	Oct. 3
2. *Jambo Means Hello* I learned lots of African words.	M. Feelings	Oct. 17
3. *Charlotte's Web* I cried when Charlotte died, but I loved this book.	E. B. White	Nov. 20

FIGURE 7–15 A sample basic reading list.

of the characters in the stories. The student in Figure 7–16 humorously describes herself, in a carefully written letter, as a conquering soldier who had a laughing fit. The teacher can discuss spelling (*threw* vs. *through*), the careful self-corrections (*hysterical*), or the mechanics of writing (indentation for paragraphs, etc.).

Story Frames. Story frames, story grammars, story maps, and story boards provide insights into a student's understanding of plot, character, ability to predict, sequence, and so on. In Figure 7–17, a story board created by a fifth-grader from an inner-city school indicates how well the story was understood. This child clearly sequences and understands a multicultural tale that took place in another century and setting. The youngster's artistic ability should also be applauded and encouraged.

Venn Diagrams. As a popular tool for comparing stories, Venn diagrams can be used with primary as well as intermediate and middle school students. Two circles each detail the unique characteristics, ideas, or concepts under consideration, and the intersecting part shows their commonalities and similarities. Students can compare two pieces of literature or two authors' styles and then create a Venn diagram to visually indicate their insights. The third grader's Venn diagram in Figure 7–18 shows her understanding of the similarities and differences between two books of fantasy, *Jumanji* (Van Allsberg, 1981) and *Where the Wild Things Are* (Sendak, 1963). In Figure 7–19, a fifth-grade student contrasts and compares two different cultures, China and the United States, after reading *In the Year of the Boar and Jackie Robinson* (Lord, 1984) as part of a multicultural unit. Further readings to overcome stereotypes and learn more about Asian American literature and experiences might be suggested, such as *Dragonwings* (Yep, 1975), *Grandfather's Journey* (Say, 1993), or *Tales from Gold Mountain: Stories of the Chinese in the New World* (Yee, 1990).

Student Attitude Surveys and Self-Evaluations. Self-reflecting tools help to determine how students perceive themselves as readers (Figure 7–20). Students should ultimately learn to write narrative self-assessments (rather than complete a fill-in-the-blank form) to provide

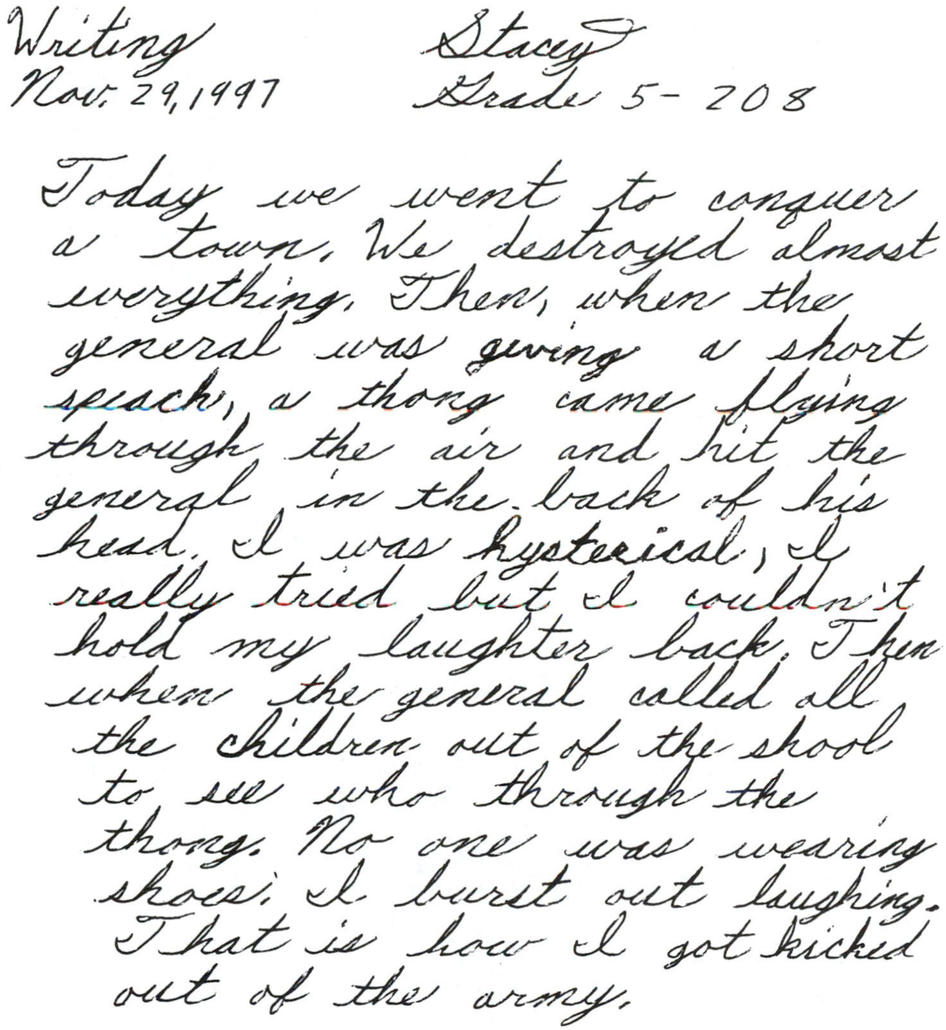

Writing   Stacey
Nov. 29, 1997   Grade 5- 208

Today we went to conquer a town. We destroyed almost everything. Then, when the general was giving a short speach, a thong came flying through the air and hit the general in the back of his head. I was hysterical, I really tried but I couldn't hold my laughter back. Then when the general called all the children out of the shool to see who through the thong. No one was wearing shoes. I burst out laughing. That is how I got kicked out of the army.

FIGURE 7–16 A character journal entry by a fifth grader.

depth and insights on where they've been and where they want to be. Some schools also ask for a reflective literacy autobiography. When did the students first start reading? Are they reading more now than a few months ago? What are their disappointments? What strengths do they see, and what areas do they want to improve?

Reading Rubrics. To clarify and guide students in terms of what is being looked at and assessed, rubrics help teachers focus on specific reading strategies and score them on a progressive scale—ranging from specific itemized strengths to specific itemized areas of weakness. Vizyak (1996a) has revised her first-grade rubrics over the years. They are fairly extensive and include predicting, recognizing print inconsistencies, knowing when meaning is lost, fluency and automaticity in reading, comprehension of text, and enjoyment of literature (see Figure 7–21).

FIGURE 7–17 A story board created by a fifth grader.

5.

Djeow Seow is being neglected by her Father.

6.

The Emperor is being Kidnapped.

The END

story board

by Tsahay

5th grade

7.

FIGURE 7–17 *Continued.*

8.

Djeow Seow is Never going to be Neglected again.

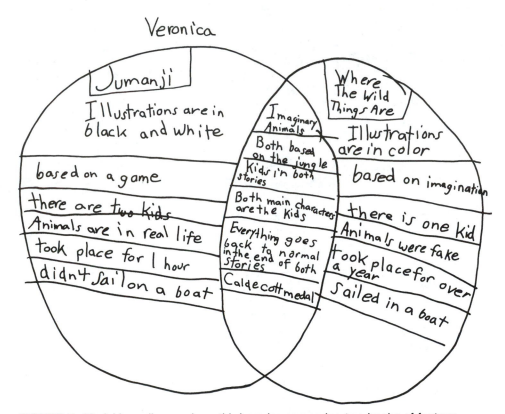

FIGURE 7–18 A Venn diagram by a third grader comparing two books of fantasy.

READING ASSESSMENT CAUTIONS

What does the teacher do with these collected "treasures" in each child's LAP? Are all of equal merit? How can one equitably assess the worth of what each student believes is precious and in which each has ego-investment? The metacognitive processes of reflection and self-assessment can be quite empowering as students analyze their growth and development.

How are the contents of the LAP to be fairly assessed by the teacher in terms of reading progress? Caution and discretion are extremely important so that judgments do not undermine the climate of trust that has been established and the philosophical underpinnings of literacy and assessment that are espoused in this book. Strickland (1995) has emphasized that "schools must provide **low-risk learning environments**" for successful learning to take place. There cannot be a mismatch between instruction (how we teach) and assessment (how we judge children's works). The LAP process contains enough selective and appropriate teacher and student material that allows for fair, collaborative, and constructive analysis and evaluation of reading behaviors and progress.

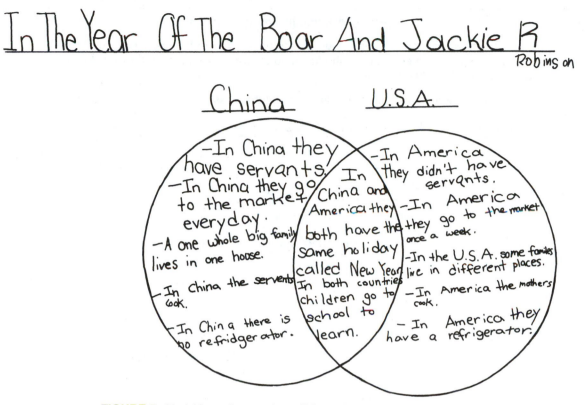

FIGURE 7–19 A Venn diagram by a fifth grader showing cultural comparisons.

CONCLUSIONS

Assessing reading means guiding reading. It entails keeping records of students' works, the teacher's ongoing notes, and formal and informal observation and evaluations. The goal of assessment is to understand each student as a person and as a reader and to change instruction so each student can improve and move forward in reading and learning. It answers the questions, What do students know, and what do they need to know to be more effective in their reading and critical thinking skills? Past and ongoing works are scrutinized, and teacher and student together determine the goals that have been met and set new goals for short-term and long-range learning. Ultimately, an in-depth reading profile emerges. Both student and teacher identify and understand the student's reading preferences; where, and if, motivation is lacking; strengths in fluency, vocabulary, and metacognitive awareness of reading strategies; self-monitoring ability; insights and critical comprehension abilities; and growth in appreciation of literature. Students know what they are doing and how they are performing. The teacher provides guidance and strategies for each child so that growth, solutions to problems, and enhancement of learning will be apparent. As Hornsby and Sukarna (1986, p. 142) caution, it's the promotion of individual achievement, not competitive assessment, that is most important.

Reading Attitude Inventory/Interview

Begin the discussion with "tell me about your favorite book" (or your favorite author) to get the conversation going. Please elaborate on the following questions and prompts (probe with "why?" or "tell me more" to get children talking).

1. How do you feel when your teacher reads a story to the class?

   I feel like there's an adventure and I would stop whatever I do and stick it in my desk and just listen to her. (S.B.)

2. How do you feel when someone gives you a book for a present?

   I like books and it's one of my number one things to do—read! (J. W.)

3. How do you feel about reading books for fun?

   I feel great, because books are like puzzles. Your mind and your books are hooked together like a puzzle. (3. G.)

4. How do you feel when you are asked to read to others in the class?

   Nice! Once I read a whole book to the whole class. (A. L.)

5. How do you feel when you are asked to read to your teacher?

   I feel good—it's sort of like putting your heads together. (3. G.)

FIGURE 7–20 A sample student attitude survey showing various students' responses. (Courtesy of Juneau, Alaska, school district.)

6. How do you feel about going to school?

It's fun and I always want to be in school. (A. S.)

7. How do you feel about how well you read?

I feel good because I get to read to myself whenever I want to read. I don't have to have a parent read to me. (O. M.)

8. How do you think your teacher feels when you read?

I've been in her class this year and last year and I've done amazing in reading. (A. B.)

9. How do you feel when you read to your family? Who do you read to? When do you read?

I like it because we read stories to each other. (C. D.)

10. How did you learn to read?

My grandpa taught me. He read me stories and then I caught on to them. (S. M.)

FIGURE 7–20 *Continued.*

Reading Rubric Grade 1

Name _____

Date _____

Shows Comprehension of Text

1	2	3	4	5
Relies on story being read by teacher or with others Retells with very little detail; sequences pictures to tell simple story Does not include inferred information when summarizing Does not differentiate real/make-believe Does not connect story events to experiences in life		Reads independently and/or relies on story being read with others Retells story in own words including characters, setting, and sequence of events Begins to include inferred information when summarizing Differentiates real/make-believe Connects story events to own life experiences		Reads independently Retells story accurately and sequentially in own words and elaborates Includes inferred information when summarizing story Differentiates real/make-believe and fiction/nonfiction Connects story events to experiences in own life and elaborates

Comments:

Shows Appreciation/Enjoyment of Literature

1	2	3	4	5
Shows limited interest in being read to Shows little interest in books Participates minimally in oral reading of familiar stories Limited use of classroom library		Enjoys being read to and wants to hear favorite stories repeatedly Reads when directed to books Participates in oral reading of familiar stories Uses classroom library when directed		Selects books he/she wishes to have read aloud and requests favorite stories repeatedly Voluntarily reads Leads oral reading of favorite stories Voluntarily uses classroom library

Comments:

FIGURE 7–21 Part of a developmental reading rubric used for first grade students by Adams County Five Star School District, Colorado.

REFERENCES

Baumann, J. F. et al. (1993). *Garden gates. New dimensions in the world of reading.* Atlanta, GA: Silver Burdett & Ginn.

Bader, L., & Wiesendanger, K. (1994). *Bader reading and language inventory.* Saddle River, NJ: Merrill/Prentice Hall.

Baskwill, J., & Whitman, P. (1988). *Evaluation: Whole language, whole child.* New York: Scholastic.

Berliner, D., & Casanova, U. (1986, January). Should you try reciprocal teaching: Yes! *Instructor,* pp. 12–13.

Clay, M. (1993). *An observation survey of early literacy achievement.* Portsmouth, NH: Heinemann.

Goodman, K. (1986). *What's whole in whole language?* Portsmouth, NH: Heinemann.

Goodman, Y. (1989). Evaluation of Students. In K. Goodman, Y. Goodman, & W. Hood (Eds.), *The whole language evaluation book.* Portsmouth, NH: Heinemann.

Hornsby, D., Sukarna, D., & Parry, J. (1986). *Read on—a conference approach to reading.* Portsmouth, NH: Heinemann.

Myers, J., & Lytle, S. (1986). Assessment of the learning process. *Exceptional Children, 53,* 138–144.

Miller, W. H. (1995). *Alternative assessment techniques for reading and writing.* West Nyack, NY: Center for Applied Research in Education.

Polakowski, C. (1993). Literacy portfolios in the early childhood classroom. In *Student portfolios.* South Brunswick, NJ: South Brunswick Schools.

Raphael, T. (1982). Teaching children question–answer strategies. *The Reading Teacher, 36,* 186–191.

Raphael, T. (1986). Teaching question–answer strategies, revisited. *The Reading Teacher, 39,* 516–522.

Rhodes, L., & Shanklin, N. (1993). *Windows into literacy.* Portsmouth, NH: Heinemann.

Sharp, Q. Q. (1989). *Evaluation: Whole language checklists for evaluating your children.* New York: Scholastic.

Shearer, A., & Homan, S. (1994). *Linking reading assessment to instruction.* New York: St. Martin's Press.

Strickland, D. S. (1995). Reinventing our literacy programs: Books, basics, balance. *The Reading Teacher, 48,* 294–302.

Templeton, S. (1991). *Teaching the integrated language arts.* Dallas: Houghton Mifflin.

Tompkins, G., & McGee, L. (1993). *Teaching reading with literature.* New York: Merrill.

Vizyak, L. (1996a). *Student portfolios: a practical guide to evaluation.* Bothell, WA: The Wright Group.

Vizyak, L. (1996b). *Using a portfolio to evaluate and enhance literacy development.* Paper presented at the IRA conference. New Orleans.

Children's Literature References

Alcock, V. (1992). *A kind of thief.* New York: Delacorte.

Cross, G. (1985). *On the edge.* New York: Holiday House.

Feelings, M. (1971). *Jambo says hello: Swahili alphabet book.* New York: Holt.

Guthrie, D. (1990). *The witch has an itch.* New York: Simon & Schuster.

Lord, B. B. (1984). *In the year of the boar and Jackie Robinson.* New York: HarperCollins.

Newman, R. (1978). *The case of the vanishing corpse.* New York: Atheneum.

Say, A. (1993). *Grandfather's journey.* Dallas: Houghton Mifflin.

Sendak, M. (1963). *Where the wild things are.* New York: HarperCollins.

Sobol, D. (1971). *Encyclopedia Brown tracks them down.* New York: Scholastic/Four Winds.

Silverstein, S. (1981). *A light in the attic.* New York: HarperCollins.

White, E. B. (1952). *Charlotte's web.* New York: HarperCollins.

Van Allsberg, C. (1981). *Jumanji.* Dallas: Houghton Mifflin.

Yee, P. (1990). *Tales from Golden Mountain: Stories of the Chinese in the new world.* Macmillan.

Yep, L. (1975). *Dragonwings.* New York: HarperCollins.

Using the Literacy Assessment Portfolio to Assess and Guide Writing Instruction

KEY WORDS AND CONCEPTS

Indirect measurement   Anchor papers
Direct measurement   Exemplars
Rubrics   Analytic scoring
Holistic scoring   Primary trait scoring
Benchmarks   Writing process approach

New York State began to use a writing competency test for fifth-grade students in the early 1980s. The test format required that all fifth graders write two different pieces in response to specific prompts. Each piece would be read and given a score from 1 to 4 (4 being the highest) by two raters. Thus, a student's score would fall on a continuum from 0 to 16.

The first group of fifth graders to take the test did so with great anticipation and eagerly awaited the results. When the data were reported to the students, one student, named Robert, was told by his teacher that he got a 14 on the test without any further explanation. He shared this news with his parents. When they asked him what he thought the score meant and what his teacher had to say about his writing, he answered "All I know is that Brian got a 16, and I think I write better." His teacher did not explain the scoring system to Robert and his parents and did not comment further about Robert's writing. The value of this assessment opportunity was lost to the teacher, to Robert, and to Robert's family. If writing assessment is to have value, it must have meaning and purpose for all who participate.

INTRODUCTION TO WRITING ASSESSMENT

Teachers today have learned the value of writing in their classrooms, not only because students should be good writers as a mark of functional literacy, but because writing has many purposes. Writing is more than a tool—it has utility in learning all subjects, it reveals a great deal about students' understanding, reactions, and cognitive strategies, and it also has personal meaning. According to Smith (1982), "Writing touches every part of our lives, and not even the illiterate escape its consequences . . . I propose to take the general utility of writing to be axiomatic; it has earned its place in any culture in which it is found" (p. 7). Writing has been found to be useful as a means of communication, for producing a permanent record, and as an art (Smith, 1982).

Renewed Emphasis on Writing Creates Controversies

The renewed interest in writing in our schools is the result of several trends. In the 1970s the public became particularly concerned about the quality of literacy instruction, and attention not only focused on the national indicators that depicted poor literacy attainment but also highlighted the deficient writing skills of many high school graduates.

In the 1980s educators began to view reading and writing as parallel aspects of children's literacy development and saw that reading and writing instruction shared cognitive dimensions that were not only linked together but reinforced each other. Consequently, reading and writing began to be taught simultaneously. Educators began writing instruction at the emergent stages of literacy development, and writing was emphasized throughout the grades in all curriculum areas. Newer theories of integrating the language arts gave teachers strategies for incorporating both reading and writing activities into daily instruction as part of whole language instruction, literature-based teaching, and thematic units.

The work of Graves (1983), Calkins (1983, 1986, 1994), and others in the 1980s popularized a new theory of writing instruction that many have called the *process approach to writing*. According to Burns, Roe, and Ross (1996), this approach is child-centered; students take ownership of their writing by creating their own pieces, are aware of audience, develop their writing through stages, and finally share their writing through publication in a supportive community of authors (p. 385). The specific classroom strategies that grew from this new approach have included writing workshops, the widespread use of journals, writing activities applied to all curriculum areas, peer editing, conferencing, computer-assisted writing instruction, students responding to literature, and re-creating meaning through writing.

The new theories about writing instruction have called for revisions in how to teach and assess writing. Several controversies have arisen about writing assessment.

Mechanics versus Content. Teachers have long faced the dilemma of whether written work should be looked at for its correctness or for the quality of ideas and content. While a composition that is full of mechanical errors can easily be red-penciled and criticized, to do so negates the thoughts and feelings that are revealed in the writing. In the past, emphasis was placed on determining if the writing was mechanically and grammatically correct, and errors were clearly marked, counted, and scored. Too frequently, students were discouraged from enjoying writing because they feared extensive criticism when assessment focused solely on mechanics.

Focus on correctness never ensured good writing. A piece of writing can exhibit good technical skills without being interesting, persuasive, artistic, or compelling. Students' knowledge of language conventions is not equivalent to their ability to use that knowledge when they write, nor does it guarantee that the writing product will be dynamic. Thoughtful educators are now more inclined to examine a piece of writing for its assets rather than deficits, which is a model that encourages students by acknowledging their accomplishments instead of highlighting their weaknesses.

Process versus Product. Educators have become more concerned about the underlying strategies children use when they write, often exemplified by organization and elaboration, and are less inclined to focus exclusively on the product. The strategies students use when they compose, such as the ability to self-edit, may ultimately be more important than attention to the writing product. According to Bratcher (1994, p. 5), we have lived through a paradigm shift in that "We no longer emphasize the products of writing to the exclusion of the process."

Grading students' writing has always been a cause for concern, but with the new emphasis on teaching through a writing process approach, an assessment dilemma persists. According to Bratcher (1994),

> On the one hand, we are committed to teaching writing as a process. . . . On the other hand, we are locked into school situations that require us to translate our response to our students' writing into letter grades or even numbers. But there is hope: teacher/grader schizophrenia can be overcome by choosing grading options that match our teaching purposes. (p. 6)

Genre Influences Writing Assessment. All forms of writing are not equivalent, and each genre requires different knowledge and strategies and ultimately succeeds because of different dynamics. Highly descriptive and colorful language used well in a poem is obviously less appropriate in a business letter. A student's ability to write a friendly letter to a pen pal (now often on a computer through e-mail) cannot be assessed in the same manner as an independent research report. Writing assessment needs to be responsive to differences in writing forms. This is especially important as classroom strategies encourage written expression in many genres including personal narratives, reports, essays, letters, poems, and articles.

Evaluation versus Description. Another dilemma for teachers is the necessity for reducing extensive analytic comments to a grade. Schools must be accountable. At the emergent literacy levels, parents and administrators may be satisfied with a thoughtful description of how a child is developing into a writer; at the upper levels, however, they want more precise assessments in the form of grades. How to reduce the thoughtful analysis of writing into a letter or number that can be recorded on a report card is difficult, and certainly students' efforts as well as the success of their products should be part of the grading equation.

Sensitivity to Individuals versus Meeting Uniform Standards. Schools are especially accountable for demonstrating results. The standards movement speaks to the concern that students should not be promoted from grade to grade without meeting developmentally appropriate standards at each level. Many feel that the schools have been too soft. By establishing and publishing uniform standards, all will know the requirements at each level, and thus education will become more rigorous.

Unfortunately, the concern with meeting standards becomes very complicated when the concept is applied to actual students in real schools. Today's classrooms are heterogeneous, composed of culturally diverse students with different educational opportunities and representing all racial, ethnic, and socioeconomic groups; growing numbers of students with foreign language backgrounds; as well as students with various handicapping conditions. Is it fair to hold all to the same yardstick? Special educators, for example, have been trained to assess students from a developmental perspective to determine if appropriate change and progress are taking place without the expectation that all students will meet a standard of performance at each grade level. The concern with uniform standards seems to negate the reality of learners with differing patterns of growth and rates of development. Today, teachers are sensitive to individual differences and want to encourage rather than discourage growth. Should the writing products of all students be assessed according to whether they meet uniform, grade-level expectations, or should the individual progress of a student be the key factor?

Indirect versus Direct Assessment. Another concern has revolved around whether writing should be assessed through indirect or direct measurement techniques. **Indirect measurement** is based on the theory that writing ability is composed of subskills (i.e., spelling, punctuation, sentence structure, etc.) that can be appraised through tests that measure knowledge. **Direct measurement** relies on the analysis of the writing product itself to determine if a writing product meets the criteria for good writing. Underlying the choice between the two approaches is the debate over which subskills constitute good writing as well as what criteria should be used to analyze a writing product.

Indirect Measurement. Indirect writing assessment has traditionally employed multiple-choice tests of knowledge of various subskills including grammar, punctuation, capitalization, and spelling. According to White (1985), these tests have a "superficial appeal" because, as with any standardized test, they seem to be objective, comparable, scientific, and statistically complex (p. 63). The tests have been severely criticized as having been developed with the simplistic notion that knowledge of mechanics alone is equivalent to good writing. Every teacher can attest to the phenomenon of a student who scores well on a spelling test but cannot apply this knowledge in daily writing. Many other attributes associated with good writing are not assessed through indirect measures, such as understanding the rhetorical task, organization, originality of thought, and quality of language usage. Indirect measures do not examine multidimensional, psycholinguistic, and cognitive aspects of the strategies students use when they write. According to White (1985), the measurement of writing through the use of standardized tests has fallen into disrepute and has been replaced or augmented by performance measures.

Direct Measurement Using Performance-Based Assessment. Direct writing assessment requires examination of the writing product and process. Now often referred to as *performance-based assessment,* direct writing assessment often involves the use of rubrics, rating scales, and holistic scoring systems. These direct measures often replace the older indirect methods, but they too have drawbacks: inefficiency caused by hand scoring and labor-intensive work, subjectivity of scorers, lack of interscorer reliability, differing opinions about what constitutes good writing, and debates over how to prioritize different writing traits. Some researchers feel that direct measures of writing are best designed at the local level and that scoring systems, even those designed for large-scale assessment programs, must be created and administered by teachers. We need to be patient while the new performance-based systems are developed and refined.

Performance-based assessment is often accompanied by rating systems used to directly measure writing samples. Holistic scoring, analytic scoring, and primary trait scoring have all been devised to assess students' writing samples.

Holistic scoring is based on the concept that the assessment of a writing sample should be based on the general or total impression and not the demonstration of different subskills. Writing samples are read quickly and separated into distinctive categories, usually assigned with score points from 1 to 4, indicating the overall quality of the writing along a continuum from unsatisfactory to excellent. This sorting process is quick, efficient, and applicable for screening students for special programs.

Several newer techniques have refined the holistic scoring process. **Writing rubrics,** for example, are scoring guides that describe qualities of writing at different levels of competency and have facilitated the ability to clearly discriminate between different levels of performance. Rubrics are easy to design and can be created collaboratively by teachers and students to reflect the specific characteristics of good writing in various forms and in response to different assignments. Examples of writing rubrics are provided later in this chapter as well as in Part IV. **Benchmarks,** or **anchor papers** (papers that exhibit the traits commensurate with each scoring point), are often used to provide assistance to scorers, whether teachers or students, so that a piece of writing can be compared with a known standard. **Exemplars**—pieces of writing that meet the highest standards and clearly demonstrate the characteristics of excellent writing—can also be used for comparison and guidance.

Analytic scoring systems are used to provide a more in-depth profile of an individual's writing ability. Here, the components of good writing are specified and prioritized, and a student's work is analyzed to determine to what extent it exhibits the targeted traits. The total score is composed of the sum of a set of subscores, although different systems have been developed to proportionately weight various aspects of writing based on their comparative importance. (The New York State system for analyzing a piece of writing shown later, in Figure 8–14, is an example of an analytic system that does not provide scores but aids in describing a writing product with the goal of providing focused instruction.) Analytic systems are similar to the informal writing evaluation that classroom teachers have traditionally used to review and mark student writing products. However, they provide more guidance by prioritizing the importance of different writing characteristics as well as by promoting a set of uniform characteristics.

A less frequently used system, but one that has often been combined with analytic scoring, is **primary trait scoring.** This system is based on the realization that different forms of writing require different components. Thus, the qualities of an excellent business letter should not be used to rate another form of writing such as a friendly letter or a personal essay. Primary trait scoring analyzes a particular piece of writing to determine if it succeeds according to its purpose, for its audience, in a given situation. This system has been used both with rubrics and analytic scoring so that a guide can be customized to the assignment and form of writing.

Along with the movement toward performance-based assessment, teachers are expected to be able to apply a variety of informal diagnostic skills with the ultimate goal of providing more effective writing instruction.

WRITING FOLDERS AND PORTFOLIOS

Widespread Application of Writing Portfolios

The emphasis on writing has resulted in the widespread use of folders and portfolios to collect student writing. While writing folders were originally a simple means to store students' work in progress, today, literacy portfolios reflect the more analytic process that promotes self-reflection and guides instruction, described in the preceding chapters.

Many teachers encourage their students to save their daily writing in work in progress folders. Classes that use a writing process approach value how a piece of writing is the result of many drafts. By saving the students' writing, the teacher, families, and students have a collection that can demonstrate developmental changes and promote self-reflection. The work for the writing folder is often chosen collaboratively and is often especially valued. Pieces can be selected to demonstrate specific characteristics of writing, examples of different genres, writing used in various curriculum projects, a personal response to reading, or change over time. The selections are then put into best works or showcase portfolios designed to demonstrate writing accomplishment. These portfolios can be created exclusively for writing work or can be combined into reading and writing portfolios.

Inside the Student's Writing Portfolio

The contents of a good writing portfolio are extensively described in Chapters 4 and 6. To summarize, Figure 8–1 contains an overview of the contents of a comprehensive writing portfolio. Examples of some important writing portfolio entries are briefly discussed next, along with their instructional implications.

- Hot topics list/writing ideas
- Self-reflections
- Goals sheet
- Artwork, webs, maps, organizers
- Lists, drafts, revisions, final copies
- Writing in many forms: reports, narratives, poems, letters, etc.
- Writing record/log
- Writing journal
- Spelling strategies
- Editing strategies, checklists
- Author's circle notes/peer conferences
- Teacher conference notes
- Family reactions

FIGURE 8–1 Contents of a student's writing portfolio.

Students' Self-Reflections. Students' self-reflections are very important to the portfolio concept. The ability to engage in thoughtful self-reflection will be affected by the student's age, skill, and training. The process of getting students to think about their writing, however, should begin at the emergent literacy level, where they need both encouragement and modeling to learn what is expected of them as part of this self-reflection. Figure 8–2 contains the self-reflections of a beginning reader and writer from the South Brunswick, NJ, school district. Portfolio assessment is an important part of this district's literacy program, and students are expected to indicate "What I Have Learned" and "What I Need to Do Better" as part of their self-reflective process.

The first grader in Figure 8–2 indicated that she knows how to write "I Love You" but also reveals that she does not know how to spell words. It's important that teachers acknowledge the student's expectations, and it would be appropriate to share with this student that spelling is an important goal. This would support this student's concern and provide reassurance that spelling is an area to be worked on.

Figure 8–3 shows the self-reflections of a seventh grader from the Lawrence, Long Island, school district at the end of the school year. This essay was prompted by a review of the entire year's portfolio. In this middle school, a portfolio evaluation and conference were used in place of a final English exam. During a conference, it would be important for the teacher to reinforce this student's positive feelings about herself as a writer of short stories, share the concern about writer's block, and discuss her feelings about being published.

Reflections can come in various forms. Figure 8–4 is a self-reflective poem that was written by a gifted fifth grader who also discusses writer's block and the intense frustration that it causes. Obviously, this student's teacher should respond to his intense frustration. Providing personal essays written by well-known writers who also experienced writer's block would be comforting and might even provide some suggestions for addressing the dilemma.

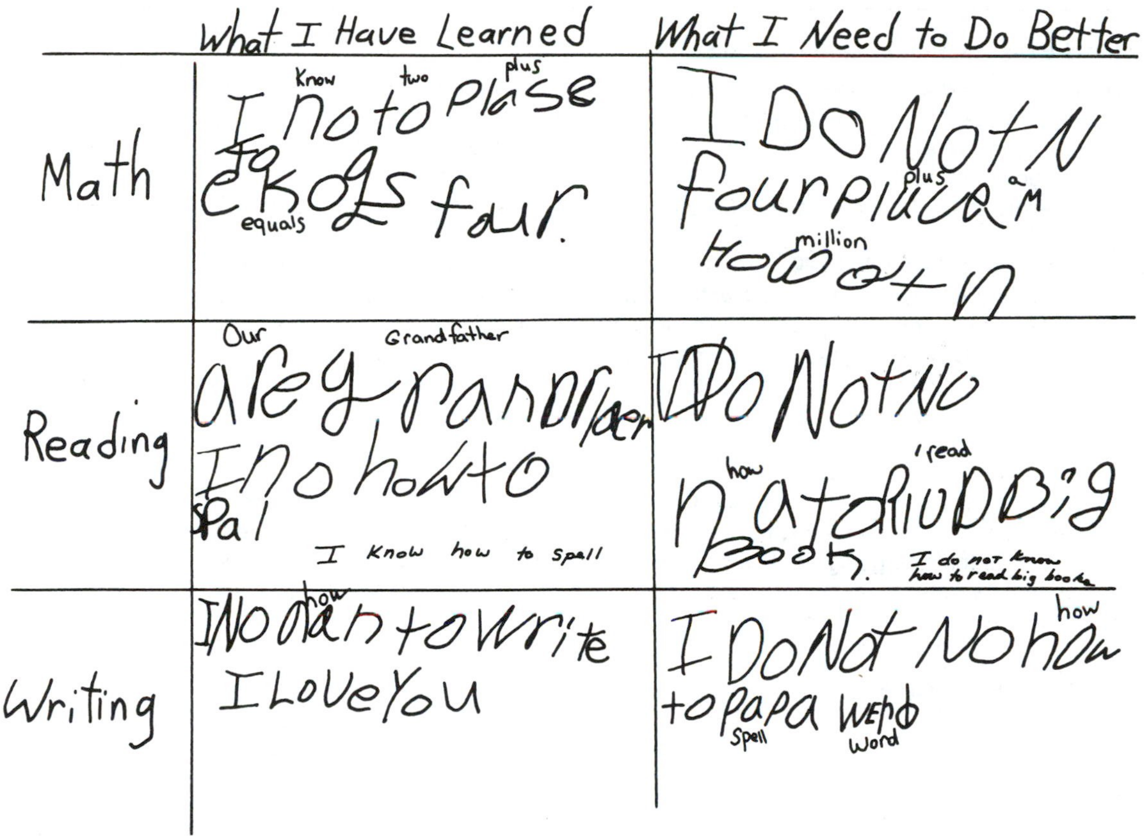

	What I Have Learned	What I Need to Do Better
Math	I no to plase *(Know two plus)* ekols faur. *(equals)*	I DO Not N fourpluea m *(plus)* Howa4n *(million)*
Reading	a regranpfaer *(Our Grandfather)* I no howto spal *(I know how to spell)*	I DO NotNO nataiuDBig *(how i read)* Books. *(I do not know how to read big books)*
Writing	I No dah towrite *(how)* I LoveYou	I DO Not No how *(how)* to papa wepd *(Spell word)*

FIGURE 8–2 Student's self-reflections from a beginning reader and writer from South Brunswick, NJ.

Writer's block would also be a good topic for a lesson, so students can explore various strategies to overcome the dilemma. Many students have found the following to be helpful techniques: discussing topics with peers, using hot topics lists, revising or extending a finished piece, reading other students' published work, and doing related reading. One teacher had the class compile a list of suggestions entitled "Things I Can Do when I Get Stuck," which all students keep in their portfolios.

Self-Evaluation and Setting Goals. Related to the process of self-reflection are the goals that students choose for their writing. Goals sheets can take many forms but certainly should be discussed as part of ongoing writing conferences between the student and teacher. Figure 8–5 contains the writing goals of a seventh grader in a writing performance self-evaluation. It is clear that this student wants to continue writing in various genres but also wants to incorporate more vivid language into her writing. This is a specific instructional message for the teacher; future lessons should focus on writing in various genres and provide exposure to examples of expressive language in published works.

Final Essay: Writing Self-Evaluation

My mom has always pushed me to write. She thinks that I have a natural talent and she wants to make sure that I develop it. I on the other hand, don't really try to develop my writing. Once in a while I might write a story for the fun of it. My mom has tried to make me keep a diary, and a journal for the books that I have read, but I am always forgetting. I write though, because once a week I write letters to my father. Also, for holidays and my mom's birthdays I write stories and give them as gifts.

The type of writing that I like to do the best, are short stories. My ideas come in the spur of the moment, and if I feel like it, I might write a story. Once I got an idea from a picture that I drew. Sometimes I might have just finished reading a book, and I might be changing something that happened in it, and from that an idea might spring.

I really get frustrated when I am writing, and I get a writer's block. I might have the best story, and know how it will end, but in the middle I will get stuck. I usually get really fed up if I can't get over a writer's block. What I do is, get up, walk around, and then go back to the story. It is all worth it when I finally come up with a great story.

The only time I have been published was in the elementary school newspaper. I would sometimes write a poem, story, joke, or recipe. Now in the Middle School, the newspaper only writes about things that are going on. I haven't been published since. It is great to be published, to see the words that I wrote on paper! I love the proud feeling that I get and I hope that I have the opportunity to be published again someday.

FIGURE 8–3 End-of-year self-evaluation by a seventh-grade student.

This is a blank page.
I do not know anything to write.
My mind is a huge brick wall blocking the path to my ideas.
Therefore, my mind is blank.
I do not have the ignition key or the ignition.
My mind is a big blob of clay.
Shapeless, useless.
And I have no hands to mold it into something useful and valuable.
I do not have the kindling to start the fire.
I only have two negative wires so I can not spark the light.
My mind is a big block of ice.
Frozen.
It is a disease without a cure.
But not death in the place of life.
Death in the place of writing.

FIGURE 8–4 "Writer's Block," a self-reflective poem written by a gifted fifth-grade student.

WRITING PERFORMANCE

Circle the appropriate letter for each item below.   (G equals GOOD EFFORT and N equals NEEDS to WORK HARDER ON THIS.)

1. Writing folder upkeep (Use of goal-setting   G   (N)
    calendar, class note taking, upkeep of skills
    and spelling list, keeping well-organized
    collection of all drafts).

2. Use of writing process (evidence of revision,   G   (N)
    conferring, editing).

3. Amount of writing submitted.   (G)   N

4. Amount of writing completed.   (G)   N

5. Trying new types of writing.   (G)   N

6. On-task behavior during writing.   (G)   N

7. Ten-week goal(s) accomplished.   (G)   N

Based on the above assessment, I believe that my overall writing grade for this ten weeks should be:

My writing goal for the coming ten weeks is:

(Write various things) (Yes)
I have accomplished this goal. I have
writtin a poem, essay & story
(To be able to creat sentences)
which contain vivid language

FIGURE 8–5 The writing goals of a seventh grader in a writing performance self-evaluation.

Early in the year, it is important for the teacher to create an atmosphere in which students think of themselves as writers and begin to develop a metacognitive awareness about how they approach writing. Figure 8–6 is an example of an inventory that a student completed in which he thought about himself as a writer. Based on this student's answer to question 6, where he reveals that it is difficult for him to write about topics he's not very familiar with, an appropriate writing goal would be to work on personal narratives that focus on first-hand experiences.

STUDENT PREFERENCE INVENTORY: <u>WRITING</u>

1.   What time of the day do you usually write?

    Afternoon

2.   How long do you usually take to write a rough draft of a narrative essay or other type of writing of approximately 150-200 words?

    20 minutes

3.   Do you ever get "writer's block"? What usually inspires you to continue writing?

    Yes, I get an idea finally

4.   What topics do you usually write about?

    Myself, sports

5.   Do you think that you write about certain topics more than others?

    Yes

6.   Would you like to vary the topics that you write about? Why do you (or don't you) think this is a good idea?

    No, it is hard for me to write things I don't know about, or have never done

FIGURE 8–6 Middle school writing preference inventory.

Figure 8–7 is a somewhat more elaborate survey that a middle school student completed at the very beginning of the school year that promotes self-awareness. It would be important to explore with this student his admiration for two writers, Roald Dahl and Michael Crichton, and the specific characteristics that make them so popular. During a conference, the teacher could assist this student by recommending other authors whose writing is similar.

7. What types of writing do you find most pleasurable to write about? (narrative essays, persuasive, descriptive, short stories, poetry?) Why?

Short stories

8. Do you like to share your writing with others? Why?

Yes they can give me advice to improve my writing

9. What pleasant/unpleasant associations do you have with writing? Can you explain why you may feel this way?

I don't like not having any ideas. It happens to me a lot

10. Would you like to see your work published? Why would this be meaningful to you?

I don't really care whether or not my work is published

FIGURE 8–6 continued

Students should be encouraged not only to edit their work but also to reflect and evaluate their writing. Figure 8–8 is a series of questions developed in the Plainedge, Long Island, schools for elementary students to help them evaluate both their nonfiction and personal narratives. These questions can be answered by the student in writing or can be discussed as part of an interview process that occurs during conferences.

Figure 8–9 is a self-editing guide developed by the same school district to encourage and assist elementary-grade students in developing editing skills and shows the importance of this phase of the writing process.

Inside the Teacher's Writing Portfolio

As part of the LAP process, we propose that teachers keep a writing portfolio for each child, or record their ongoing observations, conference notes, and other insights about each child in a notebook. The goal of this teacher portfolio is to profile a student's writing progress, processes, and strategies, with the outcome of better instruction. Also important to this process is teacher encouragement so that students have self-confidence and are motivated to write. Figure 8–10 is a summary of the typical contents of a teacher's writing portfolio for a student.

Today, teachers are keenly aware that they have many options to choose from regarding how they analyze their students' writing, both in terms of the writing product itself and the

Name _____   Date ___9/9/96___

Teacher _____   Grade ___7___

WRITING SURVEY

1. Are you a writer? _____Yes_____

    (If your answer is YES, answer question 2a. If your answer is NO, answer 2b.)

2a. How did you learn to write?

    I learned to write from my teacher and my parents.

2b. How do people learn to write?

    _____

    _____

3. Why do people write?

    To communicate and express their feelings.

    _____

4. What do you think a good writer needs to do in order to write well?

    They must be creative and check their writing-

    _____

5. How does your teacher decide which pieces of writing are the good ones?

    She looks to see how much effort was put into the writing and how the ideas were put into writing-

6. What kinds of writing do you like to do?

    I just right the best thing I can think of, regardless of what kind it is-

FIGURE 8–7 A middle school student's writing self-evaluation survey.

7.   How do you decide what to write?

The best ~~idea~~ idea I get is what I wrote

8.   Do you ever revise or edit a piece of writing? If so, describe what you do.

I check my first copy for spelling or grammar mistakes. Then I read it over to find places where it would sound better worded differently. I correct my mistakes in the next copy —

9.   Do you ever write at home just because you want to? *Yes*
     If so, how often do you write at home (just because you want to)?

I don't write at home (just because I want to) very often. But once in a ▉ I do.

10. Who or what has influenced your writing? How?

All my teachers have influenced my writing by teaching me new words and techniques.

11. Do you like to have others read your writing? *Sometimes* Who?

My parents and teachers because I trust their advice on how to improve my writing —

12. In general, how do you feel about writing?

I like to write if I get good ideas. It can be boring and frustrating if I can't come up with any —

FIGURE 8–7 *continued*

13. Among the published authors you know about (books you have read or that teacher/parent has read to you), who do you think is a good writer?

▓▓▓▓▓▓ I used to read alot of Roald Dahl books and I think he is. Now I like Michael Crichto.

What makes him or her a good writer?
(Why do you like his or her writing/books?)

His stories are imaginative and they keep me interested.

14. What do you really like about your writing?

I like my writing because it is an example of how I feel and what I'm thinking.

What would you like to improve about your writing?

I would like to keep ▓ my stories tied together and make them more enjoyable for others to ▓ read.

FIGURE 8–7 *continued*

Nonfiction (Written or Interview)

1. What did you like about this piece of writing?
2. List three things that you did well.
3. What might you change if you did this piece again?
4. Did this piece tell what you know? Why or Why not?
5. Was there something that you could have done that would have been more meaningful? Why or Why not?

Personal Narrative (Written or Interview)

1. What did you like about this piece of writing?
2. List three things that you did well.
3. What might you change if you were to do more revision on this piece?
4. What do you plan to work on in your next piece of writing?

FIGURE 8–8 Writing self-evaluation for elementary grades. (*Note.* Developed in the Plainedge, New York, school district.)

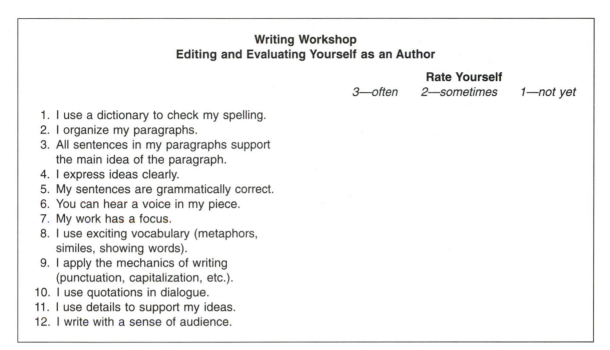

Writing Workshop
Editing and Evaluating Yourself as an Author

Rate Yourself
3—often   *2—sometimes*   *1—not yet*

1. I use a dictionary to check my spelling.
2. I organize my paragraphs.
3. All sentences in my paragraphs support the main idea of the paragraph.
4. I express ideas clearly.
5. My sentences are grammatically correct.
6. You can hear a voice in my piece.
7. My work has a focus.
8. I use exciting vocabulary (metaphors, similes, showing words).
9. I apply the mechanics of writing (punctuation, capitalization, etc.).
10. I use quotations in dialogue.
11. I use details to support my ideas.
12. I write with a sense of audience.

FIGURE 8–9 A student self-editing guide for elementary grades. (*Note.* Developed in the Plainedge, New York, school district.)

- Anecdotal/observational notes
- Developmental checklists (state or school district generated)
- Analytic measures of student's writing ability, such as

    Profile of student's writing process

    State-recommended analysis

    Writing rubrics (developed by teacher and class or school district)

    Criterion-referenced evaluations

    Assessment of different forms of writing: personal narratives, reports, stories, etc.

    Assessment of spelling, handwriting, mechanics

- Conference notes with child
- Writing goals
- Conference notes with family
- Family communications

FIGURE 8–10 Contents of a teacher's writing portfolio for a student.

process. Bratcher (1994) and Jenkins (1996) have written excellent texts for teachers who want to learn more about how children develop into writers. These authors provide elaborate descriptions and examples of different kinds of analysis teachers can do with children's writing products and processes.

The following writing assessment techniques are highlighted because they provide the means for teachers to analyze and reflect on students' writing.

Anecdotal/Observational Notes. The ongoing observation of students while they write provides excellent insights into writing strategies. To assist the teacher in daily observation, it is often helpful to create a list of target areas that the teacher wants to observe to fully understand how the student approaches writing. Figure 8–11 contains a simple writing checklist developed by Lindy Vizyak, a first-grade teacher in Colorado (see Vizyak, 1996). The

---

Name _____   **Date** _____

Writing Checklist

Spelling

_____ Student uses random letters or copies randomly.
_____ Student uses correct beginning sounds.
_____ Student uses correct ending sounds.
_____ Student uses correct middle sounds.
_____ Student uses vowels (not necessarily correctly).
_____ Student uses correct vowels.
_____ Student spells common words (*in, the, you, and,* etc.) correctly.
_____ Student appropriately copies words from charts, books, lists.
_____ Student spells harder words correctly.

Language

_____ Student capitalizes the beginning word of a sentence.
_____ Student capitalizes *I.*
_____ Student capitalizes names.
_____ Student includes end punctuation marks (.?) in writing.

Handwriting

_____ Student uses spacing between words.
_____ Student writes legibly.

Comments

_____

_____

FIGURE 8–11 A first grade writing checklist. (*Note.* From *Student Portfolios* (p. 50) by L. Vizyak, 1996, Bothell, WA: The Wright Group. Copyright 1996 by the Wright Group. Reprinted by permission.)

teacher's concerns reflect goals at the emergent stages of literacy and also are compatible with the first-grade curriculum framework. The teacher's comments are kept in chronological order on the child's writing portfolio.

Developmental Checklists and Rubrics. Many school districts have developed checklists, rating scales, or rubrics for literacy skills that correspond to different developmental levels and that are especially helpful for determining if a student is meeting grade-level expectations. Figure 8–12 is an example of a developmental writing rubric that is used by the Adams County Five Star School District in Colorado to evaluate first graders. It is critical that teachers be familiar with their school district's expectations for writing at each grade level.

State-Generated Writing Analysis Systems. Writing ability has become a very important aspect of demonstrating accountability, and therefore assessing writing is an important aspect of literacy assessment mandated by state education departments. Different states have developed their own systems for scoring students' writing samples. It is important for teachers to be aware of the system employed in their state so that their assessment practices include analysis of the competencies that their students will be expected to demonstrate. One teacher, for example, encouraged her students to take risks when writing and was dismayed when a student was penalized in a state assessment for not writing a realistic set of directions for watching a pet. Instead, this student described the care and feeding of a fire-breathing dragon. While the writing displayed a wonderful sense of humor, some evaluators felt that it did not respond to the task.

Many states use holistic scoring to rate the large number of writing samples that must be reviewed. In New Mexico, sixth-grade students are given a standard writing prompt, and their efforts are scored based on a set of criteria with score points ranging from 1 through 6 (see Rael & Travelstead, 1993). To assist scorers in using this system, they are provided a set of rubrics and anchor papers so that the scoring of narrative, expository, and descriptive papers is based on uniform criteria throughout the state. Some state systems also furnish exemplars to assist scoring by providing examples that show excellence. Figure 8–13 is a scoring rubric used to assess expository pieces done by sixth-grade students in New Mexico. It is particularly helpful because it details the criteria to be used for the different points as part of holistic scoring.

Analytic Scales. New York State also uses holistic scoring of writing samples for all fifth-grade students but includes an analysis sheet so that scorers not only provide an overall rating for a piece but can employ a process to analyze the students' writing. The purpose of the analysis is to provide individualized, appropriate instruction. Figure 8–14 is an outline of this system.

To illustrate how this system can guide instruction, see the descriptive essay in Figure 8–15 written by a fifth-grade student in response to a prompt to describe his best friend. A quick review of this essay shows it to be rather simplistic and concrete, with weakness in several areas. A more detailed analysis shows that the student also has many strengths. Figure 8–16 provides a sample analysis of this essay using the New York State guidelines.

When doing detailed analysis of writing that will lead to individualized instruction, it is important that teachers prioritize instructional goals so as not to overwhelm students. In the sample analysis in Figure 8–16, it seems that the primary goals should relate to organization and use of more vivid language. It should be noted that suggested teaching techniques include making use of oral discussion, related reading, and peer editing.

Writing Rubric—Grade 1

(Assessment Criteria)

The District Expects Most Students to Achieve Level 3 by the End of the School Year

1	2	3	4	5
Message Quality [Generates Drafts]				
■ Has difficulty generating ideas ■ Writes only a single thought about a topic		■ Generates ideas with increasing ease ■ Develops a topic by writing several sentences		■ Develops a topic by adding a variety of evidence or details ■ Organizational plan begins to emerge (beginning, middle, and end)
Drafts and Edits				
■ Lack of letter–sound correspondence (spelling) interferes with message ■ Writes with difficulty ■ Does not consider capitals or periods		■ Uses beginning, medial, and ending consonants ■ Writes some vowels ■ Uses some correctly spelled high-frequency words ■ Writes with increasing ease ■ Begins to use beginning capitals and periods appropriately		■ Writes beginning, middle, and ending sounds ■ Writes many vowel sounds correctly ■ Uses many correctly spelled high-frequency words ■ Spelling does not interfere with message ■ Writes fluently ■ Makes few errors in beginning capitals and periods
Communicates in Developmentally Appropriate Form				
■ Prints illegibly ■ Writing contains many reversals and incorrect letter forms; doesn't differentiate between upper and lower-case ■ Does not consistently write top to bottom, left to right ■ Does not space between words		■ Prints legibly enough for others to read ■ Writing contains some reversals; most letters are correctly formed; may contain some random caps ■ Writes top to bottom, left to right ■ Usually spaces between words		■ Prints letters of equal size and appropriate spacing ■ Letters are formed correctly ■ Writes top to bottom, left to right ■ Always spaces between words

FIGURE 8–12 A developmental writing rubric used by Adams County Five Star school district, Colorado.

Rubrics. The use of rubrics has been described previously, and examples can be found in Chapters 7 and 10 and Part IV. It is important to emphasize that rubrics are best created in a collaboration between teachers and students. Rubrics can be customized for specific assignments, because the evaluation criteria may be quite different with different forms of writing. Figure 8–17 is an example of a rubric created by students and teachers in the Plainedge, Long Island, school district to evaluate an independent research project that is an important part of the fifth-grade curriculum. Both the teacher and the librarian are involved in scoring the students' research papers and in the research process.

Authoring Process. More and more teachers have adopted the use of a **writing process approach** in their classes so that their students learn that a finished piece is the product of many stages from brainstorming, listing, drafting, sharing, revising, editing, to publishing. Consequently, teachers should note how well the students use the strategies appropriate for each phase of the process. Figure 8–18 shows an evaluation system developed by Cohen that can be employed to determine how a student succeeds with four stages of the writing process.

Figure 8–19 shows how a student teacher, Maureen Murphy, employed this system to describe how a second-grade student used the process strategies. It is important to note that analysis and description are used to guide instruction. The student being analyzed is Monica, who is seven years, six months old and in second grade. She is described as a friendly and cooperative child, who while not at the very top of her class, appears bright and able. She works hard to meet literacy challenges with enthusiasm. Based on an informal reading inventory, Monica is a successful second-grade reader. Monica's class devotes approximately forty-five minutes each afternoon to writer's workshop. She's had good exposure and experience with the writing process and truly seems to enjoy and look forward to the writing part of each school day.

CONCLUSIONS

The strength of the writing portfolio lies in the process of self-reflection and collaboration as well as in the use of the process to guide instruction. Several themes emerge from this chapter. Teachers should emphasize self-reflection, which needs to be modeled early in literacy instruction and throughout the grades. Collaboration must also be encouraged through classroom strategies so that students learn that they profit when they work with others. In particular, students should share their writing and self-reflections with their families. Teachers need to develop strategies to accomplish the school–family link, including periodic conferences (now often including the student or even student lead), portfolios that go home, letters to parents, photos that circulate, and exhibits for all to attend.

Portfolios can contain a wide range of materials, and there is no one right way to create a portfolio process in a classroom. However, literacy portfolios should reflect actual classroom experiences. They should also contain writing products and other entries that reveal the writing process. Student self-selections and their explanations are essential components of the process. Additionally, students should be given time to reflect on the portfolio contents and be accountable for creating an organizational system (table of contents, letter to the reader, etc.) that is coherent and clear. Of course, expectations for students will differ at different grade levels. Conferences are essential and must be held regularly so that the teacher and student both profit from reviewing portfolio contents.

New Mexico Portfolio Writing Assessment—Expository Scoring Rubric

Strong Command of Exposition Score Point 6	Generally Strong Command of Exposition Score Point 5	Command of Exposition Score Point 4
Has an effective opening and closing that tie the piece together	Has an opening and a closing	Generally has an opening and closing
Relates to the topic and has a single focus	Relates to the topic and has a single focus	Relates to the topic and has a single focus
Well-developed, complete response that is organized and progresses logically; writer takes compositional risks resulting in highly effective, vivid responses	Key ideas are developed with appropriate and varied details; some risks may be taken and are mostly successful; may be flawed, but has sense of completeness and unity	Development may be uneven with elaborated ideas interspersed with bare, unelaborated details
	Organized and progresses logically, but there may be a lapse	Some responses are organized with little, if any, difficulty moving from idea to idea; other responses may ramble somewhat with clusters of ideas that may be loosely connected, but an overall progression is apparent
Very few, if any, errors in usage	Few errors in usage	Some errors in usage, no consistent pattern
Variety of sentence and/or rhetorical modes demonstrates syntactic and verbal sophistication; very few, if any, errors in sentence construction	Syntactic and verbal sophistication through a variety of sentences and/or rhetorical modes	May demonstrate a generally correct sense of syntax; avoids excessive monotony in syntax and/or rhetorical modes; may contain a few errors in sentence construction
Very few, if any, errors in mechanics	Few errors in mechanics	May display some errors in mechanics but no consistent pattern

FIGURE 8–13 A scoring rubric to assess expository writing by sixth graders. (*Note.* From *New Mexico Portfolio Writing Assessment, Teacher's Guide, Grade 6* (no date), p. 50. Santa Fe, NM: New Mexico State Department of Education.)

New Mexico Portfolio Writing Assessment—Expository Scoring Rubric

Partial Command of Exposition Score Point 3	Limited Command of Exposition Score Point 2	Inadequate Command of Exposition Score Point 1
May not have an opening and/or closing	May not have an opening and/or closing	May not have an opening and/or closing
Relates to the topic and usually has a single focus; some responses may drift from the focus	Some responses relate to the topic but drift or abruptly shift focus	May state a subject or a list of subjects; may have an uncertain focus that must be inferred
Some responses are sparse with clear, specific details but little elaboration; others are longer but ramble and repeat ideas	Details are a mixture of general and specific with little, if any, elaboration, producing a list-like highlight response	Details are general, may be random, inappropriate, or barely apparent
Some responses have elaborated details but are interrupted by organizational flaws/lapses or by lack of transitions	Attempt at organization; some attempt to control details but few, if any, transitions	Some lengthier papers are disorganized and difficult to follow; may show no sense of planning
May display a pattern of errors in usage	May display numerous errors in usage	May have severe problems with usage including tense formation, subject–verb agreement, pronoun usage and agreement, word choice
May demonstrate excessive monotony in syntax and/or rhetorical modes; may display errors in sentence construction	Excessive monotony in syntax and/or rhetorical modes; may contain numerous errors in sentence construction	May contain an assortment of grammatically incorrect sentences; may be incoherent or unintelligible
May display a pattern of errors in mechanics NOTE: Errors may interfere with readability	May display numerous serious errors in mechanics NOTE: Errors may interfere somewhat with comprehension	May display severe errors in mechanics. NOTE: Errors may interfere with comprehension.

FIGURE 8–13 *continued*

Name _____ Grade_____ Date_____

Priority Items   Diagnostic Comments/Suggestions for Teaching

1. Task/Content

   ■ Responding appropriately to the
     requirements of the task (audience,
     purpose, form, etc.)
   ■ Providing sufficient information to
     respond adequately to the task (ideas,
     explanations, examples, etc.)
   ■ Selecting appropriate information for
     focus or emphasis
   ■ Maintaining a consistent point of view

2. Organization

   ■ Unifying the piece by means of
     appropriate generalization
   ■ Supporting generalization and
     conclusion by providing reasons,
     details, examples, etc.
   ■ Making logical connections

3. Sentence Structure

   ■ Avoiding sentence fragments
   ■ Avoiding run-on sentences
   ■ Using sentences of varied types and
     lengths

4. Language

   ■ Using specific, vivid words
   ■ Forming words correctly
   ■ Using words accurately
   ■ Avoiding unnecessary repetition

5. Mechanics/Usage

   ■ Developing spelling skills
   ■ Using punctuation correctly
   ■ Using capital letters correctly
   ■ Usage
     Subject–verb agreement
     Verb tenses
     Pronoun references
     Other:
   ■ Improving handwriting

FIGURE 8–14 New York State writing product analysis sheet for elementary grades.

200

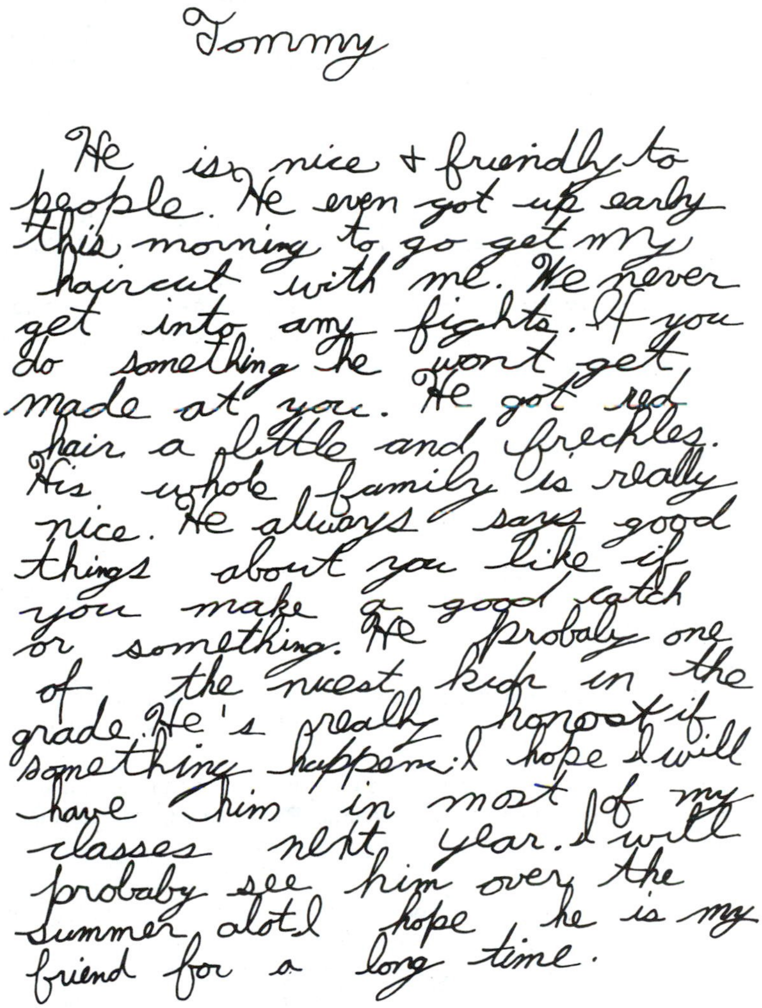

Tommy

He is nice + friendly to people. He even got up early this morning to go get my haircut with me. We never get into any fights. If you do something he wont get made at you. He got red hair a little and freckles. His whole family is really nice. He always says good things about you like if you make a good catch or something. He probaly one of the nicest kids in the grade. He's really honest if something happens. I hope I will have him in most of my classes next year. I will probaly see him over the summer alot.I hope he is my friend for a long time.

FIGURE 8–15 Sample descriptive essay by a fifth-grade student.

The essential outcomes of this writing portfolio process are to enhance student's self-esteem, promote metacognitive reflection, and guide instruction. While many teachers have begun to collect students' work in portfolios, they are still unsure how the contents should be used. Several different techniques may be used to analyze the writing contents of portfolios. The portfolio process clearly is an important tool in literacy teaching and can be a potent force for change. According to Jenkins (1996),

> the potential of portfolios to change the way we view ourselves, our children, and our curriculum will be realized only if we pursue a course of patient, persistent inquiry and continual reflection. Portfolio assessment is an evolutionary process of self-renewal that requires resolve, knowledge, and the belief that it makes a difference in children's lives. (p. 241)

1. Task/Content

This student has a clear understanding that he is supposed to describe his best friend in detail.

The student provides a great deal of information about Tommy including personal characteristics, physical description, background about his family, and examples of times they have enjoyed together. He maintains a consistent point of view and seems to have a good sense of his audience.

No specific intervention seems indicated.

2. Organization

There are significant problems with the organization of this piece of writing. The student does not organize his thoughts but tends to simply list them as they come to mind. The writing lacks topic sentences and does not display any organizing statements.

Teaching should focus on getting this student to link related ideas. Using a map or web would be helpful techniques before writing. This student should be encouraged to list his ideas and then group related thoughts under an appropriate organizer, i.e.,

How Tommy looks
    Freckles
    Red hair
Personality
    Friendly
    Nice to people

Oral discussion with a peer would be helpful before writing.

Once this student can organize his thoughts into logical categories, then attention to paragraph development can follow.

3. Sentence Structure

This student writes in well-formed, declarative sentences and seems to be quite aware of sentence structure. (Note capital letters and large periods.) There is one example of a run-on sentence.

While organization of the writing should be the primary instructional goal, it would be helpful to expose this student to a variety of sentence structures. Providing examples of descriptive pieces with variety in sentence structure would be appropriate reading.

4. Language

This student's language usage seems concrete and simple for his grade level. In particular he overuses the word *nice*. He appears to form words correctly.

This student's oral language is probably more vivid than his written language. Oral discussion should focus on using a variety of words to convey specific, vivid pictures, and certainly, substitutions for the overuse of *nice* can be developed. Again, providing reading that uses vivid language would aid awareness of descriptive language.

5. Mechanics

The student seems to have appropriate spelling skills for this level, given that he restricts language usage to simple words. The words *probably, mad,* and *honest* are misspelled. He uses terminal punctuation and begins each sentence with a capital letter. In one sentence he omitted the verb, and use of appropriate verb tense needs to be developed.

There is little evidence that the student used self-editing, and this should be developed at this grade level. Creating a checklist of items to edit would be a helpful strategy. Peer and self-editing need to be emphasized as part of this student's writing program.

FIGURE 8–16 Analysis of the "Tommy" essay using New York criteria.

STUDENT _____ TOPIC _____

TEACHER _____ LIBRARIAN _____

WRITTEN LIBRARY RESEARCH PROJECT RUBRIC—GRADE 5

	3	2	1	0
Library skills	You always located information independently. You summarized and paraphrased the information very well. You managed your time.	You usually located information independently. You showed an ability to adequately summarize and paraphrase your information. You used your time fairly well.	You sometimes located information independently or with a teacher's help. You usually copied from source. You need to manage your time.	A teacher had to guide each step.
Note taking	You always recorded meaningful information related directly to topic using index cards and abbreviations.	You usually recorded meaningful information related to topic using index cards and abbreviations.	You sometimes recorded useful information. You made limited use of index cards and abbreviations.	You need to record much more information.
Outlining	You always used logical sequencing and grouping of ideas. You used the correct format.	You usually used logical sequencing and grouping of ideas. You usually used the correct format.	You demonstrated adequate sequencing and grouping of ideas. You need to improve your format.	You need to revise your outline.
Form	You have shown that you have used the writing process extremely well. Your opening and closing paragraphs are excellent. You used specific, accurate details and examples. You have a title page and cover.	You have shown a use of the writing process. You have a good opening and closing paragraph. There is some use of details and examples. You are missing either a title page or cover.	You need some revision before it is of publishable quality. You are missing either page or cover.	You need to use the writing process to be of publishable quality. Check requirements.
Content	You have shown that you have done extensive and full research.	You have done solid research with some gaps.	Your topic needs to be more fully developed or explored.	You need to do much more research to fully develop your topic and to show that you understand your topic.
Bibliography	You have used excellent types and quality resources. You used at least three sources.	You have used acceptable sources and correct form.	You have some errors in form. You have an inadequate number or type of resources.	Needs to be revised.

FIGURE 8–17 A rubric created by students and teachers to evaluate an independent research project. (*Note.* Courtesy of the Plainedge, NY, school district.)

Four Stages of the Authoring Process

1. Prewriting: rehearsing and drafting
2. Conferencing and revising
3. Editing
4. Publishing

Rating System

0 Did not observe the use of the strategy

1 Having difficulty with the strategy

2 Developing the use of the strategy

3 Using the strategy successfully

1. Prewriting Strategies: Rehearsing and Drafting

The student is able to
- Understand the task
- Choose an appropriate form of writing
- Use appropriate beginning strategies: draws pictures; uses webs, story maps, etc.; lists; generate and discuss ideas
- Select a focus
- Generate appropriate and relevant ideas and details
- Put initial ideas on paper
- Sustain focus
- Work independently where appropriate
- Work cooperatively where appropriate
- Seek help where appropriate
- Produce a rough draft

Strengths noted: _____

Difficulties noted: _____

Teaching strategies: _____

2. Conferencing and Revising

The student is able to
- Share ideas
- Generate further, relevant ideas

FIGURE 8–18 Evaluation of a student's use of an authoring process. (*Note.* Developed by J. Cohen, Adelphi University.)

- Use feedback from classmates
- Use feedback from teacher conferences
- Modify draft
- Sustain focus

Strengths noted: _____

Difficulties noted: _____

Teaching strategies: _____

3. Editing

The student is able to
- Self-edit with attention to organization/coherence, word choice, spelling, punctuation, capitalization, grammar/sentence structure, etc.
- Seek appropriate resources
- Assist with editing others' work

Strengths noted: _____

Difficulties noted: _____

Teaching strategies: _____

4. Publishing

The student is able to
- Produce a final work in an appropriate time frame
- Produce a legible piece
- Produce a piece that has a good appearance and uses graphics appropriately (artwork, illustrations, etc.)
- Take pride in finished work
- Share with others

Strengths noted: _____

Difficulties noted: _____

Teaching strategies: _____

FIGURE 8–18 *continued*

1. Prewriting—Rating, 3

Monica is very good at planning her topics and focusing on what she needs to do to accomplish her task. The class was given an article for research about an animal. Monica handled the task of nonfiction writing with ease. Her strength is her lack of any problems in attempting the rough draft stage.

Monica should continue to receive positive reinforcement for her excellent beginning strategies and should read a variety of written forms of expression to expand her writing genre choices.

2. Conferencing and Revising—Rating, 3

The class uses peer conferencing after a rough draft is done. Again, Monica meets this phase successfully. In fact, she is one of the children who the other children most like to have a conference with because she is good at sharing ideas and posing questions that help the other students with their products. Monica also makes judgments in a nonthreatening manner.

Monica should continue to receive positive reinforcement for her excellent strategies at this stage. She should continue to be used as a resource for other students in the class.

3. Editing—Rating, 2

Monica is presently in second grade. The editing she exhibits independently is indicative of a child who is beginning to learn an editing process and continues to show growth. Her writing ability shows good spelling for this level. She uses sound–symbol correspondence as her primary spelling strategy. The sentence structure in her stories still seems choppy and shows problems with run-on thoughts. Her writing has progressed from the beginning of the year, when her sentences usually were only three to four words long.

Small group editing lessons and individual writing conferences will help Monica. She's just beginning to use self-editing strategies on a limited basis. Each editing lesson should have a simple focus with an appropriate strategy highlighted based on her recent writing. Monica should be encouraged to develop a list of skills that she can refer to when she self-edits.

4. Publishing—Rating, 3

This is a student who looks forward to completing her stories and seeing them bound with a story cover. The final products are completed neatly and in a timely manner. In this classroom, the teacher displays the finished stories on an open book rack. During snack time, I've observed Monica rereading her finished stories and sharing her stories with a friend. These stories are definitely a source of pride for her.

Monica should receive positive reinforcement for her completed work. It may be necessary to slow down her productivity at a somewhat later point so that she doesn't overemphasize the number of stories completed. Sharing stories with her family and with classmates should be continued. Monica may enjoy developing a pen-pal relationship with another second grade student from a different school to broaden her experiences and audience.

FIGURE 8–19 Authoring process evaluation for a second grader completed by a student teacher, Maureen Murphy, Adelphi University.

REFERENCES

Bratcher, S. (1994). *Evaluating children's writing.* New York: St. Martin's Press.

Burns, P., Roe, B., & Ross, E. (1996). *Teaching reading in today's elementary schools.* Boston: Houghton Mifflin.

Calkins, L. (1983). *Lessons from a child.* Portsmouth, NH: Heinemann.

Calkins, L. (1986). *The art of teaching writing.* Portsmouth, NH: Heinemann.

Calkins, L. (1994). *The art of teaching writing, new edition.* Portsmouth, NH: Heinemann.

Graves, D. (1983). *Writing: Teachers and children at work.* Portsmouth, NH: Heinemann.

Hewitt, G. (1995). *A portfolio primer.* Portsmouth, NH: Heinemann.

Jenkins, C. B. (1996). *Inside the writing portfolio.* Portsmouth, NH: Heinemann.

Rael, P., & Travelstead, J. (1993). *Statewide student assessment requirements.* Santa Fe, NM: New Mexico State Department of Education.

Smith, F. (1982). *Writing and the writer.* New York: Holt, Rinehart & Winston.

Vizyak, L. (1996). *Student portfolios.* Bothell, WA: The Wright Group.

White, E. (1985). *Teaching and assessing writing.* San Francisco: Jossey-Bass.

Conferencing and Reporting with the Literacy Assessment Portfolio

KEY WORDS AND CONCEPTS

Collecting

Collaborating

Consulting

Communicating

Teacher–parent conferences

Teacher–student conferences

Teacher–teacher conferences

Teacher–parent–student conferences

Accommodating cultural diversity

The WRITE guide

Report cards

My six year old son, David, is a cooperative child who has had his share of trouble learning to read. During the first half of first grade, he attended a reading intervention program and did well enough to graduate from it. I was scheduled for a parent–teacher conference, and I dreaded going, because my son was not having a great year.

The teacher began the conference with the flat observation that David's reading had improved, but this was the last encouraging word I heard. During the ensuing half hour, she failed to mention his attitude in class, his relationship with peers, his level of cooperation, his achievement in subjects that didn't require much reading and writing, and his ability in specialty areas. What bothered me the most was that she did not tell me anything about David as a child, or a person, even if it was "What a pain in the neck he can be!" Instead, she spent the whole conference telling me his handwriting is messy and how many spelling mistakes there were in his writing. But my back really went up when she showed me a drawing he had done to prove how carelessly he had created it and how messy it was. This was the last straw! Finally, I composed myself and carefully expressed my feelings that she had not said one positive thing about my son.

I think I made an impression. That night David's work came home with supportive comments from the teacher. Other notes came home with compliments about the expressiveness of David's pictures.

What's the moral of the story from my perspective? I did feel that I was heard at the conference, even though I had a strong and noncompliant demeanor. But I realize that my son has had problems in first grade—he rushes through work, he's young for first grade, and he does not have academic self-confidence. However, any concern this teacher had was communicated only in terms of criticism and annoyance, and there was no understanding of David as a person or acknowledgment of his efforts. This teacher's negative judgment of David during the conference may not have been spoken aloud in class but was communicated to me and to David just as forcefully as a loudspeaker announcement. Why couldn't we have discussed David and come up with some positive ideas? I hope my ruminations have some value for other parents.

A *mother's description of a spring conference with her son's elementary school teacher.*

CONFERENCING: A VALUABLE, CONSTRUCTIVE TOOL

A conference is the teacher's way of taking the pulse of the class, the individual student, and the success of various instructional strategies. It is an essential aspect of a literature-based, thematic, or integrated literacy program and a vital component and useful tool for an effective Literacy Assessment Portfolio (LAP) process. Formal LAP conferences can be held four times a year with students. This conference process should include parents and other concerned members of a child's instructional team whenever possible. All participants can review portfolio contents as the centerpiece of the conference. A literacy portfolio presents a clear picture of the student, including progress and accomplishment, and assists in developing appropriate goals and teaching strategies.

The Four C's of Conferencing

The LAP conference process is crucially dependent on four C's: collecting, collaborating, consulting, and communicating.

Collecting. **Collecting** refers to the selection of materials from reading and writing folders that will go into the LAP. The students save material daily and store it in various folders. They must select carefully, thoughtfully, and reflectively from the dynamic and plentiful assortment of these materials to create their portfolio. Choices that reflect deliberation and reflection are then placed into the LAP. De Fina (1992) points out that the distinction between a folder and a portfolio is this reflective process. The folder is a collection of *all* works; the portfolio represents selective choices.

Collaborating. In literacy-based, integrative classes, a community of readers and writers emerges. Students have learned how to interact with each other in a **collaborative,** social environment with frequent peer interaction, sharing of books and ideas, reading response groups, and ongoing communication with the teacher. Collaboration involves cooperation; and evaluating learning through the LAP becomes a cooperative venture. During a conference, participants establish goals, look for trends and patterns, discuss recreational reading interests, and acknowledge writing growth and accomplishment. The shared nature of conferencing, its collaborative spirit, promotes the child's metacognitive awareness and results in focused self-reflections and self-evaluations. Collaboration extends beyond the classroom and includes the family as well. The **teacher–parent–student conference,** which has been called "the guts of the program" by Hornsby, Sukarna, and Parry (1986), is an outgrowth of this collaborative process.

Consulting. The LAP conference provides an opportunity for the teacher to **consult** with the student, parent, and others within a focused framework. This is not merely a "How's it going?" informal question time. It is a dialogue, a discussion, a conversation, a time to question, explain, reflect, and understand. Much can be discovered at this time: Diagnoses are made, appropriate strategies for teaching can be identified and tried, and future directions are determined. The teacher consults with various participants: (1) parents who gain additional knowledge and feedback; (2) other teachers or specialists who work with and know the child (perhaps the science coordinator, reading specialist or teacher of the gifted) to share information that might require further attention; (3) administrators, if program placement, individual testing, new services or schedule changes have to be discussed; and (4) of course, the student.

Communicating. Effective communication is the essence of a language-focused, literature-based literacy program. Children learn to **communicate** in various ways—orally and in writing, in small and large groups, with peers in cooperative learning, and in one-to-one conferences with the teacher. Hopefully, they communicate with their families as well. Whether referred to as whole language, nonsplintered reading, thematic or project oriented, these literacy approaches transmit a communication ideology in a classroom environment that is perceived as a community of learners. When portfolios are used, students also learn to thoughtfully and persuasively communicate their reasons for making portfolio selections and to verbalize their reactions, feelings, and needs.

If we consider the conference a focused and directed conversation, then the key to its success is constructive communication among all participants. Can the student effectively explain why one particular work was selected rather than another? Can the metacognitive processes be verbalized and shared? How is this month's best work different from the one chosen last month? Similarly, can the teacher communicate and demonstrate interest in the student's growth and recognition of additional instructional needs in a supportive manner? It's important for professionals to use communication skills that transmit and share information in an open and nonthreatening manner.

A CONFERENCING GUIDE

The WRITE Conferencing Guide, developed by Wiener, and depicted in Figure 9–1, represents *w*ritten *r*eflections of *i*ntegrated *l*earning for *t*eacher–student *e*xchange. It can assist the communication process by guiding conference discussions. Students reflect on their LAP selections and write down their thoughts, helping them become aware of their metacognitive processes as they assess their work. The WRITE Conferencing Guide can be included in the LAP or brought along to the conference by the student.

The guide directs communication and focuses on students' self-perceptions and written reflections. If a conceptual or skill difficulty is raised, or another area of concern indicated (e.g., an item indicated from the answers to questions 5 or 6), it can be attended to during the conference, at the moment of recognized need—the teachable moment. If confusion arises over a thematic concept, a story grammar, or another entry, the concept can be taught immediately or established as a future learning goal. Written communications can also take the form of newsletters, go-homes, or weekly notes to the family, which are also incorporated into the portfolio. Kapinus (1993) reminds us that, whatever the form, "effective *communication* can be the universal clamp that holds together different aspects of a successful reading assessment program."

The teacher facilitates the four C's through thoughtful preplanning, active listening, and carefully directed and guided questioning. All these provide a focus for the students' introspective and reflective thought processes.

CONFERENCE OBJECTIVES

If assessment and evaluation techniques are neglected, underused, or poorly implemented, then the future of language-based, integrated, thematic literacy learning can be jeopardized. There must be accountability to administrators, parents, and students to guide curricular decisions and determine effective teaching and learning strategies. The conference helps to appraise student performance: Are children actively learning? Do we see evidence of growth? Can students reflect on their strengths and weaknesses and develop appropriate goals for the future? Students must recognize what has and has not been achieved, and teachers must determine which instructional strategies have been effective and which should be improved or changed.

Wiggins (1989) explains that, in traditional curriculum and content-based teaching and testing classrooms, the interdisciplinary skills of reading, writing, questioning, speaking, and

1. What is your best work? What makes it so?

_____

_____

2. How does this compare with last month's best work or other work you did not include?

_____

_____

3. After reviewing your journal responses and story maps, what comments can you make about your reading?

_____

_____

4. What are your reading goals for the next month?

_____

_____

5. What would you like to improve in your writing?

_____

_____

FIGURE 9–1 The *WRITE Conference Guide—W*ritten *R*eflections of *I*ntegrated *L*earning for *T*eacher–Student *E*xchange. (*Note.* Developed by R. Wiener, 1996.)

listening fall through the cracks, and one needs to publicly exhibit the essentials that have been taught and learned. He later (1993) cautions that portfolios may provide merely one facet of assessment and ignore or neglect another important aspect of student input, the effectiveness of the learning environment and instructional focus, and that students should provide frequent feedback to teachers regarding instruction and assessment. The LAP provides the exhibition, and the conference provides the forum for feedback and discussion.

Conferencing allows a format and structure in which one can determine if and how students are implementing what they have been taught. Traditional assessment and standardized tests can only furnish a one-dimensional look at knowledge, which is often an inflexible, impersonal judgment and constitutes only one source of information. Authentic assessment conferences provide a multidimensional picture of the child. Using the LAP as the focal point

6. How can I, the teacher, help you?

_____

_____

7. Since the last conference, what book do you want to discuss because it was (a) so good, (b) so bad, or (c) so special in some way?

_____

8. What are you most pleased about with regard to your learning?

_____

_____

9. What ideas have you been thinking about, or what piece of information have you learned that you want to discuss at the LAP conference?

_____

_____

10. What would you particularly like to share with your family?

_____

_____

FIGURE 9–1 *continued*

of conferences with parents, students, and other professionals eliminates confusion and misinformation.

Teachers need to be reminded that parents approach school conferences with different concerns and mixed reactions. Some parents dread an annual conference when the focus has traditionally been on test scores, from both standardized and other classroom tests. If the child's achievement is seen as below average, the parents may feel that blame is implied and feel guilty about being responsible for a student's not achieving at the expected level. It is common for parents in this uncomfortable position to express anger or sadness. Misunderstandings rather than shared understandings have often resulted. What does it mean to a parent that Amy is in the 70th percentile? Is Amy just passing? Are *percent* and *percentile* the same? Without an adequate explanation that Amy is doing better than 70% of the population that took that test, the parent and the child are most probably disappointed and disheartened.

Parents of students who have achieved at grade-level ability or beyond may also be disappointed by traditional conferences. While they feel proud of their child's achievement, frequently, blanket praise does not translate into an individualized assessment of the child's particular strengths and areas to be worked on. All parents profit when the teacher presents concrete information about each child through a portfolio that captures unique and personal accomplishment. Additionally, parents should feel that they can share valuable insights about their children that are often not revealed to the teacher in the school environment.

The frequency of conferences depends on the teacher and school policy. They can be called frequently, perhaps every eight weeks, or they can be held at the beginning, middle, and end of the year. They can be formally scheduled or impromptu. As mentioned, LAPs should be assembled approximately four times a year. Conferences should be scheduled, formalized, and integrated into the LAP process.

The keys to conducting an effective LAP conference are the teacher's examination and reflection about the child's LAP before the conference is held. The following general questions and concerns about literacy should be addressed before meeting with the student and others:

Generic Conference Questions for the Teacher:

1. Does the student build on prior knowledge (schema)? What evidence supports this?

2. How does the student implement higher order thinking skills?

3. Does the student reflect on what has been read? Is this evident through response journals, story maps, or self-assessment forms?

4. Has the student's repertoire of knowledge expanded? What data indicate this growth?

5. Are reading and writing substantiated by reports, response journals, lists, logs, and stated goals? Are reading and writing strategies being developed and applied in all curriculum areas?

6. Has the youngster become an active participant in the community of literacy learners? Are there anecdotal notes or other records of this?

7. Are student goals realistic and reflective?

8. Can the student use a variety of resources for finding information, and is the student developing independent learning strategies?

9. Are ideas being expressed as well in print as in speech?

10. Has self-selected, leisure time, or recreational reading increased? Is there confirmation through logs and reports?

These questions prepare the teacher to assess literacy progress that goes beyond a simple standardized test score. The materials presented in the LAP and discussed during the conference are performance-based, authentic products that are embedded in daily reading and writing tasks.

When children read in more traditional basal reading group arrangements, there may be less need for diagnostic conferencing about reading fluency, since the teacher is likely to hear the children read aloud on a daily basis. (We advocate conferences even for this reading structure, since the personal one-to-one interaction and discussion of other conferencing topics are important.) However, whenever students self-select reading material and engage in individual and independent reading, procedures must be established to monitor and assess progress. Conferences, which were always integral to individualized reading programs, are equally essential to integrated literature approaches.

CONFERENCE FORMATS

According to Pappas, Kiefer, and Levstik (1990), effective literacy conferencing should include sharing, questioning, oral reading, encouraging, and guiding. Templeton (1994) points out that in addition to focusing on reading knowledge and strategies the conference must elaborate and refine student thinking. She adds planning and record keeping as essential components. Of course, all conferences should monitor, evaluate, and guide students in a positive manner.

It is helpful to think of three phases of the LAP conference: time before, during, and after the conference. The essential features of each phase should include the following:

Before the LAP Conference

- Reviewing the student's LAP.
- Careful planning and organization of the conference agenda.
- Appropriate time set aside for the conference.
- Provision for nonintrusive note taking during the conference.
- Students informed of the conference schedule.
- Students know what to expect during the conference.
- Students have been trained how to conduct a conference.
- Students not involved in the conference know what they are expected to do while conferences are in session.
- Students not involved in the conference know when they are allowed to interrupt a conference in progress.

During the LAP Conference

- Purposeful questioning guided by the conference agenda.
- Guided portfolio review based on predetermined, shared criteria.
- Actual student reading.
- Encouraging and guiding discussion.
- Focusing on thinking and reflecting.
- Note taking and recording.
- Emphasis on two-way listening.
- Sharing ongoing literacy products (journals, logs, edited writing).
- Sharing ongoing literacy processes and strategies (self-editing guides, etc.).

■ Diagnosing basic literacy skills.

■ Trying out teaching strategies.

■ Focused teaching.

■ Sharing goals and future direction.

After the LAP Conference

■ Reviewing conference insights.

■ Recording important conference observations.

■ Evaluating effective teaching strategies.

■ Setting goals for instruction.

■ Setting agenda for future conference topics.

■ Clarifying the need for further classroom observation.

Four basic types of conferences can be implemented with LAPs: teacher–parent, teacher–parent–student, teacher–student, and teacher–teacher conferences.

Teacher–Parent Conferences

The crucial role parents play in the education of their children was discussed in Chapter 3, and its significance cannot be overstated. Educators have always known, and are now making inroads in convincing policymakers, about the importance of funding projects that create partnerships with parents for children's school success. Yet only Minnesota, Virginia, and Iowa require elementary school teachers to take classes in parental involvement. Morrow and Paratore (1993) cite numerous research studies that confirm and emphasize the gravity and significance of parental involvement, ranging from the importance of parents' reading aloud to children, to the diversity of intergenerational programs in schools, as well as to intercultural programs affecting schools and communities.

For parental involvement to be truly significant, interaction should be carefully planned and integrated into the classroom structure. A good example of this is a conference approach used at the Franklin Early Childhood School, in Woodmere, New York. Staff at this early childhood center give parents a conference sheet with cartoon-like drawings, which the parent goes over with the kindergarten child at home several weeks before the conference. Various behaviors are depicted on the conference sheet (i.e., "I share books with friends"); the parent discusses these first with the child and then at a joint conference with the parent, child, and teacher. This format clearly focuses discussion on important areas of concern that can be elaborated on in greater detail during the conference (see Figure 9–2).

Ramsaur (1992), a first-grade teacher in Alaska, has written about go-home journals and describes how useful these journals become for conferencing with parents. The go-homes were especially designed to help communicate with families in a highly transient, urban population of welfare and single-parent homes, most without telephones. Ramsaur devised a weekly go-home journal consisting of three color-coded parts: (1) a yellow teacher's reporting page that contains details about the week's activities and includes a handwritten paragraph about each child (e.g., Erik excelled in a spelling bee, Pam is sharing more with peers); (2) a white student page, where the student writes about a school or class project and asks the parent one or two questions; and (3) a blue parents' page, where parents respond to the stu-

I respect the rights and feelings of others.	I complete my tasks.	I listen while others speak.	I like listening to stories.
I can adjust to new situations.	I am able to accept limits.	I share books with my friends.	I enjoy books by myself.
I learn and play well with my friends.	I help to keep our classroom neat.	I feel confident taking part in class discussions.	I can write using temporary spelling.
I work independently.	I follow instructions.	I look after my things and keep them neat.	I read at home with my family.

To the parent(s)

     Please review these kindergarten goals with your child and add any comments in the allotted space. Please bring this "contract" to school with you at conference time. We are looking forward to sharing our mutual expectations for your child's school success.

Comments:

FIGURE 9–2 Kindergarten teacher-parent conference form. (*Note.* Courtesy of Franklin Early Childhood Center, Woodmere, NY.)

dent's questions and add personal comments. The families became so interested in the classroom program that they enthusiastically looked forward to conferencing.

Accommodating Cultural Diversity. Families newly arrived from other countries or families for whom English is not the primary language can find schools alien and frightening. Economically disadvantaged families and families of color may also feel unwelcome in schools that appear to be dominated by white, middle-class individuals (Olson, 1990). School should work toward lessening discomfort and bridging gaps created by feelings of cultural differences. Families must be helped to feel that their diversity is respected and can be a welcome part of the educational process, or they will not attend conferences or other school programs. Finders and Lewis (1994) point out that "too often the social, economic, linguistic, and cultural practices of parents are represented as serious problems rather than valued knowledge." Teachers and administrators must make the effort to create a welcoming school climate in which parents become partners in their children's education. Bilingual parent volunteers can be used to overcome language barriers, and if recruited as teacher's aides, they can facilitate better understanding of the school program.

France and Hager (1993) suggest a recruit, respect, and respond approach to promote healthy home–school interactions and rapport. Although they reported on an intergenerational research project, these three R's can be applied to all outreach efforts for family involvement. *Recruit:* Meet the challenge of attracting, recruiting, and welcoming families into the school community and keeping them involved. *Respect:* For families to remain active, they must feel they have the respect of teachers and administrators. *Respond:* React and respond to the needs of the parents, the community, or specific families.

Schools have their own culture, language, procedures, and expectations that often intimidate multicultural, multiethnic communities. Ethnocentric biases must be realized and challenged, and the entire school community must learn to become sensitive to diverse values, family systems, and traditions. Parents and other family members must feel welcomed and respected. Only then will parents be comfortable enough to participate in conferences and other school-sponsored projects. Obviously, new immigrants also become acculturated to American school practices as well as norms as they become more familiar with a new way of life. School, home, and community must form a partnership, with the goal being the enhancement of children's learning.

Conferences with parents and other family members can be informational, evaluative, or both.

Informational Parent Conferences. Informational parent conferences are essential for sharing the philosophy, structure, activities, and goals of the class so that parents know the learning experiences in which their children are engaged. What journals are to be taken home? Is the child working on a specific project? What books are their children expected to read at home? Should the parents be reading to the children, and should they be listening to their children read? How can the family become appropriately involved? The Lawrence/Inwood Public School District on Long Island is typical of many school districts that assist parents with such questions by distributing a parents' handbook called *Reading Process*. In this clearly written book, the literacy approach is explained in nonprofessional terms, stages of literacy development are described, and most importantly, specific ways for parents to support their children's literacy at home are listed. Such booklets can be distributed during conferences or at the first back to school night early in the semester or be sent home with a letter of introduction. If a school district does not have such a publication, we strongly recommend that each teacher develop one for use with parents. Professional organizations such as the International Reading Association (IRA) and the National Council of Teachers of English (NCTE) have many resources designed specifically for parents, and several are available in other languages.

The conference allows a positive relationship to develop between student, teacher, and parent. It is a time to provide guidelines that inform parents how they can assist the child to be a successful learner. The climate should not intimidate but be comfortable enough for families to ask questions and share concerns. Some teachers arrange for very early morning conferences with refreshments, so working parents can attend before leaving for their jobs. Evening conferences should be organized for others who can't attend during the day. Collins (1994) reports on schools where teachers are encouraged to be creative in scheduling conferences. Some accommodate parents by arranging home visits when necessary, weekend conferences at community centers, or even meeting with parents at fast-food restaurants. Certainly, in the absence of an actual meeting, a friendly telephone call can establish an open line of communication.

Evaluative Parent Conferences. Conferences must do more than inform parents; they must also assess the student's performance. As parents confer with the teacher and their child and examine and discuss the contents of the LAP, they see tangible evidence of progress, comparing current work with past performance. It is important for children to be present for most conferences so they can exercise their metacognitive awareness as they reflect on their work and explain to their parents how the portfolio is representative of their growth, why a certain piece was included, or what they were trying to accomplish. This concrete demonstration of skills and problem-solving abilities, rather than a single evaluative grade, is meaningful to parents. It translates into knowing about what the child has accomplished, how the child has progressed, and where assistance is needed.

The conference is an ideal time to share with the family the district literacy expectations for the grade level. A clear curriculum chart for literacy should be available for the parents to keep after it is explained during the conference. Because accountability is being stressed and standard curriculum goals are a national trend, it is important that parents be made aware of typical literacy behaviors for students at the grade level. Understanding this will facilitate parents' acceptance of grading practices that are often part of school district philosophy. While we believe in the concept of continuous progress and descriptive rather than evaluative grading, many school districts have adopted different grading practices. (The dilemma over grading students' literacy behavior will be further discussed at the end of this chapter.)

When conferencing with families, in addition to discussing the students' work samples, the teacher shares pertinent information from anecdotal and daily notes: the teacher's records of the youngster's reading preferences and dislikes; the interaction during peer editing; the extent of dialogue journal completion; and the performance on the running record, miscue inventory, and other informal reading inventories.

Figure 9–3 shows a teacher's observations about Christopher, a beginning reader. There is a great deal of positive information here that can be shared with the family during a conference about this child's beginning reading strategies and how Christopher can be assisted at home.

Teacher's Comments
Reading: A Guide for Observation

NAME: _Christopher_____ GRADE: ___1___ DATE: _____

Reads willingly	Attempts to read. Curious about books & print.
Expects reading to make sense (Reads—not simply decodes) Reads for a purpose—enjoyment or information	Picture reads. Tries to decode. Tries to make sense using pictures and some words.
Draws on prior knowledge What is already known is used to read new material	Very limited prior knowledge. Limited vocabulary—unable to name many common ideas, concepts.
Makes reasonable predictions (Samples, confirms, disconfirms words and/or passages)	Predicts but cannot confirm.
Reads on or skips Fluency/rate	Choppy, due to limited decoding skills.
Uses pictures for cues	Yes.
Self-corrects	Not able to at this time.
Reads in "chunks" Rapidly reads phrases, such as "Once upon a time . . ."	N/A.
Uses knowledge of letter–sound relationships	Consonants—but not aware of vowels in reading or writing.
Recognizes root words and endings	No
Observes punctuation (periods, question marks, exclamation points)	Observes periods and capital letters.
Finger points	Yes.
Expression	No.

FIGURE 9–3 A teacher's observations about a beginning reader.

For example, Christopher relies on picture clues to assist decoding, which is a typical beginning reading strategy that can be reinforced by appropriately using picture books at home.

Figure 9–4 is a page from a sixth grader's dialogue journal. It is significant that this student believes she "uses her knowledge"—applying what she has learned—in various situations, and this is an important strategy to share. Discussing background knowledge and using

Dear Rita,   #2

    Hi! How are you? I'm
fine. Thanks for the compliment
on my self conections No,
we aren't learning this in
school but, a few years
NOTE ago we did. I now use
my ^{past} knowledge on all
things I do now.

    The Trojan War has
become easier now that
we are further into the
book No, we are not finished

FIGURE 9–4 A page from a sixth grader's dialogue journal.

a K-W-L strategy (what I *know*, what I *want* to learn, and what I *learned*) before reading are appropriate instructional strategies that can be reinforced at home.

Figure 9–5A and B shows two parent–teacher conference reports for the same child in first and second grade. Accomplishments are noted and shared: Jennifer's growth with journal writing is reported, phonics application is noted, and her reading behaviors are discussed. In the second-grade report, it is noteworthy that the first-grade teacher was consulted about

PARENT–TEACHER CONFERENCE REPORTS: K–2

Student: _Jennifer_   Grade: _1_   Teacher: _Mrs. U._   School: _Longfellow_

FIRST CONFERENCE SUMMARY—DATE: _Dec. 2_

Attending: Student _____

Reading Level: _pre-primer_   Publisher: _Ginn_   Mother ___✔___

Math Level: _1_   Publisher: _Heath_   Father _____

Other _____

Jennifer is a gentle, sensitive child. She has a quiet and reserved manner. Jennifer has made a fine adjustment to the first grade. She has many friends. She is helpful and kind to others.

Jennifer is making fine progress in reading. She is developing a good sight vocabulary and is able to sound out many words. She is proud of her progress.

Jennifer is also progressing in writing. She enjoys keeping a journal and writing stories in writer's workshop. She uses invented and conventional spelling in her pieces.

Jennifer is able to add through 10, graph, pattern, subtract through 10. She enjoys using the math manipulatives.

Jennifer is exhibiting confidence in herself. She participates in small and large group discussions. Mrs. S is excited about her reading, and is pleased with her progress.

FIGURE 9–5A Parent–teacher conference reports for Jennifer in first grade.

the child's adjustment. In the second-grade class, the parent and teacher had three portfolio conferences during the school year in which they were able to specifically review Jennifer's progress and collaborate on ways to continue to boost her confidence.

Vizyak uses a student conference session form shown in Figure 9–6 A and B for her first graders to discuss both fiction and nonfiction books. The information on these forms is clear, detailed, and easy to share with families.

A different student conference record is shown in Figure 9–7. This conference was held with a bilingual youngster who has various literacy problems but very much enjoys the *Curious George* books and other funny stories. Sharing this with the family, showing the parents the *Curious George* books, and suggesting other humorous, easy reading material are all likely to help Chris's parents feel they can be useful in contributing to his future learning by finding appropriate books for him to read at home. Even if the parents have limited English themselves, sharing picture books will be good reinforcement.

Making Parents an Integral Part of the Process. Sharing portfolio contents assists parents in becoming part of the learning process. The self-selected representational work, materials in

PARENT–TEACHER CONFERENCE REPORTS: K–2

Student: _Jennifer_   Grade: _2_   Teacher: _Mrs. D._   School: _Longfellow_

FIRST CONFERENCE SUMMARY—DATE: _Nov. 17_

Attending: Student _____

Reading Level: _2_   Publisher: _Ginn_   Mother ✔

Math Level: _2_   Publisher: _Addison/Wesley_   Father _____

Other _____

Mrs. S. has been in close touch with me about Jenny's adjustment in second grade. Mrs. U., Jen's first-grade teacher, said Jen relaxes gradually to new situations.

Jenny is on grade level in all areas. Her standardized reading tests reflect good beginning second-grade comprehension and vocabulary skills, and her recent test results were excellent.

Jen enjoys reading, writing, and illustrating her work. She uses mostly inventive spelling with good phonics application. Memorizing word spellings for tests poses a challenge for her.

Jenny generally understands math concepts after working with the materials. Her lack of confidence, however, increases the difficulty. Working with counters more carefully will be helpful. She needs to memorize basic addition and subtraction math facts without using fingers.

I am encouraging Jenny to focus more on class instruction and discussion. Developing greater focus and self-confidence are important goals for this year.

FIGURE 9–5B Parent-teacher conference report for Jennifer in second grade.

progress, completed self-evaluation forms, ongoing reading journals, story drafts and rewrites, notes about peer and teacher conferences, and relevant teacher records all provide meaningful areas for conference discussions and create a clear, vivid picture of the child.

Parents may be asked to keep a list of questions or topics and bring them along to the conference. Time for discussing the parents' concerns should be allocated as part of the conference agenda. Teachers must also be prepared not only with the LAP but also with questions or comments for the parents. When parents leave a conference, they should have knowledge of their child's work in progress; current skill applications and abilities; and strengths, needs, and accomplishments in reading and writing as well as other learning and social behaviors. Having some print material that parents can take home to support what has been discussed (a summary report, work samples, district publications, etc.) is another good idea.

There are differing views on whether students should attend parent conferences. We believe they should participate in a parent–teacher–student conference at least once or twice during the year so the child can explain a report, poem, or story, share how it developed and why it was included, reflect aloud on other choices for inclusion, and answer some of the parent's questions and concerns. In addition to LAP conferences attended by the parent, stu-

Student Name: _____   **FICTION**

Date: _____

Title of the book: _____

Author: _____

Directions:
Put a check if the student can answer the following questions:

_____ 1. How did you choose the book?

_____ 2. Was this book **easy, just right,** or **challenging** for you to read?

_____ 3. Describe the setting in the story.

_____ 4. Describe the main character, and give at least three telling details.

_____ 5. What do you think was the main problem in the story?

_____ 6. How was the problem solved?

_____ 7. What was your favorite part of this book?

_____ 8. Did anything surprise you in the story?

_____ 9. How would you rate the book?

_____10. Would you like to do a Book Talk for the class?

_____11. What book will you choose to read next? Title:_____

_____

Evaluation Comments:

_____

_____

_____

FIGURE 9–6A Individual reading conferences for fiction book. (*Note.* Developed by Lindy Vizyak.)

Student Name: _____   **NON-FICTION**

Date: _____

Title of the book: _____

Author: _____

Directions:

Put a check if the student can answer the following questions:

_____1. How did you choose this book to read?

_____2. What did you like best about this book?

_____3. Tell about four new things you learned.

_____4. What did you notice about the illustrations?

_____5. Would you like to write a special report on this topic in Writer's Workshop?

_____6. What book will you choose to read next?

        Book Title: _____

_____7. Would you like to give a Book Talk to the class?

Evaluation Comments: _____

_____

_____

_____

_____

FIGURE 9–6B Individual reading conference form for non-fiction book.

dent, and teacher, one or two conferences should be held without the child present. At this time, issues might be raised, suggestions made and interpretations shared, that the parent or the teacher wishes to discuss out of the child's presence. The national Parent–Teacher Association (PTA) has a booklet "Making Parent–Teacher Conferences Work for Your Student," which is available through state and local PTA chapters.

Reading Conference Record

(Responses were dictated by the child to the teacher.)

Date: _April 25_

Name: _Chris_

Title of the book discussed: _Curious George_

Author of book _H. A. Rey_

Reason for picking this book _Because I like monkeys. They are really silly._

Tell me something interesting about this story. _He gets in really big trouble. He made a really big mess with ink._

How do you plan to report on this book? _I will draw a picture._

Have you read any other books by this author? _No._

Would you like to? _Yes, because he makes good books._

Teacher's notes: _Chris enjoys Curious George books very much. Share other books in the series with him. Provide other easy reading books that may be about animals and are humorous. Parents can follow up on this at home. Chris can also be encouraged to describe the picture he draws for his report, and an aide or another student can transcribe this. A language experience approach strategy should be continued._

FIGURE 9–7 Student–teacher conference form, bilingual first-grade student.

Teacher–Student Conferences

Teacher–student conferences can be held individually or in small groups. Both are useful in different ways. Teachers often have a spontaneous or informal conference with individuals or students who are working in groups. Jenkins (1996) refers to the "assess-as-you-go conference." This is different from a more formally planned portfolio conference, which often coincides with the end of marking periods, with report card dates, or with the semester close. During all student conferences, the teacher listens a lot and asks guided questions, evaluates, and gives feedback. The teacher provides students with an opportunity to read aloud, discuss books read, talk about their writing, or discuss reactions, problems, successes, or disappointments. LAP conferences are focused conversations, centered on demonstrated literacy behaviors.

Individual Conferences. The one-to-one teacher–student conference offers a rare classroom opportunity; it provides an intimate and private time for teacher and student to listen and interact without interference from others. An informal conference can be as short as three minutes, whereas a scheduled conference is often about twenty minutes. The goal is personalized attention and feedback from the teacher.

As much as school is a sociocultural environment, it is also a psychosocial environment that profoundly impacts children's emotional, as well as educational, needs. The individual conference allows some needed private time for teacher and student. The student doesn't have to share time with anyone but the teacher, and the focus is on the youngster and school-related issues and reactions. In addition to being an integral member of a community of learners, the student also feels distinctive and unique. Additionally, the natural egocentricity among young children and the need for attention and recognition among older students are well met in this one-to-one setting.

Group Conferences. When several students participate in a conference, the agenda and focus need to be clear. In group situations, some children can be overwhelmed by their more active peers, and the group dynamics need careful monitoring to ensure that all are profiting. Group conferences are useful in gathering information for future instruction, monitoring groups that are working together (especially for noting the dynamics of group interchange), and observing each youngster's performance in a group. This is especially important in thematic, project-oriented classrooms with a great deal of collaborative work. How does each individual child function in these small group settings and learning centers? The teacher should be aware of the dynamics inherent in group settings such as shyness or a tendency to dominate, as well as whether a group can stay focused. Assigning different roles to various group members (including a recorder to take notes during conferences) is another way of keeping group conferences productive.

Scheduling and Time Allocation. The conference is a precious time that children look forward to and treasure. It must, therefore, be carefully respected and planned for. Scheduled conference times should never be flippantly canceled or rushed. A timetable should be carefully scheduled, displayed, and rigidly adhered to so that conference time is not disrupted or delayed. Those students not involved in a conference need to be busy and should be aware of collaboratively established guidelines so that conferences are not frequently interrupted or intruded on for inappropriate reasons.

Factors to Promote Success with Student Conferences. For literacy to be effectively assessed using authentic student work as criteria, growth must be monitored to "follow student development and make appropriate adjustments in instruction" (Rhodes & Shanklin, 1993). As the LAP is discussed during a conference, the teacher notes how to change teaching strategies to meet the students' unique needs "so that students can take control of their own learning and teachers can improve their instruction" (Winograd, 1994, p. 421). Winograd says the challenge is how to assess, measure, or interpret all the information. This challenge can be best met during the conference if teachers learn to carefully ***listen*** to the children as they explain their thinking and learning processes.

In addition to focused listening, the following factors may be helpful in gaining a total picture of the student and are an integral part of the conference process: self-selection of material, rubrics and criteria setting, record keeping, self-assessment, analysis of trends and patterns, noting strengths, and attending to weaknesses.

Self-Selection. Students learn to select materials that go into the LAP from minilessons and class discussions. Some materials are easier than others to assemble. For example, youngsters go through their folders, make specific decisions and selections using certain guidelines, and then are prepared to discuss their work during the conference.

Rubrics and Other Stated Criteria. Rubrics are a set of scoring guidelines that indicate traits and dimensions of effectiveness on which the student will be assessed. They can provide structure for the conference and pinpoint standards useful for collaborative evaluation of actual work. They also provide a guide to assist the student in developing a strategy for meeting appropriate levels of performance. Figure 9–8 is a sample rubric that was developed by a group of third graders and their teacher in Garden City, New York, to help assess a piece of writing.

Record Keeping. Since conferences are vital to the success of literature-based, thematic learning, records that are kept of verbal, informal, and formal assessments of the students' learning are shared. Teachers must avoid becoming too entangled with record keeping so that they become overwhelmed or disheartened with the process. Records should be maintained in an easy, manageable style. A loose-leaf notebook with tabs for each student is uncomplicated and functional. It is also convenient to keep a clipboard and small sticker pads handy to jot down notes as individual students are observed while reading or interacting with peers in small literacy groups or in reader's and writer's workshops. These notes are later transferred to the appropriate loose-leaf page and discussed during the conference.

Stice, Bertrand, and Bertrand (1995) suggest maintaining three types of records that both document and reflect on children's growth: (1) records of children's work, dated and retained to show changes and progress over time; (2) teacher's informal observation records, including informal notes, observation summaries, and checklists, which are later incorporated into more formal records; (3) teacher's formal observations, such as miscue analysis, running records, conference notes, records of literature logs and response journals, and published works.

Students are also responsible for assisting with record keeping. For example, they can include a table of contents that lists everything in the portfolio to make conferencing easier. Of course, journals, logs, and book facts are also a form of record keeping that reveal reading summaries, reactions, and reflections. During the conference, the teacher can record a summary of topics discussed as well as any related activities or strategies that should be undertaken. A copy of this should be provided to the student, and a copy should be kept in the teacher's records. Giving the student this summary will promote student follow-up on the areas discussed.

Teaching to Needs. During the conference, the teacher does more listening than talking. De Fina (1992) emphasizes that this is not a time to criticize or point out failure but is instead an ideal time to identify areas to be improved on, to give suggestions, and to plan strategies. Jenkins (1996) also correctly points out that a portfolio conference is **not** the time to overwhelm students with their deficiencies; "I am ever mindful . . . that it is more important for [the student] to leave the conference with a sense of his accomplishments, and with two or three new learnings (across content and mechanics) which have been prioritized than with a head full of 'What I didn't do right'" (p. 231).

The conference also provides an ideal opportunity for on-the-spot teaching. As the child reads aloud or explains his work, the teacher notes not only what the youngster knows and

Writing Rubric—Grade 3

	4	3	2	1
Mechanics	You extensively use correct punctuation, spelling, and capitalization.	You usually use correct punctuation, spelling, and capitalization.	You sometimes have errors in punctuation, spelling, and capitalization. Your writing is hard to understand.	You rarely use proper punctuation, capitalization, and spelling. Your writing is difficult to comprehend.
Imaginative language	You extensively use specific, vivid language appropriately.	You often use impressive vocabulary words appropriately.	You sometimes use new vocabulary words. You depend on many of the same familiar words (e.g., *good, nice*).	You rarely use interesting vocabulary.
Organization	Your writing is well organized; you develop a clear plan. Your ideas are sequentially developed.	Your organization of ideas is usually clear. You develop your topic in an acceptable manner.	Your organization of ideas is not always clear. You have not really developed your topic.	Your organization is extremely weak. Your writing lacks a plan of organization. You rarely develop your topic.
Purpose	You take responsibility and ownership for your writing. You demonstrate a sense of audience and task.	You usually demonstrate a sense of audience and task. You are aware of your responsibility.	You sometimes do not demonstrate a sense of audience and task. You depend on others too much.	You don't establish a sense of audience.
Focus	Your ideas are clear and focused.	Your ideas and focus are usually clear.	Your writing is sometimes unfocused.	Your ideas are unclear and unfocused.
Craft	You clearly show skillful application of the writing process through attention to the use of engaging leads, interesting endings, relevant and appropriate supportive details, and varied sentence structure.	You usually show application of the writing process. You sometimes need teacher prompting.	You sometimes show application of the writing process. You often need teacher prompting.	You do not demonstrate knowledge and application of the steps of the writing process. You always need teacher prompting.

FIGURE 9–8 Sample rubric developed by a third-grade class and their teacher.

has accomplished but what he doesn't know. Allington (1994) indicates that in spite of all the rhetoric about curricula reform children still do too little reading, and teachers still do too much asking and assigning without enough actual instruction, "Children need fewer brief, shallow literary activities and many more extended opportunities to read and write" (p. 21).

Analyzing Trends and Patterns. Some of the conference outcomes will be the ability to assess what each student can do, analyze progress made, determine together what the student has not incorporated into his or her schema that must be addressed, and establish short-range learning goals. Without analyzing the children's reading and writing patterns, without looking at trends in their literacy behaviors, the LAP conference would become merely an empty exercise. Instead, the conference allows for the verbalization of a **reflective** process: The students reflect on why they included specific materials and self-assess their past performance.

In Figure 9–9, a fifth grader assesses herself as a writer. A teacher would obviously see many errors in this selection, such as word choice *(there/they're, too/to)*. But again, a conference should focus on positives, and while intervention is needed in some areas, mechanical problems should not receive overriding attention and overwhelm a student; an overcorrected, red-penciled essay serves little constructive help. It's noteworthy that this student takes pride in printing legibly, her personality, and her effective speaking ability. She's optimistic about the likelihood of self-improvement, and the number of technical errors should not diminish her accomplishments, undermine an excellent sense of self, and overpower her with too many areas for correction.

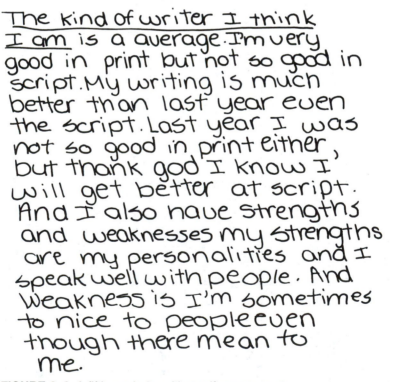

The kind of writer I think I am is a average. I'm very good in print but not so good in script. My writing is much better than last year even the script. Last year I was not so good in print either, but thank god I know I will get better at script. And I also have strengths and weaknesses my strengths are my personalities and I speak well with people. And weakness is I'm sometimes to nice to people even though there mean to me.

FIGURE 9–9 A fifth-grader's writing self-assessment.

Teachers reflect on the effectiveness of their own instructional strategies and note trends from previous conferences. The analysis of patterns indicates the student's strengths, needs, and areas that are developing slowly. Some or any of these can be addressed with demonstrations and modeling during the conference or with a focused minilesson later, or they can be the topic for a group or whole class lesson.

Conference Guidelines. Teacher–student conferences are diagnostic, instructional, and evaluative opportunities. To be effective and efficient in assessing each student's progress and performance, the conference guidelines in Figure 9–10 should be helpful.

Teaching Students How to Have a Conference. For student–teacher conferences to be productive, students must learn how to engage in a conference. Jenkins (1996, pp. 227–228) suggests an approach for teaching children about writing conferences that is useful for all student conferences. She tells her third-grade students that the purpose of a conference is to learn from one another and that students will be expected to lead the conference. The tone of the interaction is most important so that the students feel respected. A dry-run conference is conducted for all students to observe, and the teacher role plays a student who is going to share her portfolio with the teacher. The teacher, acting as the student, thinks aloud during the conference, describes the portfolio contents, explains her entries. After the role play, the class discusses what was observed and what was learned. Conference logistics are then decided including scheduling, roles, materials needed, agenda, and topics.

1. Keep topics limited.
2. Have a scheduled time for each student.
3. Set an agenda that is known to students.
4. Keep notes on meeting (to build an anecdotal history).
5. Review only two to four LAPs a day.
6. Always model good reading and writing behaviors.
7. Be an active and attentive listener.
8. Do direct teaching and minilessons on deficits as they occur during the conference. If several areas need assistance and time is limited, note the weaknesses, and demonstrate those tasks, strategies, and concepts soon after in small groups or individually.
9. Determine if students have implemented ideas, concepts, and information previously taught. (Be introspective and honest; gauge your instructional impact on their learning and make changes, if necessary, in the future.)
10. Be sure that students know what is expected, what rubrics will be used, and by what standards they are judged.
11. Encourage student reflection and self-assessment.
12. Create a collaborative conference climate.

FIGURE 9–10 Conference guidelines.

The format and topics of conferences will vary based on the purpose of the conference and the age and ability of the students. Even if students have had other experiences with conferences in prior grades, it's a good idea early in the school year to discuss how conferences will be conducted. Some teachers have a student sit in on another student's conference (after obtaining the permission of the conferee), and this can be done in tandem. However, if sensitive matters will be discussed, a conference should be confidential. Once students have learned how to have a conference with the teacher, this will of course assist them in conferring with each other as well as during parent conferences.

Teacher–Teacher Conferences

In every classroom it is not merely the students who are learning; the teacher is learning as well. Templeton (1991), Stice et al. (1995), Graves (1983), and Calkins (1983), among others, discuss the important concept of teacher as learner. As teachers learn new concepts, curricula ideas, ways of creatively presenting a direct teaching lesson, or ideas for portfolios and journals, they often share this knowledge with their colleagues. Sometimes this is done informally, over a cup of coffee in the teachers' lounge, or more formally, as in planned faculty meetings and staff development seminars. An ideal method of sharing knowledge is a teacher–teacher mentoring program: A teacher who is comfortable and familiar with student-centered learning, employing extensive use of literature, is paired with a teacher who is unfamiliar with these approaches. Portfolio practices, pedagogical strategies, and conference guidelines can thus be shared, and even an experienced teacher profits from support through dialogue with colleagues.

Teachers also need to share information about students enrolled in special programs. In teacher–teacher conferences, an instructional team learns about the child in the regular classroom setting, and the classroom teacher learns about the child in other school settings, resulting in a collaborative, reflective, and holistic perspective. Since the LAP is filled with representative samples of best works, logs and records, selected projects, and the progression of work from draft to final published writings, it should be shared with the child's future teacher as well. As mentioned in earlier chapters, the final LAP—edited, modified, and supplemented each year—should move on with the child as a permanent record.

Teacher–teacher conferences thus have at least three purposes: (1) Receive additional information, (2) understand the whole child, and (3) adapt instructional strategies to meet student needs.

To make informed decisions, teachers need information in addition to that supplied by the student and their own records and observations. This requires conferencing with others to effectively determine the child's progress and performance, as well as socialization and interactions in other school-related areas for evaluation and final reporting.

Conferences with future teachers provide authentic material, not merely a grade or test score, so that an appropriate and meaningful instructional program can be designed based on review, assessment, and evaluation of actual performance and progress. Reviewing the LAP with the students' current teachers, future teachers gain insight into students' writing abilities, reading accomplishments, and developmental achievements. This allows for appropriate instructional plans and modification of curricula and pedagogical directions. Paris (1991) indicates that the goals of portfolios and the new approaches to literacy assessment not only increase students' engagement in thoughtful reading and writing activities and provide detailed records of literacy development but also empower teachers by providing many instructional opportunities.

GRADING AND EVALUATION

What is to be done about grades and report cards in project-oriented, literature-based classrooms? How does evaluation based on a literacy assessment portfolio fit into a traditional report card structure? How can teachers who are expected to make critical judgments based on children's performance suddenly give a single grade to a youngster who has been showing progress and improvement over time?

In schools where portfolios are used for assessment, grading can be a major dilemma. This is especially so for those teachers who are philosophically committed to whole language, integrated learning, and literature-based literacy programs. Teachers try to earn children's trust and encourage them to take risks, emphasize concepts and progress, write thoughtful and encouraging comments on children's work, and then face the dilemma of having to give a single grade that cannot epitomize all work and effort. How proud and motivated will a youngster feel when the teacher writes at the end of a youngster's story, "I love puppies and kittens also. How lucky you are to have one of each," and then receives a grade of "C"?

In traditional classrooms, it is not as difficult to assign letter or numerical grades. Although difficult with primary graders, one can total up test scores from weekly exams, get an average, and assign a number or translate that number into a letter grade for intermediate students. Report cards and reporting, however, have become highly controversial topics in many schools. School boards, teachers, curricula specialists, and administrators argue the merits of grades and report cards. Some parents, they contend, especially those with children in intermediate and middle school grades, appear to want the traditional report card. Some educators, although philosophically allied to alternative pedagogy and authentic assessment, fear that the innovations, including portfolio use, will be stymied if rigor and standards do not appear to apply. Sometimes, these pioneers succumb to more traditional reporting methods. Others, like Clay (1993), Goodman (1986), and Graves (1983), hold to their philosophy and beliefs and refer to grades as nonproductive or counterproductive. They feel that students should be evaluated by the progress they make and insist that motivation, self-evaluation, comparing students with themselves and not with others, and collaboration are important areas for assessment. Therefore, they endorse the use of narrative descriptions, not single letter grades.

Still other educators believe the final report can reflect the newer pedagogy and include rigor and specificity. They implement specific criteria for assessment strategies that incorporate specially designed unit checklists (Tompkins & Hoskisson, 1995, p. 71), rubrics, and summary reports, or they hire trained evaluators to assess student LAPs in intermediate and middle schools (as in South Brunswick, NJ).

A review of reporting practices shows that currently there are three basic types of report cards: Letter grade reporting, narrative reporting, and combined reporting.

Letter Grade Reporting

A, B, C, D, and F correspond roughly to A = 90 to 100, B = 80 to 90, C = 70 to 80, D = 60 to 70, and F = failure, 59 or below. Letter grades are usually but not exclusively designed for use in intermediate and middle grades. Many school systems agree that these designations are inappropriate for younger children, and therefore other descriptors are used for the primary grades such as: E = excellent, S = satisfactory, U = unsatisfactory, and N = needs improvement.

Narrative Reporting

Next to each subject area in the report card (reading, social studies, writing, math), space is allotted for a narrative discussion indicating how well or poorly the youngster is doing. For example:

> READING: Eric has shown much improvement since the last reporting session. He reads with fluency and insight, and his inferential comprehension is now excellent. This is reflected in Erik's story grammars, literacy logs, and observations of him during regular reading time. We are still working on expanding his vocabulary, but if Erik continues reading regularly at home for recreation and personal pleasure as well as during sustained silent reading time, we anticipate growth in his vocabulary as well.

Progress, strengths, and weaknesses are reviewed and described in each of the other curricular areas as well (see Figure 9–5 A and B for examples of narrative reports used in first and second grade.)

Combined Conference and Report Card or Conference and LAP

With the combined conference and report card or conference and LAP method, the parent, child, and teacher discuss the child's progress, assess the work the youngster has selected for portfolio inclusion as well as tests, anecdotal records, and informal reading inventories. A written report summarizes the progress made and areas that still require strengthening.

Traditional versus Authentic Reporting

For classrooms that use thematic literacy programs, it is often hard for the teacher to assign a simple letter grade and even harder, in those few elementary schools where it is required, to assign a numerical grade. Letter and number grades were once thought to be excellent objective indicators of a youngster's work. Now, however, we encourage subjective evaluation, as reflected in the professional teacher's insights about each child's accomplishments. We want to see the rough drafts and the stages of edited works, not merely the final products. We want to see how the student works with peers and to record or establish growth over time.

The challenge for our schools is to use a final report format that reflects student achievements and aspirations, parental concerns, and teachers' critical judgment. It is difficult for a year's work, documented in a portfolio of accomplishments, to be distilled into a single report, letter, or grade. Each school district must adopt a reporting system that reflects its own educational directions and philosophy. Many models are available, and Azwell and Schmar's text (1995) can be consulted for samples. The South Brunswick, New Jersey, schools, for example, have worked diligently with their own faculty, outside consultants (Princeton University and the Educational

Testing Service) to develop an appropriate reporting format that harmonizes with their portfolio approach to evaluation and learning. They have progress assessment for grades kindergarten through 2 and a best works assessment for grades 3 through 12. Additionally, there is a special performance-based assessment for grade 6, which uses trained outside assessors as well as the classroom teacher to evaluate student work to ensure interrater reliability.

Other school districts use rubrics as a reliability guide for reporting. A cluster holistic method is also used in some areas to assess final LAPs according to the "three stacks approach": The teacher (or evaluator) determines if the LAP goes to stack 1, which contains excellent portfolios; stack 2, which holds average portfolios; or stack 3, for poor or weak portfolios. Grades are then assigned according to placement. A factor in this method is what Kapinus (1993) calls a balance of texts, tasks, and contexts. This means taking into account the array of reading materials encountered, tasks that have been attended to, journals, logs, books, summaries, and discussions of students' understanding of concepts and ideas, problem-solving, decision-making, and critical thinking abilities.

This struggle with reporting has not yet resulted in consensus. It is a gray area that is quite controversial and is still emerging, since traditional reporting and new pedagogy and assessment practices are often not congruent. According to Azwell (1995),

> Only recently have our assessment and evaluation systems begun to change to reflect our new understanding of the learning continuum and the implementation of a broader range of instructional strategies. We now seek information about a student's learning in an ongoing, multifaceted approach that includes observations of the processes and product, self-evaluations, as well as more traditional tests. (p. 7)

Azwell and Schmar (1995) acknowledge that there are more questions about report cards than answers, but by raising significant concerns, educators can begin to reflect on their own practices and seek other models for guidance.

Dissension about reporting practices should be avoided, and the school district must develop policies that recognize that the entire community has a stake in the outcome of learning. The joint IRA/NCTE task force on assessment (1994) points out that reporting formats between school and home must result in parents' being able to talk productively about their children's reading and writing progress. The task force believes that the involvement of parents is essential in developing new reporting procedures. If parents and administrators are not comfortable with final reporting strategies, all the work done with dynamic literacy programs and portfolio assessment may be futile. Therefore, compromises may have to be made, not with project-oriented, thematic learning principles, but with the structure, purpose, and format of final reports.

CONCLUSIONS

Many questions regarding portfolio assessment remain unanswered. Some schools, like those in Lawrence, New York, use portfolios instead of final exams. Many hold conferences in conjunction with portfolios, and others hold conferences along with report cards. The New Brunswick, New Jersey, schools have an exit portfolio for graduation, with outside judges assisting in the assessment. Bennington College now requires their students to create a portfolio of all their school activities and accomplishments as a graduation requirement.

We are currently investigating reporting procedures and are especially interested in newer report card designs from schools that have implemented portfolio assessment. Our review of report card practices on Long Island shows many schools have begun to use portfolios, but usually these portfolios are not graded, and the portfolios are not specifically reflected on report card evaluations. Changes in pedagogical and assessment practices appear to precede changes in reporting. Many administrators we surveyed candidly stated that they are wrestling with various issues: How should portfolios be assessed? Should standardized formats be used for all teachers and grades? Should primary, intermediate, and middle schools have different standards? Should outside assessors be involved? What is the role of report cards? These and other questions are being addressed in many schools, and various teacher committees have been established to discuss and design new report cards and reporting strategies. Several administrators stated that parents were more satisfied with traditional report cards than were teachers and administrators.

The primary purpose of assessment, grading, and reporting is to provide helpful and reliable information about how children are learning. The LAP is an excellent means to this end and should not be undermined by a reporting system that demeans the process of rich and varied data collection.

REFERENCES

Allington, R. (1994, September). The schools we have. The schools we need. *The Reading Teacher, 48,* 14–27.

Azwell, T. (1995). Messages about learning. In T. Azwell & E. Schmar, *Report card on report cards.* Portsmouth, NH: Heinemann.

Azwell, T., & Schmar, E. (1995). *Report card on report cards.* Portsmouth, NH: Heinemann.

Bratcher, S. (1994). *Evaluating children's writing: A handbook of communication choices for classroom teachers.* New York: St. Martin's Press.

Calkins, L. (1983). *Lessons from a child: On the teaching and learning of writing.* Portsmouth, NH: Heinemann.

Clay, M. (1993). *An observation survey of early literacy achievement.* Portsmouth, NH: Heinemann.

Collins, C. (1994, November 24). The teacher conference: A team effort. *The New York Times,* p. C9.

De Fina, A. (1992). *Portfolio assessment: Getting started.* New York: Scholastic.

Finders, M., & Lewis, C. (1994, May). Why some parents don't come to school. *Educational Leadership, 51,* 8.

France, M., & Hager, J. M. (1993, April). Recruit, respect, respond: A model for working with low-income families and their preschoolers. *The Reading Teacher, 47* (7), 568–572.

Goodman, K. (1986). *What's whole in whole language?* Portsmouth, NH: Heinemann.

Graves, D. (1983). *Writing: Teachers and children at work.* Portsmouth, NH: Heinemann.

Hornsby, D., Sukarna, D., & Parry, J. (1986). *Read on: A conference approach to reading.* Portsmouth, NH: Heinemann.

International Reading Association/National Council of Teachers of English Joint Task Force on Assessment. (1994). *Standards for the assessment of reading and writing.* Newark, DE: International Reading Association.

Jenkins, C. B. (1996). *Inside the writing portfolio.* Portsmouth, NH: Heinemann.

Kapinus, B. (1993, September). Reading assessment: The balancing act. *The Reading Teacher, 47,* 62–64.

Morrow, L. M., & Paratore, J. (1993, November). Family literacy: Perspective and practices. *The Reading Teacher, 47,* 194–200.

Olson, L. (1990, April). Parents as partners: Redefining the social contract between families and schools. *Education Week,* p. 18.

Pappas, C. C., Kiefer, B. K., & Levstik, L. S. (1990). *An integrated language arts perspective in the elementary school: Theory into action.* New York: Longman.

Paris, S. G. (1991, May). Portfolio assessment for young readers. *The Reading Teacher, 44,* 9.

Ramsaur, M. C. (1992, August/September). From teacher to parent to child. *Teaching K–8,* pp. 78–80.

Rhodes, L. K., & Shanklin, N. (1993). *Windows into literacy: Assessing learners K–8.* Portsmouth, NH: Heinemann.

Stice, C. F., Bertrand, J., & Bertrand, N. (1995). *Integrating reading and the other language arts: Foundations of a whole language curriculum.* Belmont, CA: Wadsworth.

Templeton, S. (1991). *Teaching the integrated language arts.* Dallas, TX: Houghton Mifflin.

Tompkins, G., & Hoskisson, K. (1995). *Language arts: Content and teaching strategies.* Saddle River, NJ: Merrill/Prentice Hall.

Wiggins, G. P. (1989, April). Teaching to the authentic test. *Educational Leadership,* pp. 41–47.

Wiggins, G. P. (1993). *Assessing student performance: Exploring the purpose and limit of testing.* San Francisco: Jossey-Bass.

Winograd, P. (1994, February). Developing alternative assessments: Six problems worth solving. *The Reading Teacher, 47,* 420–423.

Implementing Literacy Portfolios

Implementing Authentic Literacy Assessment in the Classroom, School, and School District

by
Dr. Giselle Martin-Kniep
Executive Director, Learner Centered Initiative, Ltd.
Sea Cliff, New York

KEY WORDS AND CONCEPTS

Learner outcomes	Scoring criteria
Outcome indicators	Analytic rubrics
Learning opportunities	Holistic rubrics
Assessment tasks	Anchor papers
High- and low-stake assessment	Exemplars

The last ten years have seen many changes in the questions that researchers, educators, and policy makers are asking about testing and assessment. Many of these questions relate to the implementation of authentic literacy assessments at the classroom, school, and school district levels. Some of these questions concern the design and use of these assessments, and other important questions relate to the implementation and use of these assessments independently or as a supplement to other forms of testing.

This chapter addresses these and other questions related to the implementation of authentic literacy assessment at the classroom level.

Much of the material in this chapter is based on my work with more than 150 teachers from 75 school districts in New York State. These teachers are participants in two regional multiyear projects related to the design and implementation of alternative forms of assessment in their schools. The overall goals of this project are to (1) increase teachers' capacity to design and use classroom-based alternative student assessments; (2) generate a collection of alternative assessment measures of literacy and communication for kindergarten through twelfth grade; and (3) identify exemplary student work related to literacy and communication for different grade levels. As part of this project, teachers work in teams, design, and validate alternative forms of student assessment, use action research as a means to address questions related to their teaching and assessment practices, and develop strategies for facilitating the work of other teachers in their schools related to assessment.

DESIGN AND IMPLEMENTATION AT THE CLASSROOM LEVEL

What Does the Process of Design Entail?

Designing authentic literacy assessments involves much more than coming up with a project or performance, assembling a collection of student work, or putting together a rubric. Teachers who use authentic literacy assessments recognize that the implementation of authentic tasks and processes requires a significant investment of time and that it is difficult to justify this investment in light of an expanding curriculum and increased student demands. In fact, negotiating assessment in the classroom means pursuing a new kind of partnership between teachers and students and a redefinition of the teachers' role centered on a philosophical stance consistent with learner-centered pedagogy. Unless teachers can rethink their entire curriculum goals along with their assessment purposes and understand how authentic assessment is a valuable tool, they will have a difficult time rationalizing their use of authentic assessment in the classroom.

Teachers' design and implementation of authentic literacy assessments cannot be separated from their beliefs and knowledge base concerning how literacy should be taught and what theoretical models are subscribed to. This is supported by research conducted by Lamme and Hysmith (1991), who found that teachers who embrace a whole language philosophy and provide students with authentic learning experiences had significantly fewer problems using portfolios in their classroom than other teachers.

Research on the questions and concerns expressed by teachers reveals that teachers undergo a distinctive developmental process in their implementation of authentic literacy assessments that is characterized by significant changes in their thinking and practices related to curriculum, instruction, and assessment (Martin-Kniep, 1995). Even teachers who have extensive teaching and assessment experience have many significant questions about tests, assessments, and grades when they begin to seriously explore the use of authentic assessment. Predominant among these are questions related to ways of implementing different forms of assessment and learning how to reconcile them with conventional tests and grades. As teachers become more proficient and comfortable with the use of authentic assessments, their questions become increasingly specific and profound, and they begin to explicitly link assessment implementation with curriculum and instructional issues.

Teachers' Learning about Assessment as a Developmental Process

Portfolios are particularly appealing to teachers who are interested in assessing literacy and communication, primarily because they offer the possibility of documenting students' progress and effort as communicators and not just their achievement. However, there are marked differences in teachers' abilities to effectively design and use portfolios. According to Stowell and Tierney (1994), teachers' use of classroom portfolios can be understood in terms of two different continuums. One continuum may be termed *student-centered*, or *inside-out*, versus *teacher-directed*, or *outside-in;* the other might be termed *bottom-up* versus *top-down*. The first continuum represents the range of differences that may exist in terms of the basic purposes of the portfolio, its management, and perceived outcomes. The second continuum represents the range of differences that may exist in how portfolios are mandated, derived, analyzed, and used. When initially exposed to portfolios, teachers tend to like the idea of student-centered and bottom-up portfolios. More often than not, however, their first attempts at designing and implementing these assessments result in teacher-directed and top-down portfolios. As teachers become increasingly familiar with some of the assumptions underlying the use of authentic assessment, and develop more practice in terms of assisting students in the analysis and reflection of their learning, their portfolio designs become more student-centered, or inside-out. Indeed, it is impossible to fully implement authentic literacy assessments without at the same time attending to the curriculum and instructional conditions that will accompany such assessments.

Assessment Design Framework

My framework for the design of authentic assessments includes five key elements: outcomes, outcome indicators, learning opportunities, assessment tasks, and scoring criteria and rubrics. This design framework (see Figure 10–1) begins with an articulation of learner outcomes that guide the teacher's thinking in terms of defining appropriate curriculum and assessments. The use of learner outcomes as the basis for curriculum and assessment design has been endorsed by many different state-wide and national curriculum and assessment efforts. As described later, learning outcomes are the basis for the identification of specific learning opportunities and of assessment tasks and processes that can elicit students' achievement and performance. The design of tasks leads to the identification of performance criteria and, in some cases, the use of scoring rubrics, which help students understand the teacher's expectations and monitor their own performance.

The design process itself is recursive rather than linear, with teachers often moving back and forth from one component to another. It is not uncommon, for example, to use indicators as the basis for the development of standards and rubrics and then to redefine the learn-

Outcomes: What do I want students to know and be able to do?

Indicators: What will that look like in my classroom?

Learning Opportunities: What do I need to teach, or have them experience, so they will attain the outcomes?

Assessment: What do I need to collect or administer to prove that students have grown toward and/or achieved desired outcomes?

Standards/Rubrics: How will I communicate what *mastery* or *accomplishment* means?

FIGURE 10–1 Assessment design framework.

ing opportunities to ensure that the student has enough background information and skills to succeed in the assessment.

Learner Outcomes

Learner outcomes are statements that describe what students are able to do, know, or value as a result of their schooling. These statements provide teachers with a framework from which to make informed decisions about how to best use available curriculum resources. They also shift teachers' attention from what they need to teach to what students need to learn; and finally, they reorient teachers and schools to a curriculum that is present- and future-informed rather than one that replicates past practices.

Outcomes are derived from educational goals, which are representations of shared cultural and societal values related to the purpose of education and schools. Sample goal statements include "Students will be critical thinkers" and "Students will be effective communicators." Goal statements respond to the question, "What will students be educated as or for?" Outcomes can be generated for a specific grade level (seventh-grade students will write a business letter); for a program (students in this class will explore and effectively use the narrative and expository genres); or for the end of schooling (on completion of twelfth grade, students will know how to effectively write, listen, and speak for social interaction).

To generate outcome statements, teachers often find it useful to imagine their best students and then describe their learning at the end of the year. Good outcome statements (1) describe what students ought to know and are able to do; (2) are stated in result-focused, observable, measurable, or inferable terms; (3) are developmental; (4) reflect broad goals; (5) are comprehensive and broad enough to be interdisciplinary; (6) are flexible in terms of how students attain them; and (7) are specific enough to form the basis for outcome indicators and performance standards. Based on my experience with teachers in many school districts, some of the most typical outcomes related to literacy have included the following:

1. Students will communicate in writing using a variety of genres to meet different purposes and for different audiences.

2. Students will communicate orally using a variety of genres to meet different purposes and for different audiences.

3. Students will read and listen attentively for information and understanding by anticipating, summarizing, interpreting, analyzing, and evaluating contextual information including various literary types, other written material, and media.

4. Students will appreciate the relationship between people's language and their culture.

5. Students will explain how their writing changes in order to take into account the differences among audiences.

6. Students will use writing as a strategy for personal learning and clarification of thinking.

Outcome Indicators

Because literacy outcomes are often broad and apply to many subject areas and disciplines, they are not immediately useful in terms of helping teachers decide what or how to teach and assess. Therefore, individual teachers need to operationalize outcomes into more specific outcome indicators. **Outcome indicators,** or **manifestations,** are statements describing the specific knowledge, characteristics, and performances that are likely to demonstrate students' attainment of learner outcomes for a specific grade level and, in some cases, subject. In some settings, these statements are also known as content standards. Obviously, these indicators translate the broad outcomes into specific goals that can more readily be operationalized. The following is an example of an outcome and its respective indicators developed by a sixth-grade teacher:

Outcome: Students will write clearly for a variety of purposes and audiences.

Indicators:

1. Students will write clear, well-developed, multiparagraphed compositions during the course of the school year.
2. Students will discuss, in writing, a given piece of literature with specific reference to plot, character, setting, theme, mood, and/or author's purpose.
3. Students will select various pieces of work and comment on them with regard to process, quality, end result, and/or changes that may be made.

Generating outcomes is not nearly as difficult as using them to develop curriculum and assessment tasks. In fact, in a room full of parents, teachers, and administrative staff who are identifying learner outcomes, all groups often generate similar, if not the same, outcomes (Kniep & Martin-Kniep, 1995). Current curricular and pedagogical strategies vary quite widely, however, and may not be consistent with the use of broad outcomes. Too often, they appear to favor the discrete teaching of isolated skills and the delivery of self-contained activities, not often intrinsically linked to one another.

A growing trend in literacy instruction has been the development of integrated, interdisciplinary learning units that focus on enhancing literacy skills, often with a focus on the use of quality literature and trade books instead of conventional subject area textbooks. But growing curricular demands, along with the necessity to address the needs of very different kinds of learners, make it difficult for teachers to design integrated curriculum units that allow for an in-depth exploration of topics via a limited but significant number of learning and assessment opportunities. Finally, inertia is not easy to fight. It is a lot more convenient for teachers to reuse existing lesson plans, teachers' guides, and packaged instructional systems than to develop a new, year-long curriculum based on student outcomes and then ponder the extent to which daily and weekly activities are likely to result in their attainment. Fortunately, literacy instruction is undergoing significant changes, and more and more teachers are adapting their instructional strategies in reading and writing and becoming increasingly comfortable with thematic, integrated curricular units that lend themselves to a variety of new teaching and assessment opportunities.

Learning and Assessment Opportunities

Learning opportunities are generated in the process of articulating the scope and sequence of the curricular and instructional experiences that are necessary for students to attain desired learning outcomes. Essentially, the teacher asks, "What kinds of experiences and learning opportunities must I provide so that my students can attain the outcomes I want from them?" Learning opportunities should be stated in sufficiently general terms so that they allow for the emergence of teachable moments and avoid becoming redundant to lesson plans. At the same time, they should be specific enough so that teachers can use them as a way to lay out the scope and sequence of their curriculum. Learning opportunities ought to be informed by district- and state-mandated curriculum guidelines as well as current research on effective literacy instruction. There are wide variations in teachers' ability to implement their own curricula in reading and writing. In many districts, lessons must reflect the specific district philosophy and choice of instructional systems as well as practical concerns about the availability of instructional resources.

Following are two examples of learning opportunities associated with the outcome "Students will interact with different kinds of reading material with understanding":

1. The teacher will provide students with varied kinds of literature throughout the school year, including autobiographies, fiction, poetry, fantasy, and nonfiction.
2. The teacher will provide guided and independent opportunities for students to read samples of literature and analyze, in writing, plot structure, methods of characterization, importance of setting, creation of mood, use of theme, and author's purpose.

The adequate use of performance- and portfolio-based assessment in authentic learning situations requires that teachers provide students with multiple and ongoing learning opportunities related to literacy so that students can (1) experience the inherent connections between reading, writing, listening and speaking; (2) read and write in realistic contexts and for diverse purposes and audiences; (3) experience and value the process of writing, not only for the sake of writing more and better, but as a means to clarify their own thinking; and (4) relate their backgrounds and experiences to the material presented. In short, authentic learning opportunities demand sustained and in-depth work on the part of teachers and students. Such opportunities are often missing when teachers rely on decontextualized, skills-based programs, which have been the basis of traditional reading programs. These older programs tend to mask the relationship between prior knowledge and reading comprehension by using short passages on many different topics; rely on literal comprehension test items; rarely go beyond finding the main idea of a paragraph or passage; underemphasize the importance and process of revision in the writing process; and use tests that fragment reading and writing into isolated skills. Traditional forms of multiple-choice testing reinforce the notion that reading and writing ability are based on attaining mechanical subskills.

Depending on the extent to which the teacher already uses a learner-centered, authentic curriculum, teachers will have to invest more or less time designing authentic assessment tasks and learning opportunities. If teachers rely primarily on teacher-centered pedagogical approaches or use fragmented curricular approaches that emphasize rote learning of isolated skills, they will have to work harder at designing alternative curriculum and assessment tasks and at transforming the nature of teacher–student interactions. In either case, teachers should aim at designing a limited number of assessment tasks per year and devote at least two if not three years to the design and implementation of student portfolios for specific outcomes, rather than assume that they can generate comprehensive portfolios or tasks for every curriculum unit.

More important than defining learning and assessment opportunities is intrinsically linking tasks to specific outcomes. Ideally, a teacher should create a matrix that maps the entire curricula and accompanying assessments and determine whether or not the teacher has sufficiently addressed and assessed desired learning outcomes. This map should reflect district, state, and national mandates, as well as current research on effective literacy programs.

AUTHENTIC ASSESSMENT STRATEGIES AND TASKS

Having identified learning opportunities, teachers can proceed with the determination of the kind of curriculum-embedded evidence that could be used to document students' progress and achievement of the learner outcomes or of the kinds of tasks or events that would produce such evidence. At this point teachers have to generate short- and long-term goals for their assessment design. This is important because the development of **authentic assessment tasks** and products takes a significant amount of time, not just to design but also to refine them based on a systematic review of students' work and performance. Teachers need to use their assessments with at least two different groups of students to sufficiently refine the language within the task, the scoring criteria, the rubric, and even the task- or portfolio-related guidelines.

Matching Teachers' Purposes with Assessments

In general, assessment can be used for the following:

1. To determine what students know, are able to do, and value, the teacher can use
   a. Diagnostic assessment to determine knowledge/skills before (baseline) or during instruction.
   b. Formative assessment for instructional or curricular decisions regarding students' needs; to communicate expectations, achievements, and progress to students, parents, and communities; and to help all students learn;v and to intervene to prevent students from failing.
   c. Summative evaluation to determine achievement and produce grades.
2. Help teachers improve on their instructional practice.
3. Determine curriculum and/or program effectiveness.
4. Develop means by which schools, districts, communities, and the state can hold themselves accountable for focusing on the needs of learners.

Teachers need to ascertain the specific purposes for which their assessments will be used. At the classroom level, it is important that teachers use assessments primarily to meet the first two purposes, to monitor students' learning and improve on their own professional practice. One of the problems teachers face in many districts is that they often feel the need or are pressured to orient their curriculum and teaching toward tests that have been designed for program evaluation and/or to meet district and state accountability mandates through the use of standardized, state-wide testing programs. This is exacerbated by the fact that many states are incorporating the use of standardized, performance-based assessment into mandated testing programs. Students will behave differently when assessment results in relatively minor, safe consequences in **low-stakes assessment** (reviewing students' portfolio goals to help them set more attainable learning goals) as opposed to **high-stakes extra assessment** (using the end-of-year test or portfolio as the primary basis for the students' grade), which results in significant consequences.

Finding the appropriate balance between the use of assessments and tests to meet a variety of purposes is not easy. In the process of continued curriculum, instruction, and assessment refinements, it is important for teachers to seek a parsimonious system; that is, one in which a few assessment tasks are required to assess a large number of outcomes. For example, teachers should use portfolios to showcase students' literacy abilities and their application across the curriculum.

Balancing Different Forms of Testing and Assessment

Teachers and administrative staff frequently question what is the appropriate balance between authentic assessments and traditional tests. The answer is contingent on many factors such as the desired student outcomes for a particular course and grade level as well as the necessity for teachers to use traditional assessment mandated by their district or state. Students with special needs—students referred for interventional teaching, English as a second language (ESL) programs or special education—often are required to take batteries of tests to identify areas of weakness or to qualify for specific instructional support, because funded programs and those mandated by the government always specify the kinds of assessments to be used. However, to the extent that we want students to apply and process their acquired knowledge and skills, we should use authentic and performance-based assessments. Not all outcomes and indicators call for the use of authentic assessment. Sometimes, a teacher needs a quick assessment of students' knowledge and recall; on other occasions, a teacher may simply want to keep students focused and accountable for doing specific kinds of tasks. In both of these cases, it might be more efficient to use traditional forms of testing and assessment. In general, it is desirable to use a variety of assessment tasks and processes to elicit many different outcomes and to address different assessment purposes. Some of these tasks and processes may be authentic, whereas in some cases, the use of conventional tests might be advisable. In yet other cases, assessment data may be easily obtained from the learning opportunities themselves. For example, one could videotape a debate in which students discuss the merits and shortcomings of specific historical figures. The debate could be used as both an opportunity for students to discuss different points of view and as a means to assess outcomes such as students' ability to communicate ideas orally or ability to use different research sources to read, analyze, and present historical issues or events.

Rather than thinking in terms of which kind of assessment is needed, teachers should concentrate on matching specific learning outcomes and indicators with appropriate assessment tasks and measures. They should also realize that different students prefer different kinds of assessment modalities and should provide all students with at least some opportunities to make learning evident by using their preferred learning modality.

Some of the questions that teachers should ask themselves as they consider the use of different assessments include the following: (1) Does the proposed assessment support the learning process for students and teachers? (2) Is the assessment generally formative (provides feedback during the learning process) or summative (provides a single judgment at the end)? (3) Will the assessment provide students with meaningful learning opportunities?

Performance Standards, Scoring Criteria, Exemplars, and Rubrics

Explicit standards and **scoring criteria** provide teachers and students with powerful images and pictures of what is deemed to be of high quality. This is important because often we assign work without really knowing what it is that students will produce; we do this because we consider the assignment important, because students seem to like doing it, or because we have assigned the work in the past. In these cases, teachers tend to discover excellence as they examine and grade the work of those students that produce exemplary work. The timing of this discovery does not allow a teacher to use newly acquired clarity in terms of examples of good work to help other students. Many students need to be guided toward producing work of good quality, because the students are unfamiliar with what is expected of them, the assignments are vague or unclear, or they have not received specific information about criteria guiding the assignment. When teachers accompany their assignments with clear and descriptive performance criteria, and provide rubrics and models, they convey their expectations in ways that students can understand and use. This makes it possible for students to identify the attributes of exemplary work, helps them monitor their own performance and achievement, and helps them refine and improve their work or performance.

Beyond their usefulness in the classroom, clear standards and criteria allow others (parents, supervisors) to understand what the teacher values and is looking for in students' work or performance, and they can help justify and validate grades. The use of exemplars, scoring criteria, and rubrics can result in an assessment system in which a teacher's judgment regarding grades can become more reliable and defensible.

The process of designing performance standards is recursive, or cyclical. Teachers begin this process by describing the attributes of a product or process that is considered exemplary. For example, in defining the attributes of an excellent oral presentation, teachers may generate criteria such as the following:

> The material presented was well researched, accurate, and relevant. The presentation was well organized and supported by visuals that clarified the most important points. The presentation was thought provoking and interactive. The presenter was assertive, clear, and understandable. The student provided both an introduction and a conclusion to the presentation.

These criteria can be further refined by translating them into language that is student-generated, or at least, is clearly understood by students. The criteria can also serve as the foundation for the development of a **scoring rubric,** which is a scale that differentiates levels of student performance on a task or process.

Scoring rubrics are very useful in assessment because they (1) convey teachers' expectations for students' work and achievement in ways that students can understand and use; (2) help teachers clarify what they want from students; (3) make it possible for students to identify the attributes of exemplary work; (4) help students monitor their own performance and achievement; (5) serve as scaffolding devices by assisting students in moving from one performance level to another; (6) allow other stakeholders—parents, resource staff, and supervisors—to understand teachers' criteria for judging students' work; (7) can help justify and validate grades; and (8) can lead to an overall increase in the quality of students' work. Sharing rubrics with students and their families makes the evaluation system public knowledge and clearly demonstrates the kind of criteria students will be judged by. Too often, grading has been the result of highly subjective evaluations by teachers who employ very different or unknown standards.

Two of the most commonly used kinds of scoring rubrics are holistic and analytic rubrics. **Holistic rubrics** assign a single score to a student's product with regard to overall performance, are defined on a rather narrow scale, rely on multiple descriptors, and are limited in value in terms of providing precise diagnostic information. However, they are efficient for sorting student work into comparative and discrete levels of achievement along a continuum from poor to excellent.

An **analytic rubric** describes and scores each of the task attributes separately, uses limited descriptors for each attribute, uses a scale that can be both narrow and broad, and allows for specific diagnostic feedback. Analytic rubrics translate well into providing personalized instruction and are useful for diagnostic purposes, whereas holistic rubrics lend themselves to efficiently grading and making comparisons between different levels of achievement.

Figure 10–2 is a writing rubric used by a second-grade teacher and her students. It is noteworthy that this rubric was created by both the teacher and her students, allowing them to share an understanding of the important traits in a piece of writing as well as the characteristics that would be used to grade the writing. Analytic rubrics are good starting points, as they allow for a clear and separate articulation of each scoring dimension. Such articulation provides students with very specific feedback on the strengths and weaknesses of products and processes. One must be careful not to be too formulaic and narrow when constructing rubrics; a successful piece of writing is more than the sum of its parts. As teachers and students become more comfortable with using rubrics and more familiar with the products and processes expected, they can rely more on holistic rubrics, which, by design, shorten the time required for scoring.

Rubrics can be created for many purposes: to assess processes (cooperative learning, interviewing strategies); products (portfolios, research papers, exhibits, artistic products); and performances (oral presentations, panel discussions). Without multiple samples of students' work, it is difficult to generate precise scoring rubrics or even to determine precisely how many levels of performance should be described. Thus, teachers should assume that initial rubrics are subject to significant revision. After using a rubric for the first time, teachers can refine it by stacking students' work into piles that share similar characteristics. By analyzing and describing how the stacks differ from one another, teachers can enhance the description of the rubric levels and help students use them to monitor their work as well as to provide more specific instruction based on students' needs.

When teachers begin to use rubrics, they may encounter a variety of problems. Rubrics can be anxiety producing for students when used too early and without student participation

Name: _____

Title: _____

Writer's Workshop Criteria

(face 4)	(face 3)	(face 2)	(face 1)
My story . . .	My story . . .	My story . . .	My story . . .
idea is very exciting and interesting to the reader.	idea is very good.	idea is OK.	idea is boring to the reader.
has lots of added details.	has some added details but needs more.	has few added details.	has no added details.
makes sense. My reader won't have any questions.	makes sense. My reader may have few questions.	makes little sense. My reader will have some questions.	doesn't make sense. My reader will have many questions.
creates a crystal-clear picture for my reader.	creates a clear picture for the reader.	creates a little bit of a picture for the reader.	doesn't give the reader any pictures.
will make my reader feel happy, sad, surprised, . . .	will give my reader some feelings.	will give my reader little feelings.	doesn't give the reader any feelings.
has a great beginning and ending.	has a good beginning and ending.	Has a beginning or ending that's OK.	doesn't have a beginning and/or an ending.
has many interesting words.	has some interesting words.	has few interesting words.	has many dull words.
has almost no proofreading mistakes.	has few proofreading mistakes.	has some proofreading mistakes.	has lots of proofreading mistakes.
has many neat and detailed illustrations.	has some neat and detailed illustrations.	has few neat and detailed illustrations.	has sloppy illustrations.

FIGURE 10–2 A writing rubric for second graders. (Courtesy of Lorraine Perrego, Hudson Valley Development Project.)

in their creation. If the rubrics are formulaic and narrowly defined, they can also dilute the characteristics of authentic tasks or be constraining and inhibit students' imagination and creativity. This tends to happen when teachers define work or performance in terms of quantitative descriptors, which may inhibit the range of performance. The following illustration is typical of a narrowly construed descriptor based on quantity rather than quality.

> The report should be typed in no less than twelve and no more than fifteen pages. It should include the use of at least three books, only one of which can be a general reference book like an encyclopedia.

This description is problematic for several reasons: It describes the form of the report and some of its components but fails to address the content and qualities that would make this report a good one, and there is no rational justification for a paper's length. Rubrics should indicate the range and types of sources to be considered in writing a substantial report. Many students want specific guidelines about the mechanical concerns in their work, and these concerns should be discussed and presented in the context of examining authentic products and performances produced outside of school.

When unaccompanied by models, rubrics may not fully convey what we want students to do. On the other hand, when teachers systematically use rubrics with accompanying exemplars and **anchor papers** (i.e., examples of performance for the intermediate levels of a rubric or scale) to provide students with visual representations of quality work, they find an overall increase in students' performance.

Exemplars are models that teachers and students can use to depict desired attributes of quality in products and performances. These models embody standards and scoring criteria that provide teachers and students with powerful images and pictures of what is considered to be of high quality. Exemplars can guide students' thinking, planning, development, and performance.

Teachers need to use multiple and different exemplars to provide students with an opportunity to internalize attributes of quality, rather than perceive the work to be done as driven by a formula. Using one or two exemplars often leads to students' treating the exemplars as recipes and copying them. Therefore, teachers should show students at least three different exemplars that depict very different approaches to producing quality work. One kind are those produced by students in the teacher's class in the current or in prior years or by students in the same grade level but in other classrooms. Another kind are exemplars from students in subsequent grades that represent a higher educational level. Finally, teachers can also use writing produced by people outside schools engaged with authentic experiences (e.g., professional published work, commercial brochures, or political debates).

Teachers need to determine whether an exemplar truly models an excellent product and is the result of good strategies. Teachers and students can compare what they consider exemplary with writing produced by other students or by professional writers using publicly defined standards. For example, a fourth-grade teacher who wants students to create a travel brochure to document learning about different regions could show students exemplary brochures done by her students in prior years and travel brochures obtained from travel agencies or Chambers of Commerce.

In some cases, the attributes of exemplary quality can be identified by examining work that does not meet exemplary status. This could be done by asking students questions such as, "How could we make this picture book better so that it would be truly excellent?" or "What would have made this presentation even better?" Even work that is not excellent can be used to depict the attainment of one outcome and not another.

Teachers today are encouraged to use a wide array of good children's literature—picture books, fiction and nonfiction trade books, newspapers, and magazines—to provide students with samples of materials found to be of high quality. Such works can be analyzed by students to see effective component features (i.e., a high-interest headline or story lead) that might be incorporated into their own work.

A problem using and interpreting exemplars relates to determining the extent to which they were produced independently by the student or whether they were supported by the teacher or by others. Producing an exemplary product within prespecified time constraints is not the same as doing it with help or with unlimited time. It is important for teachers to annotate exemplars by describing the contextual and support-related factors that led to their creation. This situation often prevails if a teacher is working with a special needs population for whom assistance is appropriately provided or time limits are eliminated. It is very possible that no student will reach the standards for a given performance or product on a given grade. However, not reaching such standards does not mean we should not use them as a means to stretch our students. The use of analogies such as the Olympics might be helpful in conveying the difference between standards and expectations. Not all will get the perfect 10, but that does not mean one shouldn't try. The goal is to assist students in bettering their individual performance through self-analysis and understanding of what successful products look like rather than to foster unhealthy competition or set unrealistic goals. Students' sincere efforts to meet desired standards of quality need to be acknowledged.

Teachers must decide how they will translate standards into expectations in terms of grades. With some rubrics, it is possible to have a one-to-one correspondence between the rubric and the grade; for others, the conversion might entail equating a lower point on the rubric to the top grade. Nonetheless, reconciling assessments and grades requires much more than technical solutions. In essence, grading is a normative process informed as much by political and philosophical issues as by technical concerns. Because of this, rational grading and reporting mechanisms can be defined only after having substantive conversations among students, parents, teachers, administrative staff, and policy members regarding the use and value of grades and report cards. These conversations should be based on the shared definition of learner outcomes and performance standards with accompanying representative student work.

STUDENTS' ROLE IN THE ASSESSMENT PROCESS

Students are more motivated to learn what is taught when they feel they have control of their own learning, and this can be attained by involving students in the design or use of classroom-based assessments. A number of strategies involve students in the design and use of authentic literacy assessments: (1) Articulate desired learning outcomes with the teacher; (2) identify the forms of evidence by which students will demonstrate their knowledge, skills, or understandings (produce a skit, poem, research paper); (3) identify processes or time lines for producing evidence of performance or work (a team-developed collage or performance that is done over one week, an individual report produced over three days); (4) define performance standards (audience engagement, use of sources, good introduction); and (5) present their work to their peers and assess their peers' work.

When teachers involve students in the assessment process, they often discover that students become more motivated and seek higher levels of performance. As teachers learn to value and foster reflections, students, in turn, become better self-assessors and increase the quality of their learning. The following excerpt from a fourth-grade student's self-evaluation of her writing from September to February illustrates the value of reflection.

> A lot of different things have changed in my writing this year. My vocabulary has grown, my handwriting has improved, I find that I'm writing with more exciting action words, and my responses to poems and stories have improved a lot.

AUTHENTIC LITERACY ASSESSMENT AT THE DISTRICT LEVEL

State-wide and national educational assessments are often naively expected to serve as credible barometers of educational quality, even though tests are often administered not just to discover how well schools or students are doing but rather to obtain external confirmation that they are not doing very well at all (Linn, 1993). In the United States, unlike many other industrialized countries, there is some support for the use of assessment as instruments of reform because traditional tests are largely unreliable and often not valid bases for making judgments about an individual's literacy development (Darling-Hammond, 1991; Stallman & Pearson, 1990).

The use of standardized testing for high-stakes decisions and program evaluation often drives teachers toward curriculum models that enhance teaching of isolated skills and knowledge tapped by these tests rather than toward integrated knowledge-in-use elicited by authentic assessment. Obviously, teachers do all they can to enable students to do well on tests that are used to assess teaching and schools. Ironically, even though many of the standardized tests currently in use in states like New York were originally designed to drive instruction in pedagogically sound ways (the New York State fifth-grade writing test), such tests foster a decontextualized and contrived approach to writing that is far removed from the natural act of writing as an expression of one's thinking. Teachers perceive that the best way to prepare students to do well on such tests is to have students practice skills and content in isolation. For example, the New York State high school competency test in writing requires that students produce a business letter in response to a problem situation, and failing the test prevents a student from earning a high school diploma. Consequently, remedial teachers may drill students on memorizing the business letter format without understanding the rhetorical task that requires the business letter response.

The predisposition to use assessment to improve instruction and enhance student learning and the assumption that authentic assessments are uniquely suited to enhance and even produce learning have resulted in many different efforts to use authentic assessment for accountability purposes. It is not surprising then that school districts consider the possibility of developing district-wide authentic literacy assessments to improve instruction, enhance learning, and provide accountability data. Many states are presently developing a range of authentic assessment tasks as part of state-wide testing as well as part of the standards movement.

ISSUES RELATED TO THE STANDARDIZATION
OF AUTHENTIC LITERACY ASSESSMENTS

Serious questions have been asked about the appropriateness of standardized authentic assessment for large-scale testing programs and high-stakes decisions. Concern has been raised about the use of a standard writing task for students with different background knowledge and interests. This variability has been known to impact performance regardless of writing ability and therefore raises significant questions about test appropriateness (Dyson & Freedman, 1990; Freedman, 1991; Moss et al., 1991)

Similar concerns can be raised about the use of portfolios beyond the classroom. As portfolios become a widespread application of authentic assessment, more individual teachers, school districts, and even state evaluation programs are considering their adoption. The use of portfolios for large-scale assessment requires comparability across classrooms, and assessment with portfolios must be shown to be reliable and valid. Portfolios are currently being experimented with in states such as Vermont, Kentucky, Pennsylvania, Hawaii, and Maryland. However, there is an inherent dilemma because standardization may interfere with teachers' instructional practices and with the use of portfolios for diagnostic and formative purposes. How can a portfolio individually reflect many different classroom practices and yet provide evidence of both validity and reliability? While reliability can be attained through the standardization of assessment protocols and rubrics, such standardization often creates contrived assessment task conditions and undermines the authenticity of the task.

Additional concerns with standardization include the use of portfolios to determine whether students have met graduation or promotion criteria. The measurement community is struggling to produce explicit means to determine the validity and reliability of these portfolios, raising the possibility that these assessments might not hold up to legal challenges when promotion or graduation are denied. It is doubtful that standardized portfolios can truly depict the range and quality of student work in the context of producing authentic work. In short, it may well be that standardization and authenticity lie at two opposite extremes of an assessment continuum.

An added problem in making valid judgments about student performance on the basis of standardized portfolios relates to separating student performance from the context and support that surround performance. Portfolios are constructed in a social context. As indicated by Gearhart and Herman (1995),

> Portfolios contain the products of classroom instruction, and good classroom instruction according to pedagogical and curriculum reforms involves an engaged community of practitioners in a supportive learning process. . . . Exemplary instructional practice supports classroom performance. (p. 3)

Whereas a specific teacher may have little difficulty differentiating students' performance and initiative from the surrounding context, others outside that classroom would not be able to do so. Recent evaluation studies conducted on the use of elementary portfolios in several schools in California (Gearhart, Herman, Baker, & Whittaker, 1992) confirm that teachers vary dramatically in their understanding and use of specific assessment tasks and on the amount of support they provide for students' performance.

Perhaps the answer to these conflicts lies in seeking an appropriate balance between the use of standardized performance tasks that elicit a broad range of outcomes and authentic classroom-based assessments that demand that students produce high-quality work.

Beyond the issue of standardization, districts need to realize that other significant barriers to the use of authentic literacy assessment exist at the classroom level. These barriers include (1) lack of adequate preservice training in assessment (Aschbacher, 1994; Stiggins, 1991); (2) low-level literacy assessment awareness among educators in general (Stiggins, 1991; Stiggins et al., 1992); and (3) the lack of attention paid to the needed congruence between a learner-centered curriculum and authentic assessment (Soodak & Martin-Kniep, 1994).

Schools and classrooms themselves are not organized in ways that foster the use of authentic assessment. Some of the structural constraints to the implementation of authentic assessment include (1) the segmentation of the school day into rigidly defined time blocks when teachers or students move from one subject to another without explicit linkages and (2) the use of a subject-centered and compartmentalized curriculum. Perhaps some teachers' apparent reluctance to embrace the use of authentic assessment is, in part, a reflection of the organizational practices in schools that work against teaching and evaluating students' conceptual understanding (Moon, 1992).

From a programmatic point of view, it is also difficult to implement authentic assessments given the excessive amount of pull-out and special programs that interrupt instructional flow. Many school districts are beginning to use push-in models of support services for remedial readers and handicapped learners rather than the pull-out programs that fragment the students' day and provide little contact, coordination, and communication between the classroom teacher and specialist. Similar barriers preclude the use of alternative assessment at the middle and secondary levels. These include the large number of students that teachers instruct daily; inflexible contact hours; reliance on teacher-directed, whole class teaching; emphasis on meeting curricular requirements instead of evaluating students' ability to absorb content; focus on content instead of learning strategies; excessive use of multiple-choice tests of content knowledge; parental pressure for numerical grades rather than descriptions about learning; and having teachers develop a departmental identity rather than an interdisciplinary one.

Finally, teachers' reliance on traditional curricula and older instructional strategies are not necessarily consistent with the use of authentic assessments. The use of authentic literacy assessments implies a conceptual and philosophical shift for teachers and administrators, many of whom are not grounded in current theories of learning and instruction, curriculum development, or assessment. While many are beginning to adopt newer models of literacy teaching, assessment strategies often still reflect outdated notions based on subskill theory and drill and practice programs.

From a curriculum standpoint, the pressure to cover more, rather than to teach something well, drives teachers to focus attention on what they are teaching and distracts them from carefully examining what students are actually learning. This is exacerbated by a curriculum that continues to expand, by the fact that teachers do not often write the curriculum they use, and by continuing pressures for schools to do it all. The long-term effect of national standards on teachers' perceived need to cover more curriculum is yet to be determined. One possibility is that the concern over curriculum coverage will require teachers to focus on more content and skills. There is also concern that because of national, state, and local curriculum articulation efforts, teachers may perceive some curriculum content as more important than others, thus leading to a streamlining effect in curricular content.

STRATEGIES FOR SUPPORTING TEACHERS' DESIGN AND IMPLEMENTATION OF AUTHENTIC LITERACY ASSESSMENTS

Classroom Level

In many school districts, professional staff are beginning to explore a portfolio process as an integral part of both classroom and district-wide assessment. Similarly, many individual teachers have learned about portfolios and are eager to try them out. In both situations, teachers need guidance in how to initiate a portfolio process. Without guidance, teachers may be overly ambitious or unfocused or may quickly discard a good concept out of frustration. The guidelines in Figure 10–3 are designed to counter some of the barriers and constraints to the use of successful authentic assessment and to help teachers use portfolio assessment in their classrooms.

Experience has taught that every year that a teacher uses portfolios to document and assess students brings new learning about portfolios and usually a new portfolio design. In essence, classroom portfolios become a mirror of curriculum, instruction, and assessment practices. As teachers examine this mirror, they discover areas that need major changes or minor refinements. The teacher then becomes, like the student who produced the portfolio, a true learner.

School and District Levels

At the school and district levels, a number of strategies offset some of the barriers and constraints to the use of authentic assessment. One strategy involves the creation of action research and collaborative input from groups of teachers. An environment that allows teachers to transform beliefs and practices requires active participation in a community in which teachers can experience themselves as learners, thinkers, and professionals. Such a community provides teachers with opportunities to work on projects that connect curriculum, instruction, and assessment. It encourages the use of collaborative inquiry and research to reshape teaching in the most comfortable manner. In such a community, teachers receive constructive feedback in a nonthreatening and supportive environment. In turn, they can make connections between changes in their teaching and changes in their students' attitudes and performance. Interdistrict collaborative projects can provide access to communities of learning for teachers. Districts can also create their own communities of learning (see Martin-Kniep; Sussman, & Meltzer, 1995).

Another strategy involves the development of exit outcomes for the district and the use of these outcomes as the basis for developing and aligning curriculum, instruction, and assessment. The identification of exit outcomes should be informed by a vision of what the learner should know or be able to do. Such a vision should be informed by the needs of different stakeholders in the educational system, including parents, teachers, administrative staff, and students. Once exit outcomes are identified, the professional staff must articulate existing curriculum, assessment, and reporting systems, and must identify areas in need of change. In addition, efforts should be made to define grade-level responsibilities related to the teaching, enabling, and assessment of outcomes to eliminate unnecessary duplication and redundancy. Finally, time should be allocated for teachers within and across grade levels to

1. Choose a primary purpose and audience for the portfolios. If you cannot make a decision between two primary audiences or purposes, develop two different portfolios. Suggested audiences can include parents, the students, and administrators.

2. Identify the learning outcomes that will drive the portfolio design.

3. Inform parents of your plans to use portfolios and include a schedule or time line for sharing students' work.

4. Create your own portfolio, and share it with your students. A teacher portfolio might take a number of different forms, such as a collection of work that the teacher used to get hired in the district; a portfolio of the teacher's own writing; or a teacher-as-assessor portfolio. The latter might include (a) desired learner outcomes and indicators, (b) learning opportunities linked to outcomes and indicators, (c) assessment tasks and scoring rubrics, (d) a letter guiding the reader through the portfolio and articulating the process used by the teacher in designing the portfolio, and (e) sample portfolios and exemplary student work.

5. Set up a place and filing system for portfolios (i.e., milk crates, pizza boxes, file cabinets with folders, etc.).

6. Identify possible portfolio contents and a schedule for selecting them. Link contents to the learning outcomes you identified in step 2. Decide which contents will be required or optional, and identify who will do the selection.

7. Generate criteria for selecting and judging contents (preferably with students). Integrate criteria into classroom activities.

8. Have students assess their work on a regular basis using the criteria generated. Showcase good examples of portfolio choices and reasons. Poor examples can be improved during periodic, individual conferences.

9. Encourage students to make portfolio selections on a regular basis and discuss ways in which they can update their portfolios. Promote the sharing of selections and reasons among students.

10. Use portfolios to communicate with parents individually and as a group (i.e., Portfolio Night, student-led portfolio conferences).

11. Develop a strategy for allowing teachers in other grades to access and use student portfolios. For example, encourage students to take their portfolios to the next grade level and to use them as a means to introduce themselves to their new teacher.

FIGURE 10–3 Steps for setting up portfolios at the classroom level.

systematically study children's work and to use it as the basis for generating commonly shared standards for students' work and performance.

A different strategy for supporting teachers' use of authentic literacy assessment involves having teachers identify and compare samples of students' work that they consider exemplary. An ongoing dialogue centered on quality student work can lead to the shared identification of performance standards, the creation of libraries of exemplars and anchor papers for rubrics, and the formation of communities of teachers, students, and community members who have a shared understanding and appreciation of school-related work. These strategies can begin to offset some of the structural and programmatic barriers to the use of authentic assessments and can help to transform schools into learning communities.

The following comment from a teacher involved in a collaborative research project addresses the value of action research in transforming teachers' beliefs and practices.

> I continue to change in my teaching style and way of thinking. The biggest change I have experienced is the amount of confidence I place in my students. Things that I never thought they would comprehend and use correctly have been very successful. I am not as worried about letting my students take control and make decisions that will ultimately affect them.

It seems clear that the application of authentic assessment and specifically the use of literacy portfolios can be a means to reform teaching and learning as well as assessment.

REFERENCES

Aschbacher, P. R. (1994). Helping educators to develop and use alternative assessments; Barriers and facilitators. *Educational Policy, 8,* 202–223.

Darling-Hammond, L. (1991). The implications of testing policy for quality and equality. *Phi Delta Kappan, 73,* 220–225.

Dyson, A. H., & Freedman, S. W. (1990). *On teaching writing: A review of the literature* (Occasional paper No. 20). Berkeley: University of California, Center for the Study of Writing.

Freedman, S. (1991, May). *Evaluating writing: Linking large-scale assessment testing and classroom assessment* (Occasional paper No. 27). Berkeley: University of California, Center for the Study of Writing.

Gearhart, M., & Herman, J. L. (1995, Winter). Portfolio assessment: Whose work is it? Issues in the use of classroom assessment for accountability. *Evaluation Comment.*

Gearhart, M., Herman, J. L., Baker, E. L., & Whittaker, A. K. (1992). *Writing portfolios at the elementary level: A study of methods for writing assessment* (CSE Technical Report No. 337). Los Angeles: University of California, Center for Research on Evaluation, Standards, and Student Testing.

Kniep, W., & Martin-Kniep, G. O. (1995). Designing schools and curriculums for the 21st century. In J. A. Beane (Ed.), *Toward a coherent curriculum: ASCD yearbook.* Alexandria, VA: Association for Supervision and Curriculum Development.

Lamme, L., & Hysmith, C. (1991). One school's adventure into portfolio assessment. *Language Arts, 68,* 620–629.

Linn, R. (1993). *Educational assessment: Expanded expectations and challenges* (CSE Technical Report No. 351). Los Angeles: University of California, Center for Research on Evaluation, Standards, and Student Testing.

Martin-Kniep, G. O. (1995, April). *What do the "cultivated" assessment-related questions and measures of teachers tell us about what they can do in the area of student assessment?* Paper presented at the annual meeting of the American Educational Research Association, San Francisco.

Martin-Kniep, G. O., Sussman, E. S., & Meltzer, E. (1995). Action research as staff development: A collaborative inquiry into alternative assessments. *Journal of Staff Development, 16*(4), 46–51.

Moon, J. (1992, October 28). Common understanding for complex reforms. *Education Week,* p. 23.

Moss, P. A., Beck, J. S., Ebbs, C., Herter, R., Matson, B., Muchmore, J., Steele, D., & Taylor, C. (1991, April). *Further enlarging the assessment dialogue: Using portfolios to communicate beyond the classroom.* Paper presented at the annual meeting of the American Educational Research Association, Chicago.

Soodak, L. C., & Martin-Kniep, G. (1994). Authentic assessment and curriculum integration: Natural partners in need of thoughtful policy. *Educational Policy, 8,* 183–201.

Stallman, A. C., & Pearson, P. D. (1990). Formal measures of early literacy. In L. M. Morrow & J. K. Smith (Eds.), *Assessment for instruction for early literacy* (pp. 7–44). Saddle River, NJ: Prentice Hall.

Stiggins, R. J. (1991). Relevant classroom assessment training for teachers. *Educational Measurement: Issues and Practice, 10*(1), 7–12.

Stiggins, R., Sullivan, P., Aschbacher, P. R., Anderson, E., Flaming, N., Loughron, S., & VanScoyt, S. (1992, June). *Assessment literacy: The foundation of sound assessment policy and practice.* Paper presented at the ECS/CDE Assessment Conference, Boulder, CO.

Using Portfolios with Students Who Have Learning and Behavioral-Emotional Problems

by
Dr. Leslie Soodak
Assistant Professor, Department of Educational Psychology
Graduate School of Education
Rutgers, S.U.N.J.
New Brunswick, New Jersey

KEY WORDS AND CONCEPTS

Public Law 94-142	IEP
IDEA	Constructivist model
Mental retardation	Multidisciplinary team
Specific learning disability	Holistic orientation
Emotional disabilities	Deficit model
Reductionist theory	Inclusion
Diagnostic-prescriptive model	

Assessment has always been an integral part of special education, providing the basis for determining eligibility for services and for developing instruction. However, controversy over the definitions of disabilities and uncertainty as to what constitutes an appropriate education highlight the need for student assessment to be comprehensive, accurate, and informative. Present conditions suggest that traditional approaches to assessment are inadequate for distinguishing students with disabilities from other students who experience failure in school. Alternative approaches to assessment, based on the notion that students actively strive to make sense of their world, may provide an opportunity for educators to understand and more effectively teach their students and for students to better understand themselves. This chapter will focus on (1) why portfolio assessment is a suitable approach to the assessment of students with disabilities; (2) how portfolios may be used to foster the development of the cognitive and affective skills of students who are learning disabled, emotionally disturbed, or mildly intellectually challenged; and (3) why portfolio assessment facilitates the inclusion of all students in general education. Before assessment is addressed, definitions of terms with respect to special populations will be discussed and clarified.

STUDENTS WITH MILD LEARNING AND BEHAVIOR PROBLEMS

Who Is Being Served?

In every classroom, teachers expect to see individual differences among students. Some students assimilate new information effortlessly, while others need repeated practice or modified instruction; some students can sit for long periods of time, while others cannot attend for the duration of a class. Most relevant to literacy instruction is that some students can acquire reading and writing skills even when presented in a decontextualized manner, while other students are unable to use this information to communicate effectively in actual situations. Differences among students pose a significant challenge to the teacher, who must address the learning needs of all students in the class. Perhaps most importantly, individual differences in learning may adversely affect the student who is struggling to keep up or fit in.

Individual differences among students must be recognized so that appropriate instructional modifications can be made. Schools are mandated to identify and educate students with special needs. The initial legislation, **Public Law 94-142,** was passed in 1975; it was renamed **IDEA—the Individuals with Disabilities Act**—in 1986. This landmark legislation, which provides for a free and appropriate education for all students has given rise to a system of service delivery that is designed to ensure the educational rights of students with disabilities. During the past twenty years, the number of children in special education has continued to grow to such a degree that over 10% of all school-age children presently receive special education services (U.S. Department of Education, 1993). This figure represents an increase of nearly 20% since 1977. During the 1991 to 1992 school year, 5.02% of all children were labeled as having a learning disability, which reflects an increase of nearly 150% in the past 16 years. The percent of school children labeled as having an emotional disturbance has been estimated to be .89, which reflects a more modest increase of 36% since 1977 (U.S. Department of Education, 1993). During the 1991 to 1992 school year, 1.14% of all schoolchildren were considered to have mental retardation. The number of students classified as having mental retardation has, however, dropped significantly since the passage of PL 94-142 in 1975, with a reduction of 38% as of 1990 (U.S. Department of Education, 1991). The growing number of students with learning disabilities has occurred simultaneously with a decrease in the number of students identified as having mental retardation. This population shift may reflect the change in the cutoff for mental retardation, which was lowered from 1 to 2 standard deviations (SD) below the mean in intelligence, as well as a preference for the more acceptable label of *learning disabilities*. Thus, there has been a tremendous rise in the total number of students being served in special education, which is largely accounted for by gains in the number of students being identified with learning disabilities.

Disability Categories or Ability Continuum?

Although it may be convenient to think of disabilities as discrete categories, it is probably more accurate to conceptualize disabilities as conditions on a learning continuum. All children vary in their ability to learn and behave in school; the point at which the differences warrant labeling is not absolute. The definitions that we use for cognitive and behavioral disorders do not offer exact criteria for diagnosis but, rather, provide guidelines for making determinations. Thus, the means by which we assess disabilities have profound implications for who will be classified, the number of students identified, and which students receive differentiated program placement. A brief review of the definitions of each of the mild disorders highlights the notion that cognitive, affective, and behavioral differences between students who are labeled and those who are not are a matter of degree, not kind.

Although the definition of *learning disabilities* remains controversial, the most widely accepted definition is included in the *Federal Register* (U.S. Office of Education, 1977): "a **specific learning disability** [emphasis added] means a disorder in one or more of the basic psychological processes involved in understanding or in using language, spoken or written, which may manifest itself in an imperfect ability to listen, think, speak, read, write, spell, or to do mathematical calculations. . . . [The] term [learning disabilities] does not include children who have learning problems which are primarily the result of visual, hearing, or motor handicaps, of mental retardation, of emotional disturbance, or of environmental, cultural, or economic disadvantage." Learning disabilities are presumed to be neurologically based disorders that typically impede the otherwise intellectually competent individual's ability to adequately use written or spoken language. Although the accepted definition of learning disabilities assumes an underlying processing deficit, in practice the classification of learning disabilities is based on the determination of a discrepancy between ability and achievement. The use of a discrepancy formula operationalizes an otherwise obscure definition; however, the lack of valid measures of ability and achievement as well as disagreement as to what constitutes a significant discrepancy have made the use of discrepancy formulas controversial.

Several characteristics have been associated with learning disabilities. Mercer (1997) noted that 85% to 90% of all students with learning disabilities experience reading problems. This may explain why the term *dyslexia* (a severe reading deficit or inability to process print at the word recognition level) has been closely associated with learning disabilities. Other characteristics include attention deficits, perceptual difficulties, the failure to use learning strategies, and poor metacognitive skills. Each of these deficits is likely to affect academic performance, as well as students' ability to function in social situations. Furthermore, because of repeated experience with academic failure, many students with learning disabilities lose motivation, self-esteem, and confidence in the value of effortful strategic learning. The term *learned helplessness* has been used to characterize the condition that stems from experiences with repeated failure. Students who develop learned helplessness tend to attribute poor performance to internal factors such as ability and attribute success to external factors such as luck (Pearl, Bryan, & Donahue, 1980). The psychological and academic characteristics associated with learning disabilities are not unique to this population. Ysseldyke, Algozzine, Shinn, and McGue (1982) have demonstrated that remedial students and slow learners have similar traits and are not necessarily distinguishable from students with learning disabilities. Similarities between students with learning disabilities and other low-achieving students coupled with weakness in the definition of learning disabilities may explain why students with learning disabilities now comprise almost one-half of those served in special education (U.S. Department of Education, 1993).

Students with mental retardation also experience academic and social deficits, although the intellectual deficits associated with this disability typically result in more pervasive problems than those associated with learning disabilities. By definition, students with **mental retardation** have both subaverage intelligence and deficits in adaptive behavior that are manifested during the developmental period (Grossman, 1983). Deficits associated with mental retardation not only influence cognitive functioning (language and academic skills) but also affect the individual's ability to function in everyday situations. Because both intelligence and adaptive behavior are continuous in nature—they represent phenomena that exist in degrees—it is difficult to determine the exact point at which mild mental retardation actually begins. The widely accepted definition of mental retardation indicates that a person must score 2 SD below the mean on a test of intellectual functioning to be considered mentally retarded (Grossman, 1983). However, this cutoff is determined more by prevailing social tolerance than by scientific evidence. In fact, a more inclusive cutoff of 1 SD below the mean was included in the definition used before 1973. The identification of mental retardation is further complicated by the assessment of intelligence in general. IQ scores may not represent an individual's true ability but also may reflect the individual's culture, language, or emotional status and may be markedly influenced by environmental factors such as testing conditions. The choice of an assessment instrument can easily alter IQ performance and consequently determine who is considered mentally retarded.

Characteristics most often associated with mild mental retardation include deficiencies in memory and use of learning strategies, limitations in conceptualization and problem solving, and difficulties in generalizing learned skills in new contexts. Inadequate social skills and experiences with failure and labeling often result in poor self-concepts. Students with mild mental retardation experience academic difficulties, but academic difficulties alone do not differentiate them from other students with learning difficulties. Cawley and Parmar (1995) compared poor readers and students with mild mental retardation and found significant differences based on reading ability rather than classification.

The most difficult disabilities to define are **emotional disabilities,** perhaps because they refer to a host of conditions, syndromes, and disorders that interact with environmental factors to influence students' ability to learn and behave in school. Emotional disorders differ from those described previously because it is presumed that the learning problems result from the individual's emotional and/or behavioral difficulties. Based on Bower's (1981) description of emotional disorders, the definition in the *Federal Register* (Office of the Federal Register, 1991) includes the following behaviors: (1) an inability to learn not attributed to intellectual, sensory, or health factors; (2) an inability to build or maintain satisfying relationships, (3) inappropriate behavior, (4) a general pervasive mood of unhappiness or depression, and (5) frequent complaints of a physical nature. The definition also specifies that the observed pattern must adversely affect educational performance. In practice, students experiencing transient problems (temporary changes in students' affect or behavior that perhaps are due to specific life stresses) that do not seem to have lasting effects on students' learning usually do not warrant labeling. Although students with emotional disorders tend to fall below average on measures of intellectual ability, their scores reflect a wide range—from being mentally retarded to gifted (Kauffman, 1997). Significantly, researchers have reported that students with emotional disturbance are behind their nondisabled peers in literacy and mathematical learning (Bower, 1981; Kauffman, 1997).

Cognition, Language, and Self-Concept: Similarities among Students with Disabilities

Although we speak of disabilities as conditions that can be distinguished from one another, students with learning or emotional disabilities share many characteristics. It is not uncommon for students with learning disabilities, mental retardation, or emotional problems to exhibit similar deficits in cognition, metacognition, and language. Characteristics that individuals with learning disabilities and emotional problems *may* demonstrate include attention deficits, high distractibility, low motivational levels, external locus of control, lack of strategy use, and poor self-regulating behaviors. Although not all students experience each problem and not each problem is manifested in the same way or to the same degree, learning, language, and self-concept are factors to consider in each of these disabilities.

There are two reasons similar characteristics may be seen in students with mild disabilities. First, the definitions of the disabilities include many of the same factors. For example, academic failure is a criterion for diagnosing learning disabilities and emotional disturbance; deficits in adjustment are expected of children with emotional problems as well as of individuals with mental retardation. Second, deficits in one area of development almost invariably influence performance in another. Cognitive ability, for example, is inherently tied to language ability. We use intelligence and learning in communication, and conversely, we use language to facilitate thinking. Similarly, our emotions are entwined with our learning abilities such that repeated academic failure suppresses motivation and lowers self-esteem. Given the interaction between emotional and cognitive functioning, it is easy to understand that students with emotional problems may have difficulty engaging in learning and may experience negative feelings about their own self-worth. Thus, children with learning disabilities, mild mental retardation, and/or emotional disorders may exhibit similar traits that need to be considered in educational planning.

SPECIAL EDUCATION: RETHINKING BASIC ASSUMPTIONS UNDERLYING ASSESSMENT AND INSTRUCTION

In recent years, the number of students identified as having disabilities has grown at an alarming rate. This has caused concern based on the high expenditures needed for special education, including both the cost to the individual, in terms of the psychological effects of labeling

(Ysseldyke, Algozzine, & Thurlow, 1992), and to society, in terms of the allocation of limited resources (Lipsky & Gartner, 1989). Concern also stems from the overrepresentation of students from minority and low-income backgrounds who are classified and placed in special education (Cummins, 1984). As educators grapple with cutoff scores and debate new categories, students continue to be labeled and served in various settings. The ease with which students are identified, which Ysseldyke and Algozzine (1982) have characterized as an "overidentification phenomenon," coupled with the unlikely event of decertification (Gottlieb, 1985), has led to concern over current practices. Questions have arisen as to whether it is wise to expose children to labels that do not reflect distinguishable categories and whether the educational services provided to students are effective (Lipsky & Gartner, 1989; Ysseldyke et al., 1992). The efficacy of the strategies used to teach students with disabilities, particularly in the area of literacy instruction, has also been challenged (Thomas & Barksdale-Ladd, 1994). Underlying all of the questions that need to be answered are concerns about the assumptions on which current practices have developed. Specifically, the reductionist approach to special education, which has prevailed for the past twenty years, is being challenged.

A Reductionist Approach to Students with Disabilities: Effects on Assessment and Instruction

Reductionist theory maintains that phenomena—people, ideas, concepts, etc.—are best understood when their component parts are identified and analyzed. Thus, a person is known when discrete skills and behaviors are evaluated; ideas are best understood when each component thought has been examined. In special education, reductionist theory has helped promote a deficit model of service by implying that the source of a student's problem is within the student; that is, disabilities are something that individuals have and that identification of the deficit is needed to provide appropriate intervention. This assumption has had a profound effect on policies and practices in special education. A belief in the intrinsic nature of disabilities can be noted in each of the definitions provided earlier in this chapter. Based on this biological/psychological interpretation of disability, the identification of disabilities takes place through an assessment process that focuses almost exclusively on revealing and analyzing the individual's deficits. Standardized, norm-referenced measures of intelligence and achievement are used to identify disabilities because, theoretically, they enable the evaluator to identify areas in which the individual is atypical. The student's identified deficits are then used as the basis for determining the disability category and to develop an appropriate educational plan for remediating the identified deficits.

Linking assessment and instructional practices based on an individual's weaknesses is commonly known as the **diagnostic-prescriptive model** of teaching. In special education, identified deficits are formally linked to educational goals in the student's **Individualized Education Plan (IEP).** Thus, skills in which the student is deficient become the basis for the student's curriculum. The teaching method that follows from this **deficit model** typically involves breaking down, or task analyzing, the targeted skill into its component parts and teaching each discrete unit using drill and practice. This method of teaching, often referred to as *direct instruction,* has been the most popular method of teaching in special education.

Although practices based on reductionist theory have an appealing simplicity, learning is not so simple. It is a complex process through which individuals attempt to make sense of their environment. It involves not only the use of specific skills but the individual's background knowledge, experience, and emotions, as well as the interaction of these factors within the learning environment. According to Vygotsky (1978), development does not necessarily precede cognitive readiness for instruction; rather, a child's instruction interacts with the child's development. For students with learning and emotional problems, the importance of considering environmental factors in assessing performance is critical in that both intrinsic and extrinsic factors have been implicated in learning disabilities, emotional disorders, and mental retardation. Students' learning and emotional problems may or may not be caused by environmental factors; however, they are most definitely influenced by environmental factors such as the demands of the learning task and the social climate. Therefore, understanding a student's learning and emotional problems requires more than identifying isolated deficits; intrinsic and extrinsic factors must be assessed before determination of disabilities is made.

A second problem with applying reductionist theory to students with disabilities lies in its effects on curriculum and instruction. Basing instruction on an individual's deficits results in a splintered curriculum with no coherent framework for determining what is taught. Teaching isolated skills through drill and practice decontextualizes learning and hinders students from connecting and integrating new knowledge to that which was previously learned. Since higher order thinking requires students to make connections among learned facts and principles, instruction that focuses on the mere acquisition of discrete parts does not promote this level of learning.

An Alternative Approach to Students with Disabilities

Those concerned with the deficit model imposed by reductionist theory have attempted to explore alternative approaches. One theoretical framework that has gained interest posits that we learn through a **constructivist model.** Rather than viewing the learner as a passive recipient of discrete skills, those adhering to a holistic interpretation view the learner as actively constructing meaning and therefore as an integral part of the learning process. Learning occurs not because information has been reduced and repeated but because it has meaning in light of the learner's background knowledge. Instruction based on holistic principles meets the needs of students with learning and emotional disorders because it accommodates diverse learning styles without sacrificing the richness associated with higher level learning. Most importantly, educational practices based on constructivist thinking encourage consideration of a multiplicity of factors that contribute to learning before arriving at diagnostic or instructional decisions. The overriding question therefore changes from, "What is wrong with the student?" to "Why is the student not learning?"

Constructing Knowledge through Integrated Literacy Instruction

In the teaching of literacy to students with mild disabilities, the importance of employing a **holistic orientation** to learning becomes salient. Traditional approaches to language learning often view reading, writing, and speaking as discrete areas of functioning. On the assumption that smaller is better, component skills within each of these areas are taught to students in an effort to build competency and simplify learning. In integrated literacy instruction, language learning is viewed as a natural process that incorporates all modes of communication. Since learning is context embedded, meaning and social function are inherent in what one learns. Providing a real purpose for reading, writing, and speaking motivates students to learn. Whole language teachers focus on understandings and interpretations; the connections students with learning disabilities and emotional problems would otherwise be expected to make on their own are woven into the curriculum.

In holistic instruction, obtaining the right answer is deemphasized as comprehension gains importance, thereby reducing stress on learners accustomed to failure. Thomas and Barksdale-Ladd (1994) point out that whole language literacy instruction provides a psychologically safe environment that encourages risk taking and reduces students' fear of failure. In fact, students are expected to assume responsibility for their own learning; they are given choices regarding the methods and materials they will use to acquire information and share their knowledge. Teachers who use holistic instruction can accommodate greater diversity than teachers who promote discrete skill instruction because the emphasis is on forming a community of literate learners; both the goals and the methods encourage interaction and acceptance. Heterogeneous instruction, where students are not labeled or separated by disability or achievement, is often used in holistic classrooms because cooperative learning is valued as a way of discovering how others think and learn. Attention to individual needs is provided for during individual conferences and by instruction in small groups that are flexibly formed and often are of short duration. This type of instruction accommodates diversity and is particularly important as we move away from segregated instruction of disabled students to mainstream instruction.

The potential benefits of using integrated literacy instruction with disabled students are only recently being realized as special education teachers begin to abandon drill and practice methods in favor of more holistic approaches to language instruction. Teachers consistently point out that the benefits exceed academic gains because this approach enhances students' self-esteem and motivation to learn (Brazee & Haynes, 1989; Scala, 1993). Teachers indicate that the structured flexibility inherent in holistic teaching allows them to accommodate a wide range of student abilities and learning styles.

Constructivism and Assessment: Completing the Circle of Change

Constructivist thinking has the potential to change the way special education students are taught, as teachers focus on student strengths and provide greater meaning, function, and context to what is being taught. Integrated, thematic literacy instruction provides an opportunity for students with special needs to assume active and interactive roles during learning. However, unless the assumptions underlying these instructional modifications are extended to the assessment of students' learning, real and important change will not occur. For example, if the diagnosis of learning disabilities continues to be based on deficits identified through standardized testing and a student's curriculum is derived exclusively from these deficits, it is unlikely that the student's instructional plan will reflect the coherence associated with holistic instruction. Furthermore, and most importantly, the growth students experience within an integrated literacy program may not be evident on traditional measures of student achievement. For curricular innovation to be complete, assessment of learning must capture the richness of new instructional processes. Too often, curricular innovations are not reflected in teachers' assessment practices, even when the apparent incompatibilities between the two are recognized (Soodak & Martin-Kniep, 1994). It is critical that curricular reform in all educational settings be extended to the assessment of student learning in a deliberate and rational manner.

The changes needed to align assessment practices with the goals of integrated literacy instruction are not radical, because special education teachers already assess students in valid, informal ways whenever they observe, teach, conference, and question their students. Effective special educators engage in ongoing assessment and base clinical judgments and educational decisions on a body of information they gather about their students. Many of the essential elements of authentic assessment are reflected in what is already being done on an informal basis by teachers who have long recognized the limitations of the formal evaluation process used to assess students in special education.

ASSESSMENT IN SPECIAL EDUCATION: INTENT AND REALITY

The Unique Role of Assessment in Special Education

Assessment plays a critical and unique role in the education of students with disabilities. Public Law 94-142 and IDEA mandate that special education services be based on student assessment and provide specific guidelines for conducting the required evaluations. Assessment in special education serves three interrelated purposes:

1. *Identification and diagnosis:* The initial goal of assessment is screening to identify students who may have a disability. Students suspected of having disabilities are referred to special education, and eligibility for services depends on whether a student is classified as disabled. Thus, diagnostic evaluations are conducted before a student's placement in special education.

2. *Instructional planning/IEP development:* Based on a student's identified needs, an IEP is developed for each student in special education. It is mandated that this plan specify the student's classification, placement, instructional goals, and support services.

3. *Accountability:* The programs that serve special students are required to demonstrate progress toward students' goals. This information is used to inform subsequent instructional decisions.

Public Law 94-142 provides guidelines for conducting evaluations for the purposes described earlier. The Protection in Evaluation Procedures (PEP) provisions are designed to ensure that assessment is fair and nondiscriminatory. Student assessment is to be conducted by a multidisciplinary team, and decisions about students must be based on more than performance on a single test. The purpose of requiring the involvement of professionals from more than one discipline is to ensure multiple perspectives on students' needs and abilities. Requiring multiple measures of student performance acknowledges the complexity of student functioning and potential weaknesses in any given assessment instrument. The PEP provisions also specify that assessment should be unbiased by requiring that it be conducted in the student's native language. Designed to encourage parent participation in educational decisions pertaining to their children, Section 615 of PL 94-142 ensures the student's parents or guardians due process in decision making and mandates that student assessment be conducted only after obtaining written consent from the student's parents or guardian. Although PL 94-142 provides guidelines for conducting fair and unbiased student evaluations, it does not mandate what types of assessment measures should be used in determining eligibility, developing instructional plans, or monitoring student progress.

Testing within a Diagnostic/Prescriptive Model

The interpretation of the laws regulating assessment in special education reflects prevailing reductionist notions about disability. The assessment process involves a comprehensive evaluation of the student by a **multidisciplinary team,** usually comprising an educational evaluator, a psychologist, and a social worker. Additional professionals such as a speech and language clinician or a physical therapist are involved in the assessment on an as-needed basis. The evaluation typically involves the administration of several standardized, norm-referenced tests to obtain measures of achievement, behavior, and intelligence. The evaluation results form the basis for determining whether a disability exists, whether the student is eligible for special education, and the instructional modifications needed to remediate the identified deficits.

Prevailing assessment practices are based on three erroneous assumptions:

Assumption 1. Educational disabilities exist exclusively within the individual. By assuming that educational problems are based only within the individual, the student becomes the sole focus of testing. This assumption inadvertently blames the student for failure. Furthermore, because the individual is seen as possessing the problem, educational assessment is conducted apart from the student's natural instructional setting, thereby excluding consideration of environmental factors that contribute to learning from the evaluation, such as task demands, instructional methods, management strategies, and motivational techniques.

Assumption 2. Standardized norm-referenced tests can be used exclusively to accurately diagnose educational disabilities. This assumption is problematic because of the lack of clarity in the definitions of the disability categories as well as weaknesses within the tests themselves. Without a clear understanding of how students with disabilities differ from nondisabled students or students with other disabilities, it may be presumptuous to base classification on normative comparisons. Furthermore, the technical adequacy of many standardized tests used in special education has been challenged (Salvia & Ysseldyke, 1995). Following a systematic review of standardized tests used in special education, Fuchs, Fuchs, Benowitz, and Barringer (1987) pointed out that the majority of tests did not include students with disabilities in their norm samples, potentially threatening the validity of scores obtained for individuals who are suspected of being disabled.

Assumption 3. Standardized norm-referenced tests are useful in instructional planning. Standardization calls for replicable conditions; thus, these tests usually contain objective, multiple-choice questions that are administered during a single test session. Keefe (1992) described many problems in basing the development of IEPs on the results of tests that do not provide information pertaining to how students arrive at their answers or how students perform over time in their natural learning environments. Further complications, such as depressed test scores, arise because standardized tests are usually administered by individuals unfamiliar to the student (Fuchs, Fuchs, Dailey, & Power, 1985). The misuse of grade-equivalent scores as absolute measures of performance may be due to the need to derive instructionally relevant information from tests that otherwise provide little assistance in instructional planning.

Standardized Tests: Confirming Failure without Revealing Reason

To understand the full impact of the limitations of standardized assessment in special education, it is necessary to return to the initial intent of mandated assessments, which is to base diagnostic and instructional decisions on information derived from the fair and nonbiased assessment of student needs. Recently, several researchers have questioned the assessment practices used in special education, claiming that inappropriate placement and eligibility decisions are often made (Lipsky & Gartner, 1989; Ysseldyke, et al., 1992). The disproportionate number of students from minority and low-income backgrounds who are classified and placed in special education is indicative of biases in the assessment process (Cummins, 1984). The overidentification of culturally diverse students is attributable to various factors: bias inherent in the tests (use of culture-specific test questions); the underrepresentation of some cultural groups in the norm sample (Clarizio, 1982); and an insensitivity to social, cultural, and linguistic differences on the part of those administering the tests (Huebner & Cummings, 1986). Given that teachers' referral decisions almost invariably lead to classification and special placement (Ysseldyke et al., 1992), it is also likely that the overrepresentation of culturally diverse students stems from biases in teachers' decisions to refer some students or some groups to special education that are not corrected during the subsequent evaluation process (Podell & Soodak, 1993). Despite legal safeguards preventing bias in the assessment of students, current assessment practices do not seem to adequately distinguish between cultural and linguistic differences and learning disabilities.

Assessment in special education is intended to be collegial and collaborative, involving both professionals and parents in educational decisions. The manner in which assessments are conducted, however, may undermine rather than facilitate shared decision making. Ysseldyke et al. (1992) note unequal participation among multidisciplinary team members in decisions pertaining to student placement and instruction. Kauffman (1997) attributes discrepancies in decision making to the lack of consistency in the interpretation of assessment data. Recognizing weaknesses in team functioning, the National Mental Health and Special Education Coalition (Forness, 1988) has called for greater interdisciplinary cooperation among professionals working with students believed to have emotional disorders. Perhaps most importantly, parents rarely consider themselves to be full, participating members of the teams responsible for the educational decisions pertaining to their children. When asked about their role in team planning, parents specifically mention feeling disenfranchised and unable to participate in discussions about the results of standardized tests (Soodak & Erwin, 1995). Although parents have knowledge about their children that can be used to provide important information and to verify clinical judgments, it is unlikely that parents will contribute to a discussion about stanines, percentiles, and equivalencies. Certainly, many parents do not possess the knowledge to challenge decisions and are intimidated by professionals who seem to have scientific data, and frequently parents do not have the resources needed to employ a trained advocate to represent the child's best interests.

The overriding intent of the assessment process in special education is to obtain a comprehensive and accurate picture of the child on which to craft an appropriate individualized educational program. The overreliance on standardized tests as measures of student achievement and potential may be counterproductive to this goal because they reveal little about how students think, learn, use prior knowledge, and monitor their own learning and instead focus on recall and recognition of information assumed to have been taught. According to Bartoli and Botel (1988), "standardized test formats, by their very definition, eliminate the use of the individual background and experience of the student . . . that is central to learning in the fullest sense of the word" (pp. 187–188).

The limitations of standardized tests are readily apparent in reading assessment. Because objectivity is central to standardized testing, standardized reading tests focus on skills that can be easily scored for accuracy, such as word recognition and comprehension skills. Standardized tests do not reveal how students use written and spoken language to communicate, including their ability to convey meaning, take the perspective of the listener/reader, and comprehend implicit as well as explicit meaning. Thus, these tests cannot provide a complete picture of students' literacy.

The use of standardized tests is further complicated by the potential sources of error that are introduced by the "one-shot" approach to testing, which is typically used in administering this type of test. Students are usually tested once, outside their classrooms by specialists they may or may not know. Clearly, students' performance is likely to be negatively affected by such factors as limitations in students' attention, the artificiality of the testing environment, and unfamiliarity with the tester. Bartoli and Botel (1988) argue that the use of tests that focus on isolated skills and look at performance at an arbitrary and static point in time underestimate student ability and may result in the diagnosis and treatment of a disability stemming from the evaluation procedures rather than an actual problem in need of correction. It is particularly troubling that standardized tests are used to confirm the existence of a disability, given that students are often referred for evaluation because of poor performance on these same tests.

Given the limitations of standardized tests, why are they so heavily relied on in making educational decisions pertaining to students with learning and emotional disabilities? As educators have attempted to meet the three assessment goals (diagnosis, instruction, and accountability), accountability may have taken precedence. The perceived objectivity of numerical scores based on comparisons with norm groups gives the impression of diagnostic accuracy, which is important in justifying decisions. However, information about students derived from standardized tests is not very useful and may be detrimental in making diagnostic and instructional decisions.

AUTHENTIC ASSESSMENT: EVALUATING THE STRENGTHS OF STUDENTS IN SPECIAL EDUCATION

Changes in the assessment of students in special education are being called for by professional organizations (Executive Committee of the Council for Children with Behavior Disorders, 1989), researchers (Gahagan, 1994; Salvia & Ysseldyke, 1995), and classroom teachers (Crowley, 1989; Hobbs, 1993). Reflecting the move toward a **holistic orientation** toward learning and learners, attention is being drawn to the use of authentic assessment. Several models of authentic assessment have been proposed as alternatives to standardized testing, including Bartoli and Botel's (1988) concept of an ecological evaluation, Glazer and Searfoss's (1988) continuous assessment of language model, and Rhodes and Dudley-Marling's (1988) outline and observation approach. Although each of these models differs to some degree in definition and emphasis, a number of important factors are common to each. Consistent with authentic assessment, each proposal recognizes the need for assessment to be (1) curriculum-embedded, (2) continuous, (3) varied in method, (4) varied in context, and (5) appropriate and sensitive to the student's developmental and cultural background. Perhaps most importantly, authentic tasks and contexts are used to sample both process- and product-oriented dimensions of learning (Valencia, 1990). Additionally, the principles underlying alternative assessment are consistent with broader definitions of literacy by viewing reading, writing, and speaking as integrated and interrelated processes. Thus, advocates of whole language and integrated literacy instruction recommend the use of authentic assessment.

Several differences between authentic assessment and traditional approaches relate to assessing students with learning and emotional problems. Authentic assessment focuses on students' ability to construct and use knowledge, whereas traditional assessment, consistent with reductionist theory, focuses on isolating and identifying deficits. Figure 11–1 outlines important differences between authentic and traditional assessment methods in special education.

Perspectives on Portfolios

Portfolios are one form of authentic assessment that has particular relevance in special education. As an organized collection of student work, portfolios can include many other forms of authentic assessment, such as work samples, observation records, and interview data. The collection must include student involvement in selecting contents, the criteria for selection of entries, the criteria for judging merit, and documentation of student self-reflection (Paulson, Paulson, & Meyer, 1991). Many educators have made convincing arguments for the use of portfolios in the literacy assessment of students in general education (Graves & Sunstein, 1992). The needs of students with learning difficulties coupled with the unique role of assessment in special education provide the basis for an equally compelling argument for the use of portfolios in special education. This argument can be made from three perspectives: the student, the parents, and the teacher.

Portfolio assessment has the potential to facilitate affective and cognitive development in a population of learners characterized as having deficits in both these areas. Reversing the negative effects of experiences with repeated failure involves restoring the students' sense of control over their own learning, which is achieved through experiencing earned success (Deshler, Schumaker, Lenz, & Ellis, 1984). Portfolios can assist in reversing feelings of learned helplessness by providing an opportunity for students to showcase work representing their accomplishments, thus focusing on strengths rather than on deficits. Furthermore, involving students in the selection of work to be included as well as in the development and use of criteria for evaluating the work may empower otherwise passive learners by actively engaging them in the evaluation process. Borkowski, Milstead, and Hale (1988) suggest that students' reflections on successful and unsuccessful outcomes discourage faulty attributions and depersonalize the effects of failure. Crowley (1989) describes how self-evaluation in portfolio assessment increased the self-esteem, motivation, and risk-taking behaviors of seventh-grade students who had been labeled learning disabled for most of their school careers. According to Crowley (1989), "each, in his own way and in his own time, learned to value himself as an able learner" (p. 244).

Students with learning disabilities, and other poor readers, often lack the strategies needed to comprehend text, and then they fail to self-regulate their learning. Wong (1991) postulates that students' failure to spontaneously mobilize strategies may be related to, and perhaps caused by, their expectations of failure and lack of initiative stemming from experiences with failure. Therefore, encouraging students to reflect on their own growth, to learn

Authentic Assessment	Traditional Assessment
1. The primary goal of assessment is to inform instruction.	1. The primary goal of assessment is the diagnosis of deficits.
2. The focus of assessment is on the processes underlying students' natural learning (e.g., the use of prior knowledge, learning strategies, and self-monitoring skills).	2. The focus of assessment is on the products of learning, that is, the recall of information assumed to have been taught.
3. Assessment is ongoing and continuous; conclusions are tentative.	3. Testing occurs once; results are assumed to be conclusive.
4. The assessment documents changes over time, allowing the individual's growth to be evaluated.	4. Assessment involves comparisons to a "norm" group, which may or may not be representative of the test taker.
5. Assessment is curriculum embedded; performance is evaluated in light of teacher expectations and instructional methods.	5. Assessment employs artificial tasks; setting and task demands are excluded from the assessment.
6. Students' cultural and linguistic backgrounds are considered in the evaluation.	6. Homogeneity of students' cultural and linguistic background is assumed.
7. The assessment process recognizes the interrelationships among literacy, academics, social skills, and classroom behavior.	7. The assessment considers each domain and skill to be discrete.
8. Multiple sources of information are used to confirm tentative conclusions regarding the students' performance.	8. Each source of information is used to provide a unique perspective on student functioning.
9. The classroom teacher plays a critical role in assessment; clinical judgment is valued.	9. The classroom teacher plays little or no role in assessment; objectivity is valued.
10. Students actively participate in the assessment; self-evaluation is an integral part of the assessment.	10. Students' participation in the assessment is minimal; students are rarely informed of test results.

FIGURE 11–1 Comparison between authentic and traditional assessment methods in special education. (*Note.* Adapted from "A Holistic/Wellness Model of Reading Assessment: An Alternative to the Medical Model" by L. W. Searfoss, 1993, *Reading and Writing Quarterly,* 10, p. 109. Copyright 1993 by Queens College Press.)

how to use metacognitive strategies, and to evaluate the areas in which additional learning is needed—as is done in the development of a literacy portfolio—all provide the motivation for students to think about their own learning. Because student work is evaluated over time and growth is valued in portfolio assessment, students are given a reason to review and question the quality of their performance and are credited for revising and improving their own work. Based on his experiences in using portfolios with students with learning disabilities, Hobbs (1993) suggests two ways in which portfolios can be used to increase strategy use. First, he suggests that teachers use portfolios to document a student's progress in acquiring a new strategy by including work reflecting the absence of a skill and work that shows proficiency in the use of the strategy. Second, he suggests that by teachers including and analyzing assignments with different requirements, students are given an opportunity to see how their strategies are regulated by task demands. Portfolios provide a meaningful context for students to develop and use learning strategies, to reflect on their knowledge, and to derive satisfaction from their accomplishments and efforts.

The second group to benefit from the use of portfolios comprises parents. Although the need for parent involvement is widely recognized, their involvement is usually limited to formal discussions at IEP meetings and parent–teacher conferences. Standardized test scores and teacher grades are the indices typically provided to characterize achievement. Portfolios not only facilitate parents' participation in decisions pertaining to placement but involve them in instruction. One parent said, in response to being asked her impression of her daughter's reading portfolio, "It's nice to know what's being done; sometimes the answer to 'How was school today?' is a little too vague." Parents, in reviewing portfolios, are given an opportunity to analyze achievement on real tasks; they can interpret performance within the context of what is expected. Because portfolios include work samples collected throughout the year (and perhaps longer), parents see progress that is often hidden in grade reporting. By providing parents with examples of student work that are selected and evaluated by both the teacher and child, the parent is given the unique opportunity to interpret progress from each perspective.

Portfolios provide parents with the information needed to help their children be more successful. They can observe what is being taught and gain understanding about the criteria for evaluating performance. Furthermore, portfolio conferences give parents the opportunity to provide information about their child's literacy involvement and other behaviors at home—information that can be used to plan and evaluate instruction. A resource room teacher notes the power of portfolios in enhancing communication with parents:

> When I sent the portfolios home for the parents to review, most of them responded in writing to many of the items included. This opened a whole new avenue of two-way communication. Some of the comments were directed at me, and some were notes of encouragement and praise for their child. Through the portfolios the parents became more involved in their child's education. (Hobbs, 1993, pp. 250–251)

Teachers can benefit from the use of portfolios in several ways. First, teachers will profit from working with students who are actively engaged in learning and parents who participate in their child's education. Second, the assessment process will facilitate teacher reflection. Evaluating students through teacher-made assignments allows teachers to consider the appropriateness of students' goals and the effectiveness of their own instructional methods and to truly individualize instruction based on student needs. Teachers may be able to use students' self-evaluations to understand how instruction is perceived by the learner. Third, portfolios aid communication among the team of teachers who work with the child (the special education teacher, speech and language therapist, and mainstream teacher). Last, portfolio assessment provides a unique opportunity for special educators to develop standards of performance within the field that challenge students and prepare them for participation in the mainstream. Instruction in remedial and special education has been characterized as ineffective, fragmented, and unrelated to the goals of general education (Lipsky & Gartner, 1989). Perhaps by making the curriculum, methods, and criteria for evaluation explicit, educators will recognize the need to make instruction more coherent and effective.

Portfolios and the IEP Process

In special education, the IEP is an essential and mandatory document specifying what, where, how, and why instruction will be provided to a student with a disability. Each student's IEP is developed and reviewed annually with the input of professionals and parents. Portfolios facilitate the development and implementation of a student's IEP by providing authentic, jargon-free information about student performance. Portfolios can be used throughout the IEP process, beginning when a referral to special education is initiated. At this point, the information included in the portfolio characterizes the student's abilities within the context of the teacher's expectations so that prereferral interventions can be made. Once a student is deemed eligible for special education, the portfolio is instrumental in the selection of instructional goals. Clearly, it is more appropriate to base instructional goals on samples of student work evaluated by both the teacher and the student than it is to select goals from deficits identified on standardized tests interpreted by clinicians who do not know the child well, if at all. The use of real work samples ensures that the student's individualized goals are relevant and functional.

As on ongoing record of student progress, the portfolio facilitates the mandated review of IEP goals. First, the portfolio provides an opportunity to reflect on the appropriateness, frequency, and effectiveness of instructional opportunities directed at meeting the identified goals. Second, evaluation of progress toward goal attainment occurs naturally within the instructional framework and involves both the teacher and the student. In fact, the portfolio encourages students to monitor and evaluate their own progress and to set their own goals. Last, as part of the mandated annual review of the IEP, the portfolio provides the information needed to revise goals and strategies as well as to select new goals and methods. As a representative body of student work collected over an extended period of time, portfolios provide a rich foundation from which to revise and plan instruction. What better way to decide what a student needs to learn or how a student might learn best than to look at how the student currently performs and what the student has done in the past? Students do not begin learning with each new IEP—portfolios allow past and present efforts and accomplishments to be considered in subsequent educational decisions.

Developing Portfolios for Use in Special Education

To realize the potential of using portfolios, it is critical that implementation be well planned and carefully monitored. The types of information to be included and the content covered within each document must reflect the goals of the curriculum, the methods used to teach, and the process by which the student acquires and uses new knowledge. The types of information that may comprise a special education literacy portfolio are similar to other portfolios and include the following:

- Informal reading inventories
- Writing samples (assigned and free choice)
- Multiple drafts of writing samples
- Photographs of projects
- Audiotapes of performance

- Videotapes of performance
- Transcriptions of student–teacher conferences
- Criterion-referenced tests
- Curriculum-based tests
- Story maps
- Observations of behavior
- Interviews
- Self-evaluations
- Self-regulation checklists
- Edited writing samples
- Learning or dialogue logs
- Journals
- Peer ratings
- Anecdotal records
- Behavior checklists
- Observations of learning and study skills
- Interviews
- IEPs

The selection of format depends on the student, the curriculum, and the purposes for the portfolio. For example, if the student is working toward developing learning strategies, it may be appropriate to include entries that demonstrate the student's organizational abilities, such as story maps and multiple writing drafts. If the portfolio is being used to document a student's affective development, it may be appropriate to include reflective journal entries, interviews, and self-regulation checklists. Videotapes may be useful if instruction is designed to enhance adaptive behavior or social skills or if oral expression exceeds writing abilities.

The information included in a portfolio must be organized so that a comprehensive picture of the student emerges. Because of the wealth of information students produce during a year, it is useful to create subdivisions within the portfolio. However, Bartoli and Botel (1988) caution that artificial subdivisions may fragment the learning process, as occurred with traditional assessments. Portfolio subdivisions have been proposed based on the purposes of assessment (a working folder, a teacher folio, and a student's showcase portfolio; Gahagan, 1994) and by skill area (a reading portfolio and a writing portfolio; Bartoli & Botel, 1988). Swicegood (1994) proposes a structure for portfolio development that has particular relevance to the assessment of students in special education. He proposes four categories for organizing information: (1) measures of behavior and adaptive functioning, (2) measures of academic and literacy growth, (3) measures of strategic learning and self-regulation, and (4) measures of language and cultural aspects. He suggests that multiple indices be used within each subdivision and that new subdivisions will emerge as the portfolio is developed and evaluated.

It is important that samples of student performance in the portfolio be accompanied by the date of completion and a description of the conditions under which the student completed the work. Particularly in special education, where many students require assistance before gaining independence, it is extremely helpful for the teacher or aide to add notations and comments that specify the instructional context in which the work was created. The assistance provided to the learner and/or modifications in the instructional setting, methods, or materials should be specified: for example, "this piece was written with a teacher's aide, who recorded the student's oral story," or "the student produced this piece in a one-on-one setting in a resource room." Providing information about the accommodations made to facilitate performance allows for more accurate assessment of the student's abilities, facilitates replication in other settings, and suggests ways to develop independence in subsequent lessons.

Examples of Portfolios in Special Education

There is perhaps no better way to consider the potential benefits of using portfolios in special education than to examine representative samples of students' portfolios. Toward this end, I have included sample items from special education and mainstream teachers who have shared the portfolios developed in their classes by students with disabilities (see Figures 11–2 through 11–8). Although the portfolios differ in how they were developed, they invariably reflect extensive teacher planning, ongoing student reflection, teacher input, and active parent participation, which are essential features.

In reviewing examples of portfolios used in special education, it is apparent that the number of self-evaluations (referred to by various terms, e.g., *reading responses* or *student reflections,* and using different response formats, e.g., open-ended questions or checklists) demonstrates that student input is highly valued. In fact, students' growth in skills and insightfulness can be noted in the evaluations of their own work over time. For example, the two self-evaluations in Figure 11–2 were written by a third-grade student with disabilities.

Teachers use portfolios in special education to promote independence. To reach this goal, students must be responsible for developing, and ultimately internalizing, criteria for evaluating their own work. The reasons students provide for selecting their best work reveal the factors they consider to be important. The excerpted samples of students' self-evaluations provided in Figures 11–3 through 11–6 demonstrate that third-grade special education students understand that many factors, including technical adequacy, editing, effort, and emotional reaction, are necessary components of good reading and writing. In Figure 11–7, a sixth-grade student with learning disabilities justified including his persuasive essay about piercing his ears in his portfolio because it was an example of his ability to use a new form of writing.

Overall, the students' responses reveal that they are aware of what effective readers and writers do and that they are able to evaluate their own efforts toward mastering these skills. Furthermore, the gains made in cognitive skills and metacognitive awareness ultimately enhance a students' self-esteem. For example, the letter in Figure 11–8, written by a third-grade student with learning disabilities to her parents at the end of the school year, reflects the pride she takes in her own growth and gives specific examples of how her literacy improved through the year.

In the portfolios reviewed, parents were brought into the assessment process in several ways. In addition to having students correspond with their parents about their portfolios, teachers frequently asked parents to review and comment on their child's portfolio. The parents' responses reflect their interest, recognition of growth, and insight into their child's abil-

Date: 11 – 21

Reading Response Evaluation

Why is this response important to you?

It is my best response because it is the logiste and the meales

FIGURE 11–2A Self-evaluation by a third-grade student with disabilities: November entry.

ities. The parent–teacher partnerships that emerge from portfolio assessment are reflected in one parent's use of the word "we" in the note she wrote to the teacher after listening to a tape of her child reading, which indicates she sees the teacher as a resource and partner in a collaborative relationship:

> [He] is reading more fluently and is much more accurate. He likes maps so I wasn't surprised he found the Amazon River. However, when he said "shorter" instead of "smaller" for the capitals, I think it was difficulty with his language—although he was able to correct himself, which was great. I think we're making progress. I still can't get him to read at home. So this [portfolio] allows me to see how he is doing. Maybe we could think of a way to get him to read at home. Any suggestions?

The writings of students and parents attest to how portfolios can facilitate learning within an environment that fosters independence and collaboration. Although good teachers might effect change in their students whether or not portfolios were used, portfolios ensure that students, parents, and teachers recognize and learn from the student's efforts and accomplishments. When asked about whether portfolios were responsible for the growth she had seen in her fifth-grade students, one special education teacher remarked, "Improvement could still have happened—I just wouldn't see it, and they [the students and parents] wouldn't see it."

Unresolved Issues in Using Portfolios in Special Education

Many issues need to be addressed as portfolios become more widely used in special education. Unlike standardized tests, which are neatly packaged, quickly administered, and rapidly scored, portfolios take time and energy. Teachers' accounts of their experiences consistently highlight the large investment of resources it takes to develop and assess portfolios. Teachers with the collaboration of their students must plan contents, develop activities, complete checklists, prepare questions, respond to work, and develop rubrics, among other things. Teachers must meet regularly with students to confer about and review the students' portfo-

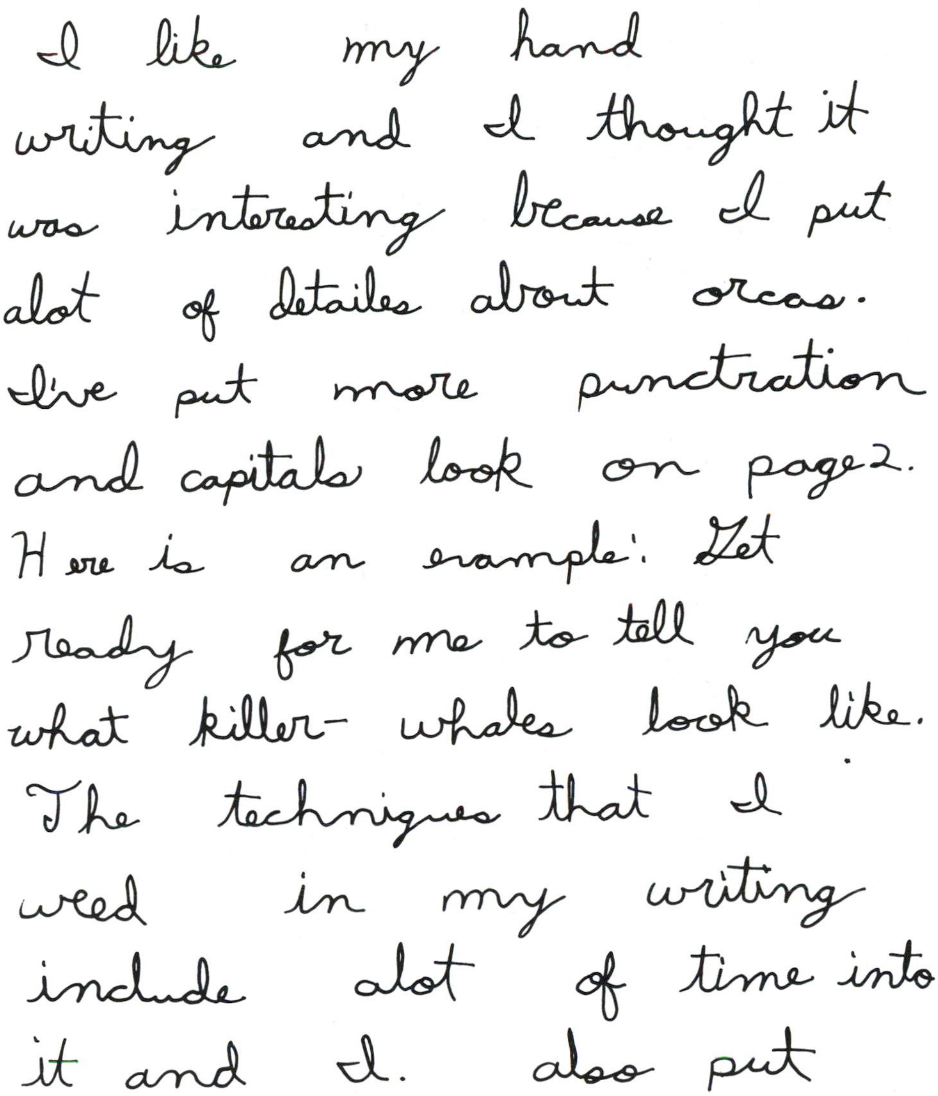

I like my hand
writing and I thought it
was interesting because I put
alot of detailes about orcas.
I've put more punctration
and capitals look on page 2.
Here is an example: Get
ready for me to tell you
what killer- whales look like.
The techniques that I
used in my writing
include alot of time into
it and I. also put

FIGURE 11–2B Self-evaluation by the same third-grade student with disabilities: June entry.

lios. They must also reflect on each student's portfolio in addition to evaluating overall process to ensure that the portfolio remains a valid and reliable measure of student performance. The expenditure of time will be justified if the results of the assessment inform teachers about their students' growth and ultimately serve to improve students' performance and self-esteem. To fulfill the many purposes of assessment in special education, explicit standards for evaluating portfolios must be developed. It is presently unclear as to how teachers will develop criteria for ensuring *reliable* scoring of portfolio contents and *valid* results. Many school districts have begun developing criteria, standards, indicators, and rubrics that are applicable to special education populations.

many details in my
report.
They made my piece
better by making it
more interesting. The
punctuation helps you stop
and breathe so you don't
keep going and going.
I would like to include
good adjestives

FIGURE 11–2B *continued*

The use of portfolio assessment reflects a new way of thinking about learners and learning that challenges the way in which decisions are presently made in special education. Therefore, implementing portfolio assessment may necessitate reconceptualization of the entire IEP process. For example, the implementation of portfolios in special education will require changes in the roles of multidisciplinary team members as classroom teachers assume greater responsibility for assessment and play a stronger role in educational decisions than is presently required. As in all educational reforms, this single change will not be a panacea for resolving the problems encountered in assessing students with learning and behavior problems. However, with deliberate planning and careful reflection on these and other yet to be identified issues, portfolio assessment may facilitate much needed change.

My best work was my dinsaur report. I selected my piece because I thought that I put a lot of information into it that the reader can under stand more better. My writing improved in getting the words right. You can see that on the second page. Now I am using capital letters. In the beginning of year I used lower case letters in the beginning of the sentence. I had a loud and clear voice when I read it to the class. It made it better to imagine that you were there. The technigve that I would like to try next is onamonpeia. It would give more excitement in my story.

FIGURE 11–3 A third grader's analysis of her best work at year's end.

I piked my scary story because I keep chaniging and revising until it's perfect

FIGURE 11–4 Self-assessment by a third-grade boy in June.

I feel this is my most interesting response because I shared my feelings and wote a lot. Also I feel it was my best response because when I hear other peoples responses I get ideas

FIGURE 11–5 A student's perceptions of her own work.

I feel this is my most interesting response because I put effortin to my report I took my time I put how I felt about Juan step father.

FIGURE 11–6 A student's recognition of her empathic response to a story character.

I. I think this is my best sample of a _persvassive · ess_
    because: _its a new form of writing and it is fun to write differendly_

FIGURE 11–7 A sixth-grade student's writing sample.

Dear Mom and Dad,

I have a reading portfolio. It contains a tape of my reading on it. It also contains a running record sheet. It also contains my respones and the thing I read also my last respon and a list of books I read. And the last thing it contains my Evaluation sheet.

It helped me by when I look back at my work I know I got better. It helped me learn from my mistakes.

The goals I accomplish were reading harder books and reading harder words. I accomplish them by reading with class and reading more at home.

It makes me a good reader by me allways reading at home and reading D.E.A.R.. Also reading with the class.

FIGURE 11–8 A third-grade student's letter to her parents.

PORTFOLIOS AND INCLUSION: FUTURE DIRECTIONS IN SPECIAL EDUCATION

The emergence of full inclusion as a conceptual framework for educating children with disabilities has generated considerable support in recent years. Concern about the nature of the student's educational experience and a firm belief in the right to full participation in all aspects of community life have led to a movement for the inclusion of all students with disabilities in general education. Proponents of inclusion argue that students with disabilities may not be best served in segregated classes and those in special education rarely return to general education classes (Lipsky & Gartner, 1989). Although there is no single definition of **inclusion,** it is seen as the right of all students with disabilities to remain in general education and to be provided with the support necessary for full participation and individual growth, such as consultant teachers, therapists, aides, and curricular adaptations. Many suggestions have been made regarding how general educators may best accommodate learners with special needs in their classes. In addition to curricular and instructional modifications, it has been suggested that changes in the assessment of students are needed to facilitate the inclusion of all students in general education (Smith & Noble, 1993).

Inclusive education can be facilitated through the use of portfolio assessment. In portfolio assessment, the focus is on recognizing a student's accomplishments and understanding how a student uses knowledge; there is no right answer or correct way of demonstrating knowledge. Students and teachers are given choices in deciding what will be assessed and a voice in developing the criteria for judging their work. The flexibility in assessment formats provided in portfolio assessment promotes accommodation and acceptance of an individual's unique learning style. Portfolio assessment also facilitates inclusion through student conferencing by providing for further individualization and collaborative goal planning. Portfolio assessment is consistent with the aim of inclusion, which is to ensure that an individual's needs are addressed within the context of the general education classroom.

Inclusion will work only if all those involved strive to make it happen. Portfolio assessment facilitates inclusion by providing flexibility and encouraging teachers to look at the development and growth of students as indicated by the students' body of work and to reflect on whether their goals and methods are effective in meeting the needs of all students, including those with disabilities.

CONCLUSIONS

Portfolios appear to be extremely useful for facilitating assessment with special education populations. Literacy growth along with movement in other curricular areas can be ascertained as students developmentally expand their knowledge and abilities. Multidisciplinary teams can review the students' work in special and mainstream classes while contributing information that is useful to the students, the parents, and other teachers with whom the children are involved. The LAP process, described in detail in Chapter 6, incorporates the educational ingredients that will facilitate learning and evaluation for students with disabilities in a manner that emphasizes positive factors: growth, development, reflection, and change by including the children's authentic works over time, with appropriate comments and notations by teacher and student. Self-esteem, so vital for this population, is immeasurably enhanced as youngsters observe their own knowledge expansion, master the ability to reflect on what they have absorbed and learned, and enjoy the personal language and literacy interactions with children and teachers as they share with pride, during conferences with parents and guardians, the products of their efforts.

REFERENCES

Bartoli, J., & Botel, M. (1988). *Reading/learning disability: An ecological approach.* New York: Teachers College Press.

Borkowski, J. G., Milstead, M., & Hale, C. (1988). Components of children's metamemory: Implications for strategy generalization. In S. Ceci (Ed.), *Handbook of cognitive, social and neurological aspects of learning disabilities* (Vol. 2, pp. 147–174). Hillsdale, NJ: Erlbaum.

Bower, E. M. (1981). *Early identification of emotionally handicapped children in school* (3rd ed.). Springfield, IL: Charles C. Thomas.

Brazee, P., & Haynes, S. W. (1989). Special education and whole language: from an evaluator's viewpoint. In K. S. Goodman, Y. M. Goodman, & W. J. Hood, *The whole language evaluation book* (pp. 249–260). Portsmouth, NH: Heinemann.

Cawley, J. F., & Parmar, R. S. (1995). Comparisons in reading and reading-related tasks among students with average intellectual ability and students with mild mental retardation. *Education and Training in Mental Retardation and Developmental Disabilities, 30,* 118–129.

Clarizio, H. (1982). Intellectual assessment of Hispanic children. *Psychology in the Schools, 19,* 61–71.

Crowley, P. (1989). "They'll grow into 'em": Evaluation, self-evaluation, and self-esteem in special education. In K. S. Goodman, Y. M. Goodman, & W. J. Hood (Eds.), *The whole language evaluation book* (pp. 237–247). Portsmouth, NH: Heinemann.

Cummins, J. (1984). *Bilingualism and special education: Issues in assessment and pedagogy.* Cleveland, Avon, England: Multilingual Matters.

Deshler, D., Schumaker, J., Lenz, K., & Ellis, E. (1984). Academic and cognitive interventions for LD adolescents: Part I. *Journal of Learning Disabilities, 15,* 108–117.

Executive Committee of the Council for Children with Behavior Disorders. (1989). White paper on best assessment practices for students with behavioral disorders: Accommodation to cultural diversity and individual differences. *Behavioral Disorders, 13,* 127–139.

Forness, S. R. (1988). Planning for the needs of children with serious emotional disturbance: The National Special Education and Mental Health Coalition. *Behavior Disorders, 13,* 127–139.

Fuchs, D., Fuchs, L. S., Benowitz, S., & Barringer, K. (1987). Norm-referenced tests: Are they valid for use with handicapped students? *Exceptional Children, 54,* 263–272.

Fuchs, D., Fuchs, L. S., Dailey, A. M., & Power, M. H. (1985). The effect of examiners' personal familiarity and professional experience on handicapped children's test performance. *Journal of Educational Research, 78,* 141–146.

Gahagan, H. S. (1994). Whole language assessment and evaluation: A special education perspective. In B. Harp, *Assessment and evaluation for student centered learning* (2nd ed., pp. 181–211). Norwood, MA: Christopher-Gordon.

Glazer, S. M., & Searfoss, L. W. (1988). *Reading diagnosis and instruction: A C-A-L-M approach.* Upper Saddle River, NJ: Prentice Hall.

Gottlieb, J. (1985). Report to the Mayor's Commission on Special Education on COH practices in NYC. In N.Y.C. Commission on Education, *Special education, a call for quality.* New York: Mayor's Commission on Special Education.

Graves, D. H., & Sunstein, B. S. (Eds.). (1992). *Portfolio portraits.* Portsmouth, NH: Heinemann.

Grossman, H. J. (Ed.). (1983). *Classification in mental retardation.* Washington, DC: American Association on Mental Deficiency.

Hobbs, R. (1993). Portfolio in use in a learning disabilities resource room. *Reading and Writing Quarterly: Overcoming Learning Disabilities, 9,* 249–261.

Huebner, E. S., & Cummings, J. A. (1986). Influence of race and test data ambiguity upon school psychologists' decisions. *School Psychology Review, 15,* 410–417.

Kauffman, J. M. (1997). *Characteristics of emotional and behavioral disorders of children and youth* (6th ed.). Upper Saddle River, NJ: Merrill/Prentice Hall.

Keefe, C. H. (1992). Developing responsive IEPs through holistic assessment. *Intervention in School and Clinic, 28,* 34–40.

Lipsky, D. K., & Gartner, A. (Eds.). (1989). *Beyond separate education: Quality education for all.* Baltimore, MD: Paul H. Brookes.

Mercer, C. (1997). *Students with learning disabilities* (5th ed.). Upper Saddle River, NJ: Merrill/Prentice Hall.

Office of the Federal Register. (1991). *Code of federal regulations* (Title 34; Pts 300–399). Washington, DC: U.S. Government Printing Office.

Paulson, L., Paulson, P., & Meyer, C. (1991). What makes a portfolio a portfolio? *Educational Leadership, 48,* 60–63.

Pearl, R., Bryan, T. H., & Donahue, M. (1980). Learning-disabled children's attribution for success and failure. *Learning Disabilities Quarterly, 3,* 3–9.

Podell, D. M., & Soodak, L. S. (1993). Teacher efficacy and bias in special education referrals. *Journal of Educational Research, 86,* 247–253.

Rhodes, L. K., & Dudley-Marling, C. (1988). *Readers and writers with a difference: A holistic approach to teaching learning disabled and remedial students.* Portsmouth, NH: Heinemann.

Salvia, J., & Ysseldyke, J. E. (1995). *Assessment* (6th ed.). Boston: Houghton Mifflin.

Scala, M. A. (1993). What whole language in the mainstream means for children with learning disabilities. *The Reading Teacher, 47,* 222–229.

Searfoss, L. W. (1994). A holistic/wellness model of reading assessment: An alternative to the medical model. *Reading and Writing Quarterly: Overcoming Learning Difficulties, 10,* 105–117.

Smith, M. L., & Noble, A. J. (1993). Toward a comprehensive program of evaluation. In J. I. Goodlad & T. C. Lovitt (Eds.), *Integrating general and special education* (pp. 149–170). Upper Saddle River, NJ: Merrill/Prentice Hall.

Soodak, L. C., & Erwin, E. J. (1995). Parents, professionals and inclusive education: A call for collaboration. *Journal of Educational and Psychological Consultation, 6,* 257–276.

Soodak, L. C., & Martin-Kniep, G. O. (1994). Authentic assessment and curriculum integration: Natural partners in need of thoughtful policy. *Educational Policy, 8,* 183–201.

Swicegood, P. (1994). Portfolio-based assessment practices: The uses of portfolio assessment for students with behavioral disorders or learning disabilities. *Intervention in School and Clinic, 30,* 6–15.

Thomas, K. F., & Barksdale-Ladd, M. A. (1994). Using whole language with children who we have failed to teach to read. *Reading and Writing Quarterly: Overcoming Learning Difficulties, 10,* 125–142.

U.S. Department of Education, Office of Special Education and Rehabilitative Services. (1991). *Thirteenth annual report to Congress on the implementation of the Education for the Handicapped Act.* Washington, DC: U.S. Government Printing Office.

U.S. Department of Education, Office of Special Education and Rehabilitative Services. (1993). *Fifteenth annual report to Congress on the implementation of the Education for the Handicapped Act.* Washington, DC: U.S. Government Printing Office.

U.S. Office of Education. (1977). Assistance to states for education of handicapped children: Procedures for evaluating specific learning disabilities. *Federal Register, 42,* 65082–65085.

Valencia, S. (1990). A portfolio approach to classroom reading assessment: The ways, whats, and hows. *The Reading Teacher, 43,* 338–340.

Vygotsky, L. (1978). *Mind in society: The development of higher psychological processes.* Cambridge, MA: Harvard University Press.

Ysseldyke, J. E., & Algozzine, B. (1982). *Critical issues in special and remedial education.* Boston: Houghton Mifflin.

Ysseldyke, J. E., Algozzine, B., Shinn, M., & McGue, M. (1982). Similarities and differences between underachievers and students classified learning disabled. *Journal of Special Education, 16,* 73–85.

Ysseldyke, J. E., Algozzine, B., & Thurlow, M. L. (1992). *Critical issues in special education* (2nd ed.). Boston: Houghton Mifflin.

Wong, B. (1991). The relevance of metacognition to learning disabilities. In B. Wong (Ed.), *Learning about learning disabilities* (pp. 231–258). San Diego: Academic Press.

Using Portfolios with Language Minority Students

by
Linda Schlam and Susan Cafetz
English as a Second Language Instructors, Columbia University, New York

KEY WORDS AND CONCEPTS

Language-Minority Student (LMS)

Limited English Proficiency (LEP)

Bilingual education

Immersion strategy

English as a Second Language (ESL)

Teaching English as a Second Language (TESL)

Teaching English to Speakers of Other Languages (TESOL)

Sheltered English

Basic Interpersonal Communication Skills (BICSs)

Cognitive Academic Language Proficiency (CALP)

Our classes are microcosms of the world, as the United States is a land of immigrants. At least 3.5 million **language-minority students (LMSs)** are enrolled in schools around the country today, a number that reflects a 68.6% increase in enrollment between the years 1985 and 1992 (Kauffman et al., 1994). If the same rate of increase continues, by the year 2000 the number of LMSs will swell to over six million children, representing a multiplicity of cultures and languages. When referring to students whose first language is not English, we prefer the term *language-minority student* to the more commonly used term, **Limited English Proficiency (LEP)** student, which emphasizes deficiency rather than proficiency. The umbrella term *LMS* presently includes children from over 170 different language groups as well as children who were born here but whose families don't speak English at home (Kauffman et al., 1994). Additionally, over one million children are from largely Spanish-speaking migrant families, who spend from a few weeks to several months in one school before moving on (Biagini, 1995). In addition to variances in language background, LMSs come from a multiplicity of sociological and political backgrounds—from rigidly hierarchical or mobile societies, countries in periods of great turmoil, or those with relative economic stability. Although many are children of poverty, others represent a broader range of economic backgrounds.

Many teachers now have LMSs in their classrooms; these students represent a wide variety of backgrounds, languages, and cultures. Addressing the literacy needs of these students poses a significant instructional challenge. Teachers who want to use a portfolio process may question how a portfolio can be applied to the LMS. This chapter addresses this concern by discussing how a portfolio process can be used both to overcome problems associated with use of standardized tests and to enhance the literacy instruction for children with limited English language skills.

THE DIVERSE NATURE OF THE LANGUAGE-MINORITY POPULATION

The reality of society in the United States is that the paradigm of the melting pot has been replaced with that of the salad bowl. First- and second-generation immigrants are no longer expected to fuse their particular cultures with the mainstream culture and lose their ethnic identity. One of the keys to a successful society and to successful schooling in the twenty-first century will be accepting cultural pluralism, with benefits that include an enhanced world perspective and first-hand exposure to many languages and cultures, which are assets in today's global community.

Children whose first language is not English have both tremendous resources and tremendous needs that require teaching and assessment that draw on their strengths and identify weaknesses. Their teachers must have realistically high expectations as well as an informed approach to second-language learning. The degree of literacy in the first language, the amount of time spent in the United States, and the type of education received in this country will have a dramatic effect on how well the students function socially and succeed academically. Because of difficulties in expressing themselves in English, LMSs need instruction and assessment that provide multiple indicators of what they can and cannot do and of what they know and don't know. Portfolio assessment, along with content-oriented, integrated or whole language teaching, can provide a context of high expectations, a language-rich environment, and multiple tools to assess language growth. It is also valuable because of the pathways it provides in setting appropriate teaching goals and strategies for maximal language growth.

INSTRUCTIONAL STRATEGIES

The schools have responded to meeting the literacy needs of LMSs with a variety of approaches and programs. Although debates continue about how best to educate non-English and limited English-speaking students, several patterns of program models seem to dominate (Tinajero, 1994). **Bilingual education** has had a controversial history in this country, but its primary mode of instruction is to maintain a student's first and primary language by providing instruction in all subject areas in that language until the student develops English proficiency. A maintenance bilingual program attempts to support and encourage both the primary language along with English so that true bilingualism is achieved. An **immersion strategy** involves teaching all instruction in English with the goal of mainstreaming students into the regular curriculum after only one or two years.

English as a Second Language (ESL) programs provide all instruction in English. These programs are also known as **Teaching English as a Second Language (TESL)** and **Teaching English to Speakers of Other Languages (TESOL).** The initial goal of such programs is to promote the acquisition of conversational language and then to equip students with English language skills so that they can succeed in the mainstream curriculum. ESL instruction has gained in popularity, especially in schools where second-language students speak many different languages. **Sheltered English** programs use a modified form of English language instruction to promote understanding.

LOOKING AT OUR STUDENTS

Cultural Differences

The influx of so many different languages and cultures in our schools will continue to have a serious impact, raising questions about what teachers teach, how they teach it, and how they assess what they have taught. Teachers need to develop an awareness of their own cultural assumptions, a sensitivity to how these cultural assumptions might conflict with those of their students, and finally, insight into how their own culture influences their curriculum, methods, and teaching.

Teachers and evaluators must also know and then take into consideration various typical behaviors for different cultures that will affect interaction with children in the classroom. A great deal of communication is nonverbal. For example, not looking the teacher in the eyes, a sign of respect in Asian cultures, can be misconstrued as disrespectful in American classrooms. In Latin America, the space between two people who are speaking to one another is much closer than in the United States. A person talking to someone from Latin America may feel uncomfortable because that person seems to intrude on personal space. Conversely, the Latin American may feel that the person is disrespectful, too cold, and too distant (Hall, 1981).

Some students are used to an educational environment where the teacher is the lecturer and the students are the note takers; they thus may have trouble adapting to our system, where interaction is an important part of the classroom environment. Attitudes about speaking up in class differ, as well. For example, in Haiti, the teacher is the authority, and to question the teacher can be interpreted as a sign of disrespect. Japanese students, because of cultural teachings, exemplified in the Japanese saying "the nail that stands out gets punched down," often communicate and achieve better when they work in small groups.

A conflict orientation is often reflected in American classrooms, because we value and encourage a multiplicity of opinions. However, Korean students, for example, avoid stating strong opinions about controversial topics, as their culture believes in the importance of mood, or *ki-bun,* "an atmosphere of good feeling" (Howe, 1988). Maintaining good *ki-bun* for oneself is important, but it is even more important to maintain good *ki-bun* for others. As with societies that have Buddhist or Confucian influences, many Koreans hold the belief that conflict reflects failure on all sides. Thus, teachers must become sensitive to and aware of various traditions that shape our world view.

Students from different countries and cultures often have gaps in their knowledge that are impediments to understanding American texts. Schema theory and brainstorming help students activate prior knowledge and fill in gaps before, during, and after reading. But, even if a student understands the meaning of individual words, differences in background between the author and the reader can create misunderstandings and confusion about simple experiences. For example, cultural background will determine if a student needs help to understand a book about baseball, Cub Scouts, or a nutritious Western diet.

Teachers must also avoid the dangers of stereotyping. Recently, there have been articles about the academic success of Asian students. In households where education is highly prized, children tend to perform well. One danger of overgeneralizing is that a teacher may then assume, for example, that no Asian child will have difficulty with any school subject. Such beliefs can have serious effects on children when they prevent them from getting the necessary help they need. The stereotype of European immigrants in the past who supposedly learned English faster than the present generation of immigrants may affect teachers' attitudes toward the realities of language learning and cultural assimilation. Additionally, there are stereotypes about culture and social class. Since some LMSs are members of a "minority caste" (Ogbu, 1978), a perception of deficiency can influence teaching, testing, and social climate. LMSs might therefore be perceived as having lower intelligence and be the object of lowered expectations, which can all too often be reinforced by low scores on standardized tests.

Performance in Social and Academic Settings

In evaluating and assessing an LMS, it is important to differentiate between how well a student functions in social settings and in academic settings. Even students who study English before coming to the United States encounter difficulty. In a junior high school English class in Japan, the teacher lectures, class participation is minimal, and English words are memorized as if they were chemistry symbols (Kristof, 1995). Only knowledge of written English is tested, and it's understandable that Japanese students can study the language for six or more years without developing the ability to speak it. Although these Japanese students might write excellent English essays on specific topics, they would probably have difficulty holding a conversation in English about what to eat for lunch. Even if a child can converse in social settings, however, this doesn't necessarily mean the child has a corresponding mastery of academic language skills. Students may communicate on the playground and score adequately on standardized tests, but because of a lack of academic instruction in their native language and in English, they may not do well in content classes. Cummins (1994) differentiates between **Basic Interpersonal Communication Skills (BICSs)** and **Cognitive Academic Language Proficiency (CALP).** He points out that in BICSs, both parties have the advantage of knowing the situation being discussed, and they make adjustments if one person does not understand correctly. The communication is context-embedded. In academic situations, however, the language must stand on its own; it is context-reduced and is much harder to understand or to produce. Cummins urges that students whose first language is not English not be removed too prematurely from support programs simply on the basis of proficiency in conversational skills. Studies show that it can take up to five years for a student from another country to catch up academically to English-speaking peers (Collier, 1987, 1989; Cummins, 1981).

It is important to note that LMSs may demonstrate the same level of skill as students fluent in English, provided they are given extra time, support activities, and various opportunities (Rigg, 1991). When allowed to demonstrate their ideas through media and to polish their writing with multiple drafts, students' progress in English and content mastery are more likely. Because LMSs have a late start in acquiring vocabulary, and their English-speaking peers are constantly acquiring new words, LMSs often lag significantly in their acquisition of academic vocabulary, even though they appear to be conversationally fluent.

LIMITATIONS OF STANDARDIZED TESTS

Confronted by linguistically and culturally diverse students, with significant variances in academic preparedness and learning styles, the standardized testing model falls far short of ideal. Differences in bilingual and LMS populations have led to questioning the value of standardized testing. Garcia (1994) notes that researchers have suggested that standardized tests may be less reliable and valid with second-language students than with monolingual students. Limitations of standardized tests that are of particular relevance to the LMS population are problems in distinguishing between knowledge of content and knowledge of the English language; emphasis on product (outcome) rather than process; a potential for cultural bias; stress on discrete points rather than real language; and difficulty in making the distinction between fluency in verbal language and an age-appropriate level of academic development. In addition, there is a potential for misplacing LMSs in special education classes because of depressed standardized test scores that do not reflect actual ability. If a test doesn't measure what it is supposed to measure, then it loses validity as an evaluative tool. The very nature of bilingualism presents particular difficulties with formal testing, because a student may be able to comprehend a particular lexical or semantic item in one language but not in the other, and the score on the standardized test will not reflect this. Moreover, time constraints compound the problem, and the student's performance may suffer unjustly.

In traditional ESL methodology, language skills were divided into the productive skills of speaking and writing and the receptive skills of reading and listening. Today we recognize the dynamic and interactive nature of all skills, but standardized tests do not adequately reveal these interrelationships. Educators need to determine how the student decodes information and need to identify particular areas of difficulty to more effectively teach the student. Perhaps the student doesn't understand a vocabulary word and has yet to learn the strategy of using the context to define it. The strategies students use to make educated guesses are not revealed by a fill-in-the-blanks exam. Moreover, formal reading tests or even verbal math problems do not reveal whether students do poorly because they lack knowledge about the subject or don't know the language. Tests may be culturally biased, especially against students from non-Western countries (Hall, Nagy, & Lin, 1984). A question may refer to George Washington, a Chevy van, or baseball, and a student newly arrived from Afghanistan may be unfamiliar with these references and consequently not be able to respond correctly.

Another problem with standardized testing is the phenomenon known to many ESL teachers in which students perform almost flawlessly on tests that call for the bits and pieces of language (i.e., use of the irregular past or the simple present and present continuous tenses), but when asked to communicate in a real or simulated situation, they can't integrate and apply the knowledge (Savignon, 1983). Conversely, other students can handle themselves well verbally but do poorly when tested on discrete bits and pieces of language. True language growth cannot be seen by relying solely on criterion-referenced standardized tests, which often focus on isolated and fragmented language skills (Taylor, 1990).

Standardized test results cannot be used as the only indicator to distinguish between different levels of English competence. Tests used to place students in appropriate instructional programs need to differentiate between BICS and CALP (Cummins, 1994). As an illustration, a student may get A's on grammar tests yet be unable to hold a conversation about the weather. The standardized test is inadequate in revealing students' strengths and weaknesses in these areas.

LMSs are often placed in classrooms where teachers have not received specialized training about language acquisition, and language development patterns have been misinterpreted as indicative of learning disabilities or other handicapping conditions. It appears that LMSs have been placed in special education classes unfairly, frequently because of a lack of proficiency in English (Ortiz & Yates, 1983). Certainly, students in low-track classes are overrepresented by LMSs, who, caught in the web of tracking and its duality of low expectations, may never rise to their true potential. Unfortunately, there is a shortage of qualified bilingual teachers who are trained in special education and evaluation to effectively determine the correct placement for an LMS. Nonetheless, all students, whether from other countries or native-born Americans, take multiple-choice and other standardized tests, which should be only one aspect of an evaluative process.

ADVANTAGES OF PORTFOLIOS IN A MULTICULTURAL CLASSROOM

As a means of assessing a student's ability to "produce, perceive, and reflect," portfolios are a valuable tool in multicultural classrooms (Brandt, 1990). To determine general language fluency, evaluate strengths and weaknesses as well as interests and ability, to self-reflect and take risks, a more authentic means of assessment, such as portfolios, is required. Because a portfolio process is flexible, it can be adapted to meet the diverse needs and backgrounds of the students. Language learning is part of a growth process, and gains made over time can be formally observed when portfolios are used. Portfolios allow for a visible and tangible body of work to be continually observed, updated, and discussed, with instruction modified accordingly. King (1993) explains that evaluation should be part of the ongoing activities in the classroom, not separate from it; evaluation should be "expansive, not reductionist" (p. 222).

LMSs, aided by their participation in the portfolio process, can be included in mainstream activities. Even when students overcome their initial difficulties in learning the basics of the language, they still need constant monitoring for a period of about five years (Cummins, 1994). The use of assessment procedures such as portfolios can help to ensure that LMSs are not unnecessarily pulled out from mainstream classes, separating them from exposure to peers who speak English. In fact, unless they have extreme difficulty in comprehending and expressing themselves in English, students should spend most of the school day in mainstream classes.

Another advantage of portfolios that is particularly relevant for LMSs is that they allow for a more authentic and integrated approach to language. The use of an assessment tool with multiple indicators can determine students' communicative and academic skills. More equitable expectations can be achieved by making the learning environment as authentic as possible, by using a variety of actual, rather than vocabulary-limited, texts, and by asking students to do the same type of performance tasks asked of native-born students. Since collaboration is encouraged, the emphasis is on interaction, not imitation, and on the natural, appropriate, and purposeful use of language. The goal is for students to have the competency to succeed in a variety of contexts in and out of the classroom.

Enright and McCloskey (1988) suggest that "teachers cannot teach language skills or literacy without integrating students' own ideas, purposes and dreams into the teaching program" (p. 10). LMSs need to feel a sense of self-worth, especially since they are in an environment where their home language has been taken away from them. It is imperative that teachers foster self-esteem by showing respect for the home cultures as well as for the students as individuals. Each child brings to the class a whole range of experiences that can be shared with others, particularly as the LMS has the advantage of knowing about at least two communities—the home country and the new country.

Student-collaboration projects should be assessed and evaluated along with individual problem-solving and critical thinking activities. Students with similar interests can work on projects together and enter the collaborative results in their portfolios. A reading response log can provide the teacher with a good understanding of the thinking strategies students employ in understanding a book or organizing ideas and should be part of the process. Logs and journals reveal interests and goals and self-reflection. Reviewing work done over time promotes self-reflection. John-Steiner (1992) emphasizes how important it is for people to be aware of the reasons and methods of their journey to a final or even intermediate objective. It leads to greater self-awareness, which is a prime indicator of future success in life.

The teacher of LMSs acts as an enabler or facilitator, and the student is acknowledged as a partner in the process with designated responsibilities. Portfolios are unique, because they require students to participate in their creation and also help teach students to judge their own work (Wolf, LeMahahieu, & Eresh, 1992). For LMSs, this has particular value as they are encouraged to be active learners and use the English-rich environment around them to improve.

> When learners are evaluated in an environment in which there are multiple opportunities to express ideas in a variety of ways and time is provided to work on a variety of topics for many purposes, to reflect on ideas, express feelings, present information . . . their learning is easier to see. (Rigg & Enright, 1986)

Thus, varied activities are necessary to make a classroom a more effective learning environment. The portfolio contents and presentations will vary from student to student, immigrants and native-born, as strengths, areas of growth, interests, and goals are highlighted.

The portfolio assessment process allows for individualized instruction for this population with varying degrees of literacy in the home language and with different problems in learning a new language and adjusting to a new culture. Portfolios document learning in cognitive, affective, and psychomotor domains.

Gardner (1983) contends that everyone has multiple types of intelligence to be developed including linguistic, mathematical-logical, musical, kinesthetic, interpersonal, intrapersonal, spatial, and visual abilities. Portfolios allow schools to tap all talents so that everyone can feel successful. Portfolio assessment can do this by including work outside the linguistic realm, that is, spatial, mathematical-logical, or visual. Particularly for students who have difficulty expressing themselves in English, the inclusion of varied elements in a portfolio is beneficial.

PORTFOLIO DESIGN ISSUES FOR LANGUAGE-MINORITY STUDENTS

The use of portfolios for LMSs can be both a delight and a burden. They contain multiple indicators of a student's progress, enabling informed decisions. Students are empowered to make judgments and take responsibility for their own progress. They see progress over time and gain heightened self-awareness. The act of maintaining portfolios provides a lens through which teachers can observe the intricacies of language acquisition and hasten its progress through appropriate intervention. However, creating a portfolio with a student who has limited English proficiency requires time, patience, sensitivity, and awareness of second-language learning.

Some issues need to be considered when portfolios are used for assessment and evaluation. Assessment is more complex when English is not the student's first language and the student has difficulty using English to communicate ideas. Instructional goals need to be clearly stated, even though some flexibility should be maintained. A way of providing baseline data and demonstrating improvement is to have students do similar types of tasks at the beginning and end of the semester, as well as at other times throughout the term. Each school should determine exit criteria and criteria for assessing evidence of continued language growth for promotion or mainstreaming. Student strengths should be highlighted. Using a task-oriented checklist is preferred to using one that demands mastery of specific language structures (e.g., the present continuous tense). Performance tasks, which include writing a short description, understanding simple directions, responding to questions, and being able to clearly retell a story, enable students to be assessed holistically.

The Contents of the Portfolio

In most ways, the contents of an LMS portfolio should not differ significantly from those of their English-dominant peers. Included should be performance-oriented tasks, defined as "any reality-based task which would require an hour and a half or less to complete" (French, 1992); exhibitions, which are displays produced over time; and reflections on both. Performance tasks and exhibitions reveal different aspects of LMS abilities. Performance tasks, such as in-class essays, give an idea of students' abilities under pressure, without feedback or reflection. Since such tasks require students to use automatic reflexes, performance tasks show how well they have integrated process, content, and form. Exhibitions, like multiple written drafts, display the students' ability to learn from feedback. They enable LMS to demonstrate mastery of subject matter by giving them extra time for comprehension and assimilation of material. Why, how, and what we teach determines what goes into the portfolio. Thus, there are many possibilities. Specifically, portfolios can include the following:

Dialogue Journals. These are journal entries in which students interact with the teacher. The teacher responds without correcting mistakes and models correct language use. By encouraging students to share their thoughts and feelings, dialogue journals can be a prime stimulus and most effective in recording language usage and growth.

Reading Response Logs. These logs have a more structured framework that encourages students to think critically and reflect on what they have read. They can be crucial in understanding where reading miscomprehension occurs and the ability to express oneself in writing.

Substitute Writing. This task encourages beginning English learners to verbally express themselves. Students use a story they are reading but substitute other nouns, verbs, or adjectives from choices given or from their imagination to create their own version of the story. For example, one sentence of the task could look like this:

The man	opened the door and	looked out.
woman	shut	smiled.
child	slammed	cried.

The words chosen must be appropriate for the context that is unfolding.

Individual Observation Logs. Students write down what is happening in the class. This activity develops observational and descriptive language skills for native speakers as well.

Oral Miscue Analysis. Teachers listen as students read aloud or retell stories and note any "repetitions, substitutions, omissions, or self-corrections" that they hear (Garcia, 1994, p. 193). Teachers, ideally with the help of a bilingual assistant, can determine if students are merely making a pronunciation error or do not understand the meaning of the words or passage. To learn whether the students understand the selection, teachers ask comprehension or inference questions. Teachers should have a copy of the passage to read along with the students. A permanent record can be made with audiotapes.

Videotapes. These can be of discussions, debates, prepared or impromptu individual speaking assignments, and skits. Students can review their discussion skills or the use of specific grammar forms. For example, in a presentation on their native country, students note their use of the present tense. Error corrections should be done on a one-to-one basis rather than in front of the whole class.

Audiotapes. These are records of students' reading aloud and then discussing the text. The teacher compares the tapes to the original passage for oral miscue analysis. Students can talk about how they read or their likes and dislikes. Tapes are kept as a cumulative record of students' ability to chunk word groups into meaningful units and of progress in intonation and pronunciation. Feedback sheets on taped oral performance tasks can be geared to pronunciation problems of particular students (e.g., es/s for Spanish-speaking students, or p/b/v distinctions for Korean students, or vocalization of final consonants for Chinese-dominant students).

Oral Interviews. Students interview others about jobs, cultural traditions, or opinions about particular issues. They can interview older people in their neighborhood or at home about life in their native country and present the responses to their class. Self-identity is closely tied to culture, and the student's body of work should reflect this. Oral interviews teach students valuable speaking and listening skills, including how to engage others in conversation and how to elicit information.

Illustrated Folktales. Students contribute their knowledge of their culture by illustrating and presenting traditional stories from their native countries. This is a way for students to share information about their culture and for the family to take part in an assignment.

Collaborative Problem-Solving Tasks. A group of students can work on task-oriented projects and experiments and on drawing inferences. For older students, an ethical problem-solving task can be determining who most deserves to get a heart transplant from a list of patients and explaining why. Computer simulations can be used for designing an ideal city. This language task naturally elicits specific language forms, such as the conditionals, "If I were the mayor, I would. . . ."

Dictations. One way to do dictations in an interactive way is for teachers to dictate while students work in pairs to transcribe the dictation, one student writing and one student listening and helping. Students can do mutual dictations with a complete paragraph on any relevant topic. In this exercise, one student presents two words of a sentence, and the other student completes it. The students dictate to each other to create meaningful sentences (Davis & Rinvolucri, 1988). Dictations focus students' attention on pronunciation, grammar, and sentence structure while remaining contextualized.

Story Retelling. The teacher can tell the first part of the story and then have the students form small groups to finish it (Morgan & Rinvolucri, 1983). Beginning students can use key words as prompts, for example, Jack, Jill, hill, fell, crown. These can be audiotaped or videotaped and then reviewed with the student. Being able to retell stories is an important element in language and literacy development for LMSs.

Classroom Observation Charts. These can be anecdotal or formalized observations particular to language and literacy acquisition. A chart records progress in reading by noting the number and types of books read, word recognition and prediction skills, and the ability to self-monitor. Verbal skills are observed in group and whole class settings, and special note can be made of pronunciation and grammar errors, as well as self-corrections. A chart reveals how comfortable the student feels while speaking English, by noting if and how the student initiates conversations with others. The notations help the teachers and students develop personal goals and mastery statements.

Self-Evaluations. Students write about their feelings about learning English. They can look back over the contents of the portfolio and write down what they notice about their language learning or particular subjects. When students notice things like, "I've always been interested in animals," or "I still find some English spellings really hard," they are developing self-awareness.

Mastery Statements. Both student and teacher can indicate what the student has achieved. The focus can be on content and language mastery. Mastery statements should concretely and accurately describe what students have accomplished to give language learners a clear gauge of their progress in English and other subjects.

Standardized Tests. Standardized tests have a place in the curriculum and in the portfolio because they are a recognized indicator of academic success and schools still rely on them to determine how students fare on academic ability. They cannot be the *only* indicator for LMSs, and in some schools, students with limited English proficiency are excused from testing.

Multimedia Presentations. Students can do more than write about "What I Did on My Summer Vacation." They can create an edited multimedia presentation, using photographs, video, and music. LMSs can show content proficiency without completely relying on written or oral language.

Each of the preceding elements can have particular value in assessing students. For example, by responding to students' journal entries, teachers can model correct forms of English and can nudge young writers into extensive responses. Authenticity of language tasks is of particular importance with LMSs. Teachers must go beyond vocabulary-limited texts and artificial dialogues to better prepare students for mainstream classes and the real world outside.

Student self-reflections and those of the teacher and family members should be integral parts of the portfolio, as true learning calls for the active involvement of all who have a stake in the student's growth. An element of the portfolio that includes this are the oral interviews. These should involve the students' first language community, including relatives. Written and taped tasks in the students' native language, such as relating traditional folktales or amusing proverbs, can be included in the portfolio. A strong argument can be made for including items in a student's native language. Their inclusion can serve three purposes: (1) Current research shows that students' cognitive ability in their first language transfers to their second language (Cummins, 1994). Rather than make the second language replace the students' first language, development and retention of the first language should be encouraged to facilitate the transfer of skills. (2) Including first-language entries enhances students' self-esteem. If the product or the task can be understood by a fluent speaker and found to be appropriate, the students' sense of self-worth can only be strengthened. (3) Because research has shown a significant transfer of prior concepts and academic skills to the second language, items written in the first language provide another indicator for evaluators in determining a student's progress. It can be used as an indicator of what the student needs in order to catch up with English-dominant peers, not only in language but in academic skills. The determination of a student's BICSs versus CALP can be made through inclusion of items in the student's first language.

In an ideal situation, the teacher or assistant teacher is fluent in the native languages of all the students in the class, but the reality is different in the majority of cases. "How can I possibly maintain portfolios with my thirty students who represent four different languages?" was a question asked by a teacher at the Fair Oaks school (Bird, 1989). To help her with material produced in students' first languages, she found senior citizens to assist with translation. This proved to be a positive and enjoyable experience for all. Other possibilities might be to check for bilingual individuals within the school—teachers, staff, or administrators—or in the community who might be willing to volunteer their time. Although including items in the first language is better pedagogy, it may not always be feasible to find someone who can help evaluate the material. In most districts, portfolios will be assessed by those who speak only, or primarily, English.

LOOKING AT THE PORTFOLIOS

A teacher should use the portfolio to note a constant progression in language development rather than the acquisition of specific forms by a certain time. The mistakes that LMSs make reflect their current and evolving knowledge of English just as invented spellings are part of a native English-speaking child's emergent language development. Proponents of whole language teaching believe that structures of language are learned nonlinearly. That is, students can appear to understand a grammatical concept and then make the same mistake before thoroughly integrating the new form. Traditionally, the teaching of grammar has been organized in a linear way, from a progression of easy to hard. At least one researcher believes that this is not necessarily the best way (O'Dowd, 1991). The order in which a language learner acquires information depends more on the types of language tasks that a learner is required to perform and the types of language exposure (or input) that the student receives. If this is the case, the use of checklists of specific grammar requirements as the sole criterion for promotion is not appropriate unless tasks and input are examined to see if the student can understand and produce them naturally and meaningfully.

For example, teachers can examine portfolio samples of LMSs' work over time and note common error patterns, which often differ from those of students who were born in the United States. At the same time, because of the flexibility of portfolios, individual attention can be given to mistakes, oral or written. Mistakes can show teachers where students' confusions lie and what has to be taught. This can mean addressing one type of error at a time and distinguishing errors that impede readers' and listeners' understanding.

Experienced second-language teachers recognize that the first language interferes, especially after the age of twelve, as demonstrated by the types of errors that students make. Regarding pronunciation, a student from Italy will have problems with the *h* sound, while Germans will have difficulty differentiating between the *w* and *v* sounds. Becoming familiar with areas of possible first-language interference can best be done by carefully observing the individual students in the class, rather than classifying them by ethnic group.

MODELS OF WHOLE LANGUAGE AND PORTFOLIO ASSESSMENT FOR LANGUAGE-MINORITY STUDENTS

The following is a description of schools in which LMSs are exposed to whole language instruction, where language is perceived as interactive and contextual. The information was gathered by personal visits and discussions with school personnel who in many ways are quite exceptional. The teachers and administrators have worked hard to create curricula that both welcome student input and are relevant to the students' needs and lives. In each of these whole language classrooms and schools, the flexibility of the portfolio is being used to full advantage, and learning and assessment are regarded as related and continual.

The International High School

At the International High School in Queens, New York, language teaching is integrated with content, and portfolio assessment is used. The mission of this school is "to enable each of our students to develop the linguistic, cognitive and cultural skills necessary for success in high school, college and beyond" (Project PROPEL, 1993, p. 16). The curriculum is experience-based. It emphasizes a collaborative approach among the student, teacher, and administration, and it includes the parents and the larger community in the projects that students create. Here the portfolio is used as evidence of this collaboration. In the tenth grade, students study interdisciplinary units on motion and visibility/invisibility that draw on material from literature, science, math, and physical education. At the end of this unit, the students assemble a portfolio that includes a personal statement section, in which they analyze their language and communication skills, individual and group work, academic growth, and general progress (Kauffman, 1994). In a mastery statement section, students "complete a word association exercise and a reflection activity." A set of evaluation guidelines assesses attendance, productivity, understanding of the classwork, ability to work with others, concentration, and growth in communication (Kauffman, 1994). Where many programs for LMSs in high schools are skills-based, rather than based on a whole language approach, the International High School stands out as a school that is determinedly experiential and whole language.

Central Park East Elementary School

Central Park East Elementary School in Manhattan is a school with a strong whole language philosophy where children create meaning through extensive reading, writing, and speaking. Located in the inner city, it stands out as a school with one of the highest reading scores in New York City. Approximately one-third of its students are those whose first language is not English. Because the staff at Central Park East believe that students don't learn any differently if their first language is not English, and because they believe in making classrooms as diverse as possible, Central Park East is committed to mainstreaming. This has been a major factor in LMSs' acquisition of English skills and in fostering a sense of their belonging to the English-speaking world. The faculty believe that through interaction with English-speaking peers, by being read to, and by engaging in a variety of work, young LMSs can become fluent in English, quickly and easily.

At weekly faculty meetings, students' work collections are examined to help teachers observe the development of writing, reading, math, science, and art skills over a period of time. The collections do not contain the students' best work, they do not contain pieces mandated by the state or some other administrative body, and they are not even totally representative of each child's work. There is a checklist of the contents of the student's collection, but there is no checklist for content required at each grade. Entries are a result of the teacher's or the student's decision. The collections are kept in big brown folders in a special room, and students can visit to peruse the contents of their folders, which include all their work from kindergarten to the sixth grade. Students interested in a topic worked on in the previous year can ask for their writing so that they can revise it with the benefit of insights and information gained in their new class. This cumulative records approach is useful for both student and teacher. In addition to the benefits that accrue with the use of the collection of students' work each semester, maintaining collections for the duration of the students' stay in the school provides teachers with extensive material for reflection on instruction and provides students with access to their work over the long term.

The Machan School

For the last seven years, the Machan School in Phoenix, Arizona, has been a whole language school with a "strongly holistic and collaborative view of teaching, learning and administering" (Rigg, 1991). The school has 900 students; two-thirds of its classes are bilingual; approximately 50% to 60% of the students are Spanish dominant; 40% to 50% of the students are English dominant. Most of the students in the school are considered at risk; 90% receive free lunch, indicating they come from low-income families. Each class has an instructional aide, which allows for more small group work. Sometimes students are grouped according to language, and at other times they are in mixed language groups. Students in all grades spend their time either in small groups, in pairs, or alone; little time is spent in whole group instruction. Students whose first and dominant language is other than Spanish or English are usually placed in ESL classes. Occasionally a child is from a home where another language is spoken (e.g., Navajo or Vietnamese), but the child speaks mostly English. This child might be placed in either an English class or a bilingual class, depending on parental choice.

The curriculum is content-oriented with extensive use of thematic units. In one lesson, students learned about the human body by outlining each other's silhouette on black paper and then, with white chalk, identifying and marking the bones while observing a real-life skeleton and feeling the bones in their own bodies. These silhouettes were then used as decorations for the traditional American holiday of Halloween, and Day of the Dead, a traditional Mexican holiday. Students used both English and Spanish in accomplishing their tasks, with the teacher responding in whatever language they were using. In small groups, students brainstormed and made lists of questions for a doctor who visited the class. The teachers read a variety of books to the class, and pairs of students researched organs such as the heart, lungs, and brain. With this information, students created visuals and wrote short reports. These were viewed by students from other classes, who asked the authors questions about them.

Draper, the K–3 project coordinator, believes that both the native language and the target language, English, need to be used, built on, and reinforced. She has observed that children in the bilingual program do better on the fourth-grade Iowa Test of Basic Skills than do children in the ESL program, who lag four to six months behind, for example, in math skills. In a bilingual class, two languages are used to promote learning, and this may account for this disparity, because students' thinking and language skills are developed through their first as well as their second language. This raises the controversy of whether bilingual classes are preferable to classes in which English is the sole language of instruction, a subject still hotly debated.

The Machan School uses a work sampling system, which incorporates a grade-level checklist, a portfolio of student work, and a narrative report to parents. Teachers and students keep two kinds of portfolios: a yearly portfolio, which can go home and is used for goal-setting conferences, and a permanent collection, which is composed of elements that the students and teacher have selected to follow the students through the years. Children are actively involved in selecting work samples for their portfolios. The district requires a writing portfolio containing genre-based samples. The school portfolios also contain sections for artwork, science, and social studies projects and math samples. The portfolios of bilingual students contain material in both English and Spanish. This is important in distinguishing if students have developed a sense of audience: Are they writing in English for an English-dominant audience, and are they writing in Spanish for a Spanish-dominant audience? Thus, having both languages in the portfolio can demonstrate the strengths of students in their choice of genre and audience. Some teachers include an audiotape of students reading and then talking about themselves as readers at various points of the school year. This tape then becomes a tangible record for the students to review their progress in reading at the end of the year and for teachers to determine what kinds of books students are selecting for their readings. If students consistently choose the same type of text or texts that are too simple, teachers can then encourage them to read something different. Portfolios are evaluated using the criteria of quantity, quality, and variety.

The school received funding to relieve small groups of teachers for two hours each month so that they could look through and discuss one another's portfolios and narrative reports. Draper feels that this should be done once a month at a minimum, to share observations and plan for future growth. The Work Sampling checklist provides a grade-level standard for language development in the child's first language. A goal for next year is to develop a series of descriptors for the child's progress in the second language. In evaluating English skills, teachers look for growth rather than a specific checklist. Teachers review the contents of portfolios with students and parents throughout the year to set new goals and make programmatic decisions such as moving to more English instruction or exiting from the bilingual program.

Additionally, teachers meet for two to three days in the summer to review their students' portfolios. This helps them reflect on what they did not collect as well as what they did. If something seems missing, is it something teachers neglected to collect or simply skimmed over? Although maintaining portfolios for each student is time-consuming, the strength of portfolio use is that teacher and student have a record over time of progress and areas that need improvement. This record is used to great advantage in helping each student develop confidence and master the English language and literacy skills.

Over the years, the Machan school has found that the deficit notion (focusing on what children can't do, their errors and mistakes) does not serve the students or the program well, and they have tried to move to observing the students' strengths and experiences. A child who comes to them from a home with strong Spanish language background has a great deal to build on. That child has the advantage of living and going to school with two good language models. Apparently, all the children want to learn English, and the reasons for improving English are everywhere—asking questions on a field trip, writing a letter requesting information, reading to a younger class, or translating for monolingual children or adults. Teachers want their students to become language virtuosos, to be able to use language for a wide variety of purposes and a wide range of audiences. While teachers spend considerable time on editing in the intermediate grades, the focus remains on the meaning and purpose of the communication, not on the errors. As teachers look back on the error or miscue pattern of individual students, it helps them view how the students make sense of the language. That knowledge is used to provide other experiences with language that will expand student understanding of and competence in English.

CONCLUSIONS

Portfolios reveal the development of language skills and various abilities of all students, including LMSs. The more samples of work that are included in a portfolio, the more multidimensional the picture of the students. Because standardized tests tend to perpetuate a deficit model of viewing an LMS rather than focus on the student's strengths, schools need a better way to assess and evaluate. There is no one way to use portfolios, and there is much room for creativity because of the inherent flexibility of portfolio design. Thus, teachers can experiment with various methodologies and strategies to see what works best for their students. When students experience progress, they will have the self-confidence to apply their language skills in whatever direction they choose.

REFERENCES

Biagini, J. M. (1995). Migratory children: A challenge for educators. *TESOL Matters, 5*(3), 1.

Bird, L. B. (1989). *Becoming a whole language school: The Fair Oaks story.* Katonah, NY: Richard Owen.

Brandt, R. (1990). On assessment in the arts: A conversation with Howard Gardner. *Educational Leadership, 47*(6), 24–29.

Chamot, A. U., & O'Malley, J. M. (1994). Instructional approaches and teaching procedures. In K. Spangenberg-Urbschat & R. Pritchard (Eds.), *Kids come in all languages: Reading instruction for ESL students.* Newark, DE: International Reading Association.

Collier, V. P. (1987). Age and rate of acquisition of second language for academic purposes. *TESOL Quarterly, 21,* 617–641.

Collier, V. P. (1989). How long? A synthesis of research on academic achievement in a second language. *TESOL Quarterly, 23,* 509–631.

Cummins, J. (1981). Age on arrival and immigrant second-language learning in Canada: A reassessment. *Applied Linguistics, 2,* 132–149.

Cummins, J. (1994). The acquisition of English as a second language. In K. Spangenberg-Urbschat & R. Pritchard (Eds.), *Kids come in all languages: Reading instruction for ESL students.* Newark, DE: International Reading Association.

Davis, P., & Rinvolucri, M. (1988). *Dictation: New methods, new possibilities.* Cambridge, England: Cambridge University Press.

Enright, D. S., & McCloskey, M. L. (1988). *Integrating English: Developing English language and literacy in the multilingual classroom.* Reading, MA: Addison-Wesley.

French, R. L. (1992). Portfolio assessment and LEP students. In *Focus on evaluation and measurement: Proceedings of the national research symposium on limited English proficient student issues* (Vol. 1). pp. 249–272. Washington, DC: ERIC Clearinghouse on Languages and Linguistics.

Fries, C. (1945). *Teaching and learning English as a foreign language.* Ann Arbor: University of Michigan Press.

Garcia, G. E. (1994). Assessing the literacy development of second-language students: A focus on authentic assessment. In K. Spangenberg-Urbschat & R. Pritchard (Eds.), *Kids come in all languages: Reading instruction for ESL students.* Newark, DE: International Reading Association.

Gardner, H. (1983). *Frames of mind.* New York: Basic Books.

Gliedman, J. (1983). Interview (with Noam Chomsky). *Omni, 6*(2), 113–118.

Hall, E. T. (1981) *The silent language.* Garden City, NY: Anchor Press.

Hall, W. S., Nagy, W. E., & Linn, R. (1984). *Spoken words: Effects of situation and social group on oral word usage and frequency.* Hillsdale, NJ: Erlbaum.

Howe, R. W. (1988). *The Koreans: Passion and grace.* San Diego: Harcourt, Brace, Jovanovich.

John-Steiner, V. (1992). Response to Joseph Walter's presentation. In *Focus on evaluation and measurement. Proceedings of the national research symposium on limited English proficient student issues* (Vol. 1). pp. 19–22. Washington, DC: ERIC Clearinghouse on Languages and Linguistics.

Kauffman, D. et al. (1994). *Content-ESL across the USA.* Washington, DC: ERIC Clearinghouse on Languages and Linguistics.

King, D. (1993). Assessment and evaluation in bilingual and multicultural classrooms. In B. Harp (Ed.), *Assessment and evaluation in whole language programs.* Norwood, MA: Christopher Gordon.

Krashen, S. D., & Terrell, T. D. (1983). *The natural approach.* San Francisco, CA: Alemany.

Kristof, N. D. (1995, July 18). Japan's schools: Safe, clean, not much fun. *New York Times,* p. A1.

Lado, R. (1977). *Lado English series.* New York: Regents.

Mehrabian, A. (1971). *Silent messages.* Belmont, CA: Wadsworth.

Morgan, J., & Rinvolucri, M. (1983). *Once upon a time: Using stories in the language classroom.* Cambridge, England: Cambridge University Press.

O'Dowd, E. (1991). *Pragmatics and morphosyntactic acquisition: A case study.* Washington, DC: ERIC Clearinghouse on Languages and Linguistics. (ERIC Document Reproduction Service No. ED 359 798)

Ogbu, J. (1978). *Minority education and caste.* New York: Academic Press.

Ortiz, A. A., & Yates, J. R. (1983). Incidence of exceptionality among Hispanics: Implications for manpower planning. *NABE Journal, 7,* 41–54.

Project PROPEL handbook: Resources for adopting sites. (1993). Long Island City, NY: La Guardia Community College.

Rigg, P. (1991). Whole Language in TESOL. *TESOL Quarterly, 25,* 521–542.

Rigg, P., & Enright, S. (Eds.). (1986). *Children and ESL: Integrating perspectives.* Washington, DC: TESOL.

Savignon, S. J. (1983). *Communicative competence—Theory and classroom practice: Texts and contexts in second language learning.* Reading, MA: Addison-Wesley.

Taylor, D. (Ed.). (1990). Assessment in whole language teaching [Special issue]. *English Education, 22*(1).

Tinajero, J. V. (1994). Are we communicating? Effective instruction for students who are acquiring English as a second language. *The Reading Teacher, 48,* 260–264.

Wolf, D., LeMahahieu, P. G., & Eresh, J. T. (1992). Good measure: Assessment as a tool for education reform. *Education Leadership, 49*(8), 8–13.

Classroom Perspectives

A. *Using a Literacy Portfolio in First Grade*

B. *Using a Literacy Portfolio Process with Gifted Students*

C. *An Administrator's Perspective: Creating Conditions for Change*

Using a Literacy Portfolio in First Grade

by
Lindy Vizyak
First-grade teacher, Cotton Creek Elementary School
Adams County Five Star Schools
Westminster, Colorado

I have been a first-grade teacher for seventeen years. I teach in a large school district eighteen miles northwest of Denver that enrolls children from five different cities. We are organized into twenty-six elementary, six middle, and three high schools. The district is composed of families from all economic groups and has both teaching English as a second language (TESL) and Chapter One classes. Six years ago I began searching for alternative methods of documenting the learning in my classroom. I had adopted a holistic philosophy of teaching, and, as my teaching had changed, so my needs for assessment changed.

My classroom is child-centered, and students are involved in many decisions that affect their learning such as classroom rules, course of study, and projects. Students know what is expected in terms of learning and behavior, and they take responsibility for both. In this class, there is a strong sense of community that values the strengths and abilities of each child. My role is that of teacher, facilitator, collaborator, and co-learner.

MY APPROACH TO LITERACY INSTRUCTION

Our reading and writing programs are literature-based. A block of two hours and forty-five minutes each morning provides the necessary time for students to read, write, illustrate, research, and share information. In my class, students are immersed in the rich language of a wide variety of genres such as environmental print, fiction, nonfiction, poetry, songs, fairy tales, and nursery rhymes. Reading material is readily accessible for all levels, whether emergent, early, or fluent readers. Our classroom has over 1,000 books with a core collection of 500 books always available for independent reading. The other 500 books are single copies and multiple-copy sets that regularly change to support unit studies, cultural studies, holidays, and other thematic projects. Shared reading, guided reading, reading aloud, and independent reading are all components of the reading program. Each format provides opportunities for involving students in making meaning to reinforce the three reading cue systems I emphasize: semantic (meaning), syntactic (structure of grammar), and graphophonic (sound–symbol relationships).

I use a variety of instructional approaches. At the beginning of the year, students are sometimes grouped by reading abilities. My goal is for each student to develop a basic sight vocabulary in addition to appropriate skills and strategies. At other times, students may be organized either in small, self-selected groups to discuss the same text or kept as a whole class to read the same text that relates to a theme study. Students are also encouraged to work independently by reading and responding to different texts. Many different reading assessments are used during the year. A teacher-made letter–sound–word screening is administered during the first week of school to obtain baseline data for each student and to identify instructional needs. A commercial miscue analysis test is given at least three times a year. I also involve the students in individual reading conferences at least once a month, when I monitor the students' progress. Figure A–1 is a sample of my reading conference notes for a student in September, October, and November. My written comments based on these individual conferences are in keeping with our school district's reading content standards for first grade.

A key component of my literacy program is daily book checkout. Parents are expected to read at home with their children. The checkout procedure is explained during the first parent conference in September. Parents sign and return slips with the titles of books read either "to child," "with child," or "by child." This information is transferred at the end of each

Name	Jenelle		
Date	Book	Oral reading	Comments
9/30	Brown Bear, Brown Bear	—Good expression ★Points and reads with a voice/print match —Corrected herself when she read too fast	Vocabulary errors: none —Seen text: class book this week —Looks to teacher for validation of correct reading
10/27	The Big Toe	Strategies: Phonics, picture clues —Beginning to self-correct errors ★Knows large print means louder voice	Vocabulary errors: a/an away in/on went (Goal:) practice "skip and come back" reading strategy —More confident reader
11/25	Come In, Boo Bear	Strategies: Picture clues, phonics, sight vocabulary (Goal) —Good rate and expression	—Unseen text/ grade-level story —Still working on "skip and come back" strategy ★ Good comprehension— could retell story Vocabulary errors: think

Figure A–1 Reading conference sheet notes.

month to a form that is kept in each child's portfolio and indicates the number of books read independently as well as the class average. Parents are also provided with a written explanation of the decoding strategies that are taught at school, and therefore I expect that they will support their child's reading development with more options than just telling the child "sound it out." Daily parent involvement has had a major, positive impact on student reading progress.

The writing program is based on a Writer's Workshop approach. Each student has a colored file folder for keeping completed writing as well as works in progress. Folders are kept in the students' desks to encourage them to write during free time as well as during our daily writing time. Students also write in spiral-bound journals. Sometimes the journals are used as diaries to record personal thoughts and events, while at other times, they serve as learning logs in which students reflect on daily activities by responding to sentence starters such as, "I

Figure A–2 Sample writing conference note.

learned that Martin Luther King Jr. . . ." Writing instruction also includes minilessons that address specific needs identified through each student's writing samples taken from their journals, writing folders, or responses to literature. The lessons often focus on author's craft, mechanics, legibility (still a concern for emergent writers), or message quality.

I meet with students individually at least once every six weeks to assess writing progress. During these conferences as students individually read their piece to me, I note spelling development, skills exhibited (capitalization, punctuation, dialogue, editing strategies, etc.), and message quality. I then identify one or two instructional goals, which I immediately address with the student. Figure A–2 shows a sample of a student's writing and my comments about what I noticed as significant.

As with reading, writing evaluation is based on district standards developed for first grade. If a student is writing at an advanced level, then the writing can be evaluated with a second-grade or above writing rubric developed by the school district. Figure A–3 is a summary of my

Name	Emily	
	Writing Progress	

Date	Topic:	Comments:
9/19	**Emily and Mom and Dad and Colton** —personal narrative	—Pattern book —Writes with a purpose —Capitalizes names/I —One sentence on each page
	Spelling: mom my is nis = nice net = neat Colton	Instructional Needs: —End punctuation (edited book) —More detail [Prompt: What could you write about your mom? dad? brother?
10/27	Topic: **We Had Halloween Fun** fiction/narrative	Comments: —Some end puctuation —"ing" (frosting)/"s" for plurals —Capitalizes I/names/beginning of a sentence —Great detail and plot development
	Spelling: fun black fases = faces had we wolle = wall frosting brothr = brother	Instructional Needs: —? —Quotation marks
11/16	Topic: Seattle —Written to tell teacher about Seattle —Personal narrative	Comments: —Above first-grade expectations —Consistent end punctuation —Some random capital letters (developmentally appropriate)
	Spelling: beach haosse = house dollres = dollars we at jellyfish cared = carried	Instructional Needs: —Correct spelling of "was" and "went" [edited book] —No periods at the end of a title
12/12	Topic: **Katie Moves to Hawaii** —narrative "I decided to write about Hawaii because we are studying Hawaii."	Comments: —Loves to write/lots of stories in her folder —Dialogue —Influenced by _American Girl_ series
	Spelling: (Strategies) —Memory/ask for help books charts, lists/sound them out agreed but move Pete know yelld = yelled	Instructional Needs: —Correct spelling of "what" "where" —"ed" ending

Figure A–3 Writing progress notes.

notes about one child after four writing conferences held in September through December. These conferences provide an excellent opportunity for individual evaluation of the student's literacy development and also for setting instructional goals appropriate for individual needs. Even in first grade, students show a remarkable range in literacy development.

My class of twenty-four first graders includes a wide range of ability levels. Three students have special educational needs, and one student receives daily pull-out services from our school's learning disabilities teacher. Two students are enrolled in a class for severe/profound cognitive and educable mentally retarded (EMR) students. These students are fully included in our class and share a specially trained paraprofessional aide. Each of these students has a portfolio that documents growth toward their Individual Educational Plan (IEP). The special circumstances of each sample of work in these students' portfolios is described: for example, "Writing was done hand-over-hand with a paraprofessional," or "When given a choice between 'happy' and 'sad' pictures, Amy chose the one that best described how she felt today and pasted it in her journal." I have more anecdotal notes about these special students than others as they have limited speech and writing skills. For example, an entry in one of these students' portfolios reads, "Raymond has memorized his *What's For Lunch* book. He points to the word that names the food pictured on each page. He holds the book and turns the pages correctly. He eagerly shares the book with the class in the author's chair." As with other students, I use observational data recorded in portfolios to plan learning experiences and note progress toward specific goals. All students in my class show growth over time, regardless of ability, race, culture, or gender. Portfolios are clearly for everyone.

STUDENT ASSESSMENT

Our school district (Adams County Five Star Schools in Northglenn, Colorado) has clearly defined content standards that align with recently developed statewide standards. At the district level, curriculum framework reports describing these standards are shared with parents and students at the first conference in September (see Figure A–4). A completed copy is included with each student's final student report card in June. There are no state requirements for testing first graders, but standardized testing occurs at fourth, eighth, and tenth grades.

I employ a portfolio system that complements my philosophy of literacy teaching and facilitates individual assessment. My student portfolios are not translated into letter grades. However, I use the contents to evaluate student understanding and application of reading and writing skills and strategies. The portfolio contents clearly support the report card evaluation and information shared during parent conferences. Figure A–5 is a sample of a student evaluation that is given to the parent with report cards distributed each quarter. It can also serve a larger purpose of guiding instruction and evaluating teaching strategies.

USING A PORTFOLIO PROCESS

The first year of using a portfolio approach to evaluation, I began very slowly. I attended workshops and read current research on portfolio assessment. Working with our school's reading resource teacher, my initial focus was on reading and writing progress. I collected handwriting

Name _____

FIRST GRADE

Reading

	1	2	3	4	5
I. Develops Fluency and Automaticity					
A. 65 High Frequency Words	0–75%		85–90%		95–100%
B. Fluency: After three readings of an average class book, @50-word passage	0–75%		84–88%		95–100%
II. PREDICTION: Predicts logically from title and/or pictures.	Never		Occasionally		Frequently
III. Confirms Text: From independent word recognition strategies (picture clues, sight vocabulary, phonics, structural analysis, skips and reads for more information, rereads, logic sub., background information) student uses:	No strategies		2 strategies		4 or more strategies
IV. RESPONDS TO TEXT	No comprehension		Literal comp.		Interpretive comp.

Writing

	1	2	3	4	5
I. Development as a Writer					
A. 20-word Developmental Test	Uses letters that may not represent speech sound		Uses some sounds heard in words. May not read words		Uses consonants and some vowels correctly
B. Spacing	Letters strung together		Inconsistent spaces large and small		Consistent spaces between words
C. Writes Legibly	Unreadable, unrecognizable letters		Fairly regular size most letters legible		Letters conform to standard and rest on line
D. Uses Periods	No punctuation		Random periods		Period at end of perceived sentence
E. Uses Capital Letters	No capitals		Random capitals		Capital letter begins sentence and uses "I"

II. Development of Writing

	1	2	3	4	5
A. Use of Letter/Sound Knowledge	Use of letters that may not represent speech sounds		Use of some sounds heard in words, may not be sure of what word is		Use of consonants and some vowels correctly
B. Word Use	Strings letters together; no use of words		Uses only high frequency words		Willing to use best known word, even if hard to spell
C. Sentence Use	No identifiable sentences		3–4 word sentences		6 or more words in many sentences
D. Story Writing	Random words, wrong or no meaning		Pattern, concept, and personal narrative stories		Uses character, setting, problem/solution in stories
III. Shares and Publishes	Does not share		Shares only when requested		Willingly shares

Speaking and Listening

I. Speaking

	1	2	3	4	5
A. Content	Unrelated		Approximate meaning; no elaboration		Complete response
B. Clarity	Speech not understandable		Some difficulty in pronunciation		Clear speaking
C. Volume	Too loud or soft				Appropriate volume
II. Listening	No comprehension		Literal comprehension		Interpretive, follows directions

Teacher _____

Date _____

FIGURE A–4 Curriculum framework report. (Courtesy of Cotton Creek Elementary, Northglenn, Colorado.)

samples, reading conference observations, and independent reading logs. I also developed forms, checklists, and tests to provide a means for recording data. I now include mathematics, social studies, and science samples in the portfolios. My specific suggestions for implementing a portfolio process in primary grades are fully described in a handbook I've written, which also includes many reproducible forms, surveys, and checklists (Vizyak, 1996).

The portfolio model I have developed is comprehensive and shows a student's educational experiences and growth during the school year in many different areas (see Figure A–6). It is a carefully selected collection of student work that provides clear evidence to the

---

Name __John_____   Date __3-11_____

Reading: John is reading independently at a 3^2 level (above grade level.) He uses many strategies to figure out new words: phonics, sight vocabulary, logical substitutions, and rereading. He has excellent expression when he reads out loud. He chooses to read for free time and has a good at-home reading record.

Writing:
Punctuation: Consistently uses correct end punctuation.

Capitalization: Usually capitalizes the first word in a sentence, "I" and people's names.

Spelling: Spells most words correctly. Examples of spelling taken from his writing: my, brown, five, had, away, leve = leave. Enjoys writing in his journal during free time.

Math: Tasks completed this grading period:
Subtraction:
____ Uses counters   ____ Uses counters and strategies   ✓ Uses strategies
  John has strong mental math skills.
  ★ Writing by ones to 100   ★ Identifies coins
  ★ Writing by fives to 100   ★ Knows value of coins
  ★ Writing by tens to 100   ★ Counts groups of pennies
                                        ★ Counts groups of nickels
                                        ★ Counts groups of dimes
Problem Solving: John is a good problem solver. He usually applies a process that leads to a correct answer. Strategies we are learning: draw a picture, look for a pattern, guess and check, and write a simple equation.

Science/Social Studies: Tests given this grading period:

Dinosaurs: 9/9   Japan: 10/10
John is very excited about our units. He often brings things to share with the class.

Comments:
John is considerate, kind, and very helpful.

FIGURE A–5 Sample student evaluation

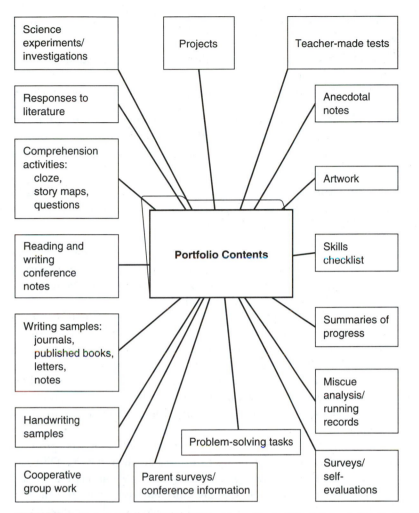

FIGURE A–6 A portfolio model. (*Note.* From *Student Portfolios—A Practical Guide to Evaluation* (p. 22) by L. Vizyak, 1996, Bothell, WA: The Wright Group. Copyright 1996 by the Wright Group. Reprinted by permission.)

student and others of the student's knowledge, skills, strategies, concepts, attitudes, and achievement in a given area or areas. My portfolio system has two major components: Student-Managed portfolios (S-M portfolios) and teacher-managed Teacher/Student assessment portfolios (T/S assessment portfolios—see also Vizyak, 1995, 1996). S-M portfolios are kept by the students, and they can include whatever they want in these portfolios. During periodic conferences, each student and I jointly select work from their S-M portfolio to consider for inclusion in the T/S assessment portfolio. This process is student-centered, and students both select and comment on their choices. I store both portfolios in 13-by-14-inch plastic milk crates that hold vertical files, and I use standard-sized folders for the portfolios. This storage system allows for materials to be filed easily without removing folders, and portfolios are readily accessible both to me and my students. The T/S assessment portfolio contains self-selected work, surveys, projects, tests, conference, and anecdotal notes, evaluation data, self-assessments, and works in progress gathered throughout the school year.

Figure A–7 is a time line of how I gather assessment information about my students throughout the school year.

Items are selected for the students' portfolios to document growth in these areas:

1. Evidence of self-reflection and self-evaluation demonstrated through samples of published writing, surveys, or reading and writing conference notes

2. Evidence of progress toward clearly defined learning goals based on district, building, and classroom assessments

3. Evidence of developing literacy skills including samples collected at regular intervals during the year to show growth over time in such areas as handwriting, journal writing, and responses to literature

My portfolio system reflects my concern that portfolio contents provide clear evidence of both learning process and resulting products to the students themselves, parents, and other educators. It is a process that both encourages self-evaluation from the students and requires parental involvement in the child's learning.

For the T/S assessment portfolio, we collect data and student work samples in a manila folder. On the front cover, I created three vertical columns titled, reading, writing, and math. On the back cover, information about science and social studies is recorded. Under each heading, I record in chronological order observations from classwork or individual conferences and testing information. Self-adhesive labels are handy for recording my daily observations and can be easily affixed on the folders. Products and notes inside the folder support all comments on the cover. I find this information especially useful for parent conferences and to complete report cards.

Not everyone in the district is currently using a portfolio process, but an increasing number of teachers are beginning to use classroom portfolios. Different models are used, depending on the purpose(s) of the portfolio. Some teachers use *showcase portfolios,* which contain examples of best work, while other models document achievement and contain a wider range of process and product work samples as well as testing data. Our school district fully supports the development of portfolios as an authentic form of assessment. Classes have been provided through the staff development department. The building principal has consistently supported efforts at the building level by providing staff development, encouraging teachers to attend workshops/conferences, sharing current research articles, and purchasing books for our professional library. Such encouragement is necessary to establish the appropriate school climate. Because we do not have a school-wide portfolio system, I give a copy of the portfolio covers to the next year's teacher as a summary of the student's progress in first grade. *The actual portfolio belongs to the student and is taken home at the end of the year.*

Parent support is an important component of this evaluation process. At the first conference in September, I tell parents about the portfolios, which will be kept for each student. I show a completed portfolio from the previous year. During the year, I share portfolios with parents at conferences and at special portfolio nights. In December and again in April, families are invited to come to school for an evening celebration. The parents at our school have been actively involved in requesting that portfolios be continued as students move beyond first grade. For the past five years, surveys indicate that parents value having samples of their child's work, understand information contained in a portfolio, and can easily see growth over time. Parent comments on the surveys include, "I know more about Jeff than I have ever

September

Letter–sound–word screening
Miscue analysis, as needed
Drawing sample
Writing sample
Parent survey for back-to-school
 conference
Interest survey
Math computation and problem-
 solving pretest

October

Writing conference
Student self-evaluation
Portfolio conference with student
Report card/summary of
 progress

November

Writing conference
About Me self-evaluation
Developmental spelling test

December

Parent/student survey from
 Portfolio Night

January

Writing conference
Self-selected journal writing
Miscue analysis for all students
Student self-evaluation
Portfolio conference with student
Report card/summary of
 progress

February

Writing conference
Parent evaluation
Student evaluation by teacher,
 student, parent

March

Writing conference
Self-selected journal writing
Portfolio conference with student
Report card/summary of
 progress

April

Writing conference
Self-evaluation

May

Writing conference
Miscue analysis for all students
Self-selected journal writing
Drawing sample
About Me self-evaluation
End-of-year survey
Math computation and problem-
 solving post-test
First-grade spelling test
Developmental spelling test
Portfolio conference with student

June

Report card
District Curriculum Framework
 Report to parents for literacy
 and math

Monthly Assessment

Voluntary reading record
Reading conference
Handwriting sample
Response to literature

Ongoing Assessment

Writing sample evaluation by
 teacher and student—two
 published books per year
Mathematics evaluation of skills
 and concepts
Social studies/science unit tests

FIGURE A–7 Assessment time line. (*Note.* From *Student Portfolios—A Practical Guide to Evaluation*, p. 10, by L. Vizyak, 1996, Bothell, WA: The Wright Group. Copyright 1996 by the Wright Group. Reprinted by permission.)

known about any of my children," and "It was wonderful to see Jennelle's work. What a great opportunity for building self-esteem!"

THE PORTFOLIO MODEL CHANGES

Over the past three years, I have made changes in my portfolio model. As I continued my research about alternative methods of assessment, I became increasingly uncomfortable with my teacher-controlled model of portfolio entries in which student participation and access were limited. It did not align with current research that stresses the importance of students' applying the processes of self-reflection and self-evaluation to set *personal learning goals.*

Two years ago, I put my research-based knowledge into practice and changed my portfolio process at the beginning of the year. I provided blank file folders for the children to collect their work. Some students collected work samples, but most did not. At the end of the year, I reflected back on this less than successful experience and made several discoveries. I had not properly modeled the process, nor had I discussed possible contents of a portfolio or reasons for selecting the contents with my students. No wonder these very young children had difficulty. This realization prompted my decision to provide a structure the following year that would support my goal of developing a *collaborative assessment model.*

I implemented my new plan by introducing the term *portfolio* during the first week of school. To provide a clear model, I shared my own portfolio with the class. I had decorated the cover of an 8-by-12-inch manila folder with items of personal significance to me including a drawing of the cover of a favorite children's book, a drawing of my family, and a University of Colorado logo, because my son is a recent graduate. I also shared the contents of my portfolio with the students and explained why each entry was included, based on the significance of each piece. Then I gave my students blank folders to decorate and share with the class. This first step created instant ownership and certainly enhanced the students' personal commitment to a portfolio collection.

Several times each week, students shared pieces from their portfolios and explained the reasons for their selections. During these conferences, I focus on the many positive things I see about the children's development. Figure A–8 is an example of items that Tiffany and I discussed during her conference about things that she recognized about her own literacy skills early in the school year at the end of October.

At the beginning of the year, students have no previous experience with this process, and most found it difficult to explain their choices or responded in a very concrete manner. Ryan shared a story he had written about his dog and said, "I put this in my portfolio because it is about my dog and I like my dog." I wanted to model other possible reasons for Ryan to include the story in his portfolio, so I said, "I know that Ryan loves to write and often writes at home and during his free time; I also see that he has a title for his story." Ryan promptly added, "Oh, yeah. I also have a summary on the back of my story." I asked him where he got the idea of including a story summary, and he said that he noticed that many of the books I read to the class had a summary on the back. Ryan had clearly made a connection between reading and writing!

The students clearly needed more direction about the portfolio process. Drawing on my experience with writer's workshop minilessons, I structured portfolio minilessons. These lessons focused on the content of S-M portfolios and reasons for selections. Most impor-

THINGS I CAN DO

Tiffany

FIGURE A–8 Notes about a student's accomplishments during October conference. (*Note.* From *Student Portfolios—A Practical Guide to Evaluation* (p. 32) by L. Vizyak, 1996, Bothell, WA: The Wright Group. Copyright 1996 by the Wright Group. Adapted by permission.)

1. Name on paper
2. Date on paper
3. Spacing between words
4. Title
5. Number the pages
6. Illustrations
7. Genre: nonfiction/personal narrative
8. Punctuation: (.)
9. Dedication
10. "oh"
11.
12.

tantly, these lessons provided the language needed for self-reflection. It became quite clear that my young students needed to be shown how to become more self-aware. The majority of the first student selections were examples of best work. As the year progressed, minilessons explored other reasons for selecting portfolio pieces including the following:

■ Something new you have learned (growth)

■ Something that took a long time (effort)

■ Something that was challenging (risk taking)

■ Something that shows interests outside of school (holistic learning)

The students also generated a chart listing "Things That Can Go in a Portfolio." It includes a story or book, science projects, letters, notes, cards, best work, math papers, artwork, photographs, things from home, challenging things, things that show improvement, and work from the student's favorite subject. The list is ongoing and expands as students discover new categories of possible portfolio inclusions. As a result of these efforts, the students' portfolios are becoming much more expansive. My students are also learning self-selection and seem to take great pride in their large collections. Each Friday, anyone who has a new portfolio entry (including me) is invited to share it with the class. These regular share sessions have resulted in improved metacognition and opportunities for building self-esteem and confidence as students develop a voice in the assessment process.

Once every nine-week grading period, students meet with me individually to choose two or three pieces from their S-M portfolios to include in our T/S assessment portfolio. The student completes an entry form to explain the student's reason(s) for each choice and attaches it to the appropriate piece. Students choose entries for various reasons. For example, one student included a computer-generated text and illustrations in his portfolio because it was his first composition on the computer, and he was very proud of his accomplishment. Students may select anything they have collected in their S-M portfolios. This process gives them practice in selecting meaningful work and reflecting on those selections. It also provides valuable information about each student's ability to self-reflect. Figure A–9 illustrates how Teri was

Name: _Teri_____   Date: _5-3-97____

WRITING SAMPLE EVALUATION

Title of student's writing _Dinosaurs With Envelopes_____

Student's Self-Evaluation:

Why did you choose to publish this writing? _It is good. (Why?) Some of my words are spelled right._____

Where did you get the idea? _I wanted to make a funny book._____

What do you like about writing? _I like when the dinosaurs get their own envelopes._____

What would make your writing better? _If I could spell it all right._____

Teacher's Evaluation:

   Writing Stages:

   ____ *Emergent:* scribbles, recognizes letters and letter names, writes random letters or numbers or copies randomly, displays some knowledge of letter sounds

   ✓ *Early:* repeats sentence patterns, uses temporary spelling, consistent spacing, displays a sense of story, uses some correct capitalization and punctuation

   ____ *Fluent:* writes with a purpose, varies writing, spells most words correctly, usually uses correct capitalization and punctuation

   Language Mechanics:

      ✓ Capitalizes the first word in a sentence
      ✓ Capitalizes the word "I"
      ____ Capitalizes names
      ✓ Includes correct end punctuation (?.).
      ____ Uses legible handwriting—sometimes

COMMMENTS: _Creative idea. Teri continues to write simple books. Beginning to take some spelling risks: ovulops = envelopes, eiksided = excited, wnderfll = wonderful "s" for plurals_

INSTRUCTIONAL NEEDS: _Add more detail to stories._____

FIGURE A–9 A student's writing self-evaluation, teacher's evaluation, and instructional goals. (*Note.* From *Student Portfolios—A Practical Guide to Evaluation* by L. Vizyak, 1996, Bothell, WA: The Wright Group. Adapted by permission.)

able to self-evaluate a piece of writing and includes my evaluation of Teri and instructional goals. I feel confident that this new T/S assessment portfolio is a successful marriage of student self-reflection and self-evaluation as well as teacher accountability.

BENEFITS OF LITERACY PORTFOLIOS

A portfolio approach to evaluation enables me to provide authentic assessment that serves as a record of a student's learning, development, behaviors, and attitudes over time. It provides a collaborative, developmentally appropriate model that reflects my program and philosophy of teaching because it focuses on the students' many unique talents, strengths, and abilities and not their shortcomings, which had often been the focus of classroom assessment. For a portfolio process to work, it should be a natural extension of teaching and individualized to meet each teacher's needs and goals.

Before starting a portfolio process, here are a few last tips. Be sure to start slowly and gradually integrate portfolios into your class. Set realistic goals by reflecting on your philosophy of teaching, your school's curriculum requirements, and your teaching needs. I've found that establishing a four- to five-year time line (Vizyak, 1995) may be helpful to develop a good system. Be consistent, and set aside time each day for assessment and record keeping. Make sure to commit sufficient time to working with individual students as well as small groups each day, and be sure to distribute your time fairly with all students. Involve parents at every phase by having them complete surveys, attend portfolio conferences (which can be run by the students after training), and attend portfolio night celebrations. Parent involvement can also be stimulated through newsletters. My experience has shown that a portfolio process can certainly be done with students as young and diverse as even my first-grade class. I truly believe that a portfolio process enhances both literacy instruction and student growth.

REFERENCES

Vizyak, L. (1995). Student portfolios: Building self-reflection in a first-grade classroom. *Reading Teacher, 48,* 362–364.

Children's Literature References

Martin, B., Jr. (1967). *Brown Bear, Brown Bear.* New York: Henry Holt.
McPhail, D. (1986). "Come in, Boo Bear." In *Bells.* Boston: Houghton-Mifflin.

Vizyak, L. (1996). *Student portfolios—A practical guide to evaluation.* Bothell, WA: Wright Group.

Melser, J., & Cowley, J. (1980). *The big toe.* Aukland, New Zealand: Shortland Public, Ltd.

Using a Literacy Portfolio Process with Gifted Students

by
Virginia Bushart and Irene Berman
Teachers of the Gifted, Mount Elementary School
Three Village School District
Setauket, Long Island, New York

Our teaching situation is rather unique. The school district in which we teach is located on the north shore of eastern Long Island in a community with a major university and an internationally recognized research laboratory. Consequently, our student population is multicultural, with families from all over the world, is quite cosmopolitan, and strongly values education, academic achievement, and accomplishment. Our school has self-contained classes for gifted children, who come from all over the district starting with third grade. Both of us teach gifted fifth-grade students in this program, but because of our mutual interests and close relationship, we team teach.

OUR READING PROGRAM

We knew the horizons of our traditional reading program well. Spanning several grade levels, the spectrum of the reading program began and ended with a basal reader. Workbooks, worksheets, word lists, and printed exams formed the strands that permeated the basal program and established fixed horizons at the beginning and end of fifth grade. Our extremely capable students would one day move beyond these horizons to a world of literature that had no bounds, while we, as fifth-grade teachers, would remain behind to function within the confines of the traditional elementary school reading program unless we set forth to explore other possibilities. And so, our journey that was destined to lead us to a portfolio process began for the reasons that most memorable journeys begin: restlessness, curiosity, the need to breathe fresh air, the lure to explore the unknown, and the thrill of taking a risk. Energized by the spirit of adventure, we cast off our anchorage and headed toward the horizon to see what lurked beyond.

THE TRANSITION FROM TEACHING
READING TO TEACHING LITERATURE

We traveled light on our first days, and ultimately we arrived at an integrated approach to reading and writing instruction that is complemented by the use of student portfolios. To explain our application of the portfolio process as an important part of our language arts program, as a means to assess learning and growth in literacy, and also to develop the specific traits of giftedness, we briefly describe our literacy program.

On day one of our first attempt to teach reading using a novel, we felt helpless as we each sat with a group of children, grasping a very small paperback, and muttering, "We thought we'd try something different today." We had only to look at the title of the novel to answer the question burning our ears, "Whatever made me do this?" As we handed a copy of the novel *Call It Courage* (Sperry, 1963) to each of our students, there was a strange silence in the classroom. We thought we detected a faint whisper, "Real books, we're getting real books!" The structures we had relied on in years of teaching reading were gone, and with only a novel in hand, we had no choice but to open to page one and begin reading. Later someone suggested discussing the cover illustration and surveying the title page. Though we didn't know it at the time, we were engaging our students in a method known as *shared guided reading*, an integral component of a well-rounded literature-based language program. We read several chapters of the novel and glanced up to discover hands waving in the air. Our

students were responding to literature without a question or directive from us. The discussion that ensued was exhilarating, and we knew we were pointed in the right direction.

It has been seven years since that first novel unfolded with our students. During our evolution, we often followed our instincts when presenting new works to our students and have followed a student-centered approach to reading in keeping with our student-centered approach to writing. Initially, our cues and inspirations were drawn from memories of our own finest moments as learners in literature classes. We also enrolled in courses and workshops designed to teach whole language and literature-based instruction and again trusted our instincts as experienced teachers when determining which elements inherent in these modes of instruction we would apply to our program. We also investigated research in the area of language arts. It was important for us to find studies that substantiated our method of presenting literature to our students while at the same time reassuring us that our instincts as educators were well grounded.

Initially, we didn't realize that we were using a method of literature instruction that presently is experiencing a great deal of attention from researchers and theorists. This method is known as *response-based* or *reader-based instruction*. The work of Langer (1994) has helped us to articulate, substantiate, and further cultivate our method of teaching and learning reading. What's more, it has invigorated and supported our application of the portfolio as a highly authentic tool for assessing student reading and language performance.

THE PURPOSES OF A LITERACY PORTFOLIO

Because our reading discussions proceed from a reader-based perspective, a portfolio provides our students an opportunity to extend their own perspectives to written expression and, further, to react and reflect not only on the literature but also on their own lives and on the lives and experiences of others. For our intellectually gifted students, the portfolio has also served as a repository for ideas in response to literature that are expressed through writing, a collector's album for writing products, and a window through which students may view themselves as writers and thinkers for the purpose of self-evaluation and reflection. For us as teachers, the portfolio has become an invaluable assessment tool. As a gifted population, our students are eager to express ideas in response to literature, and because they are both fluent and intrinsically motivated, these ideas are frequently expressed in writing. The portfolio enables us to authentically assess learning and literacy, as well as the growth in our students with respect to critical thinking, which reaches high levels of evaluation and reflects deep insight by our students. We are also able to evaluate creativity and monitor task commitment; both qualities, along with above-average ability, are included in Renzulli's (1986) Three Ringed Model for Giftedness, which we endorse.

The Portfolio as an Assessment Tool for Thinking Skills

The portfolio provides an excellent opportunity to assess thinking skills, specifically, as they relate to understanding and appreciating literature. Using criteria developed by Bloom (1956) in his *Taxonomy of Educational Objectives,* we assess our students' learning by examining their portfolios and evaluate their reactions to literature on the basis of specific descriptors of cognitive behaviors. The taxonomy presents a hierarchy of cognitive skills that informs us about the thinking strategies that should be developed in our students. As our students work

through ideas about literature through writing, we assess their learning in accordance with the hierarchy of Bloom's cognitive behaviors:

Level I. Knowledge

Level II. Comprehension

Level III. Application

Level IV. Analysis

Level V. Synthesis

Level VI. Evaluation

For example, by looking for specific learning behaviors identified by verbs associated with each of the levels in the cognitive domain, we assess the thinking skills of our students with a high degree of objectivity and reliability.

STUDENTS RESPOND TO LITERATURE

We have learned that in a literature-based reading program, summary writing is a skill that draws from the student's knowledge of a selection and indicates whether or not the student has comprehended. It can also be analyzed to determine the student's level of thinking. It is the first skill that we develop in response to a literature selection; however, we regard summary writing as a craft that we are still learning and refining ourselves as teachers and readers. Therefore, each school year we relearn summary writing with our students.

We begin by asking our students to summarize a chapter or two in a novel that we are reading together. We share these summaries, analyze them, and reach a consensus about which we think are the strongest and why. We discuss the elements of a well-written summary and model professionally written summaries for the children. We also discuss the difference between a summary and a book review. We then elicit from our students a list of the characteristics of a well-written summary, and while the list varies from year to year, it always reflects an understanding of the craft. Given the population of intellectually gifted that we teach, we are able to accomplish this goal in two sessions.

In constructing the definition of a summary, our students apply Bloom's taxonomy and are therefore required to use these thinking strategies:

Select and identify (knowledge).

Propose, explain, and expound (comprehension).

Relate, employ, and mobilize (application).

Examine, reason, deduce, and scrutinize (analysis).

Compose, construct, conceive, and formulate (synthesis).

Appraise, assay, reject, and determine (evaluation).

When our students independently write summaries, they exercise cognitive skills because in summary writing they cite, select, arrange, omit, and identify information from a literary work. Further, they must also translate, reword, retell, qualify, infer, outline, and define in the process of comprehending what they are reading. We then can assess the students' comprehension by evaluating their summaries using Bloom's model as our criteria.

A well-constructed summary likely would not include higher level thinking skills such as analysis or evaluation. Teachers know that gifted students are eager to engage in the higher level thinking skills, because it is difficult for them not to judge or criticize something that they're reading. However, summary writing is a valuable skill for bright students to learn, not only because it taps their knowledge and comprehension of literature but because it requires them to exercise intellectual discipline and to think objectively. Our students invariably include summaries in their portfolios because they are avid readers and lovers of books, and a summary for them is a memento of a favorite book. The student's summary in Figure B–1 shows the quality of the summaries our students write. This summary certainly reflects knowledge and comprehension of a novel by an extremely capable fifth-grade student. In a program for intellectually gifted students, work of this quality is typical. In a heterogeneous classroom, this summary might serve as a model for peers to follow, but even in a more homogeneous class such as ours, we find peer modeling a powerful motivator and instructor.

When our students become comfortable with the craft of summary writing, they quickly realize that there is more to literature than summarizing plots. They are naturally compelled to react to literature, and as highly verbal children and avid readers, they cannot help but comment on the material they have read. At this time, we introduce the concept of reacting or *responding to literature,* for which higher level thinking skills are more appropriately included. Since we employ a reader-based perspective in our literature discussions, our students are free to explore many possibilities in reacting to literature. It is only natural for us to extend this response-based instruction to written expression. We now ask our students to distinguish between summary and response writing. This leads to the construction of a definition of the essential elements of a reaction to literature.

We react to literature in more than one way, and our students may express their reactions to a piece of literature through prose or poetry. Often, at the completion of a novel, we ask students to capture the essence of the story in poetry. The student reaction to the novel *Sing Down the Moon* (O'Dell, 1970) in Figure B–2 reflects the student's feelings about the novel, which were deliberately omitted in the summary in Figure B–1.

Between the years 1863 and 1865, a Navajo girl named Bright Morning and her friend Running Bird were caught and sold by two Spanish slavers. They escaped together with another slave girl, but the white men who the Indians called "Long Knives" followed them and overtook them. Tall Boy, who Bright Morning was supposed to marry, met them and killed the Long Knive's leader, but he himself lost the use of his right arm forever.

Soon after Bright Morning was put through the Womanhood Ceremony, the Long Knives invaded their home, the Canyon de Chelly, captured them all and marched them to their new home, Bosque Redondo. This is known in history as the Navajo Long Walk. When they arrived there Bright Morning married Tall Boy. However she was determined that her son would not be born in Bosque Redondo, so she and Tall Boy ran away to Elk-Running Valley, where their son was born. They then returned to Canyon de Chelly and made a home there, in a secret place where they could live happily.

Figure B–1. A sample student summary of *Sing Down the Moon* by Scott O'Dell (1970).

This is an adventurous but deep and moving book about a Navajo girl named Bright Morning. She and her tribe go through many adventures together fighting off both the Spaniards and other white men called the Long Knives. When the Navajo tribe does not comply to a heartless Long Knife threat to leave the canyon—or else be taken prisoner—the Long Knives attack. They soon come upon the fleeing Navajo band, taking them captive. The next few years are heart breaking and devastating for the Navajos. They are forced to work in a valley far from Canyon de Chelly and happiness is only found once when Tall Boy, a Warrior from Bright Morning's village, marries Bright Morning.

The author uses galvanic language and poetic imagery in describing the returning of Tall Boy and Bright Morning to their homeland. For example: "The yellow cliffs rose on both sides. The spring flowed from the rock and made a waterfall that spun out over the meadow . . ." This is just one instance of imagery used with great authenticity in this book. Others are: "I saw the high ramparts against the northern sky. They were crimson in the setting sun, even the tall trees along their edges were crimson." These two sentences both demonstrated poetic emotion. I feel that in truth the Navajos won the over all war not by fighting and killing but by keeping peace.

Figure B–2. A sample student reaction to *Sing Down the Moon* by Scott O'Dell (1970).

Clearly, many high-level thinking processes were involved in the formulation of the reaction in Figure B–2, including evaluation not only of the story but also of the author's writing. This reaction is a highly literate one—perhaps *literary* is the more appropriate term, even within the context of our special program. It offers a clear contrast to the summary of the same novel in Figure B–1. Figure B–3 is another sample of a student reaction to literature—in this case, a poem ("The Trap", Beyer, 1966)—showing use of higher level thinking skills. This sample is typical of a piece that students might choose to include in their portfolios. When responses to poetry are included in portfolios, we suggest that copies of the poems be included as well. Again, we assess each student's response for *thinking skills* using criteria from Bloom's (1956) cognitive domain.

In Figure B–3, the student demonstrated a variety of thinking skills in his written response to the poem: He cited, identified, and quoted (level 1, knowledge); he qualified, inferred, explained, proposed, and projected (level 2, comprehension); he applied knowledge by relating and using material in the poem to put forth his own theory (level 3, application); he examined, deduced, scrutinized, and reasoned in his writing (level 4, analysis); he constructed, conceived, and formulated his own theories (level 5, synthesis); and finally, he judged, appraised, determined, and criticized (level 6, evaluation).

This student's reaction as well as summary writing represent typical writing activities used in our literature program. When students include these entries in their portfolios, we feel that the portfolio becomes a true reflection of the ongoing activities that we value as important aspects of our reading and writing program. As previously discussed, because we emphasize and value higher order thinking in our instruction, we use Bloom's taxonomy extensively as the criteria by which to assess learning and growth. However, we also react to the students'

> I think that the poem "The Trap" is very deep and moving. It has lots of vivid language like, "His eyes like cracked marbles", and "Into the deep morning corn." I assumed that the poem was about an old man trapping and wounding a fox, then feeling sorry for the fox. I think that the pressing of red berries into a pale crust is like the fox's blood in the field of corn. The old man is probably going to the fox and maybe ending its misery by killing it because of this: "Guess I'll ride into the back field, first thing. Some mighty big corn back there this year, Mighty big corn." I think the moral of the poem is if you might regret what you're doing, don't do it.

Figure B–3. One student's reaction to *The Trap* by Beyer (1966).

writing personally and individually with teacher comment cards that will be explained in the section describing our writing program.

THE LITERACY PORTFOLIO

The Portfolio as an Assessment of Giftedness

For our population of students and for any heterogeneous population, the portfolio provides an ideal opportunity to assess giftedness. We feel very comfortable with Renzulli's model of giftedness, which has provided us with criteria for both identifying and assessing gifted behaviors in our students. According to Renzulli (1986),

> Research on creative/productive people has consistently shown that although no single criterion can be used to determine giftedness, people who have achieved recognition because of their unique accomplishments and creative contributions possess a relatively well defined set of three interlocking clusters of traits. These clusters consist of above-average, though not necessarily superior ability, task commitment and creativity. (p. 2)

In our classroom, the portfolio becomes an ideal means to document these traits. It also becomes an effective tool for assessing traits indicating giftedness as well as for assessing language performance. Renzulli (1978) also makes the valid point that enrichment activities used for gifted populations can also benefit the education of other students. For example, process-oriented activities such as those that emphasize a variety of higher order thinking skills can certainly be applied with many students and should be integrated with regular curricular activities whenever possible. Though we emphasize the portfolio as an enrichment experience in a special program, we feel it is an activity appropriate for all students. Too often, emphasis on higher order thinking processes has not been included in regular curricular experiences, and it is not appropriate for teachers to assume that they are only good for gifted students. We believe that students' work in portfolios should be used as a valuable tool for assessing the literacy levels of all students and in particular a valuable measure for identifying gifted students within a heterogeneous classroom. Any teacher might therefore use a portfolio to assess reading and writing performance and to identify characteristics of giftedness in their students.

Renzulli (1986) describes three basic clusters of human traits found in gifted students; two of them, creativity and above average ability, have been widely discussed in the professional literature. However, the third trait, task commitment, defines for us an important piece of the assessment puzzle that is too often overlooked. The portfolio process provides the ideal opportunity to exercise and develop task commitment and also gives us the opportunity to assess it. From the moment children are invited to create portfolios, task commitment is required: from initiating the process, when the student has to obtain the portfolio itself, to producing the pieces that will be included in the portfolio, and to maintaining the portfolio as a work in progress. Thus, the portfolio is a valuable indicator of this important criterion for success.

A portfolio is an ideal outlet for student creativity and an excellent tool for assessing it. We expect that each portfolio will be as individual and unique as our students, and we remind them that they are limited only by their imagination and that imagination has no bounds. We are prepared to receive the portfolio that extends beyond the limits of a bound volume and exceeds our own conceptions and imagination. In fact, we anxiously await it. We feel that to overly define the nature of a portfolio would be to seriously inhibit our students' creative potential and to some extent limit their opportunity to demonstrate task commitment.

Introducing the Portfolio to Our Students: From Process to Product to Portfolio

In our program, portfolios are multifaceted and hold the collection of literacy products and thoughtful reflections that we value as part of our reading and writing program. They often house:

Students' writings

Summaries and reactions to literature

Comments from peers, parents, and teachers

Reflections about the world, a special time, or about personal growth and change

Our students are introduced to the concept of a portfolio early in the new school year, beginning with an invitation. During the first week of school, we recruit volunteers from our previous year's class to come to our classroom to share their portfolios. With little direction from us, our former students hold court and became proud presenters of their treasures. Many of the children read their favorite pieces and reflect on the process of creating them, while others explain how they assembled their portfolios. The audience of new fifth graders is always mesmerized by the quantity and quality of work of their slightly older peers. As observers of this process, we are always fascinated by the interaction between our former and present students. The former students display great pride and much authority as they become the teachers. The new fifth graders are not quite sure how to react. They seem impressed with the portfolios but are slightly bewildered and curious about where the portfolios will fit in terms of their assignments and our expectations for them.

As the facilitators of the process that leads to the development of these portfolios, we also are not exactly sure about how new classes will receive the idea of portfolios and where they will take it. It is satisfying for us to see that the excitement that our former students felt their portfolios has remained with them, and now our job is to make sure that the new ents will not only share in this enthusiasm but be successful in creating portfolios that e an authentic representation of their classroom performance in reading and writing.

The Portfolio and the Writing Program

At this point, we begin our writing program, and we do not officially mention the portfolio again for some time. As teachers of writing, we follow a process approach. The journey from *process to product to portfolio* defines our writing program. The portfolio has provided the keel that enables us to both direct and balance our writing program. Before we used a portfolio in our program, we often struggled to strike a balance between creativity and mechanics and between process and product. Now it is the portfolio that drives our writing program, which is an integrated language arts program that focuses on vocabulary expansion, imagery and figures of speech, grammar, and dictionary and thesaurus use. These are all taught in the context of the craft of writing. The portfolio has created an environment in which each aspect of our writing program can be nurtured in its logical and appropriate place. It represents for us the culminating opportunity to assess the skills and growth that we value as teachers of writing.

Each of our students has a notebook, which we call the writer's journal. In this journal ideas are collected and writings are composed. The writing is done completely *in school,* and the children write daily for at least forty-five minutes. We follow the guidelines for a classroom writing workshop described by Donald Graves (1983). From the very beginning, the children are free to choose their own writing topics. Teachers of highly literate fifth-grade students know, however, that when left alone to write, their students are notorious for producing twenty-page sagas of unfocused writing. Therefore, our next step is to model good writing by exposing the children to quality literature in a variety of literary genres.

It is important to mention that the writing journal is organized into several sections that become valuable assets for the writer. The journal contains students' compositions, records of their activities, reactions, and deep feelings. These records may inspire and launch future writings. Students can also record other things in the journal, such as examples of language that they want to remember. We call these selections "delicious language."

When a piece of writing is finished, the editing process begins. The children edit with each other and have devised their own method for correction. A red pen is used to mark a spelling or grammar error, while a purple pen is used to suggest that a word such as *beautiful* might be replaced with a more vivid one (e.g., *radiant, elegant, enchanting*). Revision becomes a way of life, and the children look forward to making each piece better to assist their peers. After editing with a number of peers in both individual and group conferences, the student makes final revisions, and then it is time for group share.

During group share, we can enjoy the work that has been done. S~ listen to and respond to each other's writings, and the children re~ what was liked as well as gently making suggestions for improver~ small group decides which pieces might be shared with the entir~ be handwritten or typed, and at this point, students decide whe~ product in their portfolio. As students complete their pieces, they~ ownership of their products; we hope that many of these will be inclu~

If and when a product is included in a portfolio, then comment c~ by peers, teachers, or parents preserve the reactions to the finished prodi~ cards compliment an author, comment on how the author has grown, o~ personal reflection or reaction to a particular writing. Children design thei~ cards and include special insignias, which are easily recognized by others. W~

every piece of writing in the portfolio, and at regular intervals during the school year, we write comment cards to our students sharing our thoughts on their growth as writers.

We also provide each student with a writing rubric such as the one used by the New York State Education Department that clearly defines characteristics of good writing and different levels of writing ability. The writing rubric also provides a language for communicating and discussing writing standards in the class.

Since we encourage the use of the portfolio by invitation, we do not ask or even hint to our students to bring portfolios in after the initial invitation. We sit and wait for the first one to arrive, which is the hardest part of the journey to the portfolio process. It would be very easy to simply ask the students to bring in a certain type of album on a certain date and easier to order a class set of the same binder or album. That is not our intent. We want the desire and interest to come from within, and so we wait. Again, gifted students are recognized for their task commitment, and once they endorse a process, it flows smoothly. After the first portfolio arrives, others—in various shapes and sizes—follow in a steady trickle. Each one is shared and applauded. Within weeks, the majority of students have chosen, bought, and decorated their own portfolios, which will soon house their individual collections. Students themselves become the encouragers and supporters of their peers and urge those who have not yet engaged in the process to do so. Soon, the portfolio process is established, and all participate willingly.

The Portfolio Encourages Self-Reflection

At various points during the school year, we ask our students to reflect on how they feel they have grown as readers and writers. This self-assessment is one of the final and deepest reflective layers of the portfolio, and it is totally authentic. We feel that this self-reflection is part of the instructional nature of a true portfolio process. Self-reflection is an ongoing and integral aspect of creating a portfolio. Students periodically evaluate and reflect about themselves as writers and readers, and this then assists them in making selections for their portfolios. Our students are adept at critical self-evaluation and can carefully evaluate each potential entry in terms of this reflection process. Samples of individual student reflections can be found in Figure B–4.

CONCLUSIONS

Our students' portfolios are as unique and individual as they are. For us they are assessment tools. For them they are treasures commemorating a year in their lives. The greatest satisfaction comes from anecdotes our children share with us regarding their portfolios. The father of one of our students had the opportunity to show his daughter's portfolio to his 90-year-old third-grade teacher. She approved.

As we relive the school year, we think about the stages our children have gone through from process to product to portfolio. As the first entry is chosen by the student, we acknowledge the development of higher level thinking skills and encourage creativity and risk taking. At the end of the school year, the children's portfolios are a true representation of their growth in language ability and authentically document that journey. On our last day together, we share our portfolios but not for the final time. We know that the children will continue to add and revise even beyond the end of our school year, because they have true

Student 1

In the past year I feel that I have grown as an author because I found talent that I never knew I had. I was more surprised than anyone else could be when poems leaked off my pen. A famous poet once said, "Most of my poems write themselves." In fact, most of my writing products are only second drafts. I love to read and now I like writing as well. I think I've grown as an author because I've grown to like writing.

Student 2

When I started fifth grade I wasn't a very good writer. Now I love writing and have grown in many ways . . . but I always think I could improve. A portfolio is a good idea because I could keep track of my writing and see how I improved. The most wonderful thing about a portfolio is that I always could look back at my writings.

Student 3

I have really evolved as a writer. I used to write dull stories but wrote good rhyming poems that made sense. Now I write good poetry. I enjoy writing more than I used to. Things that help me with my writing are using other poet's work. This shows me the different styles of writing, from Robert Frost's metaphorical poetry to Langston Hugh's jazzy poetry. I don't get inspired just by famous poet's writing but also poetry of people in my classroom.

Figure B–4. Samples of student self-reflections.

ownership of their work and consider the portfolio a work in progress. We also know that some of our students will return to assist us with new students next year and be proud presenters of their treasures.

As stated, the portfolio process clearly relates to Renzulli's (1986) concept of giftedness. Each portfolio is as different and unusual as its owner. The child's creativity can be analyzed from the type of book that is chosen, to the cover, layout, design, and format that are presented. There are no rules. As one student in our class once pointed out, "Your limit is your imagination." We can see the risk takers, the original thinkers, and those with imaginations free of boundaries.

The children in our program, although each clearly exceptional, come to us with various degrees and types of abilities, and the portfolios allow us to see growth in higher level thinking skills. There is no question that the portfolio is an authentic tool for measuring task commitment. We find out immediately which students are self-motivators, which students need more time to blossom, and especially which students continue to carry out the task with full force. It is most gratifying to see the late bloomers take pride in their portfolios. The portfolio is not a mere folder that houses the writings and reflections of students during fifth grade. It is an interactive assessment among the student, the teacher, the parents, and the other children in the classroom. When we started this journey, we were restless, curious, and needed to explore the unknown. We have become energized by this adventure, and we like what we have found. We will continue to explore beyond the horizon, but for now we have lowered our anchors just for a while and feel satisfied that this portfolio process exemplifies the aspects of gifted education that we value.

REFERENCES

Bloom, B. S. (1956). *Taxonomy of educational objectives, Handbook I: Cognitive domain.* New York: David McKay.

Graves, D. H. (1983). *Writing: Teachers and children at work.* Portsmouth, NH: Heinemann.

Langer, J. A. (1994). A response based approach to reading literature. *Language Arts, 71,* 203–211.

Renzulli, J. S. (1978). What makes giftedness? Re-examining a definition. *Phi Delta Kappan, 60,* 180–84, 261.

Renzulli, J. S. (1986). *Systems and models for developing programs for the gifted and talented.* Mansfield Center: Creative Learning Press.

Children's Literature References

Beyer, W. (1966). The trap. In S. Dunning (Ed.), *Reflections on a gift of watermelon pickle.* New York: Scott, Foresman.

O'Dell, S. (1970). *Sing down the moon.* Boston: Houghton Mifflin.

Sperry, A. (1963). *Call it courage.* New York: Macmillan.

EXAMPLE

C

An Administrator's Perspective: Creating Conditions for Change

by
Dr. Kathleen Gooding
Former Assistant Superintendent for Curriculum and Assessment
Plainedge, New York
Presently, Assistant Superintendent East Meadow School District East Meadow, New York

THE ADMINISTRATOR'S ROLE

Getting Started

Every innovation needs someone to lead the charge. So it was in my district with alternative assessment. Teachers alone cannot change a system; they can only change what goes on in their own classroom. An administrator was needed to spearhead the efforts of changing assessment strategies that would impact all classrooms, and this had to do be done in an organized, comprehensive manner. Although significant new initiatives normally fall into the lap of an assistant superintendent or director in charge of curriculum, instruction, or assessment, they do not necessarily start there. Because of their background in language arts and writing process, quite often, one of the first people to push for assessment change is a language arts or reading coordinator or director. In some situations, the change to alternative assessment is initiated by an individual principal who is concerned with the shortcomings of current assessment strategies and who wants to help collaborate on the process that will ultimately result in improved student performance.

In my former school district, Plainedge, New York, it all began in the art and music department and as part of an arts-infused social studies curriculum. Regardless of how the initiative begins, at some point, the district has to make a commitment to change the way it is assessing students. This was not an easy process. We had to convince the administrative staff of (1) the importance of and benefits derived from the adoption of alternative means of assessment and (2) that teachers would have the appropriate amount and type of training to develop and implement alternative strategies. To ensure success of the process, administrative efforts concentrated on four major areas: provide ongoing support, avoid mixed messages, monitor efforts, and focus on consistency.

Ongoing Teacher Support

Classroom teachers had several needs that had to be addressed. They needed (1) to feel the desire for change, (2) the camaraderie of other teachers working toward the same goal, and (3) administrative encouragement and support. Therefore, ongoing training and support were essential, since this method of assessment did not lend itself to a single in-service course offering or intensive one-time training effort. Teachers who attempted implementation of alternative methods of assessment wanted to bounce ideas off their peers as they proceeded, and they needed to maintain contact with someone knowledgeable in the field for technical assistance and guidance to overcome hurdles or to surpass initial expectations as new opportunities arose.

Time was another essential factor. Time is one of the best support mechanisms an administrator can give teachers beginning to implement new assessment activities. Teachers needed time to review and personally reflect on student work and student portfolios; time to discuss student assessments and portfolios with others including the principal, parents, and members of the support staff; and time to revisit and revise what they were doing in the classroom and refocus efforts based on evidence presented in the portfolio.

Avoiding Mixed Messages

Administrators often confuse teachers by encouraging them to become familiar with many new instructional innovations and ideas without the appropriate follow-up. It is not unusual to see teachers take one course in whole language, another in cooperative learning, and yet another on enhancing self-esteem. Sometimes administrators encourage teachers to get involved in four or five new directions at one time. This apparent lack of focus contributes to beliefs often expressed by teachers and parents that new ideas in education are only passing fads. It also helps to explain why many new and effective instructional strategies are never institutionalized.

Therefore, when asking teachers to implement new methods of assessment, I ask that they focus only on assessment and encourage them to take workshops or courses related to new assessment methods and strategies. This is not as limiting as it appears. Performance assessment and portfolios incorporate many of the concepts and theories of the most effective educational innovations: integrating curriculum and using thematic or interdisciplinary instructional and assessment techniques; adapting instruction and assessment to differing learning styles and intelligences; incorporating cooperative learning strategies into group assessment and/or projects; individualizing instruction and goal setting; documenting reflections; enhancing self-worth; developing information literacy through research and use of technology; and designing assessments to accommodate the inclusion of both special education and gifted populations. Our administrators helped teachers see these connections and geared training toward the use of these instructional strategies within the assessment process to improve both student learning and the quality of the assessment.

Monitoring

It was important to help teachers avoid developing bad habits or resorting to old, comfortable ways of doing things. Change is always difficult, and this particular methodology, although it reflects good pedagogy, was unlike anything the teachers had done before. In my introductory training discussions, I refer to the concept of the *backward curriculum* because it isn't until teachers have attempted to design multiple assessment units that they proclaim, "This is like doing everything backward!" Under normal circumstances, teachers decide what and how they are going to teach and later how they will evaluate. This method demands the reverse. First, teachers must decide the outcomes—what they want students to know and be able to accomplish. Then they should determine and design (along with the students if at all possible) the type of task that will produce the desired product, end result, or document. Finally, they must plan instructional activities that provide access to content knowledge and skills needed to promote the behaviors necessary to successfully complete the task. In addition to the challenge of backward curriculum design, this method requires teachers to document student learning on an ongoing basis rather than at the conclusion of a unit or lesson. This presents an additional challenge in terms of time and effort for teachers. It is much easier for teachers to implement one or two assessments or tests when needed than to constantly be concerned with gathering and storing pertinent information.

Other concerns when monitoring these new assessments are the issues of validity and reliability. How much coaching of students is too much? How do we know the assessments are measuring what they propose to measure? How should certain performance standards be established? There are many ways of addressing this issue. One is to use outside or independent evaluators as part of the process. Independent evaluators take an objective look at implemented assessment products. They are often experts in the field, sometimes trained community members, parents, business associates, or teachers from a different grade level or school who provide different perspectives, depending on the focus and type of assessment.

In Plainedge, independent evaluators are used in a variety of ways. First, we have an Assessment Advisory Council, which consists of teachers, students, parents, and administrators. The council interacts with the district's Workforce Partnership Consortium. Between these two groups, all formal assessments and evaluative measures are reviewed, suggestions made for improvement or revision, and the results of assessment pilots evaluated before formal implementation. Second, Plainedge is affiliated with the New York State Pacesetter's District Consortium (Center for Learning Assessment and Student Success, CLASS). As part of this affiliation, we have the option of networking with other districts throughout New York State and can work directly with members of the CLASS staff. As assessments are piloted, they can be shared with other consortium members for a critique, or they can be critiqued directly by staff members of CLASS. Finally, at strategic points in the assessment process, teams of trained evaluators actually evaluate or grade the student portfolios or performances. Depending on the assessment, the teams can consist of experts in the field being assessed, knowledgeable adults other than the student's teachers, and possibly an older student. With this model, the teacher is assigned the role of coach and helps the student prepare the portfolio or performance. Outside evaluators are used because the emotional connections between students and teachers, who have a shared ownership in the products, are less likely to bias an independent observer or evaluator.

Developing Consistency

I found that the difficult part of implementing an alternative assessment system on a district-wide basis was in giving the teachers enough freedom to appropriately meet the needs and learning styles of the students in their class while at the same time ensuring some consistency among schools and between classrooms. Whenever possible, it was beneficial for teachers on the same grade level across the district to meet as a team to design assessments. Teachers needed to agree on benchmark standards of performance and the types and format of assessment tasks, so that consistency could prevail. In Plainedge, the Assessment Advisory Council's role was to decide how much or how little freedom would be permitted on assessments as students proceed through the grades. Submitting ideas and criteria to an advisory council made things easier. Even though tasks appeared different, trained assessors identified the common components and offered suggestions that blended various proposed assessments into one complete whole. Without some group or individual overseeing the design and implementation of these varied assessment suggestions, the entire process would have been unmanageable and ineffective.

THE PARENT'S ROLE

Involvement

Although I have heard many educators indicate that parents are resistant to the new forms of assessment, I have not found that to be true. What I have found, instead, is that most parents are skeptical because they do not know what educators are talking about. Most parents have only minimal knowledge about the present types and quality of assessments being used with their child. Therefore, they have little if any basis for supporting or rejecting change and would, for lack of understanding, prefer staying with the familiar.

Awareness

Parents needed to be made aware of why changes in assessment strategies were being considered and how the new proposals would benefit their children. Parents responded positively to the concepts of learning styles and multiple intelligences. All parents can tell you exactly where their child excels and where the child has a weakness. This information is important for the teacher and the assessor. It's important for parents to know that we wish to accurately document what their children can do without any bias that may be reflected as a result of identified weaknesses. For example, many parents can tell you their children understand what they read but are unable to perform well on the short-answer recall or written assignments that customarily assess reading comprehension. The parents needed to become aware of the new system where drawings and verbal communications as well as writing and short answer questions might be used to document literacy abilities.

Training

Parents usually have a keen desire to learn about new educational innovations in their children's classes. In our district, we offered parents training to enlist their support for the assessment process. Parents learned about the new methods and how they could help to adequately prepare their children to perform well. Parents who know what is expected and how their child will be assessed are more likely to be supportive than parents who are unaware. Desired outcomes and standards must be known so that everyone involved—parent, child, and teacher—knows what is expected and how performance will be documented and assessed. Also, parents should have an understanding of rubrics, reflection, and goal-setting activities. We encouraged parents to take an active part in guiding their children to improve in areas of weakness and to flourish in areas of strength while providing constructive feedback.

Listen to What They Have to Say

It was interesting when we heard parents say "I got my first rubric today," as if it was a unique accomplishment on their part. We listened carefully to their criticism and comments. In discussions with parents, we identified inconsistencies, repetitions, and assessment criteria that were unrelated to the task being performed in the rubrics parents received at home. We also heard wonderful things about the effect of the rubrics and new assessment methods on specific students' motivation to perform, sense of self-worth, and desire to be an individual rather than follow the crowd. We let the parents know that the assessments were not cast in stone and that their input would be an essential part of the success of the new process.

Getting Parents Involved

Since these new forms of assessment are so time-intensive, many teachers have used parents as helpers in the classroom during assessment activities. For example, one of our teachers wanted to document and record the beginning readers on audiotape. On the day that the teacher worked with individual students in the learning corner, a parent volunteer helped supervise independent work. This second set of eyes in the room permitted the teacher to observe and document the students' reading behaviors as they read into the recorder. On another occasion, parent volunteers worked the tape recorder for students in the learning corner while the teacher interacted with others in the class. Other teachers had parents help students file entries in their portfolios.

There is an interesting sidelight to this activity. Teachers are often concerned about parents doing most of the work on projects and reports that are done at home; sometimes the activity submitted represents more parent than student work. However, when parents are actively involved in the classroom and the new assessment processes, they become sensitized to the need for student independence. We have asked parents to become partners in the process by helping us set up procedures and design evaluation criteria that reward students for hard work but discourage and even reject parent's work submitted in the name of the child.

Parents as Mentors and Independent Evaluators

Many of our parents have expertise that has been put to good use in our classrooms. Parents, as well as others active in the community, bring real-world concerns and experiences with them when they are involved in their local schools. We ask parents to serve as mentors to students other than their own children. For example, if a student has a particular interest in animals and there is a veterinarian in the community, we get them to connect with each other. We ask parents to help plan meaningful assessment activities for students, activities that reflect real-life experiences and may necessitate occasionally taking students out of the school building. We also believe in training community members to understand the criteria being used in assessment. They then become evaluators, and, to promote objectivity, they are assigned to schools where their own children are not enrolled.

THE STUDENT'S ROLE

Getting Students Involved

Students often ask the teacher questions such as, "How do I do this?" "Is this right?" "Is this long enough?" Too frequently, children become dependent on the teacher to guide them every step of the way. The more teachers can help students develop independence through activities that involve self-reflection and self-awareness, the more the students will gain the confidence and commitment to learn independently.

Is This O.K.?

Students should be provided with some form of criteria for determining if what they have done is what was wanted. For youngsters, a simple checklist is suggested; older students can work directly from a scoring rubric or portfolio coversheet. Teachers should reinforce the use of the criteria, and our students are encouraged to assess the quality of the work they have completed and to gain confidence when they feel they have met the criteria. In this way, rather than looking for the teacher to determine the validity of what has been done, students say, "Look at what I have done" with pride. Once our students have learned to independently use the assessment criteria, we involve them in the next process, which is goal setting. At this point, they reflect on and identify what they have done well and what areas of the project or activity still need work, and then they set short-term goals for the next project.

Internalizing Criteria

Another method we use in involving students in the assessment process is to engage them in the development of assessment criteria or guidelines. Four stages evolved for internalizing criteria: brainstorming, defining, using, and revising.

1. *Brainstorming:* Have students discuss how the assignment or project should be assessed, what makes a quality project, what resources and procedures are available, what are some possible objectives and organizational strategies, and what did they like about other projects or presentations?
2. *Defining:* Ask students to carefully define the criteria. This can be done by analyzing various examples and prior projects or through teacher role modeling.
3. *Using:* After the criteria are agreed on, students use their designed criteria to evaluate their own work and the work of peers. They discuss their findings and reactions.
4. *Revising:* Ask students how they would revise the criteria for future use. These activities can be used with the youngest of children under teacher leadership if appropriately simplified. Even if students have not designed their own criteria, they should discuss and use established criteria to self- and peer assess.

CONCLUSIONS

As can be seen, our teachers engaged in quite a paradigm shift. School leadership played a very important role in staff development and encouragement of innovation. We allowed for creative problem solving and had a shared mission and a supportive environment.

We realize that teaching is a craft and that there is a need to balance collaboration and individual integrity to maintain a teacher's sense of artistry, imagination, spirit, and inspiration. These factors were crucial to the quality of the assessments designed and implemented.

Actual implementation and successful use of alternative assessments occurred more frequently when performance standards were established for each child. The absence of or lack of clarity regarding standards and guidelines restricts the use of student self-assessment strategies. Teachers reported that it was important for them to develop and discuss their ideas, models, possible standards, and yardsticks with other teachers, and they encouraged their students to confer, debate, and use the established criteria. Apparently, common expectations, clear standards, and a collaborative environment are extremely important.

In summary, teachers cannot successfully undertake new assessment initiatives without administrative support and commitment. The research available on implementation of alternative modes of assessment indicates the need for training, encouragement, standard setting, a shared mission, collaborative goals, and a supportive environment. Staff development and collaboration allow teachers to assume new roles in their own development and in the education of their students. Although the process of transformation was time-consuming and challenging, not only did we significantly change assessment practices, but other changes occurred as well. Through the process of changing from traditional assessment to authentic practices, we also noted important changes in pedagogy, curriculum, and new relationships that developed among administrators, teachers, parents, and students.

Index

Dr. Roberta Behr Wiener (left)   Dr. Roberta Wiener is a Full Professor of Reading and Literacy at Adelphi University in Garden City, New York; the former Associate Dean of the School of Education and a practicing psychotherapist focusing on psycho-social-educational issues of children, adolescents, and adults. Her career began as a junior high school teacher of gifted adolescents. She then taught in the elementary schools in New York and was a reading specialist on Long Island. Additionally, Dr. Wiener has directed the graduate programs in Adult Learning & Development, Multilingual/Multicultural Teacher Education Program, as well as the Computer Applications for Educators program. She teaches undergraduate and graduate reading and literacy courses, working with pre- and in-service teachers, and conducts a Stress Reduction Workshop for Educators each summer.

Dr. Wiener received her B.A. & M.A. from Brooklyn College, her M.S. & Ed.D from Hofstra University, and her M.S.W. from Adelphi University. She makes presentations frequently at national and international professional conferences, has more than 25 publications in the field of literacy, including journal articles, book reviews, book chapters, literacy materials—kits, computer programs, and high-interest/low-vocabulary books. Many of these publications for the schools have been co-authored with Dr. Cohen.

Judith H. Cohen, Ph.D., J.D. (right)   Judith Cohen is an Associate Professor of Education at Adelphi University, Garden City, New York. Dr. Cohen teaches both graduate and undergraduate courses in literacy. She began her teaching career as a junior high school English/Reading teacher for the Board of Education, New York City. After completing a Master's degree at Syracuse University in Reading Education, she returned to New York and worked as a reading intervention specialist on Long Island. Her doctoral studies were completed in Reading Education with a specialization in Special Education at Hofstra University and she has been a teacher educator for 26 years.

Dr. Cohen has authored curriculum projects, a textbook on resource room teaching, many articles, textbook chapters, and law review articles and is an active inservice educator working with school district personnel. As a reflection of her longstanding concern for children's welfare, she completed legal studies at Hofstra University and was admitted to the New York State Bar as an Attorney in 1989. She works as a child advocate in school districts and the courts of New York. For the past 30 years her professional career has been devoted to advocating for children both in the context of schools as a teacher, as a university professor devoted to teacher education and as an attorney promoting child welfare both in terms of literacy improvement and legal rights.